MODERN JEWISH COOKING

LIST OF METRIC EQUIVALENTS

CONVENTIONAL	METRIC	CONVENTIONAL	METRIC
Teaspoons		*Cups*	
¼	1 ml	1	250 ml
½	2 ml	1¼	300 ml
¾	4 ml	1⅓	325 ml
1	5 ml	1½	375 ml
1½	7 ml	1¾	425 ml
2	10 ml	2	500 ml
Tablespoons		2¼	550 ml
1	15 ml	2¼	550 ml
1½	20 ml	2⅓	575 ml
2	25 ml	2½	625 ml
3	45 ml	3	750 ml
4	50 ml	3½	875 ml
Cups		4	1 liter, 1000 ml
(4 Tbsp = ¼ cup)		5	1250 ml
¼	50 ml	6	1500 ml
6 Tbsp = ⅓	75 ml	7	1750 ml
½	125 ml	8	2 liters, 2000 ml
⅔	150 ml	9	2250 ml
¾	175 ml	10	2500 ml
1	250 ml		

MODERN

JEWISH COOKING

BONNE RAE LONDON
Illustrated by Fran Gazze Nimeck

A HERBERT MICHELMAN BOOK
CROWN PUBLISHERS, INC.
NEW YORK

Inquiries should be addressed to Crown Publishers, Inc., One Park
Avenue, New York, New York 10016

Printed in the United States of America

Published simultaneously in Canada by General Publishing Company Limited

Library of Congress Cataloging in Publication Data

London, Bonne Rae.
Modern Jewish cooking.
"A Herbert Michelman book."
Includes index.
1. Cookery, Jewish.   2. Kitchen utensils.
I. Title.
TX724.L63 1980   641.5′67′6   79-25362
ISBN: 0-517-539357

Book design and calligraphy by Fran Gazze Nimeck

10 9 8 7 6 5 4 3 2 1

First edition

To
my husband, Martin,
who taught me that you never really
know a man until you let him taste-
test your cookbook recipes, and

To
my parents, Albert and Clara Goldstein,
who have always loved everything I
have ever cooked

CONTENTS

Part Three.

MENUS AND OTHER INSTRUCTIONS

ACKNOWLEDGMENTS

First and foremost, I wish to express my deepest appreciation and gratitude to Anne Griggs, Product Specialist, Sues, Young and Brown, for her encouragement, professional guidance and advice from the very beginning of this project.

To Dodie Sway, for reading and critiquing the entire manuscript and offering valuable suggestions and comments.

For assistance in compiling the chapter "How to Keep Kosher": Dr. R. David Freedman, University of California, Davis; Rabbi Joseph Feinstein, Los Angeles; Rabbi Joseph Goldman, Mosaic Law Congregation, Sacramento; and to my husband, Cantor Martin London.

For guidance and suggestions in preparing the chapter "Special Diets": Dr. Evelyn Mar, Professor, Home Economics, California State University, Chico.

To Herbert Michelman, Crown Publishers, Inc., for his help in organizing and structuring this book into its final form.

For tirelessly and endlessly proofreading: Susan Halpern and Sue Sault.

Finally, to my family and friends who graciously shared their recipes, advice and culinary expertise.

BRL

INTRODUCTION

Times change. As years and decades pass and as one generation creates another, values and standards subtly shift. This change is reflected in many areas, not the least of which is the family kitchen.

A large, busy kitchen was the center of my grandmother's family life. As the eldest of her nine grandchildren, I remember the icebox that really held a block of ice, the aromatic steam slowly rising from the old stove and filling the room with the fragrance of chicken soup. Grandma's "recipe" for preparing gefilte fish began with taking the live fish out of the bathtub. Her idea of a convenience food was a tin of macaroons at Passover.

My mother is a good cook too, but her approach stresses convenience and speed. Mom's kitchen counter resembles a store display. The lineup includes mixer, toaster, blender, can opener and knife sharpener. The overflow—popcorn popper, waffle iron, muffin warmer and griddle—found its way to the cupboard. Each electrical outlet in Mom's kitchen has an extender so that three appliances instead of one can be plugged in at once. If all of her appliances were turned on at the same time, I imagine that the city of Los Angeles would be plunged into total blackout.

My own kitchen, decorated with hanging plants and children's artwork, is a busy place. I enjoy cooking and I like experimenting and adapting recipes, trying a new idea or an old one on a new appliance. From my grandmother I have inherited a love and respect for the Jewish tradition. From my mother I seem to have acquired a passion for pressing buttons to make motors whir and the attitude that if there is an easier way to do something then I want to try it.

I think the day has arrived when we can use modern appliances to indulge a love of traditional cooking without the labor that was once involved.

Traditional Jewish cooking means preparing and serving foods in accordance with the Jewish dietary laws, or kashruth. I have tried, in writing

Modern Jewish Cooking, to offer a contemporary guide to keeping kosher, explaining the "why," "what" and "how" of the dietary laws. In addition to the introduction which follows, a detailed explanation entitled "How to Keep Kosher" appears at the end of the book.

Each recipe contained here is designed as *fleishig* (for recipes containing meat or poultry), *dairy* (for recipes that contain milk products) or *pareve* (for recipes with neither meat nor milk products: "neutral" recipes). When a recipe is followed by variations, refer to the basic recipe for full instructions.

This book contains over 500 traditional, holiday and everyday recipes, all of which are kosher and adapted to five of the latest kitchen appliances. Not everybody will own all of these appliances, but most families will have at least one or two and may use this book as a guide toward purchasing others.

The following five appliances have been selected for their versatility, popularity and true labor- or time-saving qualities:

MICROWAVE OVEN—for superfast cooking of meats, fish, poultry, vegetables, soups and desserts

CROCK POT—for slow or superslow cooking, especially good for cholent, tzimmes and soups

FOOD PROCESSOR—for superfast chopping, slicing, shredding, and mixing pastry and bread doughs

BLENDER—for lovely sauces, salad dressings, beverages and desserts

MIXER WITH DOUGH HOOK—for cakes, breads, rolls and bagels

It is apparent at this writing that the American kosher homemaker will eventually be using the metric system of weights and measures. The federal government, which established our current system of pounds and quarts, has legislated a gradual change to the metric system of grams and liters currently used throughout the world, including Israel.

All the recipes in this book specify both the conventional and metric weights and measures. Approximate, rather than actual, comparison measurements are used, except in the case of exact can, bottle or package measures and weights.

It is my hope that *Modern Jewish Cooking* can be useful to both the new cook and the experienced cook using new appliances and new measures, so that ultimately the art of maintaining kashruth and the science of using modern appliances will result in an experience that is convenient and fun and food that is absolutely delicious! *Betayavon.*

BONNE RAE LONDON

INTRODUCTION TO KASHRUTH

WHY KEEP KOSHER?

Do you remember when you asked your Jewish grandmother or great-grandmother why she kept kosher? She probably gave you a look that indicated you were in a state of insanity—hopefully temporary—as she answered, "Because I am Jewish."

As time passes, people often forget why they do things. A certain pattern or routine is established—sometimes because of social pressure, perhaps because of guilt, maybe just because of habit. Often the original motivation or explanation gets lost or forgotten.

The word *kosher* today is often used rather loosely. *Kosher-style* is frequently a description of a pastrami sandwich on rye—even if the pastrami is not kosher and is consumed along with a glass of milk. Today, in many places, there appears to be an emphasis more on kosher "style" than on content. One reason, perhaps, is that people are questioning the need to maintain kashruth, the observance of the Jewish dietary laws, and wonder, "Why should I bother to keep kosher? Why?"

The 613 commandments contained in the Torah (the first five books of the Bible) make tradition and ritual an integral part of the Jewish religion. The observance of these commandments is designed to bring a high spiritual meaning and awareness to both the ordinary routines and special events of our lives. To religious Jews, a relationship with God is not confined just to synagogue on Shabbat or the holidays. It is possible to express and renew a relationship with God dozens of times a day—to bring a touch of spirituality and holiness to our lives in many ways. One of the most important is through the process of preparing and eating food.

By keeping kosher observant Jews uplift and make holy the act of eating. Food prepared in this manner fulfills the commandments and transforms a commonplace act into something spiritually meaningful.

Health standards are *not* the primary reason for keeping kosher—although it is certainly healthful. We keep kosher because it is the Jewish way—our

1

way—of making the cooking and eating processes holy, on a high spiritual level. Keeping kosher fulfills the commandments of the Torah and strengthens our relationship with God.

Grandma, upon reflection, would certainly agree.

A GUIDE TO
THE DIETARY LAWS

All kosher food can be divided into three categories: *fleishig* (meat and poultry products), *milchig* (milk and dairy products) and *pareve* (foods which are neither meat nor milk but can be consumed with either). All foods which do not meet kosher standards are *trefah* or forbidden.

FLEISHIG

Before meat or poultry may be eaten, it must fulfill all of the following:

Acceptable Species
Meat must come from an acceptable (not forbidden) species. To be acceptable, animals must both chew the cud (eat grass) and have a cloven hoof. The only species of poultry generally accepted as kosher are domestic chickens, ducks, geese, turkeys and doves.

Ritual Slaughter
Acceptable animals and birds must be slaughtered in the ritual manner, shehitah, which minimizes pain and drains off most of the blood. Afterward the body and internal organs must be examined by a mashgiach, a pious and knowledgeable person specially trained for the job. Only healthy animals, free from disease and lesions, qualify as kosher.

Properly Butchered
For meat to be kosher, it must come from a section of the animal that one is permitted to eat. The consumption of blood, the sciatic nerve (which runs through the hind section) and certain other areas are forbidden. Meat which meets all of the above requirements can be purchased in a kosher butcher shop.

Kashered
Meat must be kashered, that is, drained of excess blood. This procedure may be accomplished either by salting or by broiling (see "Guide to Kashering Meat and Poultry").

Separate Pots, Dishes and Utensils
Kosher meat must be cooked in pots and pans that have no contact with either nonkosher meat or poultry or with any dairy products. The dishes and utensils used to serve kosher meat must also have no contact with either nonkosher meat or poultry or with any dairy products.

Any by-product of kosher meat is fleishig. This includes fat, special emulsifiers and certain kosher monoglycerides and diglycerides.

MILCHIG

Milchig is the term used to describe milk products and dairy foods. These foods must meet all of the following requirements before they can be considered kosher:

Kosher Species
Milk and all dairy products must be derived from a kosher species of animal.

Separate Pots, Dishes and Utensils
Milchig foods must be cooked in pots and pans that have had no contact with any meat or poultry products or with any nonkosher foods. The dishes and utensils used to serve milchig foods must also have no contact with fleishig or with nonkosher foods.

Any by-product of milk is considered milchig. This includes milk fats, nonfat dry milk solids, whey, sodium caseinate and lactose.

PAREVE

The following foods are considered pareve, or neutral, and may be cooked and eaten with either fleishig or milchig:

Fish
Fish must have both fins and scales in order to be considered kosher. All other species of sea life (crustaceans, mollusks, amphibians), as well as reptiles and insects, are forbidden. The complicated process of shehitah (ritual slaughter) and kashering (removal of blood) does not apply to fish.

Some people consider fish in a category separate from other pareve food. At a fleishig meal the fish would be eaten before meat, from separate plates and utensils.

Vegetables, Fruits and Grains
All foods that grow from the soil are kosher; however, these foods must be carefully examined before being used to make sure they are free of insects (which are not kosher).

Eggs

Eggs from kosher birds are kosher and pareve; however, when the egg is cracked and there is a blood spot inside, the egg is nonkosher. An egg found inside poultry at the time of slaughter is fleishig.

Honey

Honey is the only exception to the rule which forbids the consumption of a product of a nonkosher animal. Honey is considered a product of nectar from flowers, rather than a product from bees.

Nondairy Products

There are on the market many items which resemble such dairy products as coffee cream, sour cream and whipped cream both in taste and appearance but actually are pareve. These are customarily served in the original container to show that the product is pareve despite the dairy appearance.

SEPARATION OF FLEISHIG AND MILCHIG

You shall not boil a kid in its mother's milk.
Exodus 23:19 and 34:26, Deuteronomy 14:21

This commandment, which appears three times in the Torah, describes a separation that is one of the most basic and important foundations of the dietary laws. In practice, this separation between fleishig (meat) and milchig (dairy) requires careful and deliberate preparation.

Kitchen items must be designated fleishig or milchig and may be used only for foods within the category; however, either may be used for pareve foods. These items include all utensils, dishes, china, silverware, metal pots, pans, knives, Pyrex or Corning casseroles and plastic storage containers. Also, separate table linen, napkins, dish towels, placemats and sponges are required.

Fleishig and milchig must never be consumed together. After fleishig has been eaten, a certain period of time must elapse before milchig is consumed. There are different practices as to the length of this waiting period, usually three to six hours. The waiting period that separates milchig from fleishig, however, is considerably shorter. In fact, after eating milchig, if one rinses the mouth and eats a pareve food, fleishig may be eaten immediately. Hard cheese, because it clings to the palate, is an exception to this practice and requires a longer waiting period.

PART ONE

APPLIANCES

MICROWAVE OVEN

A publicity agent for one of the leading microwave oven manufacturers has boasted with unbounded enthusiasm that microwave ovens are the "greatest cooking discovery since fire." Although that statement may be open to discussion, the general impact of microwave ovens on the art of cooking is remarkable. Microwave ovens provide a completely different method of cooking and are exciting kitchen appliances.

HOW A MICROWAVE OVEN WORKS

A microwave oven is an insulated metal box which contains a magnetron tube. It is inside this special tube that microwaves are produced. Microwaves, like all radio waves, are invisible and travel at the speed of light. They move along a metal wave guide and enter the oven cavity through an opening in the top or side panel.

Microwaves react differently to different substances. They are *reflected* (or bounce off) the metal interior of the oven; they are *transmitted* (or pass through) the glass, paper or plastic cooking utensils recommended for microwave cooking; and they are *absorbed* by foods and liquids.

When microwaves penetrate foods, they are attracted to the fat, sugar and water molecules, causing these molecules to vibrate. The resulting friction produces heat that in turn cooks the food.

HOW TO BUY A MICROWAVE OVEN

Federal laws regulate the frequency of microwave transmissions and set the safety standards for microwave ovens. Because these are the same for all, other features must be considered when selecting a microwave oven.

Variable Power

Selecting an oven with variable power settings is wise. These ovens have at least 4 settings and often many more, depending on the manufacturer. Despite the confusion this creates, these settings are labeled with various descriptions of cooking methods, such as Bake, Roast, Simmer, Fast, Reheat and so forth. The important settings—and consumers should learn which setting labels on their ovens correspond to these—are high, medium high (two-thirds or 70 percent setting), medium (one-half or 50 percent setting) and low (one-third or 30 percent setting). A majority of ovens also feature a lower one-tenth or 10 percent setting, often labeled warm.

Wattage and Capacity

When selecting a microwave oven, look for a wattage of 650 and at least a 1 cu. ft. (cubic foot) capacity, as these are the figures that conform to current industry standards. Most microwave cookbooks and recipes are designed for such ovens.

Although the following factors do not affect the quality of cooking in a microwave oven, they are also important features to consider when making a purchase:

Warranty

A microwave oven manufacturer will usually offer two warranties: one on the magnetron tube and another on the rest of the unit. Some manufacturers offer in-home service. Information supplied by the manufacturer will usually elaborate on what damage is covered under the warranty and what is not. In order for a warranty to be effective, the appliance must be used according to the manufacturer's specifications.

Interior

The interior of a microwave oven may be high-quality stainless steel or an acrylic coating over metal. Acrylic, over the years, can pick up odors, stains and scratches.

Timers

All ovens have timers. These can be dials, digital timers or microprocessor panels with lighted numbers to count off the seconds. Although many people assume that the fancier timers are more likely to break, these microprocessor panels are usually solid state and the easiest of all to repair.

Convenience Features

Manufacturers may offer a variety of features such as clocks, temperature probes, removable racks, automatic starters, memory recalls, humidity sensors, temperature converters and carousels or turntables. While these additions do not affect the quality, taste or appearance of the food cooked, they may be very desirable.

BROWNING IN THE MICROWAVE OVEN

Ovens with browner units really deserve a separate category. These ovens have, on the ceiling of the cavities, calrod elements that look like the coils in an electric broiler, but they are not as powerful. Food cooked in these ovens is first microwaved and then browned.

A browner unit is not a necessity, because any food cooking in a microwave oven for 8 to 10 minutes will start to brown provided it has some natural fat. It is easy to enhance the appearance of food cooked in a microwave oven with spices, bastes and sauces (see introduction to Poultry chapter, pages 151 and 152).

A browner element will heat the oven cavity and cause food to stick, making cleanup difficult. Despite this drawback, however, microwave ovens with browners do offer some decided advantages. The introduction of dry heat adds to the range and variety of foods that can be cooked by microwaves. A microwave oven with a browner will cook fish sticks, reheat frozen french fried potatoes or Tater Tots and make them brown and crisp. Meringue will set and brown. Muffins, biscuits, cupcakes, cakes and pie shells can acquire a conventional-looking brown top crust.

SAFETY

Three agencies regulate the safety standards for microwave ovens: the Federal Communication Commission (FCC), Underwriters Laboratory (UL) and the Department of Health, Education and Welfare (HEW).

The door of the microwave oven should remain securely closed while food is cooking. Do not attempt to place objects between the front of the oven and the door, and keep the area around the door seal clean. Never attempt to operate the oven with the door open. If the oven is damaged in any way, including a bent door, broken or loosened latches or hinges, and so forth, only a qualified service person should make the adjustment or repair.

COOKING TECHNIQUES

Choose the Right Setting
The variable power settings on a microwave oven regulate the microwave energy and control the speed at which the food cooks. The higher settings cook food more quickly than the lower settings; however, many foods achieve best results when clooked slower. Use the variable power settings in the following manner:

HIGH SETTING is used for fish, poultry and vegetables. Cook precooked or very tender meat, such as hotdogs, ground meat or Beef Frye, on a high setting. Use this setting to boil liquids and to make many gravies and sauces. Rice, grain and pasta dishes may be brought to a boil on a high setting, then reduced to a lower setting to finish cooking. Most reheating is done on a high setting.

MEDIUM-HIGH SETTING is used for cakes, muffins and bakery items. Use this setting for eggs and many cuts of meat.

MEDIUM SETTING is used for less tender cuts of meat. Use this setting also for foods that are "sensitive" to microwave energy due to a high sugar content, such as Pecan Pie, or high fat content, such as most cheese and egg dishes.

LOW SETTING is used mainly for defrosting foods. It can also be used for cooking less tender cuts of meat.

Select the Right Dish

Accessories and cooking containers suitable for microwave ovens are generally made from glass, paper or plastic. Microwaves pass through these substances just as light passes through a window. Avoid all dishes that contain metal or have metal paint or trim.

To determine if a dish or container is safe to use in a microwave oven, place the empty dish in the oven. Operate the oven on a high setting for 30 seconds. The dish should remain cool or slightly warm to the touch. If at the end of this time, however, the dish is hot, it is not suitable for use in the microwave oven.

During actual cooking, a dish may become hot owing to transference of heat from the food. When a dish is covered during cooking, much of the steam is contained, making the dish and handles hot.

Proper Covering

The coverings used most frequently in microwave cooking are plastic wrap, wax paper and paper towels.

Use *plastic wrap* when a tight cover is required. When plastic wrap is properly used, the edges of the plastic around the sides of the dish are tightly sealed; however, the covering over the top of the dish should be rather loose and "puffy." As food cooks, the plastic wrap fills with steam and looks like a balloon-top over the dish. Always vent plastic wrap by puncturing 1 or 2 holes to allow some steam to escape. If plastic wrap is not properly vented, the steam will build up, then force its way out, causing the plastic wrap to tear.

Plastic wrap (more effectively than a casserole lid) holds in the steam and heat needed for cooking vegetables, many fish recipes, and rice, grains and pasta.

Wax paper is used to prevent spatter. Poultry and meat (especially ground beef) should be covered with wax paper. Wax paper is often used as a covering during the first half of the cooking time when baking heavy batters, such as Cornbread and Brownies.

Use *paper towels* to absorb spatter or excess moisture. Place a paper towel under baked potatoes when cooking or under rolls and muffins when reheating. Place a paper towel over foods with a dry or crumb coating such as Oven-"Fried" Chicken.

Less tender cuts of meat often require a covering. Either a glass casserole lid or a plastic cooking bag held closed with a string or rubber band (do not use a metal twist) are effective.

Food Arrangement
The arrangement of food in a microwave oven can affect the evenness of the cooking. A bagel shape is ideal because there are no corners to overcook and no center to undercook. In a rectangular or square dish, the thickest part of the food should be placed toward the outer edge of the dish.

Turning Food
Turning, stirring, rotating or rearranging food is necessary in some recipes. Meat and poultry need to be turned over halfway through the cooking time. Soups, gravies and certain casseroles should be stirred occasionally for best results. A carousel or turntable in an oven usually eliminates the need to rotate or rearrange the food. Without a carousel, rotation of dishes every quarter or third of the total cooking time is recommended.

Removing Excess Liquid
In conventional cooking, liquid is cooked away by dry heat and often it is necessary to add extra liquid to keep food from burning. In microwave cooking, however, there is no dry heat present to evaporate liquid. Many microwave recipes, therefore, specify less liquid than is needed in conventional cooking. Liquid can actually attract microwave energy and draw microwaves away from the food. Therefore, when roasting meat or poultry on a rack, one must occasionally remove the accumulated liquid, which collects under the rack because it would otherwise slow the cooking time.

Standing Time or Aftercooking
When the microwave energy has been turned off, food continues to cook internally. As the temperature equalizes, the center of the food gets hotter and finishes cooking. This period may be called standing time, aftercooking or equalization time.

An important technique of microwave cooking is deliberately undercooking food and allowing it to finish cooking during the standing time. The time allowed for aftercooking should be about a third of the prescribed microwave cooking time, or a maximum of 15 minutes. The times stated in recipes refer to microwave cooking time only. All microwave oven recipes take into consideration the standing time. Therefore, allow the dish to stand for the specified time before serving.

Special Accessories

Many fancy and expensive accessories are sold for microwave cooking. In my opinion, the two indispensable accessories are a microwave oven thermometer (if the oven does not come equipped with a special temperature probe) and a kitchen scale. Microwave cooking time is often determined by the weight of the food, and if one is guessing the weight, then one is also guessing the cooking time.

WHAT TO EXPECT FROM A MICROWAVE OVEN

In addition to speedy defrosting and reheating, one can expect a microwave oven to perform about 90 percent of *all* cooking jobs. Microwaves do a superior job of cooking fish. Vegetables remain a lovely natural color and have a crunchy texture. Meat and poultry stay juicy and flavorful when cooked in the microwave oven. Cakes and baked items may rise higher and be lighter and fluffier than if cooked conventionally. Less tender cuts of meat, egg and cheese dishes and other foods having a high fat or sugar content can be cooked very successfully if proper techniques are used.

KEEPING KOSHER WITH A MICROWAVE OVEN

In maintaining a kosher kitchen it is best to avoid placing food directly on the glass tray or turntable which comes with the oven (unless, of course, you have two separate trays and can tell them apart—one tray for milchig and one tray for fleishig). It is always preferable to use a clean dish or paper plate to hold food when cooking.

HOW TO ADAPT THE RECIPES IN THIS BOOK TO YOUR MICROWAVE OVEN

All of the microwave oven recipes in this book are designed for ovens with 600 to 700 watts. If the oven has a lower wattage, the cooking time may be somewhat longer.

All of the following recipes use the phrases *high setting, medium-high, medium* or *low setting.* These phrases correspond to the following power settings:

high setting	=	100% power (600 to 700 watts)
medium-high setting	=	70% or ⅔ power (425 to 475 watts)
medium setting	=	50% or ½ power (300 to 350 watts)
low setting	=	30% or ⅓ power (175 to 225 watts)

Consult your manufacturer's guide or owner's manual to learn how these designations correspond to the settings on your oven.

CROCK POT

Having an appliance that cooks s-l-o-w-l-y, in hours instead of minutes, can be a definite advantage to a busy person because it widely separates the meal preparation time from the eating time. This "set-it-then-forget-it" attitude can often turn a dinner from a last-minute rush into a leisurely meal.

Long, slow cooking is part of the Jewish heritage. For generations Jewish women have prepared meals in large, heavy pots and put them into slow ovens on Friday afternoon. There they remained, cooking slowly until after synagogue services on Saturday. The traditional recipes for Cholent, Tzimmes and stews adapt beautifully to modern-day crock pots.

HOW A CROCK POT WORKS

The crock pot is an appliance that cooks food at a slow, even temperature of 200° F (95° C) on a low setting and 300° F (150° C) on a high setting. Food will not burn or scorch in a crock pot because the heat is not concentrated on the bottom, but rather is distributed evenly around the pot.

HOW TO BUY A CROCK POT

At last count there were about three dozen crock pot models on the market. Although they differ in such features as capacity, size, shape and color, they all operate in basically the same manner.

Settings
The important settings are at the levels of 200° F (95° C) and 300° F (150° C). These settings are usually labeled low and high. In addition, some models offer higher temperature settings for browning meats and deep-fat frying.

Liner
The interior lining of a crock pot may be crockery, glass, Teflon, aluminum, porcelain or stainless steel. Some pots have removable liners, which are an advantage in serving or cleaning. The capacity of the various crock pots ranges from about 2½ quarts (2½ liters) to 8 quarts (8 liters).

SAFETY

Crock pots usually have a very short electrical cord. When this cord is permanently attached, the pot must not be immersed in water.

Many models are insulated as a safety feature. This means that the outside does not get hot, even after a full day or night of cooking.

COOKING TECHNIQUES

Keep Covered
The crock pot should remain tightly covered throughout the cooking time. As steam condenses on the lid, it drops back into the pot. This steam atmosphere helps the food to cook from the top. Removing the lid to peek inside usually means the food must cook an extra 15 to 20 minutes to make up for the loss of steam and heat.

Reduce Liquids
Liquids do not boil away in a crock pot. It is advisable to reduce the amount of liquid by half when adapting conventional recipes to a crock pot.

Underspice
Spices and flavors may become more pronounced in slow cooking. Foods should be deliberately underspiced and then tasted to correct seasonings before serving.

Little Stirring
Stirring is generally not required in crock pot cooking.

WHAT TO EXPECT FROM A CROCK POT

Soups, stews, dekel (pot roast), braised meat and poultry, beans and many vegetables turn out excellent when cooked slowly in a crock pot. Fruits, puddings, beverages, desserts, breads and cakes all adapt well to crock pot cooking.

When a recipe calls for rice or pasta, it is better to cook it conventionally before adding it to the mixture in the crock pot.

Dairy products do not adapt particularly well to crock pot cooking. When a recipe specifies milk, cream or cheese, it is best added during the last hour of cooking.

Gravies will not thicken in a crock pot as they do in a conventional oven. It may be necessary to add a thickening agent such as flour or cornstarch to achieve the desired effect.

KEEPING KOSHER WITH A CROCK POT

A crock pot liner needs to be designated either fleishig, milchig or pareve. The same base electrical unit can be used with separate liners.

HOW TO ADAPT THESE RECIPES
TO YOUR CROCK POT

When the term low setting is used for crock pot recipes in this book, it means that the food should cook at 200° F (95° C). A high setting indicates a steady 300° F (150° C) temperature is required.

Crock pot recipes are wonderfully flexible. Most recipes requiring 8 hours of cooking on a low setting can just as easily cook 4 hours on a high setting.

When the crock pot is used to "bake" breads and cakes, a high setting is recommended. The pot lid should not be lifted for at least the first 2 hours of cooking.

FOOD PROCESSORS

A food processor, more than any other kitchen appliance, helps to bring haute cuisine and a gourmet touch to the family menu. Although food-processing machines have been available for many years and are standard restaurant equipment, the introduction of the Cuisinart on the consumer market in 1973 had a strong impact on the home cook. Food processors are credited with revolutionizing and modernizing the way Americans now prepare food and often the quality of the meals they eat.

HOW A FOOD PROCESSOR WORKS

There are two styles of food processors. The Cuisinart type is a machine with interchangeable blades that chop, slice, shred, mix and blend foods in seconds. The second type is a multipurpose food-preparation unit. This comes with a variety of appliances to attach to one motor base. These attachments include blenders, mixers, dough hooks, juicers and meat grinders as well as devices to chop, shred and slice.

HOW TO BUY A FOOD PROCESSOR

In selecting a food processor, one has a basic choice between the multipurpose unit with all the attachments and the Cuisinart-type appliance. The top-of-the-line prices of these alternatives are about the same.

The Multipurpose Unit
The multipurpose unit has the advantage of doing what the Cuisinart does, plus a whole lot more. Someone who does not already own a mixer and blender may save considerable money and storage space by buying this all-in-one unit rather than buying each appliance separately. Multipurpose units are very popular in Israel and Europe, where kitchen space is minimal.

The Cuisinart-type Unit
The Cuisinart-type food processor is slender, compact and takes up relatively little counter space. The attachments, four cutting blades, also need minimal storage space. The Cuisinart-type unit is easy to assemble, change attachments and clean. It is also simple to operate—in fact, it is nearly foolproof (although many a chopped liver has accidentally turned into a pâté). Using a Cuisinart-type food processor, even the most inexperienced cook can produce a French-type creation (in the best American tradition) "faster than a speeding bullet." The original Cuisinart machine inspired many imitators and there are now over a dozen varieties to choose from. Some of the features to consider when selecting this type are:

WEIGHT—The weight of a Cuisinart-type food processor affects the performance because the lighter models have a tendency to dance around the counter when working with full loads. The heavier models are sturdier and more stationary.

CONTAINER DESIGN—Many models, including the Cuisinart, have direct-drive mechanisms, meaning that the containers and blades sit directly on top of the motors. Other models employ belt-driven mechanisms. Both designs work effectively but those with belt-drive, in which the containers sit to one side of the motors, take up more counter space.

Some Cuisinart-type units are turned on and off by manually rotating the lid from side to side. An on-off button is a desirable feature because it frees the hands. Some models feature a pulse button, which gives short bursts of energy and allows the user to start and stop the machine rapidly.

A handle attached to the container on some models makes lifting and handling more convenient.

QUALITY OF MATERIALS—Whether selecting a multipurpose unit or a Cuisinart-type food processor, consider that the quality and type of materials used in construction of the unit affects the price as well as longevity. Better-built machines have more metal than plastic parts or utilize higher-quality plastic. A metal base to protect the motor, good-grade plastic used for the container and cover, as well as rust-resistant metal blades will certainly increase the longevity of the appliance.

SAFETY

The cutting, slicing and shredding blades of a Cuisinart-type food processor are *very* sharp and the same caution and respect should be exercised as with the sharpest kitchen knife. A steel cutting blade attachment, accidentally falling from the counter toward the floor, is like a miniature guillotine, threatening severance to anything in its path.

The shape and length of the feed tube on the plastic cover of a Cuisinart-type unit is meant to keep fingers out as well as to guide food. These models are designed to operate only when the lid is securely closed. It is advisable not only to wait until the blades have completely stopped before reaching inside but also to unplug the cord when removing or inserting the blades.

Many food processors have automatic overload protection. This is a safety feature that automatically turns the unit off if the motor becomes too hot. Some models have a reset button that must be pressed to reactivate the motor, but other models automatically reset when the motor cools down.

It is advisable to keep the Cuisinart-type container bowl in the off position when it is not in use, even if the unit is unplugged. Keeping the bowl in the on position can wear out the spring mechanism. The pusher should be stored separately, outside the feed tube, when not in use because air circulation allows the container bowl to remain fresh.

COOKING TECHNIQUES

Measure Foods

The amount of food processed at one time in a Cuisinart-type food processor is limited by the size of the container and by the requirement that liquid and food should not rise higher than the top of the blade stem. The following guide represents the maximum load that should be processed at one time:

> 1½ cups (375 ml) hard vegetables (potatoes, carrots)
> 2 cups (500 ml) soft vegetables (onions, mushrooms)
> ½ lb (250 grams) meat
> 1 cup (250 grams) nuts, seeds
> ½ cup (125 ml) hard cheeses

The guide for processing liquids is:

> 2½ cups (625 ml) thin liquids
> 3½ cups (875 ml) purees
> 4 cups (1 liter) thick batters, doughs

Choose the Proper Blade

Four attachment blades are usually included with a Cuisinart-type food processor. The attachment used for about 90 percent of all processing is the S-shaped steel blade. It is used primarily for chopping, pureeing, forming bread dough and mixing. The shredding disc, another blade attachment, can be used for most cheeses, vegetables and fruits. The slicing disc works well for vegetables and for meat. The plastic blade attachment can be used for whipping cream, making mayonnaise, salad dressing or sauces, and for whipping egg whites (which will "set" but not increase greatly in volume).

How to Process Foods

To chop coarsely or to combine ingredients, the proper technique is to turn the unit on and off rapidly in short, one-second pulses or bursts of energy. For fine chopping or pureeing, the blades are allowed to process continuously until the proper consistency is reached. Very hard cheeses or ice cubes can be chopped by inserting the steel blade attachment, starting the motor and then adding a few pieces at a time through the feed tube.

When using the slicing or shredding disc, the food is first cut into chunks and then guided through the feed tube using the pusher. Meat slices best when it is well chilled or even partially frozen.

WHAT TO EXPECT FROM
A CUISINART-TYPE FOOD PROCESSOR

Whatever model of food processor you select, it will probably do an excellent job of blending and making pastry dough, purees, dips, sauces and mayonnaise. Most models will shred food well and chop or slice more or less evenly, depending on the quality of the model. The real power test of a food processor is how it performs in chopping raw meat and combining bread dough ingredients.

A Cuisinart-type unit is not designed to liquefy foods, handle large volumes or grind coffee beans. These are jobs for a blender or a multipurpose-unit food processor. A Cuisinart-type unit will whip cream and egg whites, but not as well as a mixer.

KEEPING KOSHER WITH A FOOD PROCESSOR

All attachments and accessories of a food processor, including blades, bowls or containers, covers, pushers or spatulas, must be designated milchig, fleishig or pareve. If separate sets of attachments and accessories are owned, the same motor base can be used with each.

HOW TO ADAPT THESE RECIPES
TO YOUR FOOD PROCESSOR

All of the food processor recipes in this book are designed specifically for the Cuisinart-type unit. Directions will specify which of the four blade attachments to use—steel blade, shredding disc, slicing disc, or plastic blade.

Owners of multipurpose units may use their appliance, with the appropriate attachments, for all blender, mixer and mixer-with-dough-hook recipes. Food processor recipes can be adapted for use by processing individual foods (using the attachments for slicing, shredding or grinding) and then combining these processed foods manually or, in the case of batter-type foods, using the mixer attachment.

BLENDER

A blender, the least expensive of all the appliances discussed in this book, is a handy appliance to own. The main job of a blender is to liquefy solids and to aerate liquids. In fact, another name for a blender is a liquidizer. The blender, like the Cuisinart-type food processor, grinds nuts and breads into crumbs; purees dips and spreads; and chops pieces of vegetables and fruits.

HOW A BLENDER WORKS

A blender appliance consists of a tall glass or plastic goblet with revolving blades at the bottom and a tight-fitting lid. This unit sits on top of a small electric motor. When the motor is turned on, the blades spin at an incredibly fast rate. The whirlpool or spiraling action created by the blades draws the food down to the bottom of the goblet, where the blades reduce it to fine particles.

HOW TO BUY A BLENDER

There are many features to consider when purchasing a blender:

Capacity

The capacity of the goblet determines how much food can be blended at once. In figuring usable capacity remember to allow extra space for the rise in volume that the whirlpool effect creates when the blender is operating.

Height

The height of the various blender models may vary from 10 to 18 inches (25 to 46 cm). Although taller units often are fancier or larger in capacity, they may be too tall to fit under a kitchen cabinet.

Speed Selection

The number of motor speeds on a blender may be as high as 20, however only 2 are really necessary—a high and a low (although to a beginner these 2 speeds may seem like high and higher) with perhaps a medium speed included for variety. A very large selection of speeds is confusing and makes for difficult cleanup because dust and food particles can collect in the crevices between the buttons.

Other Features

A blender needs a tight-fitting lid to prevent spatters. The most convenient lids have 2 pieces. They are designed with a smaller opening that can be exposed for adding ingredients while the motor is running.

Other convenience features on blenders may include timers, pulse buttons, goblets with graduated measurement markings and removable blade assemblies. This last feature is a great aid in maintenance because the blades are easy to clean when they can be taken apart and then reassembled.

SAFETY

Never, under any circumstances, should you put your hand inside the blender goblet while the motor is running. Never put hard wood or metal objects inside. If it is necessary to scrape the sides of the goblet while the motor is running, always use a rubber scraper or spatula.

Blender motors can overheat and burn out from misuse; therefore, care should be taken not to run the unit too long at a time and to keep the load fairly light and manageable.

COOKING TECHNIQUES

Dry Grinding

To turn bread, matzah, cookies or crackers into crumbs, break them into pieces, place in goblet, then blend. The following amounts each yield approximately ½ cup (125 ml) crumbs:

1 slice bread   16 very small cookies
8 graham crackers   2 matzahs
16 soda crackers

To dry grind foods such as nuts or coffee beans, best results are achieved when a relatively small load of ½ to 1 cup (125 to 250 ml) is blended at a time.

Liquefy Fruits and Vegetables
The blender is not a juice extractor but will do a good job of breaking down the fibrous parts of fruit and vegetable pieces to release the flavor and nutrients into a liquid. The food should first be cut into 1-inch (2.5-cm) chunks and added to ½ to 1 cup (125 to 250 ml) liquid. A fairly small amount of food (one apple or three carrots or two celery stalks) can be liquefied at one time. If desired, the liquid can be strained after blending to remove the small fibrous particles.

Chopping Food
A blender is not the best appliance to use for chopping foods (a food processor is) but all of the blender manufacturers suggest techniques for performing this task. The chopping technique which is easiest on the blender motor is the water method, in which the vegetables or fruit pieces are cut into 1-inch (2.5-cm) chunks, placed in the goblet, covered with water and, by use of a pulse button or short on-off bursts of energy, reduced to smaller pieces. In a second technique, the dry method, the food is cut into very small (¾-inch [2 cm]) pieces before being placed in the goblet. A variation of this technique is to start the motor running and drop the food pieces down through the opening in the lid.

Reconstitute Milk and Frozen Drinks
The proper technique is to add the dry milk or frozen juice to a measured amount of liquid in the goblet, cover and blend.

WHAT TO EXPECT FROM A BLENDER

A blender is designed to handle liquids and liquefy fruits and vegetables in water. It will do an excellent job of making mayonnaise and salad dressings, mixing and blending sauces, removing lumps from sauces and puddings and pureeing cooked vegetables and fruits. A good blender will dry grind nuts, coffee beans and breads.

A blender will not chop raw meat, mash potatoes or chop ice (unless liquid is added to form a slush drink). Blenders do not do a particularly good job of whipping cream or egg whites.

KEEPING KOSHER WITH A BLENDER

Each goblet, blade assembly and lid of a blender needs to be designated milchig, fleishig or pareve. However, if separate sets of these items are owned, the same motor base can be used with each set.

HOW TO ADAPT THESE RECIPES
TO YOUR BLENDER

All of the blender recipes in this book specify putting ingredients into the blender goblet and then blending on low, medium or high speed until the desired consistency is reached. If your machine has a variety of speeds to select from, always choose the lowest speed possible for the job.

Often, when using a blender, it is necessary to scrape the sides of the goblet using a rubber spatula. This helps to guide thick batters and heavy foods onto the blades for even blending and uniform consistency.

MIXER

Mixers have been popular in American kitchens since before World War II, particularly portable hand mixers that are lightweight, inexpensive and require no counter space. Food processing units, with mixer and dough hook attachments, have also been on the consumer market a long time. It is only in the last few years, however, since less-expensive, lighter-weight models have become available, that these electric mixers with dough hook attachments have soared in popularity.

HOW A MIXER WITH A DOUGH HOOK WORKS

A dough hook is an attachment that fits into the beater shaft of a table-model electric mixer. It will automatically mix and knead heavy yeast doughs. Kneading is necessary to develop gluten in bread dough, and adequate kneading results in a firm, shiny, smooth, well-developed dough ready for rising and baking. A dough hook supplies the muscle power to knead dough for the long periods of time necessary to result in a well-formed and well-textured loaf of bread.

A table mixer works in one of two ways. Either the beaters remain station-ary and the bowl revolves around, or the bowl remains stationary and the beaters revolve around the bowl. The latter method is called planetary ac-tion. Planetary action results in more thorough mixing because there is greater contact between the mixer attachment and the food.

HOW TO BUY A MIXER WITH A DOUGH HOOK

Motor

A governor-controlled motor is a desirable feature of the better table-model mixers. This maintains a constant speed as the food load is increased or decreased.

The wattage of the motor is printed on the nameplate or in the manufac-turer's guide. The wattage tells whether the motor is capable of handling heavy mixtures. If the mixer will be regularly used to make bread dough, a very strong motor is probably the most important feature to consider.

Design

Some table mixers have a detachable head that can be removed from the base and used as a portable mixer. Although not as lightweight as other portable mixers, they can still be carried around and used to beat foods in a saucepan or double boiler.

Attachments and Accessories

A table-model mixer with a dough hook usually includes attachments for mixing, whipping and beating. These can take the form of flat or round-shaped beaters, wire whisks or whips. Often a rubber spatula is included in the ensemble.

Some mixers, particularly the food processor multipurpose-type models, come with optional attachments, such as a blender, juicer, grinder, sausage filler, can opener, silver buffer and even an ice-cream maker.

Mixers come with one large bowl, usually about 4-quart (4-liter) capacity. Stainless steel bowls are probably the most durable, but glass and plastic bowls are very popular too. Many models feature in addition a smaller bowl, usually 2-quart (2-liter) size.

SAFETY

Keep fingers, hair, clothing and hard objects away from the beaters and dough hook while the motor is running.

Unplug the mixer when cleaning or changing an attachment or when the unit is not in use.

Be sure the mixer bowl is securely in place before turning on the motor.

COOKING TECHNIQUES

Using the Dough Hook Attachment
When mixing and kneading bread dough, use the dough hook attachment and, with most mixers, at low speed. Mixers generally can accommodate recipes calling for up to 8 cups (2 liters) of flour.

Using the Beater Attachment
The beater attachment can be used with a variety of speeds to achieve the desired results when preparing foods in the mixer.

Use the beaters on low speed to combine cake ingredients, mix heavy dough, such as those for cookies and noodles, and for making mashed potatoes.

Use medium speed to cream shortening and sugar for cake batters, to beat cakes and to combine icing ingredients.

Use high speed to whip egg whites, whip cream and pareve dessert whip, and beat boiled icings.

WHAT TO EXPECT FROM A MIXER
WITH A DOUGH HOOK

A table-model mixer with a dough hook can perform all of the mixing, beating and whipping jobs of a portable mixer. In addition, because of a more powerful motor, the mixer can also perform heavy-duty work, such as kneading yeast dough and mixing cookie dough.

Do not expect the mixer to handle a bread recipe using over 8 cups (2 liters) of flour.

KEEPING KOSHER WITH A MIXER

The bowl and attachments of a mixer must be designated for either pareve, milchig or fleishig use, however, separate sets may be used on the same mixer base.

HOW TO ADAPT THESE RECIPES
TO YOUR MIXER

Each mixer recipe in this book advises whether to use the beater or dough hook attachment and indicates the desired speed—low, medium or high. If your mixer has a variety of speeds, choose the lowest speed possible for the job.

PART TWO

RECIPES

BREAKFAST FOODS

Most people over the age of 6, if they have any sense of independence or survival, know how to fix breakfast for themselves. Even a dedicated "non-cook" has some familiarity with the kitchen at this time of the day.

Keeping this point in mind, we cover primarily the basics in this chapter and show how kitchen appliances can help prepare cereals, cooked fruits, eggs and beverages a little more easily, a bit faster and a little more enjoyably.

An exception, however, and an exceptional recipe is the Gourmet Omelet, which utilizes the food processor to good advantage. This recipe is an excellent choice for a fancy brunch or Sunday breakfast.

The crock pot, used with an electrical timer, can cook cereals or fruit during the night and have breakfast waiting for you when you walk into the kitchen. These timers are the same type that automatically turn on house lights in the evening when you are away. If the recipe, such as stewed prunes, needs to cook 3 hours, and you want to have breakfast at 7 A.M., prepare the ingredients in the crock pot the evening before and set the timer to go on at 4 A.M. These timers are fairly inexpensive, operate on a low voltage and are safe and convenient to use.

This chapter shows 4 very basic ways to cook eggs in the microwave oven—baked, fried, poached and scrambled. Once these recipes are mastered, the basic techniques can be applied to much fancier or more elaborate egg recipes.

Eggs are one of the most difficult items to cook successfully in a microwave oven. If you have had difficulty in the past cooking eggs in your microwave oven, the reason was probably that the eggs cooked too long or too fast (on too high a setting). One large egg cooks in about 45 seconds on medium-high (70 percent power) setting or for 1 minute on medium (50 percent power) setting. If the egg is not firm enough after this, cook for 5 or 10 seconds longer on high setting.

The blender is featured in 4 meal-in-a-glass beverage recipes. Each recipe includes milk or juice and an egg.

Serve Crunchy Granola with milk as a breakfast cereal or dry as a snack.

Crunchy Granola   PAREVE

8 cups/2 liters oatmeal
1 cup/250 ml coconut
½ cup/125 ml wheat germ
½ cup/125 ml chopped nuts
½ cup/125 ml brown sugar

¼ cup/50 ml honey
½ cup/125 ml vegetable oil
1 tsp/5 ml cinnamon
1 tsp/5 ml vanilla
½ tsp/2 ml salt

Microwave Oven Directions   Combine all ingredients in a large glass bowl. Cook uncovered on a high setting 15 minutes or until lightly toasted, stirring every 4 to 5 minutes. Cool before serving.

Conventional Directions   Combine all ingredients and spread on a large baking sheet. Place in a 325° F (160° C) oven and bake until brown and toasted, about 30 to 45 minutes. Stir mixture frequently while baking.

YIELD: About 15 servings

Oatmeal   PAREVE

NUMBER OF SERVINGS:

	1	2	6
Water	¾ cup (175 ml)	1½ cups (375 ml)	4 cups (1 liter)
Salt	¼ tsp (1 ml)	½ tsp (2 ml)	1 tsp (5 ml)
Oats	⅓ cup (75 ml)	⅔ cup (150 ml)	2 cups (500 ml)

Microwave Oven Directions   Combine all ingredients in a glass bowl. (Use a large bowl, as cereal boils very high.) Cook on high setting until mixture boils, stirring once or twice. Cover with plastic wrap and let stand 1 to 2 minutes. Stir before serving.

Crock Pot Directions   Combine all ingredients in crock pot. Cover and cook on low setting 8 hours or overnight.

Conventional Directions   Stir oats into briskly boiling salted water. Cook according to box directions, stirring occasionally. Cover pan, remove from heat and let stand a few minutes before serving.

Yesterday's Oatmeal PAREVE

One serving of oatmeal from the refrigerator, covered with plastic wrap, reheats in about 1 minute in microwave oven on high setting. Stir and allow to stand 1 minute more before serving. YIELD: 1 serving

Banana Blender Drink DAIRY

1 banana
1 cup/250 ml milk
1 egg

2 tsp/10 ml sugar
Pinch nutmeg

Blender Directions Put all ingredients into blender goblet and blend for 30 seconds on high speed. Pour into a tall glass. YIELD: 1 serving

This drink is absolutely delicious and one of the most effective quick-energy snacks I have found. For extra richness, use 2 eggs.

Chocolate Blender Drink DAIRY

1 egg
1 cup/250 ml milk

1 tsp/5 ml cocoa
2 tsp/10 ml sugar

Blender Directions Combine all ingredients in blender goblet. Blend on high speed 15 seconds. Pour into a tall glass to serve. YIELD: 1 serving

I am, for better or worse, the type of person who sleepwalks around for a few hours after the alarm blasts off. However, I find that when I make this drink for my children the sound of the ice cubes crunching around inside the blender goblet snaps me into consciousness very quickly.

Orange Juicy Blender Drink DAIRY

1 orange
1 or 2 eggs
½ cup/125 ml water
¼ cup/50 ml milk

1 Tbsp/15 ml honey
5 ice cubes
Dash ground cloves

Blender Directions Peel orange and remove seeds. Cut orange into sections and place in blender goblet. Add egg, water, milk and honey and blend on high speed 15 seconds. With motor running, add ice cubes one at a time, blending until mixture is smooth. Pour into tall glasses and sprinkle with ground cloves. YIELD: 2 servings

Mocha Blender Drink   DAIRY

2 tsp/10 ml instant coffee   Dash cinnamon
1 cup/250 ml milk   1 egg
2 tsp/10 ml sugar

Blender Directions   Put all ingredients in blender goblet. Blend on high speed
15 seconds. Pour into a tall glass to serve.   YIELD: 1 serving

---

Tomato-Yogurt Breakfast Cocktail   DAIRY

1 cup/250 ml tomato juice   Dash pepper
½ cup/125 ml plain yogurt   1 Tbsp/15 ml Worcestershire sauce
¼ tsp/1 ml onion salt   Lemon wedge

Blender Directions   Combine all ingredients except lemon wedge in blender
goblet. Blend on high speed 15 seconds or until smooth. Pour into a tall
glass. Serve with lemon wedge.   YIELD: 1 serving

When frying eggs in a microwave oven a special accessory, the browning
dish, must be used. This dish has a coating on the bottom that becomes very
hot, as does a frying pan. In using a browning dish, the proper technique is
first to preheat on high setting before adding the food.

Fried Egg   PAREVE

1 Tbsp/15 ml pareve margarine
1 egg

Microwave Oven Directions   Place empty browning dish in microwave oven
and preheat 1½ minutes on high setting. Melt margarine in dish, then carefully crack egg into it. Cover with lid. Cook on high setting 1 minute.

The technique for cooking additional batches of fried eggs is to preheat
the browning dish 30 seconds between each batch. Cook eggs on high setting
30 seconds per egg.

Conventional Directions   Melt margarine in a hot frying pan. Crack egg into
the pan and cook slowly to desired degree of firmness, basting egg with the
margarine.   YIELD: 1 serving

When poaching eggs, be sure they are completely covered with water. Vinegar added to the poaching water helps to give the egg a nice shape and prevent it from becoming stringy. It does not affect the flavor of the egg.

Poached Egg   PAREVE

1 cup or more/250 ml water   1 egg
½ tsp/2 ml vinegar

Microwave Oven Directions   Combine water and vinegar in a glass bowl. Cook on high setting 3 minutes or until boiling.

Crack the egg into boiling water. Cover dish with plastic wrap and cook on high setting 45 seconds. Let stand 30 seconds after cooking. Remove with a slotted spoon and serve immediately.

Conventional Directions   Pour water into a saucepan to a depth of 2 inches (5 cm). Add vinegar. Bring to a boil over high heat. Reduce heat and allow liquid to simmer. Carefully crack egg into a dish, then slide it into the water. Simmer 3 to 5 minutes, depending upon degree of firmness desired. Remove egg with a slotted spoon. Serve immediately.   YIELD: 1 serving

Poached Eggs and Hamburgers   FLEISHIG

1 lb/500 grams hamburger   Salt and pepper to taste
1 Tbsp/15 ml gravy coloring or   4 poached eggs
  Worcestershire sauce   Parsley sprigs, for garnish

Microwave Oven Directions   Divide hamburger into quarters and shape each into a large patty. Brush each patty with gravy coloring and place on a plastic rack in microwave oven. Cover with wax paper. Cook on high setting 3½ minutes. Turn patties, brush the other side with gravy coloring and cook on high setting 3½ to 5 minutes longer or until done to taste. Season with salt and pepper.

Top each patty with a hot poached egg. Serve garnished with parsley.

Conventional Directions   Form hamburger into 4 patties. Brush with gravy coloring. Fry in a hot frying pan until brown, turning once. Cook until done to taste. Season with salt and pepper. Top each patty with a hot poached egg and serve garnished with parsley.   YIELD: 4 servings

The exact time for baking eggs in a microwave oven will vary according to the number, size and temperature of the eggs. The following technique can be used for soft-baked eggs for breakfast or for hard-baked eggs that can be chopped and substituted for hard-boiled eggs in many recipes.

Baked (Shirred) Eggs   PAREVE

1 egg
Salt and pepper to taste

Microwave Oven Directions   Break egg into a lightly greased glass bowl or small custard cup. Cover with plastic wrap and cook on medium setting 1 minute (or medium-high setting 45 seconds) or until desired degree of firmness. Season with salt and pepper.

Conventional Directions   Break egg into a greased bowl or small custard cup. Season with salt and pepper. Bake in a 325° F (160° C) oven about 15 minutes or until egg is firm.   YIELD: 1 serving

Eggs and English Muffins   DAIRY

1 (10¾-oz)/(305 grams) can
  condensed cream of mushroom
  soup, undiluted
¼ cup/50 ml milk
1 cup/250 ml fresh mushrooms,
  sliced

3 English muffins, split,
  toasted and buttered
6 poached or microwave baked eggs
½ cup/125 ml shredded
  yellow cheese
Dash paprika

Microwave Oven Directions   Combine soup and milk in a glass bowl, stirring to form a sauce. Cook 2 minutes on high setting until very hot. Set aside.
    Place sliced mushrooms in a small glass bowl and cover with plastic wrap. Cook on high setting 1 minute. Drain and stir mushrooms into sauce.
    On a glass serving dish, arrange English muffin halves. Top each with a poached egg. Spoon mushroom sauce over eggs and sprinkle with cheese and paprika. Cook on high setting 30 seconds or until cheese is melted.

Conventional Directions   Combine soup and milk in a saucepan. Cook over medium heat, stirring constantly until bubbly. Sauté mushrooms in 2 tablespoons (25 ml) butter, then add to sauce mixture.
    Top each English muffin half with a poached egg. Spoon mushroom sauce over egg and sprinkle with cheese and paprika. Place under hot broiler until cheese is melted.   YIELD: 6 servings

This dish is especially attractive garnished with sliced tomatoes.

Breakfast Sandwich   D A I R Y

2 eggs
Salt and pepper to taste
2 Tbsp/25 ml chopped green
  pepper
1 Pita bread (see recipe in
  Yeast Breads chapter)

4 Tbsp/50 ml shredded
  cheddar cheese
1 Tbsp/15 ml chopped black olives

Microwave Oven Directions   Beat eggs with salt and pepper and pour into a
glass bowl. Cook on medium setting 1½ minutes. Stir eggs and add green
pepper. Cook on medium setting 30 to 45 seconds longer or until eggs are set.

Cut an opening in the top of the pita bread to form a pocket. Place bread
on a paper towel in microwave oven and cook on high setting 20 seconds or
until bread is warm.

Spoon cooked eggs into pita. Sprinkle top of eggs with cheese and olives.
Serve immediately.

Conventional Directions   Beat eggs with salt and pepper. Pour into a hot buttered frying pan. Add green pepper. Cook, stirring until eggs are firm but
moist. Cut an opening in the top of the pita to form a pocket. Spoon cooked
eggs into pita. Sprinkle top of eggs with cheese and olives. Serve immediately.   YIELD: 1 serving

---

Egg Puffs   D A I R Y

4 eggs
¼ cup/50 ml sour cream

Salt and pepper to taste

Microwave Oven Directions   Combine all ingredients and beat well. Pour mixture into 4 glass custard cups. Cook on medium setting 5½ minutes or until
eggs are puffy. Serve immediately.

Conventional Directions   Arrange 4 greased custard or egg-poaching cups in a
shallow pan of boiling water (a skillet is ideal). Pour egg mixture into cups.
Cover pan and simmer for 12 minutes or until eggs are puffy.

YIELD: 4 servings

There are two "tricks" to making gourmet omelets. First, use a very hot frying pan (preheated on high heat several minutes), then always mix the eggs with water instead of milk. When the water in the egg mixture hits the hot pan it instantly turns to steam and "lifts" the omelet. Milk would scorch in such a hot pan. The food processor is the perfect appliance to use to prepare quick and tasty omelet fillings.

Gourmet Omelet   D A I R Y

2 eggs   1 Tbsp/15 ml butter
2 Tbsp/25 ml water   Prepared filling (see Fillings)
Dash salt and pepper

Conventional Directions   Blend eggs, water, salt and pepper. In a very hot pan, melt the butter, then add egg mixture. Large bubbles will form as the eggs cook (if pan is too hot, lift from burner a moment to cool). Gently push cooked portion of the eggs to the center and tilt pan to allow uncooked portion to spread out. Omelet should set in about 30 seconds.

When omelet base is set, arrange filling on one side only. Using spatula, fold omelet so that the plain side covers the filled side.

Remove pan from heat. Gently transfer omelet onto serving dish. Serve immediately.   YIELD: 1 serving

Omelet Fillings
To prepare omelet fillings in food processor, use the following attachments: Use *shredding disc* for cheeses such as cheddar, jack, mozzarella and Swiss; use the *slicing disc* to slice vegetables such as mushrooms, onions or tomatoes, or fruits such as peaches and strawberries; use the *steel blade* to chop onions, green onions, green peppers, chile peppers, cooked chicken, liver or meat.

Cheese Omelet   D A I R Y

½ cup/125 ml shredded yellow cheese   ½ cup/125 ml shredded
                                       white cheese
Use cheeses as a filling.

Chicken Omelet   F L E I S H I G

1 Tbsp/15 ml pareve margarine   ½ cup/125 ml chopped cooked
¼ cup/50 ml chicken gravy   chicken
                                     ½ cup/125 ml seedless green grapes,
                                     optional

Use pareve margarine instead of butter when frying omelet. Mix gravy and chicken and use as a filling. The addition of grapes, cut into halves, gives an excellent flavor and texture.

Liver and Onion Omelet   FLEISHIG

1 Tbsp/15 ml chicken fat or pareve
   margarine

½ cup/125 ml coarsely chopped
   or sliced cooked liver
¼ cup/50 ml sliced onions

Use chicken fat or pareve margarine instead of butter when frying omelet.
Mix liver and onions and use as a filling.

Lox and Onion Omelet   DAIRY

1 (3-oz)/(85 grams) package
   cream cheese
2 Tbsp/25 ml milk

2 oz/50 grams chopped lox
¼ cup/50 ml chopped onions

Combine all ingredients, mix well, and use as a filling.

Mushroom Omelet   DAIRY

½ cup/125 ml sliced
   fresh mushrooms

¼ cup/50 ml sour cream
½ teaspoon/2 ml dill weed

Combine and use as omelet filling.

Oriental Omelet   FLEISHIG

1 Tbsp/15 ml pareve margarine
½ cup/125 ml chopped
   cooked chicken

¼ cup/50 ml drained bean sprouts
3 water chestnuts, sliced
1 tsp/5 ml soy sauce

Use pareve margarine instead of butter when frying omelet. Mix remaining
ingredients and use as a filling.

Spanish Omelet   PAREVE

3 Tbsp/45 ml chopped green onions
¾ cup/175 ml chopped tomatoes

½ tsp/2 ml Worcestershire sauce
Dash garlic powder

Mix and use as a filling.

Strawberry Omelet   DAIRY

1 Tbsp/15 ml sour cream
½ cup/125 ml sliced strawberries

½ tsp/2 ml grated orange peel

Mix and use as a filling. Fresh peaches may be substituted for the strawberries.   YIELD: Filling for 2 omelets

Scrambled Eggs   DAIRY

1 Tbsp/15 ml butter   2 Tbsp/25 ml milk
2 eggs   Salt and pepper to taste

Microwave Oven Directions   Place butter in a glass bowl. Cook on a high setting, until butter is melted, 25 to 30 seconds. Add eggs, milk, salt and
pepper, mixing well with a fork. Cook on medium setting 1½ minutes or
until outer edges of egg are cooked. Use a spoon to push cooked portions of
the egg toward center of the dish. Cook on medium setting 30 to 45 seconds
longer, until the egg is firm but not dry. Stir eggs with a fork, then cover
with plastic wrap and allow to stand 1 to 2 minutes before serving.

Conventional Directions   Beat eggs, milk, salt and pepper. Heat butter in a
frying pan and add egg mixture. Cook over medium heat, stirring occasionally, until eggs are thickened but still moist. Serve immediately.

YIELD: 1 serving

Applesauce   PAREVE

8 tart apples, peeled, cored and   ½ cup/125 ml sugar, or to taste
    quartered   1 tsp/5 ml cinnamon
½ cup/125 ml water

Microwave Oven Directions   Place apples and water in a glass bowl. Cover
with plastic wrap. Cook on high setting 15 minutes or until apples are
tender, stirring once.
   Mash apples with a fork. Stir in sugar and cinnamon.

Crock Pot Directions   Place apples and water in crock pot. Cover and cook on
low 4 to 6 hours or until apples are very soft.
   Puree apples or mash with a fork. Stir in sugar and cinnamon.

Conventional Directions   Place apples and water in a saucepan. Bring to a boil,
then reduce heat and simmer until apples are tender, adding more water as
needed to keep apples from sticking to pan. Cook until apples are tender.
   Puree apples or mash with a fork. Stir in sugar and cinnamon.

YIELD: 8 to 10 servings

Stewed Apricots   P A R E V E

½ lb/250 grams dried apricots   ¼ cup/50 ml sugar, or to taste
1 cup/250 ml water   Dash cinnamon

Microwave Oven Directions Place all ingredients in a glass bowl. Cover with plastic wrap. Cook on high setting 8 to 10 minutes or until apricots are tender and flavors have blended.

Crock Pot Directions Combine all ingredients in crock pot. Cover and cook on low 2 to 3 hours.

Conventional Directions—Cooked Combine all ingredients in a saucepan and bring to a boil. Cover and simmer gently about 30 minutes or until fruit is tender.

Conventional Directions—Uncooked Place apricots in a large jar and add sugar and cinnamon. Boil water and pour over apricots. Cover tightly and let stand overnight.   YIELD: 3 to 4 servings

Stewed Prunes   P A R E V E

1 lb/500 grams dried prunes   1 tsp/5 ml grated lemon peel
3 cups/750 ml water   2 Tbsp/25 ml sugar, or to taste
1 Tbsp/15 ml lemon juice

Microwave Oven Directions Place prunes and water in a glass bowl. Let stand 1 hour or until prunes are softened. Stir in remaining ingredients. Cover with plastic wrap. Cook on high setting 10 minutes. Serve hot or cold.

Crock Pot Directions Combine all ingredients in crock pot. Cover and cook on low setting 2 to 3 hours or until prunes are plump.

Conventional Directions—Cooked Combine all ingredients in a saucepan. Bring to a boil. Reduce heat and simmer gently, covered, until fruit is soft.

Conventional Directions—Uncooked Place prunes in a large jar and add lemon juice, peel and sugar. Boil water and pour over prunes. Cover tightly. Let stand overnight.   YIELD: 6 servings

Dried Fruit Compote   PAREVE

1 lb/500 grams dried fruit (apricots,   ¼ cup/50 ml sugar, or to taste
   prunes, peaches, apples or   1 tsp/5 ml grated lemon peel
   combination)   ½ tsp/2 ml cinnamon
2 cups/500 ml apple juice

Microwave Oven Directions   Combine all ingredients in a glass bowl. Cover
with plastic wrap and cook on high setting 15 to 20 minutes until fruit is
tender and flavors have blended.

Crock Pot Directions   Combine all ingredients in crock pot. Cover and cook
on low 2 to 3 hours or until fruit is tender.

Conventional Directions   Combine all ingredients in saucepan and bring to a
boil. Cover and simmer gently until fruit is tender.   YIELD: 6 servings

HELPFUL HINTS FOR BREAKFAST FOODS

To Heat Water for Instant Coffee, Tea or Cocoa
Water from tap, at room temperature, boils in about 3 minutes per cup on
high setting in microwave oven. Drinking temperature, however, is usually
170° F to 180° F (76° C and 82° C). This temperature is reached in about
1½ minutes on high setting.

To Warm Syrup
Remove bottle cap from a glass or plastic bottle of syrup and place bottle in
microwave oven. Cook on high setting only long enough to warm the syrup,
usually about 30 to 45 seconds for a full 16-oz (454-gram) bottle.

To Defrost Orange Juice
To defrost orange juice concentrate quickly in microwave oven, open one
end of a can. Place can open end up in microwave oven and cook on high
setting 30 seconds. Pour contents into a pitcher. Concentrate should be
melted and ready to mix with water.

To Reconstitute Frozen Juice
Place frozen juice concentrate and measured amount of water into the
blender goblet. Blend on low speed until well mixed, about 20 seconds. Juice
will be very light and foamy.

QUICK BREADS

Quick breads are made of batters and doughs that provide a product similar to yeast mixtures but, as the name implies, they produce results much faster. All the following quick-bread recipes contain baking powder or baking soda. These act as a leavening agent, making quick breads light and tender.

The microwave oven cooks quick breads more quickly than they have ever been cooked before, e.g., one muffin in less than a minute. When cooking items such as Cornbread and Ginger-Orange Bread in the microwave oven, remember to rotate the baking pans at least once while the breads are cooking. Items such as these have a heavy batter and cook best when covered with wax paper, for at least the first half of the cooking time.

Muffins in the microwave oven should be baked in either a special microwave oven muffin pan or paper-lined glass custard cups. Best results are almost always obtained when the cups are arranged in a circle. Unless the microwave oven has a carousel or turntable, muffins, like breads and cakes, need to be rotated at least once while cooking.

Use the following chart as a time guide for baking muffins in the microwave oven:

NUMBER OF MUFFINS	SETTING	TIME
1	medium-high	45 seconds
2	medium-high	1–1½ minutes
4	medium-high	2–2½ minutes
6	medium-high	2½–3 minutes

The crock pot does a lovely job of cooking quick breads and coffee cakes. Two cooking methods are presented here. Items such as Cornbread are "baked" in a baking dish placed in the crock pot with 4 or 5 paper towels laid over the top to absorb excess moisture. The crock pot is then covered. In the second cooking method, items such as coffee cakes and fruit breads are steamed, with the tightly covered baking dish placed on top of a rack or trivet inside the crock pot. Pour 2 cups (500 ml) hot water around the baking dish to provide steam for cooking. High setting is used for both of these cooking methods.

Harvest Bread, with its many variations, utilizes the food processor to great advantage. This appliance can mix 3½–4 cups of batter (just enough for one loaf) or it can combine the liquid ingredients and then you can fold them by hand into the dry ingredients.

Use the blender to mix smooth, well-formed batters for pancakes and waffles. When blending ingredients for coffee cakes and muffins, the technique is to blend liquid ingredients until smooth and then by hand, or using very short mixing times with the blender, to combine the liquid and dry ingredients. For all blender recipes in this chapter, blend carefully to avoid overmixing.

Use the mixer for recipes such as waffles that involve whipped egg whites. The mixer also does a beautiful job of mixing batters for pancakes or coffee cakes.

A variety of fruit and vegetable bread variations can be made from one basic nut bread recipe.

Harvest Bread   P A R E V E

½ cup/125 ml walnuts
1 cup/250 ml sugar
2 eggs
½ cup/125 ml pareve margarine,
  cut into 8 pieces
1 cup/250 ml pureed or shredded
  fruit or vegetable (see Variations)

½ tsp/2 ml vanilla
2 cups/500 ml flour, sifted
½ tsp/2 ml baking soda
1 tsp/5 ml baking powder
½ tsp/2 ml salt

Food Processor Directions Insert steel blade in food processor and coarsely chop walnuts. Set aside. Put sugar and eggs into container and process 15 to 20 seconds. Add chunks of margarine and blend. Add fruit or vegetable puree, vanilla and dry ingredients. Combine by turning motor on and off quickly several times. Do not overprocess. Remove steel blade and stir nuts by hand into mixture.

Pour mixture into greased loaf pan and bake in a 350° F (180° C) oven for 1 hour, or until toothpick inserted in center comes out clean. Let cool in pan 10 minutes, then turn cake out onto a rack to cool.   YIELD: 1 loaf

Variations Make the following changes in basic Harvest Bread recipe:

Apple Bread   PAREVE

1 cup/250 ml shredded apples   ½ tsp/2 ml cinnamon
½ tsp/2 ml nutmeg   ½ cup/125 ml raisins

Peel and core apples and shred in food processor, using shredding disc. Set aside. Insert steel blade in food processor and proceed with basic recipe. Add nutmeg and cinnamon along with the dry ingredients. Fold raisins into batter along with the nuts.

Carrot Bread   PAREVE

1 cup/250 ml shredded carrots
1 tsp/5 ml cinnamon

Shred carrots in food processor using shredding disc. Set aside. Insert steel blade into food processor and proceed with basic recipe. Add cinnamon along with the dry ingredients.

Orange Bread   PAREVE

1 orange, seeded

Insert steel blade into food processor, and chop walnuts as in basic recipe. Set aside. Cut orange into 16 pieces (peel and all) and remove seeds. Place orange pieces and sugar in container. Process, using pulse button or quick on-off motion until orange is chopped, then process continuously until orange is finely grated. Add eggs and proceed with basic recipe.

Peach Bread   PAREVE

1 cup/250 ml pureed peaches
¼ tsp/1 ml nutmeg

Puree canned or peeled fresh peaches in food processor, using steel blade. Set aside. Proceed with basic recipe, adding nutmeg along with the dry ingredients.

Pumpkin Bread   PAREVE

1 cup/250 ml pumpkin puree
1½ tsp/7 ml pumpkin pie spice

Puree cooked pumpkin in food processor using steel blade (or use canned pumpkin). Set aside. Proceed with basic recipe, adding pumpkin pie spice along with the dry ingredients.

Zucchini Bread   PAREVE

1 cup/250 ml shredded zucchini   1½ tsp/7 ml cinnamon

Shred unpeeled zucchini in food processor using shredding disc. Set aside.
Proceed with basic recipe, adding cinnamon along with the dry ingredients.

YIELD: 1 loaf

Ginger-Orange Bread   PAREVE

¼ cup/50 ml pareve margarine	1 tsp/5 ml ground ginger
⅓ cup/75 ml sugar	1 tsp/5 ml cinnamon
1 egg	1 tsp/5 ml salt
¾ cup/175 ml molasses	1 tsp/5 ml baking soda
¾ cup/175 ml orange juice	1 Tbsp/15 ml grated orange peel
2 cups/500 ml sifted flour	2 cups/500 ml hot water

Microwave Oven Directions Cream margarine and sugar in a large mixing
bowl. Add egg and beat well. Mix molasses with orange juice. Sift dry ingredients together and add alternately with molasses and orange juice, beating
thoroughly after each addition. Stir in orange peel.

Line an 8-inch (20-cm) square glass dish with wax paper. Pour batter into
dish and cover with wax paper. Cook on medium high setting 3½ minutes.
Remove wax paper cover and cook 3 to 4 minutes longer on medium high.
Cool slightly before serving.

Crock Pot Directions Grease and flour a 2-quart (2-liter) mold which will fit
comfortably into crock pot. Pour prepared bread mixture into mold and
cover top securely with foil, then tie the foil firmly in place with string or
strong thread. Place filled mold on a metal rack in crock pot. Pour 2 cups
(500 ml) hot water around mold and cover crock pot. Cook on high setting 3
to 4 hours or until done. Remove from mold and cool on a rack. Serve warm
or cooled.

Conventional Directions Prepare batter as directed and pour into a well-
greased 8-inch (20-cm) square baking dish. Bake at 350° F (180° C) about
30 to 45 minutes or until top springs back when lightly touched.

YIELD: 1 large loaf

Cornbread   DAIRY

1 cup/250 ml sifted flour	¾ cup/175 ml cornmeal
3 tsp/15 ml baking powder	1½ cups/375 ml buttermilk
½ tsp/2 ml salt	2 eggs, well beaten
½ tsp/2 ml baking soda	2 Tbsp/25 ml melted butter
⅓ cup/75 ml sugar	

Microwave Oven Directions Sift flour, baking powder, salt and baking soda into mixing bowl. Stir in sugar and cornmeal. Add buttermilk to beaten eggs and stir into dry ingredients. Stir in melted butter.

Line an 8-inch (20-cm) glass dish with wax paper. Pour prepared batter into dish and cover with wax paper. Cook on medium-high setting 3½ minutes. Remove wax-paper cover and cook 3 to 4 minutes longer on medium-high or until top springs back when lightly touched.

Crock Pot Directions Prepare batter as described above and pour into a well-greased baking dish that will fit comfortably into crock pot. Place dish in crock pot and lay 4 or 5 paper towels over baking dish to absorb excess moisture. Cover crock pot and cook on high setting 2 to 3 hours.

Conventional Directions Prepare batter as described above and pour into a greased baking dish. Bake at 425° F (220° C) 25 to 30 minutes.

YIELD: 1 pan bread

Cranberry Fruit Bread   P A R E V E

2 cups (½ lb)/500 ml (250 grams) fresh cranberries
1 apple
½ cup/125 ml chopped pecans
2 cups/500 ml sifted flour
1 cup/250 ml sugar
1½ tsp/7 ml baking powder
½ tsp/2 ml baking soda

½ tsp/2 ml salt
⅓ cup/75 ml pareve margarine
1 egg
1 tsp/5 ml grated orange peel
1 tsp/5 ml grated lemon peel
½ cup/125 ml orange juice
1 tsp/5 ml lemon juice
2 cups/500 ml hot water

Crock Pot Directions Put cranberries through the coarsest blade of the food grinder (or steel blade on food processor). Peel apple, remove core and dice into small pieces. Combine cranberries, apple and pecans and set aside.

Sift flour, sugar, baking powder, baking soda and salt into a large mixing bowl. Cut in pareve margarine until mixture resembles small peas. Stir in egg, orange and lemon peel, and juices. Add cranberry mixture and stir until mixture is well blended.

Grease and flour a 2-quart (2-liter) mold which will fit comfortably into crock pot. Pour mixture into mold and cover top securely with foil, then tie the foil firmly into place with string or strong thread. Place filled mold on a metal rack in crock pot. Pour 2 cups hot water around mold and cover crock pot. Cook on high setting 2½ to 3 hours. Remove mold from crock pot and turn bread onto a cooling rack. Serve warm or cooled.   YIELD: 1 large loaf

Biscuits   PAREVE or DAIRY

2 cups/500 ml sifted flour   ¼ cup/50 ml pareve margarine
1 tsp/5 ml salt   ⅔ cup/150 ml water or milk
3 tsp/15 ml baking powder   Melted pareve margarine

Mixer Directions Sift dry ingredients into mixer bowl. Cut margarine into
small chunks and drop into flour mixture. Mix on low speed until mixture
resembles cornmeal. Add water or milk and mix on low speed until dough
clings to beaters and clears sides of the bowl.

Transfer dough to a lightly floured surface. Knead lightly until smooth,
about 30 seconds. Pat or roll dough to ½-inch (1.5-cm) thickness. Cut into
circles with a 2-inch (5-cm) biscuit cutter.

Place biscuits on a greased baking sheet and brush with melted pareve
margarine. Bake at 450° F (230° C) 12 to 15 minutes. Serve immediately.

YIELD: 12 biscuits

Variations Make the following changes in basic Biscuit recipe:

Buttermilk Biscuits   DAIRY

⅔ cup/150 ml buttermilk   ½ tsp/2 ml baking soda

Substitute buttermilk for water in basic recipe. Add baking soda with dry
ingredients.

Fruit-filled Biscuits   PAREVE

¼ cup/50 ml jam or preserves

Prepare Biscuit dough and roll into ¼-inch (1-cm) thickness. Cut into circles
as directed. Place a spoonful of jam on a biscuit circle, then cover with a
second circle. Press edges together. Continue with remaining biscuits and
jam.

Orange Biscuits   PAREVE

⅔ cup/150 ml orange juice   1 Tbsp/15 ml grated orange peel

Substitute orange juice for water in basic recipe. Add orange peel to dry
ingredients.

Rich-tasting Biscuits   DAIRY

⅔ cup/150 ml sour cream

Substitute sour cream for water in basic recipe.   YIELD: 12 biscuits

Basic Coffee Cake   DAIRY

1½ cups/375 ml sifted flour   1 egg
½ cup/125 ml sugar   ⅔ cup/150 ml milk
2 tsp/10 ml baking powder   3 Tbsp/45 ml melted butter
½ tsp/2 ml salt

Mixer Directions Sift dry ingredients together and set aside. Place egg in mixer bowl, and begin mixing on low speed. Gradually add milk and melted butter. Add dry ingredients and continue mixing until flour is moistened. Pour into greased 8-inch (20-cm) cake pan. Bake at 425° F (220° C) 25 to 30 minutes.   YIELD: 1 coffee cake

Variations Make the following changes in Basic Coffee Cake recipe:

Almond Coffee Cake   DAIRY

½ tsp/2 ml almond extract   ½ cup/125 ml chopped almonds
1 egg white

Add almond extract to Basic Coffee Cake batter along with the milk. Pour batter into greased cake pan. Before baking, brush cake top with a slightly beaten egg white. Sprinkle with chopped almonds. Bake as in basic recipe.

Apple Coffee Cake   DAIRY

1 cup/250 ml apple slices   ¼ cup/50 ml chopped walnuts
2 tsp/10 ml cinnamon   1 egg
¼ cup/50 ml brown sugar   ¼ cup/50 ml milk or cream

Prepare Basic Coffee Cake batter as in basic recipe and pour into greased cake pan. Cover batter with a layer of thinly sliced apples. Sprinkle with cinnamon and brown sugar. Top with chopped walnuts. Beat egg with milk or cream and pour over top. Bake at 400° F (200° C) about 40 minutes.

Coffee Cake with Streusel Topping   DAIRY

2 Tbsp/25 ml melted butter   ½ tsp/2 ml cinnamon
¼ cup/50 ml brown sugar

Prepare Basic Coffee Cake batter as in basic recipe. Pour into greased cake pan. Combine melted butter, brown sugar and cinnamon. Sprinkle evenly over batter and bake as in basic recipe.

                                    YIELD: 1 coffee cake

Yogurt-Streusel Coffee Cake   D A I R Y

STREUSEL TOPPING

2 Tbsp/25 ml butter   ¼ cup/50 ml bread crumbs
3 Tbsp/45 ml brown sugar   ½ tsp/2 ml cinnamon
2 Tbsp/25 ml sugar   ½ cup/125 ml chopped pecans
¼ cup/50 ml flour

COFFEE CAKE

2 cups/500 ml sifted flour   ½ cup/125 ml soft butter
1 tsp/5 ml baking powder   ½ cup/125 ml sugar
1 tsp/5 ml baking soda   ½ cup/125 ml brown sugar
½ tsp/2 ml salt   1 tsp/5 ml vanilla
2 eggs   1 cup/250 ml unflavored yogurt

Blender Directions   To prepare streusel topping: Melt butter and set aside. Place remaining ingredients except pecans in blender goblet and blend on low speed until well mixed. With motor running, add melted butter, blending well. Pour streusel topping into a small bowl, stir in pecans and set aside.

To prepare coffee cake: Sift flour, baking powder, soda and salt into a large mixing bowl and set aside. Pour remaining ingredients, except yogurt, into blender goblet. Mix at low speed until smooth. Add half the yogurt and half the flour mixture. Blend on high speed until smooth. Stop motor and scrape sides of goblet with a rubber spatula. Add remaining yogurt and dry ingredients and blend until smooth.

Pour coffee cake batter into a greased 9-inch (23-cm) spring-form pan. Sprinkle with prepared streusel topping. Bake at 350° F (180° C) 45 minutes or until a toothpick inserted in the center comes out clean.

YIELD: 1 coffee cake

Variation

Sour Cream Streusel Cake   D A I R Y

1 cup/250 ml sour cream

Substitute sour cream for the yogurt and proceed as in basic recipe.

YIELD: 1 coffee cake

Caraway-Cheese Muffins   D A I R Y

2 cups/500 ml sifted flour
4 tsp/20 ml baking powder
1 Tbsp/15 ml sugar
½ tsp/2 ml salt
2 tsp/10 ml caraway seeds

1 egg
1 cup/250 ml milk or buttermilk
3 Tbsp/45 ml butter, softened
1½ cups/375 ml shredded
  yellow cheese

Blender Directions Sift the dry ingredients into a large mixing bowl. Add caraway seeds and set aside.

In blender goblet combine the egg, milk and butter. Blend on medium speed until smooth. Add cheese and blend. Pour cheese batter into dry ingredients and stir by hand until flour is moistened. Do not overmix.

Pour batter into greased or paper-lined muffin tins and bake at 350° F (180° C) about 30 minutes.   YIELD: 12 muffins

---

This is a tasty and nutritious muffin recipe, but the real beauty and convenience are that the batter stays fresh in the refrigerator as long as a month.

Forever Yours Bran Muffins   D A I R Y

1 cup/250 ml boiling water
3 cups/750 ml bran flakes cereal
1 cup/250 ml sugar
½ cup/125 salad oil
2 tsp/10 ml baking powder

½ tsp/2 ml salt
2½ cups/625 ml flour
2 eggs, beaten
2 cups/500 ml buttermilk
1 cup/250 ml raisins

Microwave Oven Directions Pour boiling water over bran flakes cereal. Stir and allow to cool.

In a large bowl, mix sugar and oil. Sift together dry ingredients and add to sugar mixture. Stir in cereal mixture, along with remaining ingredients and blend well. Cover and store in the refrigerator.

Do not stir mixture when spooning batter into paper-lined microwave oven muffin pan. Cook on medium-high setting 45 seconds per muffin or 2½–3 minutes for 6 muffins.

Conventional Directions Bake prepared batter in greased muffin tins at 400° F (200° C) 20 minutes.   YIELD: About 40 muffins

PANCAKES

Many pancake batter recipes are given in the following pages. All of the batters, once mixed, are cooked in the following manner:

Conventional Directions   Use a very hot, lightly greased griddle or frying pan. Pour ¼ cup (50 ml) prepared batter onto the griddle and cook pancakes until bubbles appear on the surface. Turn pancakes before the bubbles burst (or pancakes will be tough). Turn only once and cook pancakes on the other side. Serve immediately with butter and hot syrup or jam.

Batter for Buttermilk Pancakes may be made the night before and stored in a covered pitcher in refrigerator.

Buttermilk Pancakes   D A I R Y

3 eggs   2 tsp/10 ml baking powder
2 cups/500 ml buttermilk   1 tsp/5 ml salt
½ tsp/2 ml baking soda   2 tsp/10 ml sugar
2½ cups/625 ml flour   ½ cup/125 ml melted butter

Blender Directions   Place eggs and buttermilk in blender goblet. Add remaining ingredients. Blend at high speed until batter is smooth and bubbly. Use a rubber spatula to scrape the sides of the goblet to be sure all the flour is blended.

Pour batter directly from goblet onto hot griddle, allowing ¼ cup (50 ml) batter for each pancake.

Mixer Directions   Beat 3 eggs on medium speed until fluffy. Combine buttermilk and baking soda. Sift dry ingredients and add to eggs alternately with the buttermilk. Add melted butter.

Pour batter onto hot griddle, allowing ¼ cup (50 ml) batter for each pancake.   YIELD: About 18 pancakes

Variations Make the following changes in Buttermilk Pancakes recipe:

Banana Pancakes   DAIRY

1 banana

Slice banana thin and stir into prepared pancake batter.

Blueberry Pancakes   DAIRY

1 cup/250 ml blueberries

Drain blueberries well and stir into prepared pancake batter.

Cottage Cheese Pancakes   DAIRY

1 cup/250 ml cottage cheese
1 cup/250 ml milk

Omit buttermilk from basic recipe and substitute cottage cheese and milk when preparing batter.

Sour Cream Pancakes   DAIRY

2 cups/500 ml sour cream

Omit buttermilk from basic recipe and substitute sour cream when preparing batter.   YIELD: About 18 pancakes

Sourdough Pancakes   DAIRY

2 cups/500 ml Sourdough Batter   ½ cup/125 ml milk
   (see recipe in   1 tsp/5 ml salt
   Yeast Breads chapter)   1 tsp/5 ml baking soda
1 egg   2 Tbsp/25 ml sugar
2 Tbsp/25 ml vegetable oil

Blender Directions Put Sourdough Batter into blender goblet. Add egg, oil and milk and blend on medium speed.

Combine salt, baking soda and sugar. Sprinkle over top of batter. Using several quick on-off turns, gently combine dry ingredients into batter.

Pour batter directly from goblet onto hot griddle, allowing about ¼ cup (50 ml) batter for each pancake.   YIELD: About 12 pancakes

Packaged Pancakes

Blender Directions   Assemble and measure ingredients according to directions on package of pancake mix. Put all ingredients into blender goblet and blend on low speed until batter is thoroughly mixed.

Pour batter directly from goblet onto hot griddle, allowing about ¼ cup (50 ml) batter for each pancake.

The next time you are making pancakes on the griddle, double or triple the recipe. Freeze the leftover pancakes in individual plastic bags.

Next-Day Pancakes   DAIRY

3 frozen pancakes   2 Tbsp/25 ml syrup
1 Tbsp/15 ml butter

Microwave Oven Directions   Remove 3 frozen pancakes from the plastic bags and stack on a serving plate. Top with butter and syrup. Cook in microwave oven on high setting 1½ minutes.   YIELD: 1 serving

---

Basic Waffles   DAIRY

1½ cups/375 ml flour   2 eggs, separated
2 tsp/10 ml baking powder   2 Tbsp/25 ml vegetable oil
1 tsp/5 ml sugar   1¼ cups/300 ml milk
½ tsp/2 ml salt

Mixer Directions   Preheat electric waffle iron.

To prepare waffle batter: Sift dry ingredients together and set aside. Separate eggs and place whites in mixer bowl. Attach beaters and whip whites on high speed until stiff peaks form. In a separate bowl, beat egg yolks on medium mixer speed until thick and lemon-colored. Add oil and milk and beat thoroughly. Add dry ingredients and mix well. With a spatula gently fold in beaten egg whites.

Pour ½ cup (125 ml) batter onto preheated waffle iron and bake until crisp.   YIELD: 5 to 6 waffles

Cheese Waffles   DAIRY

2 oz/50 grams shredded yellow
  cheese
2 eggs, separated
1 Tbsp/15 ml vegetable oil

1 cup/250 ml milk
1½ cups/375 ml sifted flour
2 tsp/10 ml baking powder
½ tsp/2 ml salt

Food Processor Directions   Preheat electric waffle iron.

Insert plastic disc in food processor. Place egg whites in container and process until egg whites are thick and set (egg whites will whip but will not have a high volume. When whipping egg whites, keep feed tube open to allow some air to be incorporated. Transfer egg whites to a mixing bowl and set aside. Insert shredding disc in food processor. Cut cheese into chunks and guide through feed tube to shred.

Insert steel blade in food processor. Add egg yolks, oil and milk to cheese in container and process until mixture is well blended. Sift dry ingredients and add to cheese mixture, processing until smooth. By hand, fold cheese mixture into beaten egg whites.

Pour ½ cup (125 ml) batter onto preheated waffle iron and bake until crisp.   YIELD: 5 or 6 waffles

Chocolate Waffles   DAIRY

6 Tbsp/75 ml cocoa
1½ cups/375 ml sifted flour
2 tsp/10 ml baking powder
½ tsp/2 ml salt
2 eggs

1½ cups/375 ml milk
3 Tbsp/45 ml melted butter
½ cup/125 ml sugar
½ tsp/2 ml vanilla

Blender Directions   Preheat electric waffle iron.

Sift cocoa, flour, baking powder and salt into a large mixing bowl and set aside.

Place eggs, milk and butter in blender goblet and blend on low speed until smooth. While motor is running, add sugar and vanilla. Stop blender and add dry ingredients. Blend at low speed only until flour is combined into batter.

Pour ½ cup (125 ml) batter onto preheated waffle iron and bake until crisp.   YIELD: 5 or 6 waffles

YEAST BREADS

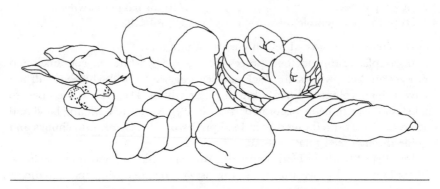

Delicious homemade bread, with a crisp crust and fragrant aroma, is much easier to make than you might think. A mixer with a dough hook eliminates the difficult task of hand kneading for making challah, other breads, bagels, rolls and yeast coffee cakes.

Challah is the egg bread traditionally eaten in Jewish homes on Shabbat and holidays. The dough is usually braided, glazed with a beaten egg and then sprinkled with poppy or sesame seeds before baking.

Every recipe in this chapter is made with active dry yeast. This can be bought in ¼-oz (7-gram) packages. Compressed yeast may be substituted, however, using a 0.6-oz (16.8-gram) cube for each package of dry yeast.

There are several tricks to making yeast dough successfully. Dry yeast should be dissolved in liquid which is 105° F (40° C) to 115° F (46° C). If the water is too cool, the yeast will not begin to rise, and very hot liquid will kill the yeast and make it inactive.

A warm spot, 80° F (26° C) to 85° F (27° C), free from drafts, is the best place for the yeast dough to rise. Usually 1½ to 2 hours are needed for the first rising. After the dough is shaped, an additional 30 minutes to 1 hour is required for the dough to again double in bulk. The microwave oven can be an ideal place for yeast dough to rise (see "Microwave Oven Hints for Yeast Breads"). The conventional oven can also provide a good environment for letting bread rise. Preheat the oven on the lowest setting for 1 minute. Turn the oven off and wait 1 minute before placing the yeast dough inside.

The mixer with a dough hook is the primary labor-saving appliance featured in this chapter for making and kneading yeast dough. Most mixers can handle up to 8 cups of flour, which produce 2 big loaves. When a bread recipe gives a range in the amount of flour to be used, always start with the smaller amount and add more only if necessary.

The usual technique in making yeast dough in a mixer is to combine the yeast and liquid ingredients with about half to two-thirds of the flour and begin mixing on low speed using the beater attachment. After a thick, smooth batter is formed, switch to the dough hook attachment. Gradually add remaining flour, ½ cup (125 ml) at a time, mixing until the dough forms a ball and clings to the dough hook, clearing the sides of the bowl. Continue mixing on low speed to knead the dough until it is smooth and elastic, usually 4 to 6 minutes longer. Without a dough hook, 8 to 10 minutes of hand kneading is usually required.

The food processor is used for several no-knead bread recipes. These delicious loaves have a crumbly texture, somewhat like quick breads. With the food processor, only one loaf can be made at a time. The best, foolproof procedure is to place the dry ingredients in the container, combine the yeast with the liquid ingredients and, with the motor running, slowly pour the liquid through the feed tube, processing until dough forms a ball and clears the sides of the container.

The use of a blender for combining liquid ingredients with some of the flour for yeast coffee cakes is demonstrated in the recipe for Basic Beaten Batter.

Special hints for using the blender and food processor to make bread crumbs are given at the end of this chapter.

MICROWAVE OVEN HINTS FOR YEAST BREADS

To Reheat and Freshen Bread
Place bread or roll on a paper towel in microwave oven. Cook on high setting 5 seconds per roll or slice of bread. If the roll is large, like a Kaiser roll, cook for 10 seconds. A very dense roll, such as a bagel, needs 15 seconds.

To Proof Bread Dough
"Proof" is the term used to describe yeast dough when it is in the process of rising. The microwave oven can be an excellent warm, draft-free area in which to proof dough. To create the proper atmosphere, bring 1 or 2 cups (250 to 500 ml) water to a boil in the oven. Turn off oven. Place dough in oven along with the hot water. The oven should stay very warm at least 30 minutes. When the oven cools, remove the dough, bring the water to a boil again, then return dough to oven.

Some microwave ovens have a very low setting (warm or 10 percent power) that can be used for proofing bread. This can be tricky, however, since it is easy to overheat the dough and destroy the yeast. Consult the manufacturer's book for specific directions.

To Proof Frozen Bread
The following method is only suitable for microwave ovens with a very low (10 percent) setting. Place one medium-size loaf of frozen dough in a greased glass loaf pan. Cover loosely with plastic wrap and heat 45 minutes to 1 hour on a 10 percent setting, or until double in bulk. Bake as directed in conventional oven.

To shape Challah, divide the dough into thirds. Roll each portion into a rope, then braid the ropes into a strand. Braiding is more even if you begin in the middle and work toward each end. Taper the ends of the loaf and press the edges together. To shape a fancy loaf of Challah, divide the dough into quarters. Roll 3 quarters into ropes and braid as described above. Divide the fourth quarter into 3 parts. Roll each of these into a rope and make a smaller braid. Press this smaller braid on top of the larger one.

Challah for Shabbat   P A R E V E

1 (¼-oz)/(7 grams) package   1 tsp/5 ml salt
   active dry yeast   ⅓ cup/75 ml oil
1½ cups/375 ml warm water   3 eggs, well-beaten
½ cup plus 1 Tbsp   1 additional egg, beaten
   (125 ml + 15 ml) sugar   Poppy or sesame seeds, optional
7 to 8 cups/1750 to 2000 ml flour

Mixer Directions   Dissolve yeast in ½ cup (125 ml) warm water. Add 1 tablespoon (15 ml) sugar. Set aside.

   Place 6 cups (1500 ml) flour, ½ cup (125 ml) sugar and salt in mixer bowl. Begin mixing on low speed to combine ingredients. Gradually add yeast mixture, oil, 3 eggs and remaining water, mixing until a very thick batter is formed.

   Attach dough hook. Add remaining flour gradually, mixing until dough clings to dough hook and clears the sides of the bowl. Continue mixing on low speed to knead dough until satin smooth, about 4 to 6 minutes longer.

   Place dough in a greased bowl and turn to grease the top. Cover with plastic wrap and place in a warm, draft-free spot. Allow to rise until double in bulk, about 2 hours.

   Punch dough down. Divide dough in half, then divide each half into thirds. Roll each piece of dough into a rope and braid 3 strands together. Place on greased baking sheets and let rise until double in bulk, at least 1 hour.

   Brush the top of the Challah with the remaining egg and, if desired, sprinkle with poppy or sesame seeds. Bake at 350° F (180° C) 45 minutes or until a rich brown color.   YIELD: 2 large loaves

Variations   Add the following ingredients to the basic Challah recipe:

Raisin Challah   PAREVE

1 cup/250 ml raisins

Add raisins along with flour when preparing Challah dough. Knead, shape and bake loaves as in basic recipe.

Onion Rolls   PAREVE

½ cup/125 ml minced onions   2 Tbsp/25 ml oil

Divide prepared Challah dough into 24 pieces and roll each into a 3-inch (7-cm) circle. Place on a greased baking sheet.

Sauté minced onion in oil until golden brown. Place a spoonful of the onion mixture in the center of each circle, fold over and press the edges firmly together. Allow rolls to rise 30 minutes. Bake at 350° F (180° C) 15 minutes or until brown.   YIELD: 2 large loaves or 24 rolls

During the summer, my children go to a day camp where, every Friday, they make Challah. When the children were younger, these little loaves never survived the car trip home. When, finally, the entire family got to taste their culinary efforts, we thought it was one of the best challahs we had ever tasted.

Kiddush Challah   PAREVE

2 (¼-oz)/(7-gram) packages yeast   1 egg
6 to 7 cups/1500 to 1700 ml flour   5 Tbsp/65 ml melted pareve
½ to ¾ cup/125 to 175 ml sugar,   margarine
   depending upon sweetness desired   2 cups/500 ml warm water
1 Tbsp/15 ml salt   1 additional egg, beaten

Mixer Directions In mixer bowl combine yeast, 5 cups (1250 ml) flour, sugar and salt. Attach beaters and begin mixing on low speed. Add eggs, margarine and water and mix until a very thick batter is formed.

Attach dough hook. Gradually add remaining flour, until dough clings to dough hook and clears the sides of the bowl. Continue mixing on low speed to knead dough until satin smooth, about 4 to 6 minutes longer.

Place dough in a greased bowl and turn to grease the top. Cover with plastic wrap and place dough in a warm, draft-free spot. Allow to rise until double in bulk, about 2 hours.

Punch down dough. Divide into 8 portions, then divide each portion into thirds. Roll each piece of dough into a rope and braid 3 strands together. Place on greased baking sheets and let rise until double in bulk, at least 1 hour. Brush the top of the Challah with the remaining egg. Bake at 350° F (180° C) 30 to 45 minutes or until golden brown.   YIELD: 8 small loaves

Variations   Prepare Challah dough as in basic recipe and shape as follows:

Bow Knots   P A R E V E

Divide dough into 24 pieces. Roll each piece of dough into a small rope. Tie each in a loose knot and place on a greased baking sheet. Let rise 1 hour, then bake at 350° F (180° C) 20 to 30 minutes or until golden brown.

Cloverleaf Rolls   P A R E V E

Form dough into small balls. Dip each ball into melted pareve margarine. Place 3 balls in each section of a greased muffin pan. Let rise 1 hour, then bake at 350° F (180° C) 20 to 30 minutes or until golden brown.

Crescents   P A R E V E

Divide dough into quarters, then roll each section into a circle, about ¼ inch (1 cm) thick. Cut circle into pie-shaped wedges. Brush with melted pareve margarine. Beginning at the wide end, roll up each wedge. Place on a greased baking sheet, curving the tips to form a crescent shape. Let rise 1 hour. Bake 350° F (180° C) 20 to 30 minutes or until golden brown.

Fan Tans   P A R E V E

Divide dough into quarters, then roll each section into a very thin rectangle. Brush with melted pareve margarine. Cut into strips about 1 inch (2.5 cm) wide. Stack 6 or 7 strips together. Cut strips into pieces 1½ inches (4 cm) long and place upright in greased muffin pans. Allow to rise 1 hour. Bake at 350° F (180° C) 20 to 30 minutes or until browned.

Parker House Rolls   P A R E V E

Shape dough into small balls. Let rest 10 minutes. Flatten each ball with the palm of your hand, then brush half of each roll with melted pareve margarine. Fold over on ungreased half and press down edge. Place on greased baking sheet and let rise 1 hour. Bake at 350° F (180° C) 20 to 30 minutes or until golden brown.   YIELD: 24 rolls

No-Knead Egg Bread   P A R E V E

1 (¼-oz)/(7 grams) package yeast	2 eggs, beaten
½ cup/125 ml warm water	2 Tbsp/25 ml melted pareve
3 cups/750 ml flour	margarine
1 tsp/5 ml salt	1 additional egg, beaten
6 Tbsp/75 ml sugar	

Food Processor Directions   Dissolve yeast in warm water. Set aside.

Insert steel blade in food processor. Combine flour, salt and sugar in container. Combine beaten eggs, melted margarine and yeast mixture. With motor running, slowly pour liquid mixture through feed tube and continue processing until dough forms a ball and clears sides of container.

Remove dough from container and shape into a ball. Place in a greased bowl, turning to grease the top. Cover and let rise in a warm place until double in bulk, about 1½ hours.

Punch dough down, then divide into thirds. Roll each piece of dough into a rope and braid the strands together. Place on a greased baking sheet. Brush the top with beaten egg. Cover and let rise until double in size, about 30 minutes.

Bake at 375° F (190° C) about 45 minutes or until golden brown.

YIELD: 1 large loaf

This recipe, like several others in this chapter, uses the "sponge" method of making bread—first dissolving the yeast and sugar in water and letting it rise before adding it to the other ingredients. It is a good technique, especially for someone new to bread making, because you can be absolutely sure that your bread will rise and the unleavened loaves can remain a Passover specialty.

Pareve White Bread   PAREVE

1 (¼-oz)/(7 grams) package yeast	5 to 6 cups/1250 to 1500 ml flour
4 Tbsp/50 ml sugar	2 tsp/10 ml salt
1¾ cups/425 ml warm water	4 Tbsp/50 ml pareve margarine

Mixer Directions   Dissolve yeast and 1 tablespoon (15 ml) sugar in ¾ cup (175 ml) warm water. Set aside.

In mixer bowl combine 4 cups (1 liter) flour, remaining sugar and salt. Attach beaters and begin mixing on low speed to combine ingredients. Add yeast mixture, margarine and remaining water, mixing until a very thick batter is formed.

Attach dough hook. Gradually add remaining flour until dough clings to dough hook and clears the sides of the bowl. Continue mixing on low speed to knead dough until satin smooth, about 4 to 6 minutes longer.

Place dough in a greased bowl, turning to grease the top. Cover and let rise in a warm place, free from drafts, until double in bulk, about 2 hours. Punch down. Let rest 15 minutes. Divide dough in half. Shape each half into a loaf. Place each loaf in a greased loaf pan. Cover and let rise until double in bulk, about 1 hour.

Bake at 375° F (190° C) 45 minutes or until nicely browned.

YIELD: 2 large loaves

Variations   Make the following additions or changes in Pareve White Bread recipe:

Cheese Bread   DAIRY

1½ cups/375 ml grated yellow cheese

Mix grated cheese with flour and prepare dough as in basic recipe.

Fruit Bread   PAREVE

1 Tbsp/15 ml grated orange peel   ½ cup/125 ml chopped dates,
½ tsp/2 ml cinnamon   prunes or raisins

Add orange peel and cinnamon along with the liquid ingredients when preparing basic recipe. Mix chopped dates, prunes or raisins with flour. Knead, shape and bake dough as in basic recipe.

Graham Bread   PAREVE

2 Tbsp/25 ml brown sugar
3 cups/750 ml graham flour

Substitute brown sugar for the sugar and graham flour for half the white flour, and prepare dough as in basic recipe.

Herb Bread   PAREVE

¾ tsp /4 ml *each* thyme,   1 Tbsp/15 ml caraway seeds
  marjoram and sage

Mix herbs and caraway seeds with the flour and prepare dough as in basic recipe.

Rye Bread   PAREVE

2 Tbsp/25 ml molasses   1 Tbsp/15 ml caraway seeds
3 cups/750 rye flour

Replace sugar with molasses and substitute rye flour for half of the white flour. Add caraway seeds along with the flour and prepare dough as in basic recipe.

Whole-Wheat Bread   PAREVE

2 Tbsp/25 ml brown sugar
6 cups/1500 ml whole-wheat flour

Replace sugar with brown sugar and substitute whole-wheat flour for white flour when preparing basic recipe.   YIELD: 2 large loaves

There are several standard indicators my husband uses to quickly evaluate the quality of Jewish life in towns or cities when we travel, such as the number of synagogues, kosher butcher shops, Hebrew day schools, Cohens in the telephone book, etc. My own personal reference point is the quality of the bagels at the local deli. A town with great bagels usually has a pretty good community to back it up.

Bagels   P A R E V E

EGG BAGELS

4 to 5 cups/1000 to 1250 ml flour	1 cup/250 ml warm water
1 (¼-oz)/(7 grams) package yeast	¼ cup/50 ml oil
2 Tbsp/25 ml sugar	2 eggs, beaten
2 tsp/10 ml salt	1 Tbsp/15 ml sugar

WATER BAGELS

4 to 5 cups/1000 to 1250 ml flour	2 tsp/10 ml salt
1 (¼-oz)/(7 grams) package yeast	1½ cups/375 ml warm water
3 Tbsp/45 ml sugar	1 Tbsp/15 ml sugar

Mixer Directions   In mixer bowl combine half the flour, yeast, 2 tablespoons (25 ml) sugar (3 tablespoons, 45 ml, for water bagels) and salt. Attach beaters and begin mixing on low speed to combine ingredients. Gradually add water (and oil and eggs for egg bagels), mixing until a thick batter is formed.

Attach dough hook. Add remaining flour, gradually. Continue mixing until dough clings to dough hook and clears the sides of the bowl. Knead on low speed 3 to 5 minutes or until dough is smooth and elastic.

Place dough in a greased bowl, turning to grease the top. Cover and let rise until double in bulk, about 2 hours.

Punch dough down and divide into 16 pieces. Roll each piece into a rope about 10 inches (25 cm) long and pinch the ends of each rope together to form individual circles.

In a large shallow pan, pour water to a depth of 2 inches (5 cm). Bring to a boil and add 1 tablespoon (15 ml) sugar. Reduce heat to low. Drop a few bagels at a time into simmering water and cook for 7 minutes, turning once.

Transfer bagels to a greased baking sheet. Bake at 450° F (230° C) 20 minutes or until bagels are brown.   YIELD: 16 bagels

Variations   Make the following changes in basic Bagel recipe:

Onion Bagels   P A R E V E

½ cup/125 ml minced onion	1 egg white, slightly beaten
2 Tbsp/25 ml pareve margarine	

Sauté onion in margarine until browned. Set aside. After boiling bagels, brush the surfaces with egg white. Sprinkle onions evenly over tops of bagels and bake as in basic recipe.

Raisin Bagels   PAREVE

2 Tbsp/25 ml brown sugar   ½ cup/125 ml raisins

Substitute brown sugar for the sugar and add raisins along with the flour.
Prepare bagel dough as in basic recipe.

You may feel like a mad chemist when you prepare this recipe, opening
every jar and box in the kitchen, but the results are worth it.

Black Bread   PAREVE

½ cup/125 ml water   ½ tsp/2 ml honey
2 Tbsp/25 ml vinegar   1 tsp/5 ml salt
2 Tbsp/25 ml molasses   ½ tsp/2 ml instant coffee powder
1 Tbsp/15 ml cocoa   ½ tsp/2 ml onion powder
2 cups/500 ml unsifted white flour   3 Tbsp/45 ml melted
1 cup/250 ml unsifted rye flour   pareve margarine
½ cup/125 ml bran cereal, crushed   1 (¼-oz)/(7 grams) package yeast
2 tsp/10 ml caraway seeds   ¼ cup/50 ml warm water

GLAZE

½ tsp/2 ml cornstarch
¼ cup/50 ml cold water

Food Processor Directions   In a saucepan, heat ½ cup (125 ml) water, vinegar,
molasses and cocoa over medium heat until boiling. Cool to lukewarm.

Insert steel blade in food processor. In container, combine flours, bran
cereal, caraway seeds, honey, salt, coffee and onion powder. Add margarine
and process 20 to 30 seconds or until mixutre is well combined.

Dissolve yeast in ¼ cup (50 ml) warm water. With processor running, add
yeast gradually through feed tube, then add molasses mixture, processing
until dough forms a ball, clearing the sides of the bowl.

Turn dough onto a lightly floured board and knead 2 to 3 minutes. Place
in a greased bowl, turning to grease the top. Cover and let rise in a warm
place, free from drafts, until double in bulk, about 2 hours.

Punch dough down. Shape into a ball and place in center of a greased 8-
inch (20-cm) round cake pan. Cover and let rise until double in bulk, about
1 hour. Bake at 350° F (180° C) for 35 to 40 minutes.

To glaze bread and give it a shiny crust, combine cornstarch and cold
water in a saucepan. Cook, stirring constantly, until mixture boils. Continue
to cook for 1 minute. As soon as bread is baked, brush cornstarch mixture
over top of loaf. Return bread to 350° F (180° C) oven and bake 2 to 3
minutes longer or until glaze is set. Remove from pan and cool on wire rack.

YIELD: 1 loaf

This is a food processor specialty and very impressive.

Brioche   DAIRY or PAREVE

1 (¼-oz)/(7 grams) package yeast
¼ cup/50 ml milk or water,
   scalded and cooled
¼ cup/50 ml sugar
2¼ cups/550 ml flour
1 tsp/5 ml salt

½ cup (1 stick)/125 ml frozen
   butter or pareve margarine
3 egg yolks
1 egg
½ tsp/2 ml lemon juice

Food Processor Directions   Stir the yeast, milk and sugar together in a small bowl. Let stand while mixing the rest of the ingredients.

Insert steel blade in food processor. In container combine the flour, salt and butter, which has been cut into chunks. Mix until crumbly. With the motor running, slowly pour the yeast mixture through the feed tube. Add the egg yolks, egg and lemon juice, processing until the dough is smooth and forms a ball, clearing the sides of the container.

Turn the dough out on a lightly floured surface and knead until smooth, about 3 minutes. Place dough in a large greased bowl, turning to grease the top. Cover, let rise in a warm place until double in bulk, about 1½ to 2 hours.

Punch dough down. Remove a small portion and form into a "teardrop" shape. Shape the rest of the dough into a smooth ball and place in a greased brioche pan. Use your finger to make an indentation in center of dough. Press "teardrop" into indentation.

Cover and let rise until double in bulk, about 1 hour. Bake at 375° F (190° C) for 45 minutes or until golden brown.

YIELD: 1 large or 10 small Brioche

Variations   Form prepared Brioche dough as follows:

Small Brioche Rolls   DAIRY or PAREVE

Divide dough into 10 portions. Form as for large loaves, including small "teardrops" for tops of brioche. Place dough in greased muffin tins. Cover and let rise until double in bulk, about 1 hour. Bake at 375° F (190° C) for 20 to 25 minutes.

Coffee Rolls   DAIRY or PAREVE

Divide dough into 8 portions. Roll each into a strip about 2 feet long. Cover and let rise about 30 minutes. Twist ends of these strips in opposite directions and shape each into a coil. Place in a greased baking pan, cover and let rise 45 minutes. Bake at 375° F (190° C) 15 to 20 minutes. Drizzle with white glaze when cool (see Cakes chapter).   YIELD: 1 large or 10 small Brioche

Pita is Arabic pocket bread, very popular in Israel for holding falafel and
sandwich fillings. This round, flat bread can also be cut into pie-shaped
wedges and used for appetizer dips and spreads. The high cooking temperature causes pita to puff during baking, producing the characteristic
"pocket."

Pita   P A R E V E

1 (¼-oz)/(7 grams) package yeast   1 Tbsp/15 ml salt
½ cup/125 ml lukewarm water   1½ cups/375 ml very warm water
8 cups/2 liters flour   2 Tbsp/25 ml olive oil
2 Tbsp/25 ml sugar

Mixer Directions Dissolve yeast in ½ cup (125 ml) warm water and set aside.
In mixer bowl, combine 6 cups (1500 ml) flour, sugar and salt and begin
mixing on low speed to combine ingredients. Add 1½ cups (375 ml) very
warm water to flour mixture and mix until absorbed. Add softened yeast
and mix until a soft dough is formed.

Add remaining flour gradually, mixing until dough clings to dough hook
and clears the sides of the bowl. Continue mixing on low speed to knead
dough until satin smooth, about 5 minutes.

Place dough in a large greased bowl and rub with olive oil. Cover and
allow to rise until double in bulk, about 2 hours.

Punch dough down and divide into 12 pieces, each orange size. Gently
form into balls, tucking underneath the ball as you round and smooth the
surface. Cover and let rest in a warm place 30 minutes.

On a lightly floured surface, roll each piece of dough into an 8-inch (20-
cm) circle. Cover and let rest in a warm place 30 minutes.

On the bottom rack of a preheated 500° to 550° F (260° to 290° C) oven,
bake bread on an ungreased baking sheet 5 to 6 minutes or until undersides
are lightly browned. Broil tops 30 seconds or until golden.

YIELD: 12 pita rounds

Use either mixer with a dough hook or the food processor to make fresh homemade dough for pizza.

Pizza Dough   PAREVE

1 (¼-oz)/(7 grams) package yeast   2 cups/500 ml flour
1 tsp/5 ml sugar   ½ tsp/2 ml salt
⅔ cup/150 ml warm water   1 Tbsp/15 ml oil

Mixer Directions   Dissolve yeast and sugar in warm water. Set aside.

Combine half the flour and the salt in mixer bowl. Attach dough hook and begin mixing at low speed. Add oil and yeast mixture, mixing until well combined. Gradually add remaining flour, mixing until dough clings to dough hook and clears the sides of the bowl. Continue to mix on low speed to knead the dough, about 3 minutes longer.

Place dough in a greased bowl, turning to grease the top. Cover and let rise in a warm place until double in bulk, about 2 hours. Pat the dough to fit into a 12-inch (30-cm) pizza pan. Add desired sauce and toppings (see Dairy Main Dishes chapter for suggestions). Bake at 400° F (200° C) 20 to 30 minutes.

Food Processor Directions   Dissolve yeast and sugar in warm water. Set aside.

Insert steel blade in food processor. Place flour and salt in container. With motor running, add oil and yeast mixture through the feed tube, processing until dough forms a ball and clears the sides of the container. Turn dough out onto a lightly floured surface and knead 2 to 3 minutes or until smooth and shiny.

Allow dough to rise, shape in pizza pan and cook as in basic recipe.

YIELD: Dough for 12-inch (30-cm) pizza

Pumpernickel Bread   P A R E V E

6 Tbsp/75 ml cornmeal
1½ cups/375 ml cold water
2 Tbsp/25 ml brown sugar
2 tsp/10 ml caraway seeds,
   optional
1 Tbsp/15 ml melted
   pareve margarine
1 Tbsp/15 ml salt

1 cup/250 ml mashed potatoes,
   unseasoned
1 (¼-oz)/(7 grams) package yeast
1 tsp/5 ml sugar
¼ cup/50 ml lukewarm water
½ cup/125 ml white flour
2 cups/500 ml rye flour
3 cups/750 ml whole-wheat flour

Mixer Directions   Mix cornmeal and cold water in a saucepan. Bring to the boiling point, stir and cook 3 or 4 minutes or until mixture is thickened. Transfer to mixer bowl. Add brown sugar, caraway seeds, margarine, salt and mashed potatoes, mixing until well combined. Cool to lukewarm.

Dissolve yeast and sugar in warm water and let stand 10 minutes or until mixture is bubbly.

Attach dough hook to mixer and begin mixing cornmeal mixture on low speed. Add yeast mixture, blending well. Combine flours and add gradually to cornmeal mixture. Even though the dough will appear very stiff and sticky, continue mixing and adding flour. When all of the flour has been incorporated, knead on low speed 7 to 10 minutes or until dough is smooth, elastic and no longer sticky.

Place dough in a greased bowl, turning to grease the top. Cover and allow to rise in a warm place until double in bulk, about 2 hours.

Shape dough into 2 round loaves and place on a baking sheet which has been greased and sprinkled with cornmeal. Cover and let rise in a warm place until double in bulk. Brush tops with cold water. Bake at 375° F (190° C) about 45 minutes. Cool on wire racks.   YIELD: 2 loaves

Rye Bread   P A R E V E

3 cups/750 ml rye flour
4 to 5 cups/1000 to 1250 ml
   white flour
¼ cup/50 ml brown sugar
2 tsp/10 ml salt
2 tsp/10 ml caraway seeds,
   optional

1 (¼-oz)/(7 grams) package yeast
2 cups/500 ml warm water
3 Tbsp/45 ml melted
   pareve margarine
¼ cup/50 ml cornmeal
1 egg white
1 Tbsp/15 ml water

Combine rye and white flours and mix well. In mixer bowl, combine half the flour mixture, brown sugar, salt, caraway seeds and yeast. In a separate mixing bowl, combine water and margarine. Attach beaters and begin mixing flour mixture on low speed. Gradually add water-margarine mixture, mixing until batter is thick and smooth.

Attach dough hook. Add remaining flour gradually, mixing until dough clings to dough hook and clears the sides of the bowl. Continue mixing on low speed to knead dough, about 4 to 6 minutes or until dough is smooth and elastic.

Place dough in a well-greased bowl, turning to grease the top. Cover and let rise in a warm place until double in bulk, about 1½ to 2 hours. Punch dough down and form into a ball. Cover and allow to rise until double, about 1 hour longer.

Sprinkle cornmeal on working surface and divide dough into 2 equal portions. Form each portion into an oval loaf. Place loaves on greased baking sheets. Cover and allow to rise 1 hour.

Brush tops with slightly beaten egg white mixed with water. Bake at 350° F (180° C) 35 to 40 minutes or until well browned. Remove from baking sheets and cool on a wire rack.   YIELD: 2 loaves

---

No-Knead Whole-Wheat Bread   D A I R Y

¾ cup/175 ml milk	1 (¼-oz)/(7 grams) package yeast
1 Tbsp/15 ml butter	¼ cup/50 ml warm water
1½ tsp/7 ml sugar	2 cups/500 ml whole-wheat flour
2 Tbsp/25 ml molasses	1 cup/250 ml white flour
1½ tsp/7 ml salt	Melted butter

Food Processor Directions Scald milk, add butter, sugar, molasses and salt. Cool to room temperature. Dissolve yeast in warm water. Combine yeast and milk mixtures.

Insert steel blade in food processor and place whole-wheat and white flours in container. With motor running, slowly pour liquid ingredients through feed tube and continue processing until dough forms a ball and clears the sides of the container.

Remove dough from container and shape into a smooth ball. Place in a greased bowl, turning to grease top. Cover and place in a warm spot to rise until double in bulk, about 1½ hours.

Punch dough down, fold and turn. Allow to rest 10 minutes. Shape dough to fit into a greased loaf pan. Brush top with melted butter. Cover and allow to rise until double in bulk, about 30 minutes.

Bake at 375° F (190° C) 50 minutes or until bread is golden brown and sounds hollow when lightly tapped.   YIELD: 1 large loaf

Sourdough batter can be used in breads, pancakes, waffles and cakes to add a very distinctive and very delicious flavor.

Sourdough Starter   P A R E V E

1 cup/250 ml flour   1 Tbsp/15 ml sugar
1 cup/250 ml warm water

Conventional Directions Combine ingredients in a stainless steel, pottery or glass bowl. Cover and let the mixture stand in a warm place 2 or 3 days or until fermented. Use starter to make basic Sourdough Batter.

YIELD: About 1½ cups (375 ml)

The evening before you want pancakes for breakfast or wish to make bread or a cake, prepare the Sourdough Batter.

Sourdough Batter   P A R E V E

1½ cups/375 ml Sourdough Starter   2 cups/500 ml warm water
  (see preceding recipe)   2½ cups/625 ml flour

Conventional Directions Combine Sourdough Starter, water and flour in a large mixing bowl made of stainless steel, pottery or glass. Mix thoroughly, cover and place in a warm spot 10 to 12 hours or overnight. Batter is thick and lumpy when first mixed, but thins down as it ferments and will be ready by breakfast time.

Remove 1½ cups (375 ml) of batter. This now becomes the starter for your next batter. Store in refrigerator in a stainless steel or pottery bowl.

Use the remaining prepared batter in recipes calling for Sourdough Batter.   YIELD: About 4½ cups (1125 ml) batter

---

Sourdough French Bread   P A R E V E

1 (¼-oz)/(7 grams) package yeast   5 to 6 cups/1200 to 1500 ml flour
1½ cups/375 ml warm water   1 tsp/5 ml sugar
3½ cups/875 ml Sourdough Batter   2 tsp/10 ml salt
  (see preceding recipe)   ½ tsp/2 ml baking soda

Mixer Directions Dissolve yeast in warm water in large mixer bowl and stir in Sourdough Batter. Add 4 cups (1 liter) flour, sugar and salt. Attach beaters to mixer and mix on low speed 3 to 4 minutes. Leave batter in mixer bowl, cover and let rise in warm place until double in bulk, about 1½ to 2 hours. Punch down.

Mix soda with 1 cup (250 ml) of the remaining flour. Attach dough hook and begin mixing on low speed. Add flour and soda mixture gradually. Add more flour as necessary, mixing until dough clings to dough hook and clears the sides of the bowl. Continue mixing on low speed to knead dough, 4 to 6 minutes or until satiny smooth.

Shape dough into 2 oblong loaves and place on a lightly greased baking sheet. Cover and place in a warm spot to rise until double in bulk, about 1½ to 2 hours.

Before baking, brush the outside of the loaves with water. Make diagonal slashes across the top with a sharp knife.

Place a shallow pan of hot water on bottom rack of the oven. Bake loaves at 400° F (200° C) 45 minutes or until crust is browned.   YIELD: 2 loaves

---

Sourdough Rye Bread   P A R E V E

3½ cups/875 ml Sourdough Batter (see recipe p. 62)	1½ tsp/7 ml caraway seeds
1 cup/250 ml rye flour	½ tsp/2 ml baking soda
1 Tbsp/15 ml brown sugar	3 to 4 cups/750 to 1000 ml white flour
1 tsp/5 ml salt	3 Tbsp/45 ml cornmeal

GLAZE

½ tsp/2 ml cornstarch	¼ cup/50 ml water

Mixer Directions   In mixer bowl combine Sourdough Batter, rye flour, brown sugar, salt, caraway seeds, baking soda and half the white flour. Attach beaters and begin mixing on low speed until batter is thick and smooth.

Attach dough hook. Gradually add remaining white flour, mixing at low speed until dough clings to dough hook and clears the sides of the bowl. Continue mixing on low speed to knead the dough until very smooth, about 8 to 10 minutes longer.

Place dough in a greased bowl, turning to grease the top. Cover and let rise until double in bulk, about 2 to 2½ hours.

Punch dough down. Shape into an oblong loaf. Sprinkle a baking sheet with cornmeal and place loaf on top. Cover and let rise in a warm place until double in bulk, about 1 to 1½ hours.

Before baking, brush the loaf with a mixture of ½ teaspoon (2 ml) cornstarch dissolved in ¼ cup (50 ml) water. Put a shallow pan of hot water on the bottom rack of the oven. Bake loaf at 400° F (200° C) for 10 minutes. Brush again with cornstarch mixture. Continue baking 20 to 25 minutes longer, until lightly browned.   YIELD: 1 large loaf

Basic Coffee Cake Batter   D A I R Y

1 (¼-oz)/(7 grams) package   ½ cup/125 ml butter
   active dry yeast   1 tsp/5 ml cinnamon
¼ cup/50 ml lukewarm water   3¼ cups/800 ml sifted flour
1 cup/250 ml milk   2 eggs
¼ cup/50 ml sugar   ½ tsp/2 ml vanilla
1 tsp/5 ml salt   Desired topping (see Variations)

Blender Directions   Dissolve yeast in lukewarm water; set aside. Scald milk
and add sugar, salt and butter. Cool to lukewarm. Place cooled milk mixture
in blender goblet. Add cinnamon and 1 cup of the flour. Blend on low speed
until thoroughly combined. Add softened yeast, eggs and vanilla, blending
well. Add remaining flour and blend until very smooth. (If blender cannot
handle all the flour, add as much as possible, then combine the rest of the
flour and batter mixture in a large mixing bowl, stirring to blend well.)

Transfer batter mixture to a large bowl, cover, and let rise until double in
size, about 1 hour. Use with different toppings to make coffee cakes. Bake
coffee cakes in a 375° F (190° C) oven for 30 minutes.

YIELD: One or two 8-by-8-inch (20-by-20-cm) coffee cakes

Variations   Prepare Basic Coffee Cake Batter and top as follows:

Apple Coffee Cake   D A I R Y

2 or 3 apples   4 Tbsp/50 ml sugar
2 Tbsp/25 ml melted butter   1 tsp/5 ml cinnamon

Use half recipe of Basic Coffee Cake Batter. Spread batter evenly in a
greased baking pan. Peel and slice apples and arrange slices on top of batter.
Brush apples with melted butter. Combine sugar and cinnamon and sprinkle over top. Let rise 45 minutes, then bake as directed.

Jam Swirl   D A I R Y

½ cup/125 ml jam   4 Tbsp/50 ml sugar   ½ tsp/2 ml cinnamon

Use half recipe of Basic Coffee Cake Batter. Spread batter evenly in a
greased baking pan. With a spoon make grooves in a swirl design on top of
batter, then fill in grooves with the jam. Combine sugar and cinnamon and
sprinkle over top. Let rise 45 minutes, then bake as directed.

Spicy Almond Coffee Cake   D A I R Y

½ cup/125 ml slivered almonds   ½ tsp/2 ml cinnamon
4 Tbsp/50 ml sugar   1 tsp/5 ml pumpkin-pie spice

Use half recipe of Basic Coffee Cake Batter. Spread batter evenly in a greased baking pan. Mix together almonds, sugar, cinnamon and spice. Sprinkle mixture evenly over batter. Let rise 45 minutes, then bake as directed.

Streusel Coffee Cake   DAIRY

2 Tbsp/25 ml melted butter   2 Tbsp/25 ml bread or cake crumbs
2 Tbsp/25 ml sugar   ½ tsp/2 ml cinnamon
3 Tbsp/45 ml flour

Use half recipe of Basic Coffee Cake Batter. Spread batter evenly in a greased baking pan. Mix together butter, sugar, flour, crumbs and cinnamon. Sprinkle mixture evenly over batter. Let rise 45 minutes, then bake as directed.   YIELD: One or two 8-by-8-inch (20-by-20-cm) coffee cakes

This recipe is courtesy of my friend Linda Freedman, who prepares it every year for breaking the Yom Kippur fast.

Honey Slices   DAIRY

3 Tbsp/45 ml sugar   1 egg, well beaten
¾ tsp/4 ml salt   3 cups/750 ml flour
3 Tbsp/45 ml butter   4 Tbsp/50 ml butter, melted
½ cup/125 ml milk, scalded   ¾ tsp/4 ml cinnamon
1 (¼-oz)/(7 grams) package yeast   3 Tbsp/45 ml sugar
¼ cup/50 ml warm water   2 Tbsp/25 ml honey

Mixer Directions   Add sugar, salt and 3 tablespoons (45 ml) butter to scalded milk. Allow to cool. Dissolve yeast in water. In mixer bowl combine yeast, milk mixture, beaten egg and half of the flour. Attach beaters and begin mixing on low speed until batter is thick and smooth.

Attach dough hook. Add remaining flour gradually, until dough clings to dough hook and clears sides of the bowl. Continue mixing on low speed to knead the dough until smooth, about 5 minutes longer.

Place and turn dough in greased bowl. Cover, let rise until double in bulk, about 1½ hours. Roll dough into a rectangle, 20 by 8 inches (51 by 20 cm). Spread with 3 tablespoons (45 ml) melted butter and sprinkle with cinnamon and sugar. Cut dough into twenty 4-by-2-inch (11-by-5-cm) strips. Place strips on edge in greased loaf pan so that layers form one long row down length of pan. Cover and let rise about 45 minutes.

Combine honey and remaining butter. Drizzle over top. Bake at 375° F (190° C) 35 to 40 minutes.   YIELD: 1 loaf

Soft Bread Crumbs   P A R E V E

1 slice pareve bread

Blender Directions   Remove crust from bread and tear bread into quarters.
Place in blender goblet and blend at low speed until coarsely chopped.

YIELD: ¾ cup (175 ml) crumbs

Fine, Dry Bread Crumbs   P A R E V E

2 slices pareve bread

Microwave Oven Directions   Place 2 slices bread on a paper towel in microwave oven. Cook on high setting 45 seconds. Turn bread over and cook 45
seconds longer. Allow to stand a few minutes. Use food processor or blender
to make fine crumbs, or grate bread on a grater, or place in a plastic bag and
crush with a rolling pin.

Food Processor Directions   Oven toast bread on a baking sheet at 300° F
(150° C) until bread is crisp and dry. Or toast in microwave oven as above.
Insert steel blade in food processor. Place toasted bread in container and
process until finely crushed.

Blender Directions   Toast bread as above. Break into pieces and place in
blender goblet. Blend on high speed until finely crushed.

YIELD: About ½ cup (125 ml) crumbs

Seasoned Bread Crumbs   P A R E V E

1 cup/250 ml fine, dry pareve bread crumbs	1 tsp/5 ml salt
	½ tsp/2 ml garlic powder
1 tsp/5 ml onion powder	½ tsp/2 ml paprika
2 tsp/10 ml dried parsley flakes	¼ tsp/1 ml dried thyme

Mix all ingredients well. Store, covered, in a cool, dry place.

Variation

Cheese-Flavored Crumbs   D A I R Y

¼ cup/50 ml grated hard cheese

Add cheese to basic recipe and mix well.

YIELD: About 1 cup (250 ml) crumbs

APPETIZERS

The recipes in this chapter are designated *dairy, fleishig* and *pareve*. The pareve category, however, can be easily enlarged by substituting pareve margarine for butter or chicken fat, or by using pareve "sour cream" instead of dairy sour cream or yogurt.

In preparing appetizers for a party or first course, appliances can be used in the following ways:

Use the microwave oven for heating canapés and dips, crisping chips and pretzels and preparing hors d'oeuvres.

Flavored butters and cheese for canapés or spreads can be prepared easily in the mixer.

Just about any leftover or tidbit can be pureed into a tasty canapé spread in the food processor. This is the perfect appliance, too, for knish fillings and chopped liver or herring.

The blender quickly produces perfectly smooth, creamy dips.

Several recipes in this chapter use liver as one of the ingredients. Each of these recipes specifies "broil liver" as a first step, since broiling on both sides is the proper method of kashering liver.

HEATING CANAPES IN MICROWAVE OVEN

Canapés are appetizers which have a bread or pastry base. The microwave oven can be a great help in quickly heating up to a dozen canapés at a time. Arrange the canapés in a single layer on a serving dish which has been lined with a paper doily or napkin to absorb excess moisture.

TIMING GUIDE FOR CANAPES

8 to 10 canapés: Cook on high setting 30 seconds, or until hot
12 canapés: Cook on high setting 45 seconds, or until hot

BROWNING DISH CANAPES

The browning dish is that special accessory described before which, when preheated, acts like a frying pan in the microwave oven. In the browning dish the canapés can be heated while the bread base is being toasted.

For 12 appetizers, cut 3 slices of bread into quarters. Spread a flavored butter on one side of the bread and place a filling on the other side. Preheat the browning dish on high setting 3 to 4 minutes. Arrange canapés on browning dish, buttered side down. Cook on high 1 to 1½ minutes until filling is hot and bread is toasted.

SOFTENING BUTTER AND CHEESE

Remove foil cover from 8 ounces (250 ml) butter or cream cheese and place in a glass dish. Cook on high setting 30 seconds to 1 minute or until soft. Combine with spices and use as a spread for canapés.

HEAT DIPS

Spoon prepared dip into glass serving bowl. For 1½ to 2 cups (375 ml to 500 ml) dip, heat in the microwave oven about 1½ to 2½ minutes on a high setting.

When cream is overwhipped, the fat particles clump together. You can create creamy, delicious natural butter by rinsing this mixture with ice water, then straining to remove the extra liquid. Butter may be pressed into a mold or formed into shapes. Chill well. This butter may be served plain or mixed with other ingredients and seasonings as a spread for canapés.

Homemade Blender Butter   D A I R Y

1 cup/250 ml whipping cream   ½ tsp/2 ml salt, if desired
½ cup/125 ml ice water

Food Processor Directions   Insert plastic disc in food processor. Pour whipping cream into container and process until cream becomes thick. With the motor running, slowly pour water mixed with salt through feed tube. Continue processing until butter forms. Strain butter.

Mixer Directions Pour whipping cream into bowl. Attach beaters and mix on high speed until cream thickens and stands in peaks. With motor running, slowly add ice water and salt. Continue mixing until butter forms. Strain butter.

Blender Directions Pour whipping cream into blender goblet. Blend on low speed until cream thickens around the blades, about 15 to 30 seconds. With the blender running, slowly pour in ice water and salt. Increase speed to medium and continue blending 1 to 2 minutes longer until butter forms. Turn the butter into a strainer to drain.   YIELD: Over ½ cup (125 ml)

This is a marvelous recipe! It is neither low calorie nor low in cholesterol, and it contains sodium, *but* it is pareve, which makes it extremely valuable in a kosher kitchen. The basis for this recipe is pareve dessert whip, a liquid which is packed in cartons and then frozen or refrigerated. Like dairy whipping cream it is whipped in a mixer until double in volume.

Pareve "Sour Cream"   P A R E V E

1 (10-oz)/(296 ml) carton pareve   ½ tsp/2 ml salt
  dessert whip   Dash pepper
2 to 4 Tbsp/20 to 50 ml lemon
  juice or vinegar (to taste)

Mixer Directions Pour dessert whip into mixer bowl. Attach beaters and begin mixing on medium speed, gradually increasing speed to high until dessert whip stands in stiff peaks. Reduce mixer speed to low and gradually add lemon juice, salt and pepper. Taste to adjust seasonings. Use in place of sour cream in dips, salad dressings and other recipes.
                                        YIELD: About 1½ cups (375 ml)

Flavored Butters and Cheeses for Canapés   D A I R Y o r
                                                   P A R E V E

½ cup/125 ml softened pareve   Flavoring or spice
  margarine or butter or cream   (see Variations below)
  cheese

Mixer Directions Use beater attachment on mixer. Cream butter or cheese until very smooth, using medium speed. Add flavoring or spice and continue mixing until mixture is light and fluffy. Spread on bread, pastry or toast pieces as a canapé base.   YIELD: ½ to ¾ cup (125 to 175 ml) canapé spread

Variations Add the following ingredients to ½ cup (125 ml) softened butter or cream cheese:

Chili Butter   DAIRY or PAREVE

¼ cup/50 ml chili sauce or ketchup   1 tsp/5 ml chili powder

Egg Butter   DAIRY or PAREVE

2 diced hard-cooked eggs   Pinch *each* of cayenne papper,
½ tsp/2 ml lemon juice   dry mustard and salt

Garlic Butter   DAIRY or PAREVE

½ tsp/2 ml garlic powder   ½ tsp/2 ml paprika

Green Onion Butter   DAIRY or PAREVE

2 Tbsp/25 ml minced green onion

Herb Butter   DAIRY or PAREVE

¼ tsp/1 ml dill weed   ¼ tsp/1 ml salt
¼ tsp/1 ml dried tarragon   2 Tbsp/25 ml chopped chives

Horseradish Butter   DAIRY or PAREVE

¼ cup/50 ml prepared horseradish

Lemon Butter   DAIRY or PAREVE

1 tsp/5 ml grated lemon peel   2 Tbsp/25 ml lemon juice

Mustard Butter   DAIRY or PAREVE

2 Tbsp/25 ml prepared mustard

Olive Butter   DAIRY or PAREVE

¼ cup/50 ml diced olives

Parsley Butter   DAIRY or PAREVE

¼ cup/50 ml finely chopped parsley
1 tsp/5 ml lemon juice   YIELD: ½ to ¾ cup (125 to 175 ml) canapé spread

Fish Spread for Canapés   DAIRY or PAREVE

½ cup/125 ml softened butter
  or pareve margarine
  or cream cheese

¼ cup/50 ml mashed fish fillets
  (anchovies, sardines, salmon,
  tuna, herring) or caviar
½ tsp/2 ml lemon juice

Food Processor Directions   Insert steel blade in food processor. Place softened butter, fish fillets and lemon juice in container. Process until mixture is smooth.
  Spread mixture on bread, toast or pastry pieces for canapés.

YIELD: About ¾ cup (175 ml) canapé spread

Vegetable Spread for Canapés   PAREVE

1 cup/250 ml vegetable chunks
  (avocado, mushrooms, asparagus)
½ tsp/2 ml lemon juice

Salt and pepper to taste
1 or 2 hard-cooked eggs,
  if desired

Food Processor Directions   Insert steel blade in food processor. Place vegetable chunks in container and process until pureed. Add remaining ingredients and process until smooth. Spread mixture on bread, toast or pastry pieces for canapés.   YIELD: About ¾ cup (175 ml) canapé spread

Meat Spread for Canapés   FLEISHIG

1 cup/250 ml cooked meat,
  cut into chunks (use beef,
  tongue, corned beef, liver,
  veal or chicken)
¼ to ½ cup/50 to 125 ml chicken
  fat (or mayonnaise,
  horseradish, pareve margarine,
  or 2 hard-cooked eggs)

1 to 2 Tbsp/15 to 25 ml finely
  chopped pickles (or use pimento,
  onion or celery)
Salt and pepper to taste

Food Processor Directions   Insert steel blade in food processor. Place meat chunks in container and process until pureed. Add chicken fat and process until meat is moistened and mixture is a spreading consistency. Add pickles and seasoning. Spread mixture on bread, toast or pastry pieces for canapés.

YIELD: About 1 cup (250 ml) canapé spread

My friend Sue, who is something of a health fanatic and always counting calories, cholesterol, milligrams, sugar exchanges, and so forth, makes a delicious chopped liver using this recipe but substituting 4 tablespoons (50 ml) chicken broth for the chicken fat.

Chopped Liver   FLEISHIG

1 lb/500 grams liver, beef or chicken	4 Tbsp/50 ml chicken fat or pareve margarine
1 large onion	2 eggs, hard-cooked
	Salt and pepper to taste

Food Processor Directions   Broil liver. Cool and trim. Cut into chunks.

Insert steel blade in processor. Place liver in container and process until finely chopped. Transfer to mixing bowl.

Peel onion, cut into eighths and place in food processor container. Process until finely chopped. In a hot frying pan melt chicken fat and sauté chopped onion until soft. Allow to cool.

Place eggs in food processor container. Process, using pulse button or quick on-off motion, until coarsely chopped.

Combine all ingredients and mix well. Season to taste with salt and pepper. For a smooth, pâté-type texture, return mixture to food processor and process until desired consistency is reached. Chill before serving.

YIELD: 6 to 8 servings

Use this recipe as a filling for canapés, as a spread on matzahs or as a first course, garnished with tomato slices.

Liver and Egg Spread   FLEISHIG

½ lb/250 grams chicken livers	3 Tbsp/45 ml chicken fat or pareve margarine
1 large onion	Salt and pepper to taste
6 eggs, hard-cooked	

Food Processor Directions   Broil liver. Cool and trim. Cut into chunks.

Insert steel blade in food processor. Place liver in container and process until finely chopped. Transfer liver to mixing bowl.

Peel onion and cut into eighths. Place onion in container and process until finely chopped. Transfer to bowl with liver.

Place eggs in food processor container. Using pulse button, or quick on-off motion, coarsely chop egg. Add to liver mixture.

Add chicken fat, blending well. Season to taste with salt and pepper. Chill before serving.   YIELD: About 2 cups (500 ml)

Meatballs in Sweet and Sour Sauce   FLEISHIG

1½ lbs/750 grams lean ground beef
1 Tbsp/15 ml onion, finely chopped
1 egg
½ cup/125 ml fine, dry bread
   crumbs

½ cup/125 ml water
1 (12-oz)/(340 grams) bottle
   chili sauce
⅔ cup/150 ml grape jelly
2 Tbsp/25 ml lemon juice

Microwave Oven Directions Combine beef, onion, egg, bread crumbs and water in a large mixing bowl. Mix until thoroughly blended.

In a 3-quart glass dish, combine chili sauce, grape jelly and lemon juice.

Shape meat mixture into small balls. Place in chili sauce. Cover dish with wax paper and place in microwave oven. Cook on high setting 12 minutes. Skim off fat and stir. Re-cover and cook on high setting 8 minutes longer, or until sauce is bubbly. Serve as an appetizer.

Conventional Directions Combine ingredients as described above, using a flameproof casserole or saucepan. Bring sauce to a boil over medium heat. Cover and simmer until done, about 45 minutes. YIELD: About 24 meatballs

---

An interesting and delicious way to use cold leftover tongue is to make pâté—or spread—and serve on crackers as an appetizer.

Tongue Pâté   FLEISHIG

1 cup/250 ml cooked tongue,
   cut into chunks

½ cup/125 ml mayonnaise
2 tsp/10 ml horseradish

Food Processor Directions Insert steel blade in food processor. Place chunks of tongue in container and process until smooth. Add mayonnaise and horseradish and process until thoroughly combined. Chill.

Blender Directions Turn blender on to high speed. Drop chunks of tongue, one at a time, into blender goblet and blend until coarsely chopped. Add mayonnaise and horseradish and continue blending until smooth. Chill before serving.   YIELD: About 1 cup (250 ml)

Knishes freeze beautifully after they are cooked. To reheat, place frozen knishes on an ungreased baking sheet. Bake at 350° F (180° C) 20 minutes.

Knishes   PAREVE

2 to 2¼ cups/500 to 550 ml flour
1 tsp/5 ml baking powder
½ tsp/2 ml salt
2 eggs
3 Tbsp/45 ml oil

⅓ cup/75 ml water
Additional oil
Prepared knish filling
    (see following recipes)

Mixer Directions In mixer bowl combine flour, baking powder and salt. Attach dough hook and begin mixing on low speed. Add eggs, 3 tablespoons (45 ml) oil and enough water to form a smooth dough. If necessary add more flour to help dough form into a smooth ball and cling to the dough hook. Knead the dough on low speed for 3 minutes.

Place dough in a greased bowl, cover and allow to stand at room temperature 1 hour.

Divide the dough in half. On a lightly floured board roll half the dough into a very thin rectangle. Brush dough with oil. Spread prepared knish filling (see following recipes) along the long side of the rectangle and then roll up dough, jelly-roll style. Cut roll of dough into 1½-inch (4-cm) slices and place the slices on a greased baking sheet, pressing down lightly to flatten.

When the knishes are arranged on the greased baking sheet, brush the tops with oil and bake at 350° F (180° C) 45 minutes to 1 hour, or until lightly browned. For very crisp knishes, turn after 30 minutes.

YIELD: 2 to 3 dozen knishes

Chicken Filling for Knishes   FLEISHIG

2 cups/500 ml cooked chicken,
    cut in chunks
½ cup/125 ml cooked kasha,
    rice or mashed potatoes

1 egg
¼ cup/50 ml chicken gravy or stock
Salt and pepper to taste

Food Processor Directions Insert steel blade in food processor and process chicken meat until finely chopped. Add kasha and egg and process until mixture is smooth. Add enough gravy to form desired consistency. Season to taste. Use as a filling for knishes.   YIELD: Filling for 2 to 3 dozen knishes

Kasha Filling for Knishes   FLEISHIG or PAREVE

1 onion, minced
2 Tbsp/25 ml chicken fat
  or pareve margarine
2 cups/500 ml cooked kasha

¼ cup/50 ml gravy or stock
  or vegetable liquid
1 egg
Salt and pepper to taste

Microwave Oven Directions   Place onion and chicken fat in a small glass bowl. Cover with plastic wrap and cook on high setting 3 minutes or until onion is soft. Combine with remaining ingredients. Use as a filling for knishes.

Conventional Directions   Heat chicken fat in a frying pan. Sauté onions until golden. Combine with remaining ingredients and season to taste. Use as a filling for knishes.   YIELD: Filling for 2 to 3 dozen knishes

Liver Filling for Knishes   FLEISHIG

1 lb/500 grams liver, broiled
  and cut into chunks
1 onion, peeled and
  cut into chunks
1 Tbsp/15 ml chicken fat,
  or pareve margarine

1 egg
¼ cup/50 ml cooked kasha,
  rice or mashed potatoes
Salt and pepper to taste

Food Processor Directions   Insert steel blade in food processor. Process liver until very finely chopped. Fry onion in chicken fat until lightly browned. Place cooked onion, egg and kasha in container along with liver and process until smooth. Season to taste. Use as a filling for knishes.

YIELD: Filling for 2 to 3 dozen knishes

Meat Filling for Knishes   FLEISHIG

1 Tbsp/15 ml chicken fat
  or pareve margarine
1 onion, minced
2 cups/500 ml cooked beef,
  cut into chunks

½ cup/125 ml cooked kasha,
  rice or mashed potatoes
1 egg
Salt and pepper to taste

Food Processor Directions   Melt chicken fat in a frying pan and cook onion until brown. Allow to cool slightly. Insert steel blade in food processor. Place meat cubes in container and process until very finely chopped. Add cooked onion, kasha and egg. Process until smooth. Season to taste. Use as a filling for knishes.   YIELD: Filling for 2 to 3 dozen knishes

Variations Substitute the following ingredients for cooked beef in basic recipe:

Hamburger Meat Filling   FLEISHIG

½ lb/250 grams hamburger

Cook hamburger meat along with onion. Drain well. Insert steel blade in food processor. Place hamburger and onion in container and process until very finely chopped. Add kasha and egg, processing until smooth. Season to taste. Use as filling for knishes.

Variety Meat Filling   FLEISHIG

2 cups/500 ml cooked
    heart or lung, cut in chunks

Substitute 2 cups (500 ml) cooked heart or lung, cut in chunks, for part or all of the cooked beef in basic recipe. YIELD: Filling for 2 to 3 dozen knishes

Potato Filling for Knishes   FLEISHIG or PAREVE

1 onion, minced   2 eggs, beaten
4 Tbsp/50 ml chicken fat   Salt and pepper to taste
    or pareve margarine
2 cups/500 ml mashed potatoes
    (see recipe in Vegetables chapter)

Microwave Oven Directions Place onion and chicken fat in a small glass bowl. Cover with plastic wrap and cook on high setting 3 minutes or until onion is soft. Combine with remaining ingredients. Use as a filling for knishes.

Conventional Directions Heat chicken fat in a frying pan. Sauté onions until golden. Combine with remaining ingredients and season to taste. Use as a filling for knishes.   YIELD: Filling for 2 to 3 dozen knishes

Stuffed Mushrooms   PAREVE

12 large mushrooms   ¼ cup/50 ml chopped black olives
3 Tbsp/45 ml oil   ¼ cup/50 ml pareve bread crumbs
¼ cup/50 ml pareve margarine   2 Tbsp/25 ml chopped parsley
⅓ cup/75 ml minced onion   Salt and pepper to taste

Microwave Oven Directions Clean mushrooms. Carefully remove stems and chop fine. Brush caps with oil and set aside.

In a small glass bowl place chopped stems, margarine and onions. Cover with plastic wrap and cook on high setting 2 minutes or until onion is soft. Add remaining ingredients and mix well.

Fill individual mushroom caps with a spoonful of vegetable mixture. Arrange mushrooms on a glass dish and cook on high setting 3 minutes or until hot.

Conventional Directions   Cook stuffed mushrooms in a hot, 400° F (200° C), oven 10 minutes or until heated through.   YIELD: 12 stuffed mushrooms

---

Falafel is a favorite snack or sandwich in Israel, sold at corner kiosks. For many tourists, it is a delicious introduction to a new type of cuisine.

As an appetizer, serve Falafel on toothpicks with a dish of Tahinah for dipping. To make a Falafel sandwich, place 3 or 4 Falafel balls inside a round Pita bread (see Yeast Breads chapter. Top with cut-up lettuce and tomatoes and pour on Tahinah and hot sauce. May be served with a piece of pickle.

Falafel   PAREVE

½ lb/250 grams dried garbanzos
   (chick peas)
¼ cup/50 ml cracked wheat
   (bulghor)
1 small onion
1 Tbsp/15 ml parsley flakes
4 garlic cloves
2 Tbsp/25 ml lemon juice
1 tsp/5 ml ground cumin

½ tsp/2 ml coriander
½ tsp/2 ml pepper
½ tsp/2 ml chili powder
1 tsp/5 ml paprika
Dash cayenne pepper
2 Tbsp/25 ml pareve bread crumbs
   (or as needed)
Oil for frying

Food Processor Directions   Soak garbanzos overnight in ½ gallon (2 liters) water. Next morning, drain. Place in a large pot, cover with water, add 1 tablespoon (25 ml) salt and bring to a boil. Reduce heat, cover and simmer 1½ hours. Drain and allow to cool.

Soak the cracked wheat in hot water for 20 minutes. Drain and set aside.

Insert steel blade in food processor. Place garbanzos in container and process until finely chopped. Transfer to a large mixing bowl. Peel the onion, cut into chunks and place in container along with parsley and garlic. Process until finely chopped. Add onion mixture and cracked wheat to garbanzos in mixing bowl. Stir in lemon juice and spices, mixing well. Add bread crumbs until mixture is firm enough to hold a shape. Shape mixture into 1-inch (2.5-cm) balls. Fry in deep hot oil until light brown and crisp.

YIELD: About 50 balls

Chatzelim (Eggplant Salad) PAREVE

2 medium eggplants (about 2 lbs/ 1 tomato
  1 kilo total weight) 1 green pepper
4 Tbsp/50 ml lemon juice 1 green onion
½ tsp/2 ml garlic powder 1 tsp/5 ml salt
½ cup/125 ml sesame paste Dash pepper
  (see recipe on page 79)

Microwave Oven Directions Use a small knife to pierce the skin of the eggplants to provide "vents" for steam. Place eggplants on a paper plate in microwave oven and cook on high setting 10 minutes, or until soft. Allow to cool a few minutes.

Cut eggplants in half and scoop out the flesh. Put in a bowl and immediately pour on lemon juice to prevent discoloration.

With a fork mash the eggplants. Add garlic powder and sesame paste. Finely dice the tomato, green pepper and onion and add to eggplants, mixing well. Season to taste with salt and pepper. Chill well. Serve on individual lettuce-lined plates or as a dip with slices of Pita bread.

Conventional Directions To cook eggplant, roast in a 400° F (200° C) oven for about 40 minutes, turning occasionally. Another method for cooking is to broil the eggplant, turning frequently, until the skin is charred and black and eggplant feels soft, about 20 minutes. Proceed with above directions.

YIELD: About 4 cups (1 liter)

Hummus is a favorite food in Israel. To serve, place Hummus on a plate and swirl with a knife to create a circle design. Garnish with chopped parsley or paprika. Pour a small amount of olive oil over the top. Serve with Pita bread.

Hummus PAREVE

1 (16-oz)/(454 grams) can ½ tsp/2 ml salt
  garbanzos (chick peas) ¼ tsp/1 ml pepper
⅓ cup/75 ml lemon juice ¼ tsp/1 ml cumin
¼ cup/50 ml olive oil ¼ cup/50 ml sesame paste
  (or use liquid from garbanzos)   (see following recipe)
1 garlic clove, minced

Food Processor Directions Insert steel blade in food processor. Place garbanzos, lemon juice and olive oil in container. Process until very finely ground. Add remaining ingredients and process until smooth.

Blender Directions Place garbanzos, lemon juice and olive oil in blender goblet. Blend on high speed until very finely ground. Add garlic salt, pepper and

cumin, blending to combine. Reduce blender speed to low. Add sesame
paste and blend until smooth.   YIELD: About 2 cups (500 ml)

Sesame paste is made from crushed sesame seeds and is used in the Middle
East as a spread on bread or as an ingredient in other recipes. Upon standing, the oil separates from the paste, so it must be stirred before use and kept
stored in the refrigerator. Although sesame paste can be bought in health
food stores under the name "tahinah" or "tahini" it is very easy to make
your own in a food processor or blender.

Sesame Paste   P A R E V E

3 cups/750 ml sesame seeds

Food Processor Directions   Insert steel blade in food processor and place sesame
seeds in container. Process until a thick, butterlike paste is formed, about 5
minutes. Stop processor several times to stir the paste and scrape the sides of
the container.

Blender Directions   Measure sesame seeds into blender goblet. Begin blending
at low speed to crush seeds, then increase to high speed until a smooth paste
is formed.   YIELD: ½ cup (125 ml)

Tahinah is a favorite Israeli sauce made from sesame-seed paste. It can be
served as an appetizer, dip, a first course or a salad dressing. This recipe
makes a thickened version, but it can easily be thinned with water to the
desired consistency.

An attractive way to serve Tahinah is to spread it on a plate, then swirl
with a knife to create a circle design. Garnish with chopped parsley or paprika. Serve as a dip with raw vegetables or with Pita bread.

Tahinah (Sesame Dip)   P A R E V E

1½ cups/375 ml sesame paste   2 garlic cloves, minced
  (see preceding recipe)   1 tsp/5 ml salt
1 cup/250 ml water   ¼ tsp/1 ml pepper
⅔ cup/150 ml lemon juice   ½ tsp/2 ml paprika

Food Processor Directions   Insert steel blade in food processor. Place sesame
paste in container. Begin processing and slowly add water and lemon juice,
pouring liquid through the feed tube. When mixture resembles mayonnaise,
add remaining ingredients and process until smooth.

Blender Directions   Place sesame paste in blender goblet. On low speed,
slowly add water and lemon juice. When mixture resembles mayonnaise,
add remaining ingredients and blend well.   YIELD: 2½ cups (625 ml)

Chopped Herring   P A R E V E

1 large herring fillet   2 Tbsp/25 ml lemon juice
2 eggs, hard-cooked   1 Tbsp/15 ml salad oil
1 small onion   2 tsp/10 ml sugar, or to taste
1 apple   Dash cinnamon
1 slice toast   Dash pepper

Food Processor Directions   Soak herring in cold water for several hours. Before
chopping, cut herring into chunks.

Insert steel blade in food processor. Place chunks of herring in container
and process until finely chopped. Transfer to mixing bowl. Place eggs in
container and process until finely chopped. Place in mixing bowl with
herring.

Peel onion and cut into chunks. Peel, quarter and core apple, and cut into
chunks. Insert shredding disc in food processor and shred apple and onion.
Add to fish mixture.

Soak toast in lemon juice, then add to fish mixture along with remaining
ingredients, blending well. Chill before serving.   YIELD: 6 to 8 servings

---

This spread is a natural on freshly baked bagels.

Lox and Cream Cheese Spread   D A I R Y

⅛ lb/60 grams lox   ¼ cup/50 ml milk or cream
1 (8-oz)/(227 grams) package
  cream cheese

Food Processor Directions   Insert steel blade in food processor. Place all ingredients in container and process until smooth and creamy.

Blender Directions   Combine all ingredients in blender goblet. Blend on high
speed until smooth and creamy.   YIELD: About 2½ cups (625 ml)

Variation   Add the following ingredient to basic recipe:

Lox, Cream Cheese and Onion Spread   D A I R Y

1 small onion

Peel onion and cut into eight pieces. Place onion chunks in blender goblet
and add remaining ingredients. Blend on high speed until mixture is smooth
and onion is finely chopped.   YIELD: About 1½ cups (375 ml)

Salmon Spread

PAREVE

1 (16-oz)/(454 grams) can salmon,
  drained and flaked
2 Tbsp/25 ml lemon juice
1 tsp/5 ml dill weed

2 green onions, cut into chunks
1 stalk celery, cut into chunks
1 cup/250 ml mayonnaise

Blender Directions   Combine all ingredients in blender goblet. Blend on high speed until vegetables are finely chopped and mixture is smooth.

YIELD: About 2½ cups (625 ml)

Stuffed Eggs

DAIRY or PAREVE

6 eggs, hard-cooked
2 Tbsp/25 ml mayonnaise
2 Tbsp/25 ml butter
  or pareve margarine

1 Tbsp/15 ml minced onion
½ tsp/2 ml prepared mustard
Salt and pepper to taste

Food Processor Directions   Insert steel blade in food processor. Peel eggs and cut in half lengthwise. Place yolks in container and process until finely chopped. Add remaining ingredients and process until smooth. Stuff yolk mixture into egg whites.

Blender Directions   Peel eggs and cut in half lengthwise. Remove yolks and place in blender goblet with remaining ingredients. Blend on low speed until smooth. Stuff yolk mixture into egg whites.   YIELD: 12 stuffed eggs

Variations   Add the following ingredients when preparing basic recipe:

Stuffed Eggs and Olives

DAIRY or PAREVE

¼ cup/50 ml chopped black olives

Stuffed Eggs and Onions

DAIRY or PAREVE

3 Tbsp/45 ml minced green onion

Stuffed Eggs and Pimento

DAIRY or PAREVE

2–3 Tbsp/25–45 ml diced pimento

YIELD: 12 stuffed eggs

Cheese Ball   DAIRY

1 cup (4 oz)/250 ml shredded
  yellow cheese
1 cup (4 oz)/250 ml shredded
  white cheese
1 (8-oz)/(227 grams) package
  cream cheese
2 Tbsp/25 ml butter

1 tsp/5 ml Worcestershire sauce,
  or to taste
⅓ cup/75 ml fresh parsley, chopped
1 tsp/5 ml paprika
½ cup/125 ml finely chopped
  walnuts

Food Processor Directions   Use the shredding disc to shred 4 ounces (250 ml) each yellow and white cheese. Transfer to mixing bowl.

Insert steel blade in food processor. Combine cream cheese, butter, Worcestershire sauce, parsley and paprika in container and process until smooth. Add to cheeses in mixing bowl and stir until well blended. Shape cheese mixture into a large ball. Roll in walnuts to give a fine, even coating. Chill well before serving.   YIELD: 1 3-inch (8-cm) cheese ball

---

Cheese Sticks   DAIRY

1 cup/250 ml flour
½ tsp/2 ml salt
½ cup (1 stick)/125 ml frozen
  butter
1 (3-oz)/(85 grams) package
  cream cheese, frozen

1 cup (4 oz)/250 ml shredded
  yellow cheese
½ cup/125 ml grated hard cheese
2 Tbsp/25 ml dry white wine
4 Tbsp/50 ml ice-cold water,
  or as needed
Paprika

Food Processor Directions   Insert steel blade in food processor. Put flour and salt into container. Cut frozen butter and cream cheese into chunks and add to flour mixture. Process, using the pulse button or a quick on-off motion, until mixture resembles small peas. Add the yellow cheese, hard cheese and wine and process. With the motor running, slowly add the ice water through the feed tube, processing until the dough forms a ball and clears the sides of the bowl.

Roll the dough on a lightly floured surface. Cut into narrow strips, about 3 inches (8 cm) in length. Place dough strips on a cookie sheet. Sprinkle with paprika and bake in a 400° F (200° C) oven about 10 minutes or until golden brown. Serve warm or cold.   YIELD: About 90 cheese sticks

---

For best results when grating cheese in the blender, cut into ½-inch (2-cm) chunks and chill in refrigerator. When blending cheeses for dips and spreads, remove from refrigerator about 30 minutes before using.

Cheese Dip Italian

D A I R Y

1 cup (4 oz)/250 ml grated
  white cheese
1 cup/250 ml dry cottage cheese
2 Tbsp/25 ml dry white wine

1 clove garlic
½ tsp/2 ml oregano
Dash salt

Food Processor Directions To grate cheese, place chunks of cheese in container and process using steel blade attachment until finely grated. Add remaining ingredients and process until smooth and creamy.

Blender Directions To grate cheese, cut into small chunks. Place chunks in goblet and blend on high speed until finely grated. Add remaining ingredients and blend until smooth and creamy.   YIELD: About 2 cups (500 ml)

Swiss Cheese and Caraway Dip

D A I R Y

½ cup/125 ml mayonnaise
3 Tbsp/45 ml dry white wine
2 tsp/10 ml caraway seeds

1 cup (4 oz)/250 ml shredded
  Swiss cheese

Food Processor Directions To shred cheese, insert shredding disc in food processor. Place chunks of cheese in feed tube and use the pusher to guide cheese onto shredding disc.

Insert steel blade. Combine cheese and remaining ingredients in container and process until smooth and creamy.

Blender Directions To shred or grate cheese, place chunks of cheese in goblet and blend on high speed until finely shredded. Add remaining ingredients and blend until smooth and creamy.   YIELD: 1½ cups (375 ml)

Dried Fruit Dip

D A I R Y

½ cup/125 ml dried fruit
  (prunes, apricots, raisins,
  peaches or any combination)

½ cup/125 ml yogurt
½ cup/125 ml cottage cheese
1 tsp/5 ml vanilla

Food Processor Directions Insert steel blade in food processor. Place dried fruit in container and chop fine, using pulse button or quick on-off motion. Add remaining ingredients and process until thoroughly blended.

Blender Directions Use scissors to cut dried fruit into small pieces. Place fruit in blender goblet. Blend at medium speed until well chopped. Add yogurt and cottage cheese and blend a few seconds on low speed to mix thoroughly. Add vanilla. Blend until creamy.   YIELD: 1 to 1½ cups (250 to 375 ml)

Mexican Guacamole Dip   P A R E V E

1 large ripe avocado
1 small onion
1 garlic clove
2 Tbsp/25 ml lemon juice

1 Tbsp/15 ml oil
¼ tsp/1 ml salt
1 tsp/5 ml chili powder

Food Processor Directions   Peel avocado, remove pit and cut avocado into chunks. Peel onion and cut into small chunks. Insert steel blade in food processor. Place avocado, onion chunks and garlic in container. Process until chopped very fine. Add remaining ingredients and process until smooth.

Blender Directions   Prepare avocado and onion as above. Place avocado chunks and lemon juice in blender goblet. With motor running add onion and garlic to avocado mixture. Blend on high speed until finely chopped. Add remaining ingredients and continue blending until smooth.

YIELD: About 1 cup (250 ml)

South-of-the-Border Bean Dip   D A I R Y

1 (16-oz)/(454 grams) can
   vegetarian baked beans
1 cup (4 oz)/250 ml shredded
   yellow cheese
½ cup/125 ml chopped green
   pepper

½ cup/125 ml chopped onion
¼ tsp/1 ml garlic powder
1 tsp/5 ml chili powder
1 tsp/5 ml salt
Dash cayenne pepper
1 tsp/5 ml vinegar, or to taste

Food Processor Directions   Insert steel blade in food processor. Place all ingredients in container and process until smooth. Serve hot.

Blender Directions   Combine all ingredients in blender goblet and blend on high speed until smooth. Serve hot.   YIELD: 3 cups (750 ml)

Tomato Blender Dip   D A I R Y

½ lb/250 grams ripe tomatoes
1 cup/250 ml sour cream
¼ tsp/1 ml garlic powder

1 tsp/5 ml dried basil
¼ tsp/1 ml salt

Blender Directions   Cut tomatoes into chunks and place in blender goblet. Blend at high speed until tomatoes are liquefied. Strain to remove liquid (use as a beverage or in another recipe).

Return tomato pulp to blender goblet. Add sour cream and seasonings and blend until smooth. Chill before serving.   YIELD: 1½ cups (375 ml)

Eggplant Dip
DAIRY

2 medium eggplants
2 lemons
¼ cup/50 ml olive oil

2 large garlic cloves
¼ cup/50 ml grated hard cheese
Salt and pepper to taste

Food Processor Directions   Broil the eggplants, turning frequently until skin is black and charred, about 20 minutes. Or eggplants may be cooked by roasting at 400° F (200° C) for about 45 minutes until flesh is soft. Allow to cool.

Cut eggplants in half and scoop out the flesh. Cut lemons in quarters and remove seeds. Insert steel blade in food processor. Place eggplant and lemon chunks in container and process until mixture is smooth. Add remaining ingredients and process until smooth and creamy.

Blender Directions   Cook eggplant as described above and scoop out flesh. Place lemon chunks in blender goblet along with eggplant. Blend at high speed until lemon is liquefied. Add remaining ingredients and blend until smooth and creamy. Taste to correct seasonings.

YIELD: About 2 cups (500 ml)

Fresh Vegetable Dip
DAIRY

1 cucumber
½ green pepper
1 green onion

1 garlic clove
1 cup/250 ml sour cream
1 tsp/5 ml dill weed, or to taste

Food Processor Directions   Wash and trim cucumbers. Peel if skin is heavily waxed. Cut all vegetables into 1-inch (2.5-cm) chunks.

Insert steel blade in food processor. Place vegetable chunks in container and process until coarsely chopped. Fold vegetables into sour cream with dill.

Blender Directions   Prepare vegetable chunks as described above.

Start blender motor running on medium speed. Drop vegetable chunks into goblet, a few at a time, blending until mixture is well chopped. Fold vegetables into sour cream with dill.   YIELD: 1–1½ cups (250–375 ml)

Crispy Snack Mix   PAREVE

¾ cup/175 pareve margarine
3 Tbsp/45 ml Worcestershire sauce
1½ tsp/7 ml onion salt
1½ tsp/7 ml garlic salt
1 tsp/5 ml celery salt
1 cup/250 ml salted mixed nuts

1 cup/250 ml salted peanuts
2 cups/500 ml thin pretzel sticks
2 cups/500 ml dry wheat cereal
2 cups/500 ml dry rice cereal
2 cups/500 ml dry corn cereal

Microwave Oven Directions   In large glass casserole combine margarine, Worcestershire sauce and salts. Cook on high setting until margarine is melted. Add remaining ingredients, mixing well until evenly coated. Cook on high setting 8 minutes, stirring every 2 minutes to distribute seasonings. Store in airtight container.

Conventional Directions   Melt margarine and combine ingredients as described above. Spread mixture on baking sheet. Bake at 300° F (150° C) 25 to 30 minutes, stirring once.   YIELD: 10 cups (2500 ml)

APPETIZER HINTS IN MICROWAVE OVEN

To Freshen Chips, Crackers and Pretzels
Place pieces in a single layer on a paper towel in microwave oven. Cook on high setting 15 to 30 seconds. Let stand 2 minutes before serving.

To Roast Nuts
Spread ½ to 1 cup (125 to 250 ml) shelled nuts in a shallow dish. Cook uncovered on high setting 6 to 10 minutes, stirring frequently. Allow nuts to stand a few minutes after roasting. They may be sprinkled with salt or vegetable oil before serving.

To Roast Chestnuts
Slash a crisscross on each nut. Spread 1 to 2 dozen nuts in a shallow glass dish. Cook on high setting uncovered 1 minute, or until the nuts pop open. Stir once. Let nuts stand for 5 minutes before removing the shells.

To Roast Seeds
Rinse fibers from pumpkin, sunflower or squash seeds and blot dry with paper towels. Place 1 cup (250 ml) seeds in a shallow glass dish. Sprinkle with salt. Cook on high setting 5 to 7 minutes or until crisp, stirring frequently. Allow to stand 5 minutes before serving.

SOUPS

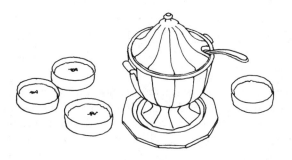

A bowl of soup can be a warm comfort on a cold, rainy day or it can be a refreshing snack on a summer afternoon. Some consider soup to be a first course, while others prefer to make it the entire meal. The soup recipes in this chapter range from traditional chicken soups (three delicious recipes), meat soups and meal-in-a-bowl chowders to elegant creamed vegetable soups. If you have never tried a chilled fruit soup, two recipes are included as an introduction to this delightful light snack.

Many of the recipes feature the crock pot, which is the perfect appliance to simmer soups slowly for a rich flavor.

The microwave oven is also featured in many recipes—both for quick-cooking soups, such as those using a prepared stock, and also for slower-cooking soups, involving meat or dried beans. These soups, which need to simmer at a lower setting to develop flavor and cook ingredients fully, still cook nearly twice as fast in the microwave oven as in conventional cooking.

Any cooked vegetable can be turned into a smooth, satisfying soup by pureeing it in the blender and adding milk or stock.

The food processor can be useful in any recipe that requires chopping, dicing, slicing or shredding of food, but it is particularly featured in several recipes where intricate preparation is involved.

Any recipe in this chapter which calls for meat stock can also be made with water and soup mix powder or bouillon cubes as a substitute. Many markets carry these powders or cubes in a pareve form, with either chicken, beef or vegetable "flavoring."

Basic Beef Stock   FLEISHIG

2 to 2½ lbs/1 kilo beef knuckle   2 tsp/10 ml salt
  or shank   4 sprigs parsley
8 cups/2 liters water   1 bay leaf
1 onion, quartered   3 whole cloves
1 stalk celery, chopped   ¼ tsp/1 ml dried thyme
2 carrots, chopped

Crock Pot Directions   In crock pot, combine beef and water. Cover and cook on low setting 3 to 4 hours. Add remaining ingredients. Cover and cook on low 3 to 4 hours longer. Strain stock, cool and refrigerate. When stock is well chilled, remove the fat which has accumulated on top and discard. Use in recipes calling for beef stock.   YIELD: About 2 quarts (2 liters)

Basic Chicken Stock   FLEISHIG

2 lbs/1 kilo chicken necks,   1 stalk celery, chopped
  backs and wings   4 sprigs parsley
6 cups/1500 ml hot water   1 tsp/5 ml salt
1 onion, quartered   Dash pepper
2 carrots, chopped   1 bay leaf

Crock Pot Directions   Combine all ingredients in crock pot. Cover and cook on low setting 6 to 8 hours. Strain stock, cool and refrigerate. When well chilled, remove the fat which has accumulated on top and discard. Use in recipes calling for chicken stock.   YIELD: About 1½ quarts (1500 ml)

Bean and Barley Soup   PAREVE

1 cup/250 ml navy or lima beans,   ½ tsp/2 ml pepper
  washed and soaked overnight   1 whole clove
¼ cup/50 ml barley   1 carrot, diced
4 cups/1 liter boiling water   1 onion, chopped
1 bay leaf   1 stalk celery, chopped
1½ tsp/7 ml salt

Crock Pot Directions   In crock pot place the beans, barley, water, bay leaf, salt, pepper and the clove. Cover and cook until beans are almost tender, 5 to 6 hours. Add remaining ingredients. Cover and cook on low setting 3 to 4 hours longer. If soup is too thick, thin with a little water.

YIELD: 6 to 8 servings

Beef Vegetable Soup   FLEISHIG

1 lb/500 grams beef short ribs
   or flanken
2 quarts/2 liters water
1 tsp/5 ml salt
1 onion, chopped
½ cup/125 ml diced celery

2 (10-oz)/(283 grams) cartons
   frozen mixed vegetables
2 cups/500 ml diced potatoes
1 (16-oz)/(454 grams) can
   tomatoes, cut up

Crock Pot Directions   Place beef, water, salt, onion and celery in crock pot. Cover and cook on low setting 4 to 6 hours. Remove short ribs. Strip meat off bones, chop and return to crock pot. Discard bones. Add frozen vegetables, potatoes and tomatoes. Cover and cook on low setting 2 to 3 hours.

YIELD: 10 servings

Quick Mixed-Vegetable Soup   FLEISHIG

1 (10-oz)/(283 grams) package
   frozen mixed vegetables

3 cups/750 ml stock
   (chicken or beef)

Blender Directions   Cook frozen vegetables in ¼ cup (50 ml) of the stock 5 minutes, or until barely tender. Place vegetables in blender goblet, adding enough stock to cover. Blend on low speed until smooth. Add pureed vegetable mixture to remaining stock in saucepan. Cook until soup is hot.

YIELD: 4 to 6 servings

After-Thanksgiving Turkey Soup   FLEISHIG

1 turkey carcass
2 quarts/2 liters water
1 tsp/5 ml salt, or to taste
½ tsp/2 ml pepper
1 onion, chopped

2 stalks celery, chopped
2 carrots, cut up
4 sprigs parsley
1 bay leaf
1 cup/250 ml cooked rice

Crock Pot Directions   Break turkey carcass into several pieces and place in crock pot. Add remaining ingredients, except rice. Cover and cook on low setting 5 to 6 hours. Strain and return soup to crock pot. Discard cooked vegetables. Strip meat from bones and return meat to soup. Add cooked rice. Cover and cook on high setting 20 to 30 minutes.   YIELD: 8 servings

Blender Borscht   D A I R Y

1 (16-oz)/(454 grams) can beets
4 cups/1 liter water
3 Tbsp/45 ml vinegar
1 carrot, thinly sliced
1 tsp/5 ml dill weed

2 tsp/10 ml pareve instant
   soup mix, beef-flavored, *or* 2 beef-
   flavored pareve bouillon cubes
1 tsp/5 ml salt, or to taste
1¼ cups/300 ml sour cream

Blender Directions   In a large pot, combine all ingredients except sour cream. Bring to a boil, reduce heat and simmer, covered, 30 minutes. Remove from heat and allow to cool slightly.

Pour soup mixture into blender goblet (in 2 or 3 "loads") and blend until smooth. Transfer to a refrigerator container and chill.

When ready to serve, place soup in blender with 3 heaping tablespoons of sour cream for each cup of soup. Blend on low speed until mixture is smooth and light pink in color. Serve in chilled mug or soup bowl. Garnish with a spoonful of sour cream.   YIELD: 6 servings

Cabbage Borscht   F L E I S H I G

1 lb/500 grams beets
1 lb/500 grams brisket
1 onion, chopped
1 garlic clove, minced
5 cups/1250 hot water
1 bay leaf

½ tsp/2 ml pepper
2 cups/500 ml shredded cabbage
1 (16-oz)/(454 grams) can tomatoes
1 tsp/5 ml salt, or to taste
¼ cup/50 ml lemon juice
2 Tbsp/25 ml sugar

Microwave Oven Directions   Place beets in a glass dish, cover with plastic wrap. Cook on high setting 7 minutes or until beets are tender. Allow to cool, then peel beets. Grate half of the beets fine; cut the rest into julienne strips. Set aside.

Cut brisket into small chunks. Place in a large glass bowl and add onion, garlic, water, bay leaf and pepper. Cover with plastic wrap and cook on high setting 10 minutes. Reduce setting to medium and cook 40 minutes longer.

Stir in cabbage, tomatoes, salt, lemon juice and sugar. Cover with plastic wrap. Cook on medium setting 15 minutes. Remove bay leaf and add beets. Cover and cook on medium setting 10 minutes longer or until beets are heated through. Taste to correct seasonings (the sugar and lemon juice combine for a sweet-sour taste). Allow soup to stand a few minutes before serving.

Conventional Directions   Peel the raw beets and grate fine. Set aside. Place meat and water in a large soup pot. Bring to a boil, then skim surface. Add remaining ingredients except sugar and lemon juice. Cover and cook over low heat 2 hours. Add the sugar and lemon juice. Cook 30 minutes longer. Taste to correct seasonings.   YIELD: 6 to 8 servings

---

Sweet and Sour Borscht   DAIRY or PAREVE

8 large beets, peeled
1 onion
2 quarts/2 liters water
1 tsp/5 ml salt, or to taste

1½ Tbsp/20 ml brown sugar
¼ cup/50 ml lemon juice
1 egg
Sour cream, optional

Food Processor Recipe   Cut the beets into chunks. Peel the onion and cut into eighths. Insert steel blade in food processor. Place beets and then onions in container and process until finely chopped.

Place beets, onion, water and salt in a saucepan. Bring to a boil, lower heat and simmer, covered, 1 hour. Add brown sugar and lemon juice, tasting to correct sweetness or tartness.

Beat the egg in a bowl. Add a small amount of the hot soup to the egg, stirring constantly. Pour the egg mixture slowly back into the soup, stirring until soup thickens. Chill and serve with sour cream, if desired.

YIELD: 8 to 10 servings

Meat Borscht   FLEISHIG

1½ lbs/750 grams brisket
1 quart/1 liter water
1 onion, chopped
1 (16-oz)/(454 grams) can tomatoes
1 tsp/5 ml salt, or to taste

½ tsp/2 ml black pepper
1 medium-size head cabbage,
    shredded
2 Tbsp/25 ml sugar
¼ cup/50 ml lemon juice

Crock Pot Directions   Cut brisket into chunks and place in crock pot. Add water, onion, tomatoes, salt, pepper and all but 1 cup (250 ml) of the cabbage (reserve for later use). Cover crock pot and cook on low setting 6 to 8 hours.

Add sugar, lemon juice and the remaining cabbage. Cook, uncovered, on high setting until cabbage is tender, about 15 minutes. Taste to correct seasonings.   YIELD: 6 to 8 servings

Some things were never meant to be changed, and no appliance yet invented can improve upon the taste of . . .

Grandma's Chicken Soup   FLEISHIG

1 large/1½ kilos stewing chicken
   (about 3 lbs)
2 to 3 quarts/2 to 3 liters cold water
3 or 4 carrots

2 stalks celery
4 sprigs parsley
1 onion, peeled
1 Tbsp/15 ml salt, or to taste

Conventional Directions Place chicken in a large pot and cover with cold water. Bring to a boil and skim. Add remaining ingredients. Cover pot, reduce heat and simmer gently 2 or 3 hours. Soup may be strained before serving, vegetables discarded and chicken saved for another use.

YIELD: 8 servings

Since word got around that I was writing a cookbook, many people have offered recipes and advice. The most outstanding recipe came from an unlikely source—the cantor of our synagogue, George Wald. I admit that I was skeptical at first—I mean, whoever heard of a chicken soup with potato and garlic—but Cantor Wald has an honest face as well as a lovely voice, and if he said it was good, I figured it was worth a try. Well, it proved to taste not just good but absolutely great, definitely a recipe to sing about.

Sweet Chicken Soup   FLEISHIG

5 carrots, quartered
½ bunch celery (top half,
   with the leaves), tied together
1 parsnip, whole
½ bunch parsley, tied together
3 garlic cloves, peeled
1 sweet potato, peeled

1 tsp/5 ml salt, or to taste
1 tsp/5 ml seasoned salt
3 or more quarts/3 liters cold water
1 large onion, peeled
1 very large/2 kilos chicken,
   4 to 5 lbs

Conventional Directions In a very large soup pot, place carrots, celery, parsnip, parsley, garlic and sweet potato. Add salt and seasoned salt and fill pot two-thirds full of cold water. Cover pot and bring mixture to a boil. Skim surface, add onion and chicken. Cover, bring to boil again, lower heat to a simmer and cook 1½ hours until chicken is tender. Skim fat from top of the soup.

Remove chicken, onion, celery, parsnips, parsley and garlic, squeezing the vegetables to extract as much liquid as possible. Save chicken for another use. Serve soup with pieces of carrots and chunks of sweet potato.

YIELD: 8 to 10 servings

Chicken Soup with Rice   FLEISHIG

3½ cups/875 ml chicken stock
1 small onion, chopped
½ cup/125 ml chopped celery

1 carrot, chopped
1 tsp/5 ml dry parsley flakes
1 cup/250 ml cooked rice

Microwave Oven Directions In a large glass bowl, combine stock, vegetables and parsley. Cover with plastic wrap, place in microwave oven, and cook on high setting 10 minutes or until mixture boils. Reduce setting to medium and cook 5 minutes longer, or until vegetables are soft. Remove vegetables with a slotted spoon and discard. Add rice. Cover dish with plastic wrap. Cook on medium setting 5 minutes or until rice is thoroughly heated.

Conventional Directions Combine all ingredients except rice in a saucepan. Bring to a boil and simmer 30 minutes, or until vegetables are soft. Remove vegetables. Add rice and continue cooking until rice is hot.

YIELD: 4 servings

Variations Omit rice and substitute following ingredients in basic recipe:

Chicken Barley Soup   FLEISHIG

¾ cup/175 ml cooked barley

Chicken Noodle Soup   FLEISHIG

1½ cups/375 ml cooked noodles   YIELD: 4 servings

Corn Chowder   DAIRY

1 Tbsp/15 ml butter
1 small onion, diced
1 (10¾-oz)/(305 grams) can
   condensed cream of celery soup
4 cups/1 liter milk

1 (16-oz)/(454 grams) can
   whole-kernel corn, drained
½ teaspoon/2 ml salt, or to taste
Dash pepper

Microwave Oven Directions Combine butter and onion in a 3-quart glass bowl. Cover with plastic wrap and cook on high setting in microwave oven 3 minutes or until onion is soft. Add remaining ingredients, stirring until well blended. Cover with plastic wrap. Place in microwave oven and cook on high setting until soup is very hot, about 8 minutes.

Conventional Directions In a soup pot, melt butter. Add onion and cook over medium heat until onion is soft. Add remaining ingredients, stirring until well blended. Cook and stir until soup reaches the boiling point, but do not allow to boil.

YIELD: 6 servings

Fish Chowder, Mediterranean Style   P A R E V E

2 lbs/1 kilo fish fillets   3 eggs
  (fresh or defrosted)   2 Tbsp/25 ml lemon juice
3 cups/750 ml boiling water   Salt and pepper to taste
1 cup/250 ml celery, thinly sliced   Parsley sprigs
½ cup/125 ml rice

Microwave Oven Directions Arrange fish fillets in a glass baking dish. Cover
with plastic wrap and cook on high setting 10 minutes or until fish flakes
easily. Drain and reserve liquid. Cut fish into chunks and set aside.

In a very large glass bowl, combine fish broth, water, celery and rice.
Cover with plastic wrap and cook on high setting 3 minutes. Reduce setting
to medium and cook 14 minutes longer or until rice is soft.

Beat eggs. Add lemon juice and mix well. Pour 1 cup (250 ml) soup into
egg mixture, stirring constantly. Pour egg mixture back into bowl of soup,
stirring until well blended. Season to taste. Add fish chunks.

Cover soup with plastic wrap. Return to microwave oven and cook on
medium setting 5 minutes or until fish is hot. To serve, garnish with parsley.

Conventional Directions Cook fish in water until fish flakes. Remove fish and
set aside. Add celery and rice to fish broth. Cover and cook until rice is
tender, about 20 minutes. Beat eggs and add lemon juice. Pour 1 cup (250
ml) of soup into egg mixture, stirring constantly. Pour egg mixture back into
the pot of soup, stirring until well blended. Do not boil. Season to taste. Add
chunks of fish. Continue cooking until fish is heated through. Garnish with
parsley.   YIELD: 6 servings

Lentil Soup   P A R E V E

1 onion, chopped   2 carrots, chopped
1 garlic clove, minced   2 tsp/10 ml salt, or to taste
2 Tbsp/25 ml oil   ½ tsp/2 ml pepper
1 lb/500 grams lentils (washed   2 cloves
  and soaked overnight)   1 bay leaf
  1 (16-oz)/(454 grams) can stewed 6 sprigs parsley
  tomatoes   5 cups/1250 ml hot water
1 stalk celery, chopped

Crock Pot Directions In a hot frying pan, sauté onion and garlic in oil until
brown. Place lentils in crock pot. Add onion, garlic and remaining ingredients. Cover and simmer on low setting 10 to 12 hours.

YIELD: 6 servings

Variation   Add the following ingredients to basic Lentil Soup recipe:

Lentil Soup with Meat   F L E I S H I G

2–2½ lbs/1 kilo soup meat   1 soup bone

Follow directions in basic recipe, but before serving remove and discard bone.   YIELD: 6 servings

---

The food processor is a great appliance to have when making this recipe because almost every ingredient needs to be sliced, diced or chopped.

Mushroom Soup   P A R E V E

1 lb/500 grams fresh mushrooms   2 stalks celery
1 small tomato, cut in quarters   ½ tsp/2 ml salt, or to taste
1 or 2 carrots   4 cups/1 liter water
1 medium onion   1 egg yolk
4 sprigs parsley

Food Processor Directions   Insert slicing disc in food processor. Arrange mushrooms in feed tube and use pusher to guide them onto cutting blade to slice thin. Place tomato quarters in feed tube and slice thin. Place mushrooms and tomatoes in a large pot.

Insert shredding disc in food processor. Cut carrots into chunks and place in feed tube. Use pusher to guide carrots onto cutting blade to shred. Add to pot with other vegetables.

Insert steel blade. Peel onion and cut into eighths. Place in container with parsley and celery, cut into chunks. Process until coarsely chopped. Add to soup pot.

Add salt and water to vegetables in soup pot. Bring to a boil, lower heat and simmer, covered, 1 hour on a low flame.

Beat egg yolk. Pour a small amount of hot soup into egg yolk, stirring constantly. Gradually return egg yolk mixture to soup. Stir until well blended. Do not boil.   YIELD: 6 servings

---

Variation   Add the following ingredient to basic Mushroom Soup recipe:

Mushroom-Barley Soup

½ cup/125 ml barley

Add barley along with vegetables. This results in a thickened soup.
                                                  YIELD: 6 servings

Onion Soup   F L E I S H I G

2 Tbsp/25 ml pareve margarine   1 tsp/5 ml sugar
3 medium onions, thinly sliced   Salt and pepper to taste
6 cups/1500 ml beef stock

Microwave Oven Directions   Place margarine and onions in a large glass bowl.
Cover with plastic wrap and cook on high setting 10 minutes, or until onions
are soft. Stir in beef stock and sugar. Cover with plastic wrap. Cook until
soup is hot, about 10 minutes on high setting. Add salt and pepper to taste.

Conventional Directions   In a hot frying pan melt margarine and sauté onions
until soft. Transfer to a soup pot and add remaining ingredients. Bring to a
boil, then lower heat and simmer until soup is hot. Season to taste.

YIELD: 6 to 8 servings

Variations   Make the following changes when preparing basic Onion Soup
recipe:

Pareve Onion Soup   P A R E V E

6 cups/1½ liters water
3 cubes vegetable bouillon

Omit beef stock and substitute water and vegetable bouillon.

Dairy Onion Soup   D A I R Y

½ cup/125 ml grated hard cheese

Follow instructions for Pareve Onion Soup, stirring in grated hard cheese
just before serving.   YIELD: 6 to 8 servings

Pareve Split Pea Soup   P A R E V E

1 lb/500 grams dried split peas   2 quarts/2 liters boiling water
1 onion, chopped   1 cup/250 ml diced potatoes
1 tsp/2 ml salt, or to taste   ⅔ cup/150 ml thinly sliced carrots
½ tsp/2 ml pepper

Microwave Oven Directions   Combine split peas, onion, salt and water in a
large glass bowl. Cover with plastic wrap and cook on high setting 10 min-

utes, reduce setting to medium and cook 30 minutes longer, or until peas are tender, stirring occasionally.

Add remaining ingredients. Cover bowl with plastic wrap and cook on high setting 20 minutes or until vegetables are tender. Taste and correct seasoning.

For a smooth texture, soup may be pureed in a blender or pressed through a sieve.

Conventional Directions   Place all ingredients in a large soup pot. Bring to a boil, lower heat, then simmer 2 to 2½ hours.   YIELD: 8 to 10 servings

---

Split Pea Soup with Beef Stock   FLEISHIG

½ cup/125 ml dried split peas
2½ cups/625 ml beef stock
1 cup/250 ml chopped cooked beef
  (optional)

1 small onion, chopped
1 celery stalk, chopped
½ tsp/2 ml salt, or to taste
¼ tsp/1 ml pepper

Blender Directions   Place peas and beef stock in a saucepan and cook over medium heat until peas are tender, about 45 minutes. Allow to cool slightly, then pour into blender goblet. Blend on medium speed until soup is smooth. Pour back into saucepan. Add remaining ingredients and cook until vegetables are tender.   YIELD: 3 or 4 servings

---

Schav   PAREVE

1 lb/500 grams schav
  (sorrel grass) or spinach
1½ quarts/1½ liters boiling water

1 egg
1 tsp/5 ml salt
1 bunch green onions

Microwave Oven Directions   Wash the schav or spinach leaves well and cut off stems. Tie the stems together. Place leaves and stems in a large glass bowl and add water. Cook on high setting 5 minutes. Remove stems and discard.

Beat the egg and salt together. Gradually pour hot soup into the egg, stirring constantly. Chill soup before serving.

To serve Schav: Finely dice the green onions and place a spoonful in bottom of each serving bowl. Pour the Schav over the diced onion.

Conventional Directions   Combine schav and boiling water in a large pot. Bring to a boil, lower heat, and simmer for 15 minutes. Stir in beaten egg mixture. Chill soup before serving.   YIELD: 8 servings

Cream of Vegetable Soup   D A I R Y

2 Tbsp/25 ml butter
2 Tbsp/25 ml flour
1 tsp/5 ml salt, or to taste
3 cups/750 ml milk

1 to 1½ cups/250 to 375 ml cooked
   vegetables (see Variations)

Blender Directions   Prepare a white sauce by melting butter in a small saucepan over medium heat. Add flour and ½ teaspoon (2 ml) salt, blending well.
Slowly add 1 cup milk, stirring constantly. Cook until mixture boils and
thickens. Set aside.

Place cooked vegetables and remaining milk in blender goblet. Blend at
medium speed until smooth. Pour into saucepan, add salt and heat until just
below boiling. Stir prepared white sauce into soup mixture, blending well.
Taste to correct seasoning.   YIELD: 6 servings

Variations   Add the following as the vegetables when preparing basic Cream
of Vegetable Soup:

Cream of Asparagus Soup   D A I R Y

1 (10-oz)/(283 grams) package frozen asparagus

Cook 1 package frozen asparagus according to package directions. Drain
asparagus, saving cooking liquid to use in preparing white sauce as a substitute for an equal amount of milk.

Cream of Broccoli Soup   D A I R Y

½ lb/250 grams broccoli

Cook the thick stems from the broccoli for soup and reserve the broccoli
flowerets for another recipe.

Cream of Cauliflower Soup   D A I R Y

½ head cauliflower

Use half of a large head of cauliflower, cooked until tender, in basic soup
recipe.

Cream of Potato Soup   D A I R Y

3 medium potatoes

Peel and cook potatoes. Cut into small chunks and use in basic soup recipe.

Cream of Spinach Soup   DAIRY

1 lb/500 grams spinach

Carefully wash spinach. There is no need to cook spinach before blending.
Proceed as in basic recipe.   YIELD: 6 servings

Old-Fashioned Cream of Tomato Soup   DAIRY

4 Tbsp/50 ml butter	¼ tsp/1 ml pepper
4 Tbsp/50 ml flour	1 bay leaf
1½ tsp/7 ml salt	½ tsp/2 ml ground cloves
2 cups/500 ml milk	1 Tbsp/15 ml minced onion
1 (16-oz)/(454 grams) can tomatoes	½ tsp/2 ml salt, or to taste

Microwave Oven Directions   Prepare white sauce by placing butter in a glass
casserole. Cook on high setting until melted, about 1 minute. Stir in flour
and salt, blending until smooth. Add milk, stirring constantly. Cook on high
setting 6 to 8 minutes, or until mixture thickens and boils (stir after 4 minutes). Set aside.

Press tomatoes through a sieve or blend until smooth. In large glass bowl
place tomatoes and remaining ingredients. Cook on high setting until boiling, about 6 minutes. Remove bowl from oven. Stirring constantly, add
white sauce. Return to oven and cook on high setting until heated through.

Conventional Directions   In a small saucepan, melt butter over medium heat.
Add flour and salt, blending well. Slowly add milk, stirring constantly. Cook
until mixture boils and thickens. Set aside.

Press tomatoes through a sieve or blend until smooth. In a soup pot,
combine remaining ingredients and bring to a boil. Lower heat and simmer
10 minutes. Pour white sauce into soup, stirring constantly. Heat thoroughly
before serving.   YIELD: 4 to 6 servings

Fruit soups are not often served in America, although they are a great favorite in Israel and Europe. Try serving chilled fruit soup as a dessert or a between-meals snack.

Apricot Fruit Soup   PAREVE

1 lb/500 grams fresh apricots, seeded   ½ tsp/2 ml grated orange peel
3 cups/750 ml boiling water   ½ tsp/2 ml cinnamon
½ cup/125 ml sugar   1 Tbsp/15 ml cornstarch

Microwave Oven Directions In a glass bowl place everything except cornstarch. Cover with plastic wrap and cook on high setting until apricots are tender, about 10 minutes. Push apricots through a sieve or blend. Return apricot puree to soup. Dissolve cornstarch in a small amount of cold water and stir into hot soup. Cook on high setting 2 minutes, or until soup is thickened. Chill before serving.

Conventional Directions Place apricots in a saucepan with cold water. Bring to a boil, lower heat and simmer gently 1 hour. Puree apricots in blender or through a sieve and return to liquid. Add remaining ingredients and cook until soup is thickened, about 30 minutes longer. Stir several times.

YIELD: 4 servings

Cherry Fruit Soup   PAREVE

¼ lemon   ¼ cup/50 ml sugar
1¾ cups/425 ml water   ¼ tsp/1 ml cinnamon
2 cups/500 ml pitted   ½ cup/125 ml sweet red wine
   sweet cherries   1½ tsp/7 ml cornstarch

Blender Directions Remove seeds from lemon, cut into small pieces and place in blender goblet. Add water and blend until lemon is liquefied. Pour into saucepan and add cherries, sugar and cinnamon. Bring to a boil, lower heat and simmer 5 minutes. Add wine. Dissolve cornstarch in a small amount of cold water and stir into soup mixture. Cook, stirring constantly, until soup is slightly thickened. Chill in refrigerator.

To serve: Remove cherries from soup with a slotted spoon and place in blender goblet. Add ½ cup (125 ml) soup and blend on low speed until cherries are coarsely chopped. Return cherries to soup mixture. Serve in individual bowls or glasses.   YIELD: 4 servings

This delicious soup has been a favorite of mine for years. The fresh vegetables are simmered gently in chicken stock and then blended until velvety smooth.

Velvety Vegetable Soup   F L E I S H I G

2 onions, sliced
2 stalks celery, cut up
2 Tbsp/25 ml pareve margarine
4 cups/1 liter chicken stock
2 medium potatoes, sliced

2 carrots, sliced
1 zucchini, sliced
Salt and pepper to taste
4 sprigs parsley

Blender Directions   Sauté the onions and celery in melted margarine. In a soup pot combine sautéed vegetables with remaining ingredients. Cook gently on low heat until vegetables are soft. Pour soup into blender (in two or three "loads") and blend until smooth. Return to soup pot. Taste to correct seasonings.   YIELD: 4 to 6 servings

MICROWAVE OVEN HINTS FOR SOUP

To Heat Individual Serving
Pour desired amount of soup into serving bowl. Cover with wax paper and cook on high setting about 2½ minutes or until soup is hot.

Canned Soup
Place an equal amount of condensed canned soup and water in a serving bowl. Stir to blend well. Cover with wax paper and cook on high setting about 1½ minutes or until soup is hot.

Dehydrated Soups
Prepare dehydrated (powdered) soups in glass measuring cup or individual serving bowls. Combine soup and hot water. Cover with wax paper and cook on high setting the same amount of time indicated on the soup package for conventional cooking. Stir and serve.

SOUP MATES

Soup mates are nourishing, tasty little items which make a bowl of soup very attractive. Some soup mates, such as dumplings or Einlauf, are served floating in the soup, while others, such as Piroshki, are served along with the soup. One of the all-time favorite soup mates in a Jewish home is Knaidlach (matzah balls), and recipes for several versions of this treat are found in the Passover chapter.

Use the mixer or the food processor for making dough for Kreplach, noodles and Piroshki. The food processor also has an amazing ability to quickly chop or puree meat, poultry and vegetables for filling mixtures.

The microwave oven can be used to cook dumplings and to crisp croutons and is featured in filling recipes which need to be cooked.

The blender is used to prepare batters, as for Einlauf.

Croutons   P A R E V E

2 slices pareve bread or Challah

Microwave Oven Directions Slice bread into ¼-inch (1-cm) cubes. Spread cubes in a single layer on a paper towel and place in microwave oven. Cook on high setting 1½ to 2 minutes, or until dry. Allow to stand a few minutes before using.   YIELD: About 1 cup (250 ml) croutons

Variations

Garlic-Cheese Croutons   D A I R Y

2 Tbsp/25 ml butter, melted   1 tsp/5 ml paprika
1 tsp/5 ml garlic salt   1 Tbsp/15 ml grated hard cheese

Brush slices of bread with a mixture of melted butter, garlic salt, paprika and grated cheese. Cut bread into cubes and cook as in basic recipe.

Onion-Herb Croutons   PAREVE

2 Tbsp/25 ml olive oil
1 tsp/5 ml salt
1 tsp/5 ml minced onion

1 tsp/5 ml parsley flakes
½ tsp/2 ml oregano

Brush slices of bread with a mixture of olive oil, salt, onion, parsley flakes
and oregano. Cut bread into cubes and cook as in basic recipe.

YIELD: About 1 cup (250 ml) croutons

Dumplings   PAREVE or DAIRY

2 cups/500 ml flour
3 tsp/15 ml baking powder
1 tsp/5 ml salt
¾ cup/175 ml water or milk

2 eggs
2 Tbsp/25 ml oil
2½ cups/625 ml or more boiling
    water

Microwave Oven Directions Combine flour, baking powder and salt. Blend
water, eggs and oil together and mix with dry ingredients until just moistened. Batter should be very thick.

Boil water in a glass casserole in microwave oven. Drop dumpling batter
by rounded teaspoons into boiling water. Cover with plastic wrap and microwave oven cook on high setting 7 to 10 minutes. Allow to stand 5 minutes
before serving.

Conventional Directions Prepare dumpling batter. Fill a large pot with 2
quarts (2 liters) water and bring to a boil. Drop batter by spoonfuls into
boiling water. Reduce heat to a simmer. Cover tightly and cook for 12
minutes.   YIELD: 4 to 5 servings

Variations Add the following ingredients to prepared dumpling batter:

Parsley Dumplings   PAREVE or DAIRY

¼ cup/50 ml minced parsley

Savory Dumplings   PAREVE or DAIRY

2 Tbsp/25 ml minced onion
2 Tbsp/25 ml minced parsley

¼ tsp/1 ml pepper
½ tsp/2 ml marjoram
                                    YIELD: 4 to 5 servings

Einlauf are egg drops or egg strips. They are a quick and easy noodle substitute and may be cooked directly in the soup.

Einlauf   P A R E V E

1 egg   Dash salt
¼ cup/50 ml cold water   3 Tbsp/45 ml flour

Blender Directions   Put egg and water in blender goblet. Blend on low speed a few seconds to combine. Add salt and flour. Blend on low speed until mixture is smooth.

Slowly pour spoonfuls of batter in a steady stream into boiling soup. Cook 5 minutes.   YIELD: Einlauf for 1 quart soup

Farfel   P A R E V E

1 egg   1 to 1½ cups/250 to 375 ml flour
¼ tsp/1 ml salt

Food Processor Directions   Insert steel blade in food processor. Place egg and salt in container and process until lightly mixed. Add 1 cup (250 ml) flour and process until well combined. Add more flour, if necessary, until mixture forms a stiff ball and clears sides of the container.

Remove dough from the container and let stand 1 hour, or until hard enough to shred.

Insert shredding disc in food processor. Break off pieces of dough and place in the feed tube. Use the pusher to guide dough through the feed tube onto the shredding disc.

Remove farfel from the container. Spread on a platter to dry, stirring occasionally. Allow to dry for several hours, then store in a covered jar.

To cook farfel, drop in boiling soup and cook 10 to 15 minutes. Farfel may be cooked in boiling water and served as a side dish as a substitute for potatoes.   YIELD: About 1½ cups (375 ml)

Kreplach   P A R E V E

2 eggs   Water as needed
½ tsp/2 ml salt   Kreplach filling
1½ to 2 cups/375 to 500 ml cups   (see following recipes)
   sifted flour

Food Processor Directions   Insert steel blade in food processor. Put eggs and salt into container with about 1 cup (250 ml) flour. Mix well. Add another ½ cup (125 ml) flour and process until it forms a ball. If necessary, add more flour or water gradually. Remove dough from container. Knead a few seconds by hand and form into 2 balls.

Mixer Directions   Sift 1½ cups (375 ml) flour and salt into mixer bowl. Drop in eggs. Attach beaters and mix on low speed until mixture becomes a very stiff paste, about 45 seconds. If mixture is too moist more flour may be added. If mixture is too dry, add water, a spoonful at a time, until proper consistency is reached. Divide dough in half and roll into two balls.

To Roll Kreplach   Prepare dough by either method. You will need a large flat surface on which to roll dough. With floured rolling pin, roll dough very thin. Turn the dough often, rolling first on one side and then the other, flouring rolling pin as needed. Roll and stretch dough as thin as possible.

Cut dough into 3-inch (8-cm) squares. Place one spoonful of Kreplach filling (see following recipes) in the center of each square. Fold crosswise to form triangles. Press the edges together to seal. Cook in boiling salted water or soup for approximately 15 minutes. Kreplach will rise to the top of the liquid when done.   YIELD: About 2 dozen Kreplach

---

Chicken Filling for Kreplach   F L E I S H I G

1 lb/500 grams cooked chicken   3 sprigs parsley
    meat   1 egg
1 small onion   Salt and pepper to taste

Food Processor Directions   Insert steel blade in food processor. Cut chicken meat into chunks and place in the container. Process until chicken is very finely chopped, then transfer to a mixing bowl. Peel the onion, cut in eighths and place in container along with the parsley. Process until mixture is finely chopped, then add to chicken along with remaining ingredients. Combine mixture well and use as a filling for Kreplach.

                                       YIELD: Filling for 2 dozen Kreplach

---

Hamburger Filling for Kreplach   F L E I S H I G

1 lb/500 grams hamburger   1 tsp/5 ml salt
½ cup/125 ml minced onion   ½ tsp/2 ml pepper
1 egg

Microwave Oven Directions   Break hamburger into chunks and place along with onions in a glass bowl. Cover bowl with wax paper and cook on high setting 5 minutes. Drain off fat and use a fork to break up and separate the meat into smaller pieces. Cover with wax paper and cook on high setting 3 minutes longer. Drain off fat. Allow meat to cool.

Beat egg and add with seasonings to meat mixture, blending well. Use as a filling for Kreplach.   YIELD: Filling for 2 dozen Kreplach

Meat Filling for Kreplach   FLEISHIG

1 lb/500 grams cooked meat   1 egg
1 small onion   Salt and pepper to taste
¼ cup/50 ml bread crumbs

Food Processor Directions   Insert steel blade in food processor. Cut the meat
into chunks and place in container. Process until finely chopped, then transfer to a mixing bowl. Peel onion and cut into eighths. Place in container and
process until finely chopped. Add to meat mixture, along with remaining
ingredients. Blend well and use as a filling for Kreplach.

YIELD: Filling for 2 dozen Kreplach

The same dough recipe is used for making both Kreplach and noodles. The
difference lies in the handling and cooking of the dough once it has been
prepared.

Noodles   PAREVE

1 recipe Kreplach dough

Conventional Directions   Prepare Kreplach dough, using either the food processor or mixer method.
   Prepare a large, flat work surface to roll dough. Cover with a floured
tablecloth or pastry cloth. Place dough on cloth. With floured rolling pin,
roll dough very thin. Turn the dough often, rolling first on one side and then
on the other, flouring cloth and rolling pin as necessary. Roll and stretch the
dough as thin as possible.
   After dough has been rolled, allow it to stand until dry, about 30 minutes,
but do not allow to become brittle. Roll loosely, jelly-roll fashion and cut
crosswise into very thin strips. Toss lightly to separate. Allow noodles to dry
at room temperature at least 1 hour.
   Store in a jar or plastic bag.
   To cook noodles, drop into boiling salted water and cook for 10 minutes.
YIELD: About 8 oz (250 grams) noodles

Variations

Noodle Puffs   PAREVE

Roll dough thin, as for noodles, and let stand until almost dry. Fold dough
in half. Use a thimble or small round cutter to cut through both thicknesses
of dough, pressing well so that the edges stick together. Fry in hot oil until
brown and puffy. Serve in soup.   YIELD: About 8 oz (250 grams) noodles

Piroshki are of Russian origin. They are savory little pies. The crust is made from a seasoned pastry dough and the filling may be just about any vegetable, meat or poultry leftover.

Piroshki   PAREVE

1½ cups/375 ml flour
¼ tsp/1 ml baking powder
½ tsp/2 ml salt
¼ tsp/1 ml pepper
½ cup/125 ml pareve margarine
1 egg

¼ cup/50 ml cold water, or as
   needed
Melted pareve margarine or 1 egg
   yolk diluted with 1 Tbsp/15 ml
   cold water
Piroshki filling (see following recipe)

Food Processor Method   Insert steel blade in food processor. Sift dry ingredients and place in the container. Add chunks of margarine and mix by using the pulse button or quick on-off motions until the mixture resembles small peas. Add the egg and process until blended. With food processor running, gradually pour water through the feed tube and process until dough forms a ball and clears the sides of the container. Chill dough in refrigerator for about 10 minutes to make handling easier. If frozen margarine and ice water are used, the dough may be rolled without chilling.

Mixer Directions   Sift flour, baking powder, salt and pepper into mixer bowl. Cut margarine into small pieces and drop into bowl. Attach beaters and mix on low speed until mixture is in lumps the size of small peas. Add egg. Gradually add enough water, 1 tablespoon (15 ml) at a time, to hold dough together. Do not overmix. Chill dough in refrigerator for about 10 minutes to make handling easier.

To Make Piroshki   Circles of dough are needed to make Piroshki. Roll the chilled dough on a floured board and cut into 3-inch (8-cm) circles.

Place 1 tablespoon (15 ml) filling in the center of each circle. Pinch the pastry together in a neat ridge across the center of the Piroshki. Place on a greased baking sheet.

Brush the Piroshki with melted pareve margarine or with an egg yolk diluted with cold water. Bake at 375° (190° C) for 20 minutes or until brown.   YIELD: About 30 Piroshki

Cabbage Filling for Piroshki   PAREVE

1 onion, chopped
3 Tbsp/45 ml pareve margarine
3 cups/750 ml finely
   shredded cabbage

2 tsp/10 ml dried dill weed
2 hard-cooked eggs, chopped
1 tsp/5 ml salt, or to taste

Microwave Oven Directions   In a glass bowl, place the onion and pareve margarine. Cover bowl with plastic wrap and cook on high setting 4 minutes. Add the cabbage, mix well, cover with plastic wrap and cook 5 minutes longer on high setting. Add remaining ingredients. Filling should be very finely chopped and blended. Use 1½ tablespoons (20 ml) filling for each Piroshki. Cabbage Piroshki should contain a little more filling than other kinds.

Conventional Directions   Sauté the onion in hot margarine. Add cabbage and cook 30 minutes or until vegetables are tender. Mix with remaining ingredients and use as a filling for Piroshki.   YIELD: Filling for about 30 Piroshki

---

Carrot Filling for Piroshki   DAIRY

1 lb/500 grams carrots, peeled
2 Tbsp/25 ml pareve margarine
2 Tbsp/25 ml sour cream

1 tsp/5 ml salt, or to taste
2 hard-cooked eggs, chopped

Food Processor Directions   Cook the carrots in boiling salted water for 30 minutes or until tender. Insert steel blade in food processor. Slice the carrots into pieces and place in container. Process until very finely chopped.

   Melt the margarine in a frying pan and sauté the carrots about 10 minutes. Add the sour cream and bring mixture to a boil. Remove from heat and allow to cool. Add salt and chopped eggs. Use as a filling for Piroshki.

YIELD: Filling for 30 Piroshki

Chicken and Liver Filling for Piroshki   FLEISHIG

1 small onion
2 Tbsp/25 ml chicken fat
   or pareve margarine
1 cup/250 ml cut-up cooked
   chicken meat

½ lb/250 grams chicken livers,
   broiled
1 slice day-old Challah
Salt and pepper to taste
Dash nutmeg

Food Processor Recipe   Insert steel blade in food processor. Peel the onion and cut into eighths. Place the onion pieces in the container and process until finely chopped. Fry the onion in chicken fat until soft.

Cut chicken meat and livers into small chunks and place in the container. Process until very finely chopped.

Trim crust from the Challah, soak in a little water and squeeze dry. Add to container with the chicken mixture. Add the cooked onions and remaining ingredients. Process until filling is smooth. Use as a filling for Piroshki.

YIELD: Filling for 30 Piroshki

Kasha Filling for Piroshki   PAREVE

½ cup/125 ml minced onion
2 Tbsp/25 ml pareve margarine
2 cups/500 ml cooked kasha

1 egg yolk
1 tsp/5 ml salt, or to taste
Dash pepper

Microwave Oven Directions   Place onion and margarine in a glass bowl. Cover with plastic wrap and cook on high setting 2 minutes. Add remaining ingredients, stirring to mix well. Use as a filling for Piroshki.

Conventional Directions   In a frying pan, sauté onion in margarine. Combine with remaining ingredients and use as a filling for Piroshki.

YIELD: Filling for 30 Piroshki

Meat Filling for Piroshki   FLEISHIG

1 lb/500 grams hamburger
1 small onion, minced
2 Tbsp/25 ml chicken fat
   or pareve margarine

2 hard-cooked eggs, finely chopped
Salt and pepper to taste

Microwave Oven Directions   Place hamburger and onion in a glass bowl. Cover with wax paper and cook on high setting 5 minutes or until meat loses its pink color. Drain off fat and crumble beef. Chop the meat very finely and blend with chicken fat, eggs and seasonings. Use as filling for piroshki.

Conventional Directions   In a frying pan melt chicken fat. Sauté onion and hamburger until meat loses its pink color. Drain off excess fat. Mix well with remaining ingredients. Mixture should be very finely chopped. Use as a filling for Piroshki.

YIELD: Filling for 30 Piroshki

CHOLENT, STEWS AND TZIMMES

This chapter is a testimony to the convenience and simplicity of the crock pot.

Cholent, a well-seasoned hearty bean dish, is the food traditionally eaten at the noon meal on Shabbat. For generations Jewish housewives have prepared Cholent, and some weeks it was tasty and other weeks it was dry and disappointing. Today, with the use of a crock pot, you can easily and predictably produce a perfect Cholent week after week after week.

If you are accustomed to making Cholent weekly, you will notice some basic differences when cooking it in a crock pot. First, the beans for Cholent do not need to presoak before being cooked overnight in the crock pot. Second, the amount of water needed in the crock pot is *less* than used conventionally (after about an hour or 2 of cooking the level of liquid in the crock pot should be barely covering the top of the bean mixture).

It is not permitted to cook food on Shabbat, although completing the cooking process and keeping cooked food warm is allowed. For this reason the Cholent should be at least one-third cooked before Shabbat begins. This can be accomplished by starting the Cholent cooking on low setting about 2 hours or on high setting about 1 hour (and then turning the setting back to low) before Shabbat begins.

Microwave oven recipes are featured along with crock pot recipes to demonstrate relatively faster methods of cooking chili, goulash and stew.

The food processor is used for one Tzimmes recipe which involves grating and fancy cutting; however, this appliance can be used in any recipe where foods need to be chopped, shredded or sliced.

Basic Shabbat Cholent   F L E I S H I G

½ cup/125 ml dry kidney beans
½ cup/125 ml dry small lima beans

½ cup/125 ml dry navy beans
1½ lbs/750 grams potatoes

1 lb/500 grams beef chuck or
flanken
1 onion, chopped
3½ cups or more/875 ml water
1 Tbsp/15 ml salt, or to taste

Pepper to taste
3 cloves garlic,
whole and unpeeled
1 Tbsp/15 ml minced parsley

Crock Pot Directions Wash beans well and set aside. Peel potatoes, cut each in half and place in bottom of crock pot. Place meat on top of potatoes and sprinkle on onions. Mix beans together and spread over top. Add water to cover. Add salt, pepper, garlic and parsley. Cover pot and cook on low setting 12 hours or longer.

Before serving Cholent, remove and discard bone and garlic cloves. Cut meat into small pieces and stir into Cholent. YIELD: 6 to 8 servings

---

Chicken Cholent with Kasha FLEISHIG

2 Tbsp/25 ml oil
1 large onion, chopped
3 garlic cloves, minced
1 cup/250 ml kasha
1 stalk celery, diced

1 or 2 carrots, chopped
3 cups or more/750 ml boiling
water
2½-lb/1 kilo chicken, cut up
Salt, pepper, paprika
and thyme, to taste

Crock Pot Directions In a frying pan, heat oil and cook onion and garlic until lightly browned. Add kasha, celery and carrot and continue cooking until mixture is well blended and hot. Transfer to crock pot. Add 3 cups (750 ml) boiling water, or more if needed to cover kasha mixture.

Place chicken in crock pot and season well. Cover and cook on low setting 12 hours or longer. YIELD: 4 to 6 servings

---

Cholent with Barley FLEISHIG

½ lb/250 ml dry lima beans
½ cup/125 ml barley
2 Tbsp/25 ml chicken fat or oil
1 onion, chopped
3 garlic cloves, minced

2 lbs/1 kilo beef chuck or flanken
Salt, pepper and paprika to taste
3 cups or more/750 ml boiling
water

Crock Pot Directions Wash beans well, combine with barley and place in crock pot. In a frying pan heat chicken fat. Add onion, garlic and beef and cook until browned. Season well with salt, pepper and paprika. Combine onion and garlic with beans in crock pot. Cut beef into serving pieces and place on top. Pour on enough boiling water to cover bean mixture. Cover crock pot and cook on low setting overnight. YIELD: 6 servings

If you are entertaining many people for Shabbat lunch, this is an excellent dish because it will serve about 15 people.

Cholent for All
FLEISHIG

½ lb/250 grams dry lima beans
½ lb/250 grams dry kidney beans
1 cup/250 ml barley
2½ lbs/1 kilo beef chuck
   or flanken
2 large onions, chopped

4 garlic cloves, minced
2 Tbsp/25 ml oil
1 Tbsp/15 ml salt, or to taste
Pepper and paprika to taste
4 cups or more/1 liter
   boiling water

Crock Pot Directions   Wash beans well. Combine with barley and set aside. In a frying pan brown beef, onions and garlic in hot oil. Place bean mixture in crock pot and combine with onions. Add 4 cups (1 liter) boiling water, or more if needed to cover bean mixture.

Place meat in crock pot and season very well with salt, pepper and paprika. Cover and cook on low at least 12 hours.   YIELD: About 15 servings

---

With the high cost of meat today, an economical and tasty alternative is a meatless Cholent. Like meat or poultry, this bean dish is high in protein but at a much lower cost.

Meatless Cholent
PAREVE or FLEISHIG

½ lb/250 grams dry lima beans
½ lb/250 grams dry kidney beans
2 Tbsp/25 ml chicken fat or oil
1 large onion, chopped
3 garlic cloves, minced
4 medium potatoes, peeled
   and cut in halves

3 tsp/15 ml pareve instant
   soup mix, beef-flavored,
   or 3 beef-flavored
   pareve bouillon cubes
3 cups or more/750 ml boiling
   water
1 (8-oz)/(227 grams) can
   tomato sauce
Salt, pepper and paprika to taste

Crock Pot Directions   Combine beans, wash well and set aside. In a frying pan, heat chicken fat and sauté onion and garlic. Place potato halves on bottom of crock pot. Cover with bean mixture. Add onion and garlic. Dissolve soup mix or cubes in boiling water and pour over beans to cover. Add tomato sauce. Season with salt, pepper and paprika. Cover crock pot and cook on low overnight.   YIELD: 8 servings

Variation   Add the following ingredients to basic Cholent recipe:

Martin's Marvelous Meatless Chili Cholent

1 green pepper, chopped   ¼ tsp/1 ml cumin
2 tsp/10 ml chili powder,
   or to taste

Sauté green pepper along with onion and garlic. Add with chili powder and
cumin when preparing basic recipe.   YIELD: 8 servings

Chili   F L E I S H I G

2 lbs/1 kilo hamburger   1 cup/250 ml water
1 green pepper, chopped   2 Tbsp/25 ml chili powder
1 onion, chopped   1 tsp/5 ml salt
1 garlic clove, minced   ½ tsp/2 ml cumin
2 (16-oz)/(454-gram) cans tomatoes

Crock Pot Directions   In a hot frying pan, brown hamburger. Place hamburger and remaining ingredients in crock pot, stirring to blend. Cover and
cook on low setting 4 to 6 hours.   YIELD: 4 to 6 servings

Variation   Add the following ingredient to basic recipe:

Chili with Beans   F L E I S H I G

2 (16-oz)/(454-gram) cans kidney beans or lima beans

                                                      YIELD: 4 to 6 servings

Quick Chili   F L E I S H I G

1 or 2 pounds/500 to 1000 grams   1 (16-oz)/(454-gram) can kidney
   hamburger   beans, undrained
1 onion, chopped   2 Tbsp/25 ml chili powder,
½ green pepper, chopped   or to taste
2 tomato sauce (8-oz)/(227-gram)   Dash cayenne pepper, or to taste
   cans

Microwave Oven Directions   Place hamburger, onion and green pepper in a
large glass bowl. Cover with plastic wrap and cook on high setting 6 minutes
(8 minutes if using 2 pounds [1000 grams] meat). Drain off fat and crumble
beef mixture. Add remaining ingredients. Cover with plastic wrap and cook
on high setting 5 minutes. Reduce setting to medium and simmer 12 to 15
minutes. Stir well before serving.

Conventional Directions   In frying pan sauté hamburger and onions until soft.
Drain off fat. Transfer mixture to a large pot. Add remaining ingredients.
Bring to a boil, then simmer, covered, 45 minutes.   YIELD: 4 to 6 servings

Beef Stew

1½ lbs/750 grams boneless beef,
 cut in small cubes
4 Tbsp/50 ml flour
1½ tsp/7 ml salt
½ tsp/2 ml pepper
2 Tbsp/25 ml vegetable oil
2 onions, peeled and quartered
5 carrots, cut in chunks
2 lbs/1 kilo potatoes, peeled
 and cut in pieces

2 stalks celery, cut up
2 (8-oz)/(227-gram) cans tomato
 sauce
2 Tbsp/25 ml Worcestershire sauce
1 cup/250 ml hot water
1 tsp/5 ml instant soup mix,
 beef-flavored, or 1 beef-flavored
 bouillon cube
1 bay leaf

Microwave Oven Directions Coat meat with a mixture of flour, salt and pepper. Heat the oil in a large frying pan and brown meat on all sides. Transfer meat to a very large glass casserole. Add remaining ingredients. Cover tightly with plastic wrap and cook on high setting 8 minutes or until mixture boils. Reduce microwave oven setting to medium and cook 1 hour longer, or until beef and vegetables are tender and sauce is bubbly. Remove bay leaf before serving.

Conventional Directions Prepare stew as described above, placing all ingredients in a large, heavy pot. Cover tightly and cook over low heat 2 to 2½ hours. YIELD: 4 to 6 servings

---

Hungarian Goulash

4 potatoes, peeled and quartered
2 lbs/1 kilo beef chuck,
 cut into small cubes
1 onion, chopped
2 garlic cloves, minced
1½ cups/375 ml tomato juice
2 tsp/10 ml beef-flavored
 instant soup mix or
 2 beef-flavored bouillon cubes

½ tsp/2 ml salt, or to taste
2 tsp/10 ml paprika
1 bay leaf
3 Tbsp/45 ml flour
3 Tbsp/45 ml pareve margarine,
 melted

Crock Pot Directions Place potatoes in bottom of crock pot. Place meat on top and cover with chopped onion and garlic. Combine tomato juice with soup mix, salt and paprika and pour over meat. Place bay leaf on top. Cover crock pot and cook on low setting 9 to 10 hours.

About 15 minutes before serving, blend flour and melted margarine together and stir mixture into sauce. Cook on high setting until slightly thickened. YIELD: 6 servings

Basic Stew   FLEISHIG

2 lbs/1 kilo meat (beef, lamb or
  veal) cut into cubes
Salt, pepper and paprika to taste
4 Tbsp/50 ml flour
2 Tbsp/25 ml oil
1 large onion, cut in eighths

6 carrots, sliced
2 celery stalks, sliced
4 potatoes, peeled and cut up
2 cups/500 ml beef stock
2 cups/500 ml tomato juice
1 bay leaf

Crock Pot Directions Coat meat with salt, pepper, paprika and flour. In a
large frying pan, heat oil and brown meat on all sides. Place in crock pot.
Place vegetables over meat. Pour beef stock and tomato juice over vegetables
and place a bay leaf on top. Cover crock pot and cook on low setting 8 to 10
hours.   YIELD: 4 to 6 servings

Savory Lamb Stew   FLEISHIG

3 Tbsp/45 ml vegetable oil
2 lbs/1 kilo boneless lamb, cut in
  cubes
4 Tbsp/50 ml flour
1 tsp/5 ml seasoned salt, or to taste
½ tsp/2 ml pepper
½ tsp/2 ml marjoram

¼ tsp/1 ml thyme
2 lbs/1 kilo potatoes, peeled
  and cut in quarters
2 onions, peeled and sliced
1 (10¾-oz)/(305 grams) can
  condensed clear chicken soup

Crock Pot Directions Heat oil in a large frying pan. Coat meat with flour and
flavorings and brown in hot oil. In crock pot, place half the potatoes. Layer
half the onions over potatoes. Arrange meat over onions. Layer with second
half of the onions then cover with remaining potatoes. Add condensed soup.
Cover and cook on low setting 8 to 10 hours.   YIELD: 6 servings

Apple and Carrot Tzimmes   PAREVE

4 apples
1 lb/500 grams carrots
2 Tbsp/25 ml barley
3 Tbsp/45 ml pareve margarine
½ cup/125 ml water

1 tsp/5 ml salt
2 tsp/10 ml honey
½ tsp/2 ml nutmeg
½ tsp/cinnamon

Food Processor Directions Quarter and core apple and cut into large chunks.
Peel carrots and cut into chunks. Insert shredding disc in food processor and
shred apples and carrots.

    Put all ingredients into saucepan. Cover and cook over low heat for 2
hours, or until barley is tender. Stir occasionally, adding more water if necessary. Serve hot as a vegetable dish.   YIELD: 6 servings

Rice and Prune Tzimmes　　　　　　PAREVE

1 cup/250 ml rice
1 cup/250 ml pitted prunes,
　coarsely chopped
3 cups/750 ml boiling water
½ cup/125 ml brown sugar

2 Tbsp/25 ml lemon juice
1 tsp/5 ml grated lemon peel
¼ cup/50 ml pareve margarine
Dash cinnamon
Dash salt

Microwave Oven Directions　In a large glass bowl combine all ingredients. Cover with plastic wrap and cook on high setting 3 minutes, then reduce setting to medium and cook 14 minutes longer, or until rice is tender.

Conventional Directions　Place prunes and water in a saucepan to soak for several hours. Add rice and bring to a boil. Reduce heat and add remaining ingredients. Cover tightly and simmer for 30 minutes.　　YIELD: 6 servings

Sweet Potato–Carrot Tzimmes　　　　　　FLEISHIG

2 to 2½ lbs/1 kilo beef brisket
2 lbs/1 kilo sweet potatoes,
　peeled and quartered
2 lbs/1 kilo carrots, coarsely grated

⅓ cup/75 ml brown sugar
1 tsp/5 ml cinnamon
Salt and pepper to taste
1 cup/250 ml water

Crock Pot Directions　In a hot frying pan, brown the brisket. Place sweet potatoes in bottom of crock pot. Cover with grated carrots. Sprinkle brown sugar and cinnamon over vegetables. Place brisket on top. Season with salt and pepper. Add water. Cover crock pot and cook on low setting 8 to 10 hours.　　YIELD: 6 to 8 servings

Tzimmes with Lamb　　　　　　FLEISHIG

2 lbs/1 kilo carrots
2 large sweet potatoes
1 lamb breast, cut into strips

½ cup/125 ml water
3 Tbsp/45 ml flour
3 Tbsp/45 ml honey

Crock Pot Directions　Peel carrots and sweet potatoes and cut into large chunks. Place vegetables in bottom of crock pot and arrange lamb strips on top. Add water. Cover crock pot and cook on low setting 6 to 8 hours or until vegetables are soft. Remove meat and set aside. Dissolve flour in a small amount of cold water and pour into crock pot, stirring until blended. Add honey. Return meat to pot. Cover crock pot and cook on high setting for 20 minutes or until sauce is thickened and very hot.　　YIELD: 8 servings

FISH

The appliance featured most prominently in this chapter is the microwave oven. Fish cooks very quickly in the microwave oven, 5 minutes per pound (500 grams) on a high setting, and it doesn't dry out but rather stays moist.

When using fish which has been frozen, it is particularly important that the fish be completely defrosted and blotted dry with paper towels before cooking in the microwave oven. The baking dish should be covered with either plastic wrap, wax paper or a casserole lid, and the dish itself should be rotated a quarter turn at least once or twice during the cooking time. Allow fish to stand 5 to 10 minutes before serving to allow for aftercooking.

Gefilte fish, the traditional favorite fish recipe for Shabbat and holidays, is made using the food processor and the mixer. The Roumanian-style version is delicious and so easy to make when adapted to modern appliances.

The blender is featured in recipes calling for batter or breading mixtures.

Poached Salmon   P A R E V E

Salmon (whole, chunk, fillets, steaks)
2 chopped onions
2 chopped carrots
3 stalks celery, chopped
6 sprigs minced parsley

2 bay leaves
½ tsp/2 ml pepper
¼ tsp/1 ml thyme
2 Tbsp/25 ml lemon juice
½ cup/125 ml white wine or water

Microwave Oven Directions   Weigh salmon on a kitchen scale. If using less than 2 pounds (1 kilo) of fish, the remaining ingredients may be cut in half.

Rinse salmon and set aside. Place remaining ingredients in a large glass baking dish. Cover with plastic wrap and cook on high setting until vegetables are soft, about 10 minutes. Strain to remove vegetables and bay leaves. Return liquid to baking dish.

Place salmon in liquid in baking dish. Cover with plastic wrap and cook on high setting 5 minutes per pound (500 grams). If using whole fish, or a thick chunk, carefully turn salmon about halfway through the cooking time.

Conventional Directions   Place everything except salmon in a large saucepan. Add 3 cups (750 ml) water. Bring to a boil and cook for 20 minutes. Pour broth through a strainer.

Place fish in a rectangular pan or fish poacher. Fish may be wrapped in cheesecloth for easier handling. Pour broth over fish. Cut wax paper to fit the top of the pan and then cut a small hole in the middle of the wax paper to allow steam to escape. Cook fish in simmering liquid 10 minutes for each inch (2.5 cm) of fish (measured at the thickest part). When cooked, drain off liquid and serve.   YIELD: Allow ⅓ to ½ lb (150 to 250 grams) per person

Traditional-Style Gefilte Fish   PAREVE

3 lbs/1½ kilos fish fillets	1 egg
(use a combination of lean	¼ cup/50 ml matzah meal
and fat fish, such as pike	1 teaspoon/5 ml salt
and carp or pike and whitefish)	½ teaspoon/2 ml pepper
1 onion	¼ to ½ cup/50 to 125 ml cold water

STOCK

1 onion, sliced	1 Tbsp/15 ml salt
1 stalk celery, diced	6 cups/1½ liters water,
2 carrots, thinly sliced	or as needed

Food Processor Directions Insert steel blade in food processor. Cut fish fillets into large chunks. Mix fish varieties as you place chunks in container so that some of each type of fish is in each load to be processed. Do not overload container, but limit load size to about 1½ cups (375 ml). Process fish until finely chopped. Transfer to a large mixing bowl and repeat procedure with remaining fish chunks.

Peel onion, cut into eighths and place in container. Process until very finely chopped, then add to fish mixture. Add egg, matzah meal, salt and pepper, mixing well. Mix in as much water as needed to make a light, fluffy mixture.

Microwave Oven Directions Combine stock ingredients in a large glass casserole. Cook on high setting 12 to 15 minutes or until stock boils. Reduce setting to medium and cook 15 minutes longer.

Wet your hands to shape fish mixture balls. Place half of the fish balls into stock. Cover with plastic wrap and cook on medium setting 10 to 12 minutes.

Use a slotted spoon to remove fish balls. Drain well. Repeat procedure using remaining fish mixture. Serve cold with horseradish.

Conventional Directions Combine stock ingredients in a deep, heavy pot. Add cold water to cover. Cover pot and bring to a fast boil. Allow stock to boil for 30 minutes, then reduce heat and allow stock to simmer gently.

Prepare fish mixture as described above. Wet hands to form fish into balls. Drop the balls into stock. Cover and simmer gently 1 to 1½ hours. The liquid should be reduced by about half. Allow stock to cool slightly before carefully removing fish balls to a shallow serving dish. The fish liquid may be strained and poured over fish balls. Refrigerate until fish is well chilled and liquid has jelled. Serve cold with horseradish. YIELD: About 20 fish balls

Recipes are traditionally passed down from mother to daughter, but this one scampered along the branches of a few family trees before it reached me. It came from my father's first cousin's mother-in-law, and it is a luscious, very low-calorie version of Gefilte Fish. A special Roumanian secret (or former secret) is the hint of sugar. It doesn't make the recipe sweet, but rather brings out the delicate flavor.

The ideal way to make this dish is to purchase 6½ lbs (3 kilos) whole fish. Choose at least two kinds, one fat and one lean. Pike, whitefish, buffalo and sucker, or combinations of these, are most commonly used. Fillet the fish and save the heads, bones and skin for stock. Put the fish fillets through the finest blade of a food grinder (or use the steel blade attachment on the food processor).

Sophie Sway's Roumanian Gefilte Fish　　　P A R E V E

STEP 1

2 or 3 onions, finely chopped
⅓ cup/75 ml salad oil

⅔ cup/150 ml water
Salt and pepper to taste

STEP 2—STOCK

Fish bones, heads and skin
2 onions, cut up
1 Tbsp/15 ml salt

1 Tbsp/15 ml sugar
Cold water to cover

STEP 3

3½ lbs/175 kilos fish fillets,
　finely ground (combination of fat
　and lean fish)
3 Tbsp/45 ml sugar

3 eggs, beaten
2 Tbsp/25 ml salt
2½ to 3 cups/625 to 750 ml water
3 or 4 peeled carrots, optional

Step 1. Precooking the onions. This step is best done ahead of time to allow the onions to cool thoroughly. Cook the chopped onions in salad oil, water, salt and pepper. Cover the saucepan and cook until onions are soft but not brown. Refrigerate onions and liquid until needed.

Step 2. Combine in a very large pot fish bones, skin and heads, cut-up onions, salt and sugar. Add water until ingredients are covered. Over high heat, allow the stock to boil uncovered for at least 30 minutes. Strain stock, discard bones, skin and onions, adjust seasonings and return stock to pot. Set aside.

Step 3. In mixer bowl, combine ground fish, onions and liquid from Step 1, sugar, beaten eggs and salt. Combine on medium speed until well mixed. With mixer running, gradually add water, ½ cup (125 ml) at a time, mixing well to allow fish to absorb the liquid. Continue mixing until fish mixture is fluffy, moist, but firm enough to hold a shape. Taste and adjust seasonings.

Step 4. Bring the fish stock to a boil. Wet your hands to form fish mixture into balls. The fish balls expand when cooking, so judge size accordingly. Drop each ball into boiling stock by rolling it off your hand (it may seem that the balls won't hold together, but they always do). Shake the pot gently after adding each fish ball. Do not crowd. It may be better to cook the fish in two batches. Add 3 or 4 peeled carrots to stock, if desired. Cover pot. Boil fish balls for 30 minutes, shaking pot occasionally. Reduce heat to a simmer and cook an additional 30 minutes (total cooking time is 1 hour). While the fish cooks, the stock will reduce, but add more water only if stock darkens and reduces very low. Let the fish balls cool in the stock for 15 minutes.

Carefully remove fish balls with a slotted spoon. Place in a pan about 2 inches (5 cm) deep. Slice carrots, if used, placing 1 piece on each fish ball. If desired, stock can be poured over fish to jell. Cool and refrigerate fish for as long as 1 week.

Serve cold with horseradish.   YIELD: 22 to 25 fish balls

Baked fish, sprinkled with dill and lemon juice or served with a tangy sauce, is a quick and easy dish to cook in the microwave oven. Fish gives off a great deal of liquid when cooking. This liquid should be drained off or removed with a baster and saved to use in preparing the accompanying sauce. The following recipes are for a basic baked fish and a choice of 7 delicious sauces to serve with it.

Basic Baked Fish   P A R E V E or D A I R Y

Fish (whole, chunk,   Prepared sauce, if desired
 fillets or steaks)   (see following recipes)

Microwave Oven Directions Weigh the fish on kitchen scale. Rinse and place in a glass baking dish. Cover dish with plastic wrap and cook on high setting 5 minutes per pound. If using whole fish or a thick chunk, carefully turn the fish about halfway through the cooking time.

If serving with a sauce: Pour the hot prepared sauce over fish, either at end of cooking time or when fish has only a minute or two left to cook.

Fish may also be served without sauce, seasoned lightly with salt, pepper and dill weed and garnished with a thick lemon wedge.

Conventional Directions Melt 4 tablespoons (50 ml) pareve margarine and brush on fish. Place remaining margarine in a baking dish. Season fish lightly and arrange in baking dish. Bake at 350° F (180° C) 25 to 30 minutes or until fish flakes easily with a fork. Season with salt, pepper and dill weed.

If cooking fish in a sauce, omit margarine and seasonings. Pour prepared sauce over fish before baking. Bake at 350° F (180° C) 25 to 30 minutes or until fish flakes easily. YIELD: Allow ⅓ to ½ lb (150 to 250 grams) per serving.

SAUCES FOR BAKED FISH

Creamy Cucumber Sauce   D A I R Y

½ cup/125 ml milk   2 Tbsp/25 ml flour
½ cup/125 ml fish stock   Salt and pepper to taste
2 Tbsp/25 ml butter   1 cucumber
1 Tbsp/15 ml minced onion

Microwave Oven Directions Combine milk and fish stock. Cook on high setting 1½ to 2 minutes, or until very hot but not boiling. Set aside.

In a glass mixing bowl place butter and onion. Cover with plastic wrap and cook on high setting 1 minute or until butter is melted and onion is soft. Stir in flour and seasonings. Stirring constantly, add milk mixture. Cook 1 to 2 minutes or until mixture thickens and boils. Stir well. Cook on medium setting 5 minutes.

Peel and remove seeds from 1 cucumber. Chop or grate the cucumber fine and add to sauce. Pour sauce over prepared baked fish.

Conventional Directions Combine the milk and fish stock and set aside. In a small saucepan, sauté onion in butter. Add flour and seasonings and stir well. Add milk and cook, stirring constantly, until mixture thickens and boils. Lower heat and simmer 15 minutes. Add chopped or grated cucumber pulp.   YIELD: About 1½ cups (375 ml)

Curry Sauce   DAIRY

¼ cup/50 ml chopped onion   Dash of pepper, thyme
2 Tbsp/25 ml butter   and cayenne papper
1 tsp/5 ml curry powder   ½ cup/125 ml milk
¼ tsp/1 ml garlic powder   ½ cup/125 ml fish stock
¼ tsp/1 ml salt, or to taste   2 egg yolks

Microwave Oven Directions In a glass mixing bowl, place onion, butter and
seasonings. Cover with plastic wrap and cook on high setting 2 minutes or
until onion is soft. Add milk and fish stock. Cook 3 minutes on high setting
or until mixture boils. Beat egg yolks. Pour a small amount of hot liquid into
egg yolks, stirring constantly, then pour egg mixture back into sauce. Cook
on high setting 1 minute longer or until sauce thickens. Taste to correct
seasonings.

Conventional Directions In a small saucepan, sauté onion in butter. Add milk,
fish stock and seasonings. Cook until mixture boils. Beat 2 egg yolks and add
to mixture as above. Stir constantly until sauce thickens. Taste to correct
seasonings.   YIELD: About 1½ cups (375 ml)

Quick Mushroom Sauce   DAIRY

1 (10-¾ oz)/(305 grams) can   ¼ cup/50 ml dry white wine
  condensed cream of mushroom   or fish stock
  soup   2 Tbsp/25 ml lemon juice
                                   Salt and pepper to taste

Microwave Oven Directions In a glass mixing bowl combine all ingredients,
stirring well. Cook on high setting 3 minutes or until sauce boils. Use as a
sauce for baked fish.

Conventional Directions In a saucepan combine all ingredients, stirring well.
Cook over medium heat until sauce boils. Serve with baked fish.

YIELD: About 1½ cups (375 ml)

Mustard Sauce   DAIRY

1 cup/250 ml fish stock or hot
  water
2 tsp/10 ml or 1 cube
  pareve onion soup mix

2 tsp/10 ml prepared mustard
2 Tbsp/25 ml sour cream
Salt and pepper to taste

Microwave Oven Directions In a glass bowl combine fish stock, onion soup and mustard. Cover with plastic wrap and cook on high setting 2 minutes, or until mixture boils. Stir in sour cream and seasonings. Use as a sauce for baked fish.

Conventional Directions In a small saucepan combine fish stock, onion soup and mustard. Cook over medium heat until mixture boils. Stir in sour cream and seasonings.   YIELD: About 1 cup (250 ml)

Variations Make the following changes in Mustard Sauce recipe:

Horseradish Sauce   PAREVE

2 tsp/10 ml prepared horseradish

Substitute horseradish for mustard in basic recipe.

Mustard-Dill Sauce   PAREVE

1 tsp/5 ml dill weed

Add dill weed to prepared Mustard Sauce.   YIELD: About 1 cup (250 ml)

Sweet and Sour Sauce   PAREVE

1 (8-oz)/(227 grams) can
  tomato sauce

½ cup/125 ml brown sugar
¼ cup/50 ml lemon juice

Microwave Oven Directions In a glass bowl combine ingredients. Cover with plastic wrap and cook on high setting 3 to 4 minutes or until sauce boils. Use as a sauce for baked fish.

Conventional Directions In a small saucepan combine all ingredients and cook, over medium heat, until bubbly. Use as a sauce for baked fish.

YIELD: About 1¾ cups (425 ml)

Fresh Tomato Sauce   P A R E V E

2 large tomatoes   ½ tsp/2 ml marjoram
3 garlic cloves, minced   Salt and pepper to taste
⅓ cup/75 ml fresh parsley, minced   ¼ cup/50 ml hot water
2 Tbsp/25 ml lemon juice   (for Conventional Directions)

Peel tomatoes by dipping in boiling water for 15 seconds or by pouring boiling water over top of tomatoes. If peel does not slip off easily, repeat procedure.

Microwave Oven Directions Chop peeled tomatoes fine and place in a glass mixing bowl. Add remaining ingredients, blending well. Cover bowl with plastic wrap and cook on high setting 3 minutes or until mixture boils, then reduce setting to medium and continue cooking 12 minutes longer. Stir well and taste to adjust seasonings. Use as a sauce for baked fish.

Conventional Directions Chop peeled tomatoes and place in a saucepan along with remaining ingredients. Bring to a boil, reduce heat and simmer gently 30 minutes. Taste to adjust seasonings.   YIELD: About 1½ cups (375 ml)

Fillets in Tomato Sauce, Italian Style   P A R E V E

2 lbs/1 kilo fish fillets   1 (4-oz)/(113 grams) can sliced
1 tsp/5 ml oregano   mushrooms, drained
1 (15½-oz)/(439 grams) jar pareve spaghetti sauce

Microwave Oven Directions Arrange fillets in a glass baking dish. Sprinkle with oregano and cover dish with plastic wrap. Cook on high setting 8 minutes. Drain off liquid. Spoon spaghetti sauce over fish and arrange mushrooms on top. Cover with plastic wrap and cook 5 to 6 minutes longer or until fish flakes easily and sauce is hot and bubbly.

Conventional Directions Combine all ingredients as directed in basic recipe. Cook, uncovered, in a 350° F (180° C) oven for 20 to 30 minutes, depending on the thickness of the fillets.   YIELD: 4 servings

Although the cooking time for fish is 5 minutes per pound (500 grams) on a high setting in the microwave oven, trout, because it is a relatively bony fish, cooks in 4 minutes per pound.

Trout Amandine   P A R E V E

¼ cup/50 ml pareve margarine   1 Tbsp/15 ml lemon juice
¼ cup/50 ml slivered almonds   1 tsp/5 ml onion salt, or to taste
4 trout, about ½ to 1 lb each/250 to 500 grams each

Microwave Oven Directions Place margarine and almonds in a glass baking dish. Cook on high setting 5 minutes, or until almonds are toasted, stirring once. Remove almonds and set aside.

Weigh the trout on a kitchen scale and figure the cooking time at 4 minutes per pound (500 grams). Arrange trout in the baking dish and brush with the melted margarine. Cover dish with wax paper and cook on high setting half of the cooking time. Carefully turn fish and cook on high setting the remaining cooking time or until trout flakes easily. Allow to stand a few minutes before serving.

To serve, sprinkle fish with lemon juice and onion salt. Arrange almonds on top.

Conventional Directions In a large frying pan, melt margarine. Dust trout with flour, salt and pepper. Sauté the floured fish over medium heat for 10 minutes, turn and cook 8 minutes longer. When golden brown, transfer to a serving dish. To pan juices add almonds and lemon juice. Sauté for 3 to 5 minutes or until almonds are golden. Pour over hot trout. YIELD: 4 servings

---

Haddock Paprikash(Hungarian Style)   D A I R Y

1½ lbs/750 grams potatoes
½ lb/250 grams fresh mushrooms
2 Tbsp/25 ml finely chopped onion
2 Tbsp/25 ml butter
Paprika

½ cup/125 ml dry white wine
2 lbs/1 kilo haddock fillets
Salt and pepper to taste
1 cup/250 ml sour cream

Microwave Oven Directions Peel potatoes, slice thin and arrange in a large glass baking dish. Cook on high setting 10 to 12 minutes or until potatoes are soft. Slice mushrooms, and arrange on top of potatoes. Sprinkle with chopped onion. Dot with butter and sprinkle with ½ teaspoon (2 ml) or more paprika. Pour wine on top.

Arrange fillets on vegetable mixture. Sprinkle with additional paprika. Cover dish with plastic wrap and cook on high setting 10 to 12 minutes, or until fish flakes easily. Season to taste with salt and pepper.

In a separate glass dish heat the sour cream on high setting until bubbly. Stir well and pour sour cream over fish and vegetables. Sprinkle top with paprika.

Conventional Directions Boil, peel and slice potatoes and arrange in a greased baking dish. Top with sliced mushrooms and chopped onions. Dot with butter, sprinkle with salt, pepper and paprika, and pour wine on top. Spread with half the sour cream. Arrange fillets on top. Sprinkle with paprika and spread with remaining sour cream. Bake at 375° F (190° C) 25 to 35 minutes or until fish flakes easily and sauce is bubbly.   YIELD: 4 servings

Israeli-Style Fish in Sesame Sauce   P A R E V E

2 lbs/1 kilo fish fillets
1 tsp/5 ml cumin
¼ tsp/1 ml garlic powder

Olive oil (for Conventional
   Directions)

SAUCE

½ cup/125 ml chopped onions
⅓ cup/75 ml lemon juice
½ cup/125 ml fish stock

½ cup/125 ml sesame paste
   (see recipe in Appetizers chapter)
Chopped parsley

Microwave Oven Directions Arrange fillets in a glass baking dish. Sprinkle with cumin and garlic powder. Cover dish with plastic wrap and cook on high setting 8 minutes, or until almost done. Drain off excess liquid. Set aside.

To make sesame sauce: Place onions in a glass bowl. Cover with plastic wrap and cook on high setting 1 to 2 minutes or until onions are soft. Slowly stir lemon juice and fish stock into sesame paste. Add onions. Pour over fish.

Re-cover baked fish with plastic wrap and return to microwave oven. Cook on high setting 4 to 5 minutes longer, or until fish flakes easily and sauce is bubbly. Sprinkle with chopped parsley. Serve hot or cold.

Conventional Directions Brush fish fillets with olive oil. Sprinkle with cumin and garlic powder. Place in a baking dish and bake uncovered at 350° F (180° C) 15 minutes or until fish is flaky. Pour sauce from basic recipe over fish. Bake uncovered 15 minutes longer.   YIELD: 4 servings

Easy "Fried" Sea Bass   D A I R Y

2 tsp/10 ml salt
½ cup/125 ml milk
2 lbs/1 kilo sea bass fillets
1 cup/250 ml seasoned crumbs
   (bread, matzah meal, crackers,
   cornflakes or other cereals)

½ tsp/2 ml paprika
Lemon wedges

Microwave Oven Directions Add salt to milk. Dip fillets into highly salted milk, then coat with seasoned crumbs. Arrange fish in a baking dish, sprinkle with paprika, then cover with a paper towel. Place in microwave oven and cook on high setting 10 minutes. Serve with lemon wedges.

Conventional Directions Bread fillets as above. Place breaded fillets on a greased baking sheet. Sprinkle with paprika. Bake at 500° F (260° C) 12 to 15 minutes. Serve with lemon wedges.   YIELD: 4 servings

Crispy Fried Fish   P A R E V E

Use blender to make a batter coating or breading to prepare fish for deep-fat frying. Select pieces of fish steaks or fillets uniform in size and not over 1 inch (2.5 cm) thick and coat generously with coating or breading mixture (see below). Heat oil to 350° F (180° C) and fry fish, a few pieces at a time, until golden brown. Drain on paper towels and serve with tartar sauce.

Blender Batter   P A R E V E

1¼ cups/300 ml flour
1 tsp/5 ml salt
½ tsp/2 ml pepper
1 Tbsp/15 ml oil

2 beaten eggs
¾ cup/175 ml beer,
    at room temperature

Blender Directions   Place everything except beer in blender goblet. Blend on low speed until mixture is smooth. With motor running, slowly add beer and blend well. This batter may be prepared ahead of time and refrigerated. Use as a batter for preparing fried fish.   YIELD: About 2 cups (500 ml)

Blender Breading   P A R E V E

1 cup/250 ml pareve crumbs
    (bread, cracker, matzah,
    cornflakes or cornmeal)
1 tsp/5 ml salt

¼ tsp/1 ml pepper
¼ tsp/1 ml paprika
1 egg, beaten
2 tsp/10 ml water

Blender Directions   Use blender to make crumbs and to combine crumbs with seasonings. Mix egg and water. Dip fish pieces in egg mixture, then coat fish with breading mixture. After fish is coated, allow to dry about 20 minutes before frying.   YIELD: About 1 cup (250 ml)

Grilled Halibut is very attractive garnished with parsley and tomato slices and served with lemon wedges and tartar sauce.

Grilled Halibut   PAREVE

1 Tbsp/15 ml pareve margarine   1 tsp/5 ml dill weed
1 Tbsp/15 ml lemon juice   1 lb/500 grams halibut steak

Microwave Oven Directions   Place margarine in a small glass bowl and cook on high setting 30 seconds or until melted. Combine margarine, lemon juice and dill weed.

A special accessory, the browning dish, is used to grill halibut. The browning dish acts as a hot frying pan in the microwave oven. It is necessary to preheat the empty dish in order to have the bottom hot before the food is added.

Preheat the empty browning dish for 5 minutes in microwave oven on high setting. Brush one side of the halibut with the margarine mixture. Place halibut, brushed side down, on preheated browning dish and cook on high setting 2½ minutes. Brush other side of halibut with margarine mixture, turn halibut, and cook an additional 2½ minutes on high setting. YIELD: 2 servings

Steamed Red Snapper Oriental Style   PAREVE

1 whole red snapper   ½ tsp/2 ml salt
  (carefully check weight)   1 tsp/5 ml ground ginger
1 Tbsp/15 ml sherry   1 green onion, sliced diagonally
1 tsp/5 ml peanut oil   10 small mushrooms, sliced
2 Tbsp/25 ml soy sauce   Boiling water
½ tsp/2 ml sugar   (for Conventional Directions)

Microwave Oven Directions   Select a glass baking dish that is shallow but large enough to hold the whole fish comfortably. If necessary, cut fish in half to fit into dish.

Rinse fish and set aside. In baking dish combine remaining ingredients. Cover with plastic wrap and cook on high setting until marinade is hot and vegetables are tender, about 2 minutes. Place fish in baking dish and spoon some of the marinade on top. Cover with plastic wrap. Calculate cooking time based on 5 minutes per pound (500 grams) for fish. Cook fish for half of the cooking time. Carefully turn fish and finish cooking.

Conventional Directions   Place fish in baking dish. Pour marinade over fish. Put baking dish with the fish into a larger pot or roasting pan that has a cover (baking dish may be placed on a rack inside larger pan). Pour boiling water into larger pan to a depth of about 1 inch. Cover tightly and steam on top of stove, about 30 minutes for a 2½-lb (1-kilo) fish, 15 minutes for a 1-lb (500-gram) fish. Serve immediately. YIELD: Allow ½ lb (250 grams) per serving

An attractive way to serve Salmon Circle is to unmold onto a serving dish and fill the center cavity with cooked peas, parsley sprigs or cherry tomatoes. This dish is good hot or cold.

Salmon Circle   DAIRY or PAREVE

1 (16-oz)/(454 grams) can salmon
¼ cup/50 ml finely chopped
   green pepper •
¼ cup/50 ml finely chopped
   green onion
¼ cup/50 ml finely chopped celery

¾ cup/175 ml crushed
   cracker crumbs
1 cup/250 ml milk (or mixture
   of half nondairy creamer
   and half water)
1 Tbsp/15 ml lemon juice
3 eggs, beaten

Microwave Oven Directions   Drain liquid from the salmon. Discard the skin and bones and flake the meat into a mixing bowl. Add remaining ingredients and mix well.

Spoon mixture into a glass ring mold, or shape mixture around a custard cup (open end up) placed in a 9-inch (23-cm) glass pie plate.

Cover dish with wax paper and cook on high setting 8 minutes.

Conventional Directions   Prepare mixture as described above. Spoon mixture into a greased loaf pan or ring mold. Bake at 400° F (200° C) 30 minutes.

YIELD: 6 servings

Variation

Tuna Circle   DAIRY or PAREVE

Omit salmon from basic recipe and substitute 2 (6½- or 7-oz)/(185- or 200-gram) cans tuna fish.   YIELD: 6 servings

Tuna Fish Patties   DAIRY

2 (7-oz)/(200-gram) cans tuna,
   drained
4 eggs
½ cup/125 ml chopped onion
1½ cups/375 ml soft bread crumbs
½ cup/125 ml milk

¼ tsp/1 ml garlic powder
1 Tbsp/15 ml chopped parsley
1 tsp/5 ml lemon juice
1 tsp/5 ml dill weed
Salt and pepper to taste.

Food Processor Directions   Insert steel blade in food processor. Place all ingredients in container and process until smooth. Form mixture into patties and fry in hot oil until golden brown on both sides.   YIELD: 4 to 6 servings

Tuna-Noodle Casserole   DAIRY

2 (7-oz)/(200-gram) cans tuna fish,   1 cup/250 ml milk
   drained and flaked   2 hard-cooked eggs, chopped
1 (10-¾ oz)/(305-gram) can   3 cups/750 ml cooked noodles
   condensed cream of celery soup   ½ cup/125 ml peas, frozen or
¼ cup/50 ml mushrooms, chopped   canned

Microwave Oven Directions Combine all ingredients and spoon into a glass
baking dish. Cover with wax paper and cook on high setting 10 minutes or
until center is hot and sauce is bubbly.

Crock Pot Directions Combine tuna, soup, mushrooms, milk and eggs in
crock pot. Mix well. Cover pot and cook on high setting 1 hour. Add cooked
noodles and peas. Cover and cook on low setting 3 to 4 hours.

Conventional Directions Combine all ingredients and place in a greased 2-
quart dish. Cover and cook at 400° F (200° C) 20 to 30 minutes, or until hot
and bubbly.   YIELD: 6 servings

MEAT

The recipes in this chapter show how modern appliances, particularly the microwave oven and crock pot, can be used to prepare favorite meat recipes.

There are many rules pertaining to the slaughter, inspection and kashering of meat (see "A Guide to the Dietary Laws" and "Guide to Kashering Meat and Poultry"). Only cuts of meat from the front part of the animal can be sold in kosher butcher shops. These are generally the less tender cuts of meat and they are beautifully suited to long, slow cooking in the crock pot.

Both tender and tougher cuts of meat can be cooked to be very tender and flavorful in the microwave oven. The important techniques to know are presented in "Roast Beef—Microwave Oven Guide and Time Chart."

The food processor is featured in two recipes in this chapter. Hamburgers and Kibbee (a lamb dish) involve the fine chopping of raw meat, using the steel blade attachment.

ROAST BEEF—MICROWAVE OVEN GUIDE
AND TIME CHART

If you own a microwave oven and have not used it to cook beef, now is the time to enjoy the benefits of this exciting way of cooking. For a meal in minutes, keep in mind that using your microwave oven will reduce your cooking time to almost half the time required to do it conventionally. On a hot summer day, you can prepare a meal without heating the house. Using the microwave oven will conserve energy, thereby reducing your utility bills.

Beef cooked in the microwave oven is juicy, moist, flavorful and, best of all, tender—provided a few simple guidelines are followed:

Insert a Thermometer
Before you start to cook the meat, insert into it a special microwave oven

thermometer so that its point reaches the center of the thickest part of the meat. The thermometer should not touch any bone, fat or gristle. It should stay in place throughout the cooking process, and therefore it must be inserted in such a way that it will not be disturbed when the meat is turned. The best method is to insert the thermometer lengthwise through the side of the meat, rather than down into the top.

Do not try to cook with a conventional thermometer in the microwave oven. Only a special microwave oven thermometer, or a probe if the oven is equipped to handle one, may be used.

Starting Temperature
Best results will be obtained if the beef is at room temperature before you start cooking. This means a minimum reading of 40° F (5° C) on a meat thermometer inserted in the thickest part of the meat. A starting temperature of 50° to 55° F (10° to 13° C) is even better.

Use a Rack
Roast the meat on a microwave oven-proof rack which fits inside a glass baking dish. An inverted saucer may be substituted for the rack.

Turn the Meat
Before starting, place the meat fat side down in the dish. Halfway through the cooking time, turn the meat fat side up. For a truly tender roast, at this halfway point, turn off the microwave oven and wait 10 minutes before turning the meat fat side up and resuming cooking.

Drain Off Excess Liquid
While the meat is cooking, liquids will collect underneath the rack. This excess liquid can slow down the cooking process. When ½ cup (125 ml) or more liquid is collected, it is necessary to drain it off or remove it with a baster (save to use for gravy).

Browning
Meat with some natural fat will begin to brown after 8 to 10 minutes of cooking in the microwave oven. To enhance the appearance of the meat by giving it a browner color, a baste of liquid gravy coloring, diluted slightly with wine, broth or water, may be used. Other items such as parsley, paprika or sliced mushrooms will help to give meat a nice taste and appearance.

Standing Time or Aftercooking
It is a characteristic of microwave oven cooking that food continues to cook after the microwave energy has been turned off. You will need to learn to undercook the meat deliberately and then allow it to stand about 10 or 15 minutes to reach serving temperature. You can figure that the temperature of the meat will rise 15° F (60° C) during this standing time or aftercooking. The meat may be left in the oven to aftercook or removed and covered with a piece of foil.

Cooking Times and Setting

Use the following chart as a guide for roasting beef in the microwave oven:

CUT OF MEAT	SETTING	COOKING TIME (per pound or 500 grams)	TEMPERATURE AT END OF COOKING	SERVING TEMPERATURE (after 15 minutes standing time)
Beef standing rib or Rolled rib roast				
RARE	medium-high	7 min/lb	120° F/49° C	135° F/57° C
MEDIUM	medium-high	9 min/lb	140° F/60° C	155° F/68° C
WELL DONE	medium-high	10 min/lb	160° F/71° C	175° F/79° C
Shoulder roast or Rolled roast				
RARE	medium	12 min/lb	120° F/49° C	135° F/57° C
MEDIUM	medium	14 min/lb	140° F/60° C	155° F/68° C
WELL DONE	medium	15 min/lb	160° F/71° C	175° F/79° C

LESS TENDER CUTS OF BEEF
MICROWAVE OVEN GUIDE AND TIME CHART

Special guidelines and techniques need to be followed when cooking less tender beef in the microwave oven, such as brisket, dekel (pot roast) and corned beef. These meats need to cook slowly in order for the tough fibers to break down and soften.

Prebrown

If desired, less tender cuts of beef may be prebrowned in a hot frying pan before cooking in the microwave oven. This not only gives a brown appearance but also seals in meat juices.

Low Setting

Cook less tender cuts of beef on a medium or low setting.

Frequent Standing Times

The practice of alternating cooking times with standing times helps greatly in tenderizing meat. If the meat weighs 3 lbs (1500 grams or 1½ kilos) and the total estimated cooking time is 66 minutes, use the following as a guide:

> 20 minutes microwave oven cooking time
> 10 minutes standing time
> 20 minutes microwave oven cooking time
> 10 minutes standing time
> 25 to 30 minutes microwave oven cooking time

Although this method may seem to be very involved, the results are very tender, flavorful and delicious. This same meat would require over 2 hours of cooking time if prepared conventionally.

Save Liquid
Less tender cuts of meat are cooked without a rack and are allowed to simmer in the collected pan juices. These liquids are not removed as when cooking tender cuts of meat. The extra volume of food that this bit of liquid provides slows the cooking process and helps to tenderize the meat.

Cover
A glass casserole lid or plastic cooking bag tied with string or rubber band (do not use a metal twist) makes a convenient cover when cooking less tender cuts of meat.

Fork Test
Less tender cuts of meat are often fairly thin and do not hold a thermometer well. Even thicker pot roasts should be tested for "doneness" using the old-fashioned fork test (in which meat is cooked until it is "fork tender").

Cooking Times and Settings
Use the following chart as a guide for cooking less tender cuts of beef in the microwave oven:

CUT OF MEAT	SETTING	COOKING TIME
Brisket, pot roast, corned beef, tongue, Swiss steak and chuck	medium or low	22 minutes/lb (500 grams)

Standing Ribs or Rolled Rib Roast   FLEISHIG

4- to 4½-lb/2 kilos rib roast
Pepper, garlic powder
   and paprika to taste
1 tsp/5 ml liquid gravy coloring

1 Tbsp/15 ml dry wine,
   stock or water
Salt to taste

Microwave Oven Directions   Place meat fat side down on a plastic microwave oven-proof rack which fits inside a glass baking dish. Season with pepper, garlic powder and paprika. Combine gravy coloring and wine and brush over surface of meat.

Cook meat on medium-high setting for 20 minutes. Turn the meat fat side up, remove liquid from the dish (save to use for gravy). Continue cooking an additional 15 to 20 minutes, or until a thermometer inserted in the thickest portion of the meat registers 140° F (60° C) (for medium). Cover meat with a piece of foil and allow to stand 15 minutes before carving. The temperature of meat will continue to rise during this standing time. Salt to taste before serving.

Conventional Directions

Standing ribs of beef: Season meat with salt, pepper, garlic powder and paprika. Insert a conventional (not microwave oven) meat thermometer. Place meat fat side up on a rack in an open roasting pan. Roast at 300° F (150° C) to desired degree of doneness. Allow 18 to 20 minutes per pound (500 grams) for rare, 22 to 25 minutes per pound for medium and 27 to 30 minutes per pound for a well-done roast.

Rolled rib roast: Proceed as for Standing Ribs of Beef, but increase roasting time by 10 minutes per pound (500 grams).   YIELD: 6 servings

---

Short Ribs in Chili Sauce   F L E I S H I G

3 to 4 lbs/1½ to 2 kilos
  beef short ribs
2 Tbsp/25 ml oil
Salt and pepper to taste
4 potatoes, peeled and quartered

4 carrots, peeled and sliced
1 onion, sliced
2 cups/500 ml chili sauce
1 cup/250 ml water

Crock Pot Directions   In a large frying pan brown short ribs in hot oil. Place potatoes, carrots and onion in crock pot. Arrange browned ribs on top. Pour chili sauce over meat. Season to taste. Cover and cook on low setting 6 to 8 hours or until meat is tender.   YIELD: 4 to 6 servings

---

Shoulder Clod Roast   F L E I S H I G

3-lb/1½ kilos shoulder clod roast
Pepper, paprika and
  garlic powder to taste

3 Tbsp/45 ml flour, optional
Salt to taste

Microwave Oven Directions   Place meat fat side down on a microwave oven-proof rack which fits inside a glass casserole. Season with pepper, paprika and garlic powder. Sprinkle with flour, if desired.

Cover dish and cook on medium setting 20 minutes. Turn the meat fat side up and remove extra liquid from the dish (save to use for gravy). Cook 20 to 25 minutes on medium setting, or until a thermometer inserted in the thickest portion of the meat registers 140° F (60° C) (for medium). The temperature of the meat will continue to rise during this standing time. Salt to taste before serving.

Conventional Directions   Combine seasonings with flour and sprinkle over meat. Place on a rack in an open roasting pan and cook in a 325° F (160° C) oven 25 to 30 minutes per pound (500 grams) for medium and 30 to 35 minutes per pound (500 grams) for well done.   YIELD: 6 servings

Brisket   FLEISHIG

3 lbs/1½ kilos beef brisket   1 package dry onion soup mix
Pepper and paprika to taste   ½ cup/125 ml chili sauce
                                     ½ cup/125 ml water, as needed

Microwave Oven Directions Place meat in a glass casserole. Season with pepper and paprika. Cover dish and cook on medium setting 1 hour, or until fork tender.

About 20 minutes before brisket has finished cooking, sprinkle onion soup mix over surface of meat. Re-cover and continue cooking.

Slice brisket thin to serve. Combine ½ cup (125 ml) pan juices with ½ cup (125 ml) chili sauce and serve as gravy.

Crock Pot Directions Place brisket in crock pot. Sprinkle with seasonings and onion soup mix. Combine chili sauce with ½ cup (125 ml) water and pour on top. Cover crock pot and cook on low setting 8 to 10 hours.

Conventional Directions Place brisket in a roasting pan. Sprinkle on seasonings and onion soup. Add chili sauce and ½ cup (125 ml) water. Cover tightly with foil and roast at 325° F (160° C) about 2 hours, or until meat is almost tender. Remove cover and baste with pan juices. Continue roasting 30 minutes longer or until brisket is browned, basting frequently.

YIELD: 6 servings

Chuck   FLEISHIG

2 large onions, sliced   2 Tbsp/25 ml flour
1 (8-oz)/(227 grams) can   2 Tbsp/25 ml oil
   tomato sauce   ½ cup/125 ml water
2 to 2½ lbs/1 kilo chuck steak   (for Conventional Directions)
Pepper, paprika and
   garlic powder to taste

Microwave Oven Directions Place onion slices and tomato sauce in a large glass baking dish. Cover dish and cook on high setting 5 to 6 minutes, or until sauce is hot and onions are almost tender. Set aside.

Sprinkle meat with seasonings and flour. Heat oil in a hot frying pan and brown meat on both sides. Transfer meat to baking dish, spooning some of the onion and sauce mixture on top. Cook on medium setting 45 minutes or until fork tender.

Crock Pot Directions Brown meat on both sides in hot oil, then transfer to crock pot. Place onion slices on top of meat and add tomato sauce. Cover and cook on low setting 8 to 10 hours or until tender.

Conventional Directions Sprinkle meat with seasonings and flour. Heat oil in a hot frying pan and brown meat on both sides. Add onion slices and brown slightly. Add tomato sauce and water. Reduce heat, cover and cook slowly until tender, about 1½ to 2 hours. Add additional water if needed.

YIELD: 4 servings

Stuffed Flank Steak

FLEISHIG

2 to 2½ lbs/1 kilo flank steak
2 cups/500 ml Challah Stuffing
(see recipe in Savory Stuffings
chapter)
3 Tbsp/45 ml oil
½ cup or more/125 ml hot beef
stock

3 Tbsp/45 ml Worcestershire sauce
3 Tbsp/45 ml soy sauce
1 Tbsp/15 ml dry white wine
¼ tsp/1 ml garlic powder
Dash ginger

Microwave Oven Directions Score flank steak on both sides. Spread stuffing on steak and roll lengthwise like a jelly roll. Fasten edges with toothpicks or tie with string. In a heavy frying pan, brown in hot oil. Place in a glass baking dish.

Combine remaining ingredients to make a sauce and pour over meat. Cover dish and cook on medium setting 30 minutes. Turn steak roll, re-cover and continue cooking 20 to 30 minutes longer or until fork tender.

Crock Pot Directions Prepare steak and sauce as described in basic recipe. Metal skewers may be used to fasten steak after filling. Place steak roll in crock pot and pour sauce on top. Cover and cook on low setting 8 to 10 hours.

Conventional Directions Stuff and roll steak as described in basic recipe. In a heavy frying pan, brown steak in oil. Increase stock to 1½ cups (375 ml) when making sauce, and pour sauce over steak rolls. Cover and simmer slowly until tender, about 2 hours, adding more liquid if necessary.

YIELD: 4 servings

Pot Roast (Dekel)   F L E I S H I G

3 lbs/1½ kilos beef chuck
Pepper, paprika and
   garlic powder to taste
3 Tbsp/45 ml oil
2 bay leaves
1 cup/250 ml hot beef stock
   or tomato juice, or as needed

1 package dry onion soup mix
4 medium potatoes,
   peeled and sliced
4 carrots, sliced

Microwave Oven Directions Sprinkle meat with seasonings and brown in hot oil. Place meat in a glass casserole and place bay leaves on top. Add beef stock or tomato juice. Cover meat and cook on medium setting 1 to 1¼ hours or until fork tender.

About 30 minutes before meat has finished cooking, turn meat and sprinkle surface with package of onion soup. Arrange vegetables in dish with meat. Re-cover and continue cooking until meat is fork tender.

Remove cooked meat to a serving platter and cover tightly with foil to keep warm. Set aside. Cover casserole containing vegetables with plastic wrap and place in microwave oven. Cook on high setting 10 minutes or until vegetables are tender. Cut meat into serving pieces and serve with vegetables and gravy.

Crock Pot Directions Sprinkle meat with seasonings and brown on both sides in hot oil. Place in crock pot along with vegetables, beef stock and onion soup mix. Cover and cook on low setting 8 to 10 hours or until tender.

Conventional Directions In a large, heavy frying pan, brown meat in oil. Add seasonings, onion soup and beef stock. Cover tightly and simmer slowly 1½ hours. Uncover and add vegetables. Cover and continue cooking until meat and vegetables are tender, about 1 to 1½ hours longer.   YIELD: 6 servings

Hot Dogs   F L E I S H I G

Hot dogs have been precooked when you buy them and really need only to be reheated. The exact cooking time depends on the size of the hot dog and how well done you like it. Generally, 30 seconds to 1 minute each is sufficient time to cook hot dogs steaming hot.

Microwave Oven Directions For 1 hot dog: Place hot dog on a paper plate and cook on high setting for 15 to 30 seconds, until barely warm. Place hot dog in a bun and cook on high setting 15 to 30 seconds longer, until both bun and hot dog are very hot.

Conventional Directions To boil hot dogs: Place hot dogs in a sauccpan filled with boiling water. Simmer gently 6 to 8 minutes.

To broil hot dogs: Place hot dogs on a broiler rack about 2 inches from flame. Broil until brown, turning to brown other side.   YIELD: 1 serving

---

Swiss steak is tender and flavorful when cooked in the microwave oven. Use a plastic cooking bag, closed with a rubber band or piece of string (*no* metal twists) to hold the meat. A convenient trick to learn is to vent the bag (poke a small hole for steam to escape) along the side rather than on the top. This way the meat can be turned, halfway through the cooking time, with no loss of juice and without opening the bag.

Swiss Steak   FLEISHIG

2 to 2½ lbs/1 kilo beef,
 sliced 1 inch (2.5 cm) thick
4 Tbsp/50 ml flour
¼ tsp/1 ml garlic powder
Salt, pepper and paprika to taste
3 Tbsp/45 ml oil
1 small onion finely chopped

¼ cup/50 ml chopped celery
¼ cup/50 ml chopped green pepper
1 small carrot, peeled
 and thinly sliced
2 cups/500 ml cooked
 or canned tomatoes

Microwave Oven Directions Sprinkle one side of meat with flour and seasonings. Pound the seasonings into the meat, using a mallet or the edge of a heavy plate. Turn meat over, sprinkle with remaining flour mixture and pound well. Cut meat into serving pieces. Brown meat in oil in a hot frying pan, turning to brown both sides.

Place meat in a plastic cooking bag and add remaining ingredients. Tie bag closed with string or fasten with a rubber band and vent the bag to allow steam to escape.

Place meat in microwave oven. Cook on high setting 5 minutes or until liquids boil. Reduce setting to medium and cook 50 to 60 minutes longer or until steak is fork tender. Turn the meat halfway through the cooking time.

Crock Pot Directions Season meat, pound well and brown as described in basic recipe. Place meat in crock pot. Add remaining ingredients. Cover and cook on low setting 6 to 8 hours or until tender.

Conventional Directions Season meat and pound well. Heat oil in a heavy frying pan and brown the meat on both sides. Add remaining ingredients. Cover pan and simmer gently until meat is tender, about 2 to 2½ hours.

YIELD: 6 servings

Corned Beef
F L E I S H I G

3 lbs/1½ kilos corned beef   1 bay leaf
1 onion, sliced   2 cups or more/500 ml water

OPTIONAL VEGETABLES

4 potatoes, peeled and sliced   1 onion
4 carrots, cut up

Microwave Oven Directions   Rinse the meat. Put the onion, celery and bay leaf into a large glass baking dish and place meat on top. Pour 2 cups (500 ml) water over meat. Cover and cook on high setting 6 to 8 minutes, or until water is boiling. Lower setting to medium and cook 1 to 1½ hours longer or until meat is fork tender. Turn meat when half done. If desired, vegetables may be added during second half of cooking time.

Crock Pot Directions   Place corned beef in crock pot with 4 cups water. Add onion, celery and bay leaf. Cover and cook on low setting 10 to 12 hours. If optional vegetables are added, arrange in crock pot before adding meat.

Conventional Directions   Place corned beef in a large pot. Add onion, celery and bay leaf, and cover with cold water. Bring to a boil, lower heat and simmer for 3 hours or until tender. Add vegetables during the last hour.

YIELD: 4 to 6 servings

Boiled Beef (Essic Fleisch)
F L E I S H I G

2 to 2½ lbs/1 kilo beef   Salt, pepper and thyme to taste
  (chuck or brisket)   1 bay leaf
2 large onions, sliced   1 cup/250 ml or more water

Crock Pot Directions   Place beef and onions in crock pot. Add salt, pepper, herbs and water. Cover crock pot and cook on low setting 8 to 10 hours or until beef is tender.
YIELD: 4 to 6 servings

Variations   Make the following changes in basic Boiled Beef recipe:

Beef and Vegetables
F L E I S H I G

5 potatoes, peeled and sliced   2 onions, quartered
5 carrots, cut up   2 quarts/2 liters water

Place potatoes, carrots and onions in crock pot and arrange meat on top. Increase water in basic recipe to 2 quarts (2 liters). Cover crock pot and cook as in basic recipe. The liquid makes an excellent soup as a first course (skim off excess fat before serving).
YIELD: 4 to 6 servings

Beef Frye   FLEISHIG

Beef Frye is the trade name for thinly sliced pieces of spicy kosher meat that can be bought in small packages. It can be used for appetizers or sandwiches or served with eggs at breakfast.

Separate meat strips and arrange in a single layer on a paper towel. Cover with a second paper towel and place in microwave oven. Cook on high setting 30 to 45 seconds per slice for hot meat strips and 45 to 60 seconds per slice for crisp strips.   YIELD: Allow 1 to 3 strips per serving

Tongue in Sweet and Sour Sauce   FLEISHIG

3 lbs/1½ kilos tongue   2 bay leaves
1 onion, sliced   2 cups/500 ml or more water

SWEET AND SOUR SAUCE

1 cup/250 ml tongue stock   1 onion, diced
⅓ cup/75 ml vinegar   ⅓ cup/75 ml raisins
⅓ cup/75 ml honey   ½ tsp/2 ml salt
½ tsp/2 ml ground ginger   1 lemon, sliced very thin

Microwave Oven Directions   Arrange onion and bay leaves in a glass baking dish and place tongue on top. Pour 2 cups (500 ml) water over the meat. Cover and place in microwave oven. Cook on high setting 6 to 8 minutes or until water is boiling. Reduce setting to medium and cook 1 to 1½ hours or until tongue is fork tender, turning tongue when half done. Cool slightly, then remove skin and roots. Slice and serve with sweet and sour sauce.

To make sauce: Combine all ingredients in a glass mixing bowl. Cover with plastic wrap and place in microwave oven. Cook on high setting 5 minutes or until mixture boils. Reduce setting to medium and cook an additional 5 minutes. Serve over sliced tongue.

Crock Pot Directions   Place tongue in crock pot. Add onion, bay leaves and 4 cups (1 liter) water. Cover and cook on low setting 9 to 12 hours or until tender. Serve with sweet and sour sauce.

Conventional Directions   Place tongue, onion and bay leaves in a large pot. Cover with cold water and bring to a boil over high heat. Reduce heat and simmer gently 3 to 4 hours or until tender. Combine sauce ingredients in a saucepan. Cover and cook over medium heat until mixture boils. Reduce heat and simmer, stirring occasionally, about 10 to 15 minutes.

YIELD: 6 servings

To fry tender steak in the microwave oven, a special accessory, the browning dish, is used. The empty dish is preheated on high setting so that the bottom becomes very hot, acting like a frying pan. When the meat is added, it browns and cooks at the same time.

Pan-Fried Steak   FLEISHIG

8 oz/250 grams minute steak or cube steak
Salt and pepper to taste

Microwave Oven Directions   Place empty browning dish in microwave oven. Preheat dish by cooking on high setting 6 minutes. Carefully place steak in browning dish. Cook on high setting 2 minutes. Turn steak and cook 1½ minutes longer (for medium). Season to taste.

Conventional Directions   Heat a frying pan and grease lightly. Place steak in hot pan and brown very quickly on both sides. Reduce heat. Cook slowly until steak is done, pouring off fat as it accumulates. Season with salt and pepper before serving.   YIELD: 2 servings

GROUND BEEF RECIPES

There really is a difference in taste between hamburger meat you chop yourself in a food processor and meat which has been ground. Freshly chopped meat is juicier and very flavorful.

Hamburgers   FLEISHIG

1 lb/500 grams lean tender beef,   1 tsp/5 ml salt, or to taste
   cut in chunks   ¼ tsp/1 ml pepper
1 small onion

Food Processor Directions   Insert steel blade in food processor. Place half the meat chunks in the container. Process, using the pulse button or a quick on-off motion, until the meat is coarsely chopped. Transfer to a mixing bowl and repeat procedure with remaining beef.

   Peel onion, cut into chunks and place in container. Process until chopped very fine. Add to meat mixture. Season with salt and pepper. Mix all ingredients lightly, trying not to handle the meat any more than necessary. Shape mixture into 4 patties, about 1 inch (2.5 cm) thick.

4 hamburger patties   1 Tbsp/15 ml water
1 Tbsp/15 ml gravy coloring   (for Microwave Oven Directions)
   (for Microwave Oven Directions)   Salt, as needed

Microwave Oven Directions Arrange patties on a plastic or microwave-oven-proof rack which fits inside a glass dish. Brush patties lightly with a mixture of liquid gravy coloring and water. Cover with wax paper. Cook on high setting 4 minutes. Turn patties and cook 3 minutes longer, or until done.

Conventional Directions To pan fry hamburgers: Heat a frying pan until very hot. Sprinkle the pan lightly with salt to prevent sticking. Arrange patties in pan, reduce heat to medium and cook 8 minutes on each side, or until done.

To broil hamburgers: Arrange patties on a broiling rack and broil about 6 minutes on each side or until done.   YIELD: 4 servings

---

Spaghetti and Meat Balls   FLEISHIG

MEATBALLS

1 lb/500 grams lean ground beef	Salt and pepper to taste
⅓ cup/75 ml bread crumbs	1 egg
1 Tbsp/15 ml minced parsley	2 Tbsp/25 ml dry red wine
2 Tbsp/25 ml minced onion	1 Tbsp/15 ml olive oil
½ tsp/2 ml oregano	

SAUCE

2 onions, chopped	½ cup/125 ml dry red wine
3 garlic cloves, minced	1 tsp/5 ml salt, or to taste
2 Tbsp/25 ml minced parsley	½ tsp/2 ml pepper
2 Tbsp/25 ml oil	1 tsp/5 ml oregano
2 (16-oz)/(454-gram) cans tomatoes	1 bay leaf
1 (6-oz)/(165-gram) can tomato paste	

1 lb/500 grams spaghetti

Crock Pot Directions Mix ground beef with other ingredients except olive oil. Shape into meatballs. Heat oil in a large frying pan and brown the meatballs on all sides. Transfer to crock pot.

To prepare sauce: In the hot frying pan, sauté onions, garlic and parsley in oil. Add remaining ingredients except spaghetti and pour into crock pot. Cover and cook on low setting 8 to 10 hours. Cook spaghetti according to package directions. Drain well. Serve meatballs and sauce over cooked spaghetti.   YIELD: 4 to 6 servings

A good meat loaf in the microwave oven is not really a loaf at all but circle-shaped. Form the meat mixture into a ring around an inverted custard cup. As the meat cooks, then stands afterward, much of the fat will collect inside the custard cup. Cut the meat ring into thirds and transfer to a serving platter before removing the cup. An attractive way to serve the meat is with cooked peas or carrots piled in the center.

Meat "Loaf"   FLEISHIG

2 to 2½ lbs/1 kilo lean ground beef
½ cup/125 ml bread crumbs or
   matzah meal
1 egg

1 (8-oz)/(227 grams) can
   tomato sauce or 1 cup/250 ml
   chili sauce
1 package onion soup mix

Microwave Oven Directions   Combine all ingredients. On a large glass dish, or 10-inch (25 cm) glass pie plate, form mixture into a ring shape around an inverted custard cup. Cover dish with wax paper and place in microwave oven. Cook on a high setting 18 minutes. Allow to stand 5 minutes for fat to collect inside cup.

   To serve, cut meat into thirds and reassemble on serving dish.

Conventional Directions   Press meat mixture into a greased loaf pan. Bake at 350° F (180° C) 1 to 1½ hours. Unmold onto serving dish.

YIELD: 6 servings

Stuffed Green Peppers   FLEISHIG

1 lb/500 grams green peppers,
   cut in half and seeded
1 lb/500 grams lean ground beef
1 egg
½ cup/125 ml cooked rice
1 Tbsp/15 ml chopped parsley

1 (8-oz)/(227 grams) can tomato
   sauce
3 Tbsp/45 ml dry red wine
½ tsp/2 ml oregano, optional
1 cup/250 ml water
   (for Conventional Directions)

Microwave Oven Directions   In a glass baking dish, place green peppers, cut side up. Mix together the ground beef, egg, rice, parsley and 2 tablespoons tomato sauce. Stuff peppers with this ground-beef mixture. Combine remaining tomato sauce with wine and oregano and pour over peppers. Cover dish with plastic wrap and place in microwave oven. Cook on high setting 18 to 20 minutes, or until done.

Conventional Directions   Stuff peppers as in basic recipe and prepare sauce, adding an additional 1 cup water. Cover and bake at 350° F (180° C) for 1 hour.   YIELD: 4 servings

One-Dish Spaghetti   F L E I S H I G

1 lb/500 grams lean ground beef
1 small onion, chopped
2 cups Marinara Sauce
   (see recipe in Gravy and Savory
   Sauces chapter)
1 cup/250 ml water

½ tsp/2 ml salt
1 tsp/5 ml oregano
½ tsp/2 ml garlic powder
½ cup/125 ml sliced mushrooms
¼ lb/125 grams spaghetti

Microwave Oven Directions In a large glass bowl place ground beef and chopped onion. Cover with wax paper and cook on high setting 5 minutes. Drain the fat from the meat and crumble with a fork. Add Marinara Sauce, water, flavorings and mushrooms, stirring well. Cover with plastic wrap and cook on high setting 4 minutes, or until sauce boils.

    Break spaghetti into 2-inch pieces and stir into sauce mixture. Cover bowl with plastic wrap. Cook on high setting 6 minutes. Stir mixture. Re-cover with plastic wrap and cook on high setting 6 minutes longer. Let stand, covered, at least 5 minutes before serving.   YIELD: 4 servings

Savory Stuffed Cabbage   F L E I S H I G

1 large head cabbage
1 lb/500 grams lean ground beef
½ cup/125 ml cooked rice
1 onion, chopped
1 egg, slightly beaten
1½ tsp/7 ml paprika

1 tsp/5 ml salt
¼ tsp/1 ml pepper
1 (1-lb)/(454 grams) can sauerkraut
1 (8-oz)/(227 grams) can tomato
   sauce
½ cup/125 ml water
3 Tbsp/45 ml sugar

Crock Pot Directions Cook whole cabbage in boiling water until leaves are pliable. Drain, remove large outer leaves and set aside.

    Combine beef, rice, onion, egg, paprika, salt and pepper. Place a large spoonful of meat mixture on each cabbage leaf. Fold in sides of cabbage leaf and roll up, tucking in the ends securely.

    Drain and rinse sauerkraut. Place in bottom of crock pot. Arrange cabbage rolls over sauerkraut. Mix tomato sauce, water and sugar, and pour over cabbage rolls. Cover and cook on low setting 7 to 9 hours.

YIELD: 4 to 6 servings

Sweet and Sour Stuffed Cabbage   FLEISHIG

1 large head cabbage
1 lb/500 grams lean ground beef
1 small potato, peeled and grated
1 carrot, grated
1 onion, peeled and grated
1 egg

1(8-oz)/(227 grams) can tomato
  sauce
¼ cup/50 ml lemon juice
½ cup/125 ml brown sugar
1 cup/250 ml water (for
  Conventional Directions)

Microwave Oven Directions Wash cabbage and check weight on a kitchen scale. Place cabbage in a glass bowl, cover with plastic wrap and place in microwave oven. Cook on high setting 5 minutes per pound (500 grams). Separate the cabbage leaves and set aside.

In a mixing bowl combine the beef, grated vegetables and egg. Place a spoonful of this mixture in the center of each cabbage leaf and roll up, tucking in the ends securely.

In a large glass baking dish, arrange the cabbage rolls. Combine tomato sauce, lemon juice and brown sugar and pour over cabbage. Cover dish with plastic wrap and place in microwave oven. Cook on high setting 5 minutes. Reduce setting to medium and cook 15 minutes longer, or until cabbage is tender and sauce is bubbly.

Conventional Directions   Boil cabbage until leaves are pliable. Combine filling ingredients and use to stuff cabbage leaves as described in basic recipe. Combine tomato sauce, lemon juice and sugar in a large, heavy frying pan. Add cabbage rolls and 1 cup (250 ml) water. Cover tightly and cook over moderate heat 30 minutes. Reduce heat to low and simmer 30 minutes longer.   YIELD: 4 to 6 servings

Variation   Omit potato from basic Stuffed Cabbage recipe and substitute the following:

1 cup/250 ml cooked kasha or 1 cup/250 ml cooked rice

Braised Lamb

1 breast of lamb,
  with pocket for stuffing
Salt
About 2 cups/500 ml Rice
  and Vegetable Stuffing
  (see Recipe in Savory Stuffings
    chapter)

1 Tbsp/15 ml flour
¼ tsp/1 ml *each* paprika,
  pepper and garlic powder
1 cup/250 ml chili sauce
1 or 2 cups/250 or 500 ml water
1 envelope onion soup mix

Crock Pot Directions Sprinkle inside of cavity with salt and stuff with Rice and Vegetable Stuffing. Fasten edges together with toothpicks. Combine flour, 1 teaspoon (5 ml) salt, spices, and garlic powder, and sprinkle over outside of lamb.

Place lamb in a roasting pan and roast in a preheated 450° F (230° C) oven 15 to 20 minutes to brown the lamb and to render the excess fat.

Transfer lamb to crock pot. Combine chili sauce, 1 cup (250 ml) water and soup mix, and pour over lamb. Cover and cook on low setting 10 to 12 hours, turning after about 8 hours of cooking. Skim fat from gravy before serving.

Conventional Directions Prepare lamb as described in basic recipe. After browning lamb in 450° F (230° C) oven for 15 to 20 minutes, reduce heat to 325° F (160° C). Prepare sauce as described above, increasing water to 2 cups (500 ml). Pour sauce over lamb, cover tightly and roast at 325° F (160° C) for 1½ hours or until done. YIELD: 4 to 6 servings

Lamb Chops

Lamb chops
Salt, pepper and garlic powder to taste

Microwave Oven Directions A special accessory, the browning dish, can be used to brown and cook lamb chops in the microwave oven. The technique is first to preheat the browning dish 6 minutes on high setting, so that the bottom becomes very hot and acts like a frying pan.

Carefully check the weight of the chops on a kitchen scale. Place the chops on the preheated browning dish and return to microwave oven. Cook on high setting, uncovered, 10 minutes per pound (500 grams), turning the chops when half done. Season to taste with salt, pepper and garlic powder.

Conventional Directions Preheat a large frying pan. Sprinkle chops with salt, pepper and garlic powder. Brown chops on one side, then turn to brown the other side. Reduce heat to low and continue cooking until chops are done.

YIELD: Allow ⅓ to ½ lb (150 to 250 grams) per serving

Lamb Roast

4- to 5-lb/2 kilos lamb
   shoulder roast
1 garlic clove
3 Tbsp/45 ml lemon juice
¼ tsp/1 ml *each* curry powder,
   dry mustard and marjoram

½ tsp/2 ml pepper
¼ cup/50 ml blackberry or currant
   jelly
1 cup/250 ml dry red wine

Microwave Oven Directions   Rub lamb with cut garlic clove. Combine lemon juice and spices, and rub mixture evenly over lamb. Cover the lamb with plastic or foil and refrigerate several hours or overnight.

When ready to cook, place the lamb, fat side down, on a microwave oven–proof rack that fits inside a glass baking dish. Best results are obtained when a special microwave oven probe or thermometer is used to monitor the temperature of the lamb during cooking (do *not* attempt to use a conventional thermometer in the microwave oven). Insert the thermometer lengthwise through the lamb, so that the tip rests in the middle of the thickest part but does not touch bone, fat or gristle.

In a saucepan, combine jelly and wine, heating until jelly is melted. Brush over lamb. Place in microwave oven. Cook on high setting 25 minutes.

Turn the lamb, placing fat side up. Drain off any excess liquids which have collected in the dish (save to use as gravy). Brush lamb with any remaining wine-jelly mixture or with pan drippings. Return lamb to micro-wave oven and cook on high setting until the thermometer registers 165° F (74° C), approximately 5 to 30 minutes longer, depending on the weight of the lamb.

Allow the lamb to stand, covered with a tent of foil, for 10 to 15 minutes. The temperature of the meat rises during this time. The final serving temperature for lamb is 180° F (82° C).

Skim fat from pan drippings, taste to adjust seasonings and serve as a gravy.

Crock Pot Directions   Marinate lamb as described in basic recipe. When ready to cook, place meat in a roasting pan in a preheated 450° F (230° C) oven 15 to 20 minutes to brown the surface and to render the excess fat. Transfer lamb to crock pot. Combine jelly and wine and pour over lamb. Cover crock pot and cook on low setting 8 to 9 hours. Skim off excess fat from gravy before serving.

Conventional Directions   Marinate lamb overnight as described in basic recipe. Roast lamb, uncovered, at 325° F (160° C) 30 minutes per pound, or until meat thermometer registers 180° F (82° C). Combine jelly and wine and baste lamb frequently with mixture.

YIELD: Allow ¼ to ⅓ lb (125 to 150 grams) per serving

Lamb Shanks
FLEISHIG

2 Tbsp/25 ml oil
4 lamb shanks, cracked
2 tsp/10 ml curry powder
¼ tsp/1 ml *each* dry mustard,
    sugar, cumin and allspice

2 garlic cloves, minced
1 large onion, chopped
2 stalks celery, chopped
1 (10¾-oz)/(305 grams) can
    condensed clear chicken soup

Crock Pot Directions Heat oil in a large frying pan and brown the lamb shanks. Transfer to crock pot. Combine spices and sugar and sprinkle over lamb. Add garlic, vegetables and soup. Cover crock pot and cook on low setting 8 to 9 hours, or until lamb is tender.   YIELD: 4 servings

Shish Kebab
FLEISHIG

1 lb/500 grams lean lamb, cut in small cubes

MARINADE

¼ cup/50 ml olive oil
1 Tbsp/15 ml lemon juice
1 garlic clove, minced
1 onion, finely chopped

1 Tbsp/15 ml chopped parsley
1 tsp/5 ml salt
¼ tsp/1 ml pepper
½ tsp/2 ml ground thyme

VEGETABLES

1 green pepper cut up
8 large mushrooms

8 cherry tomatoes

Microwave Oven Directions Cut up lamb. Combine the oil, lemon juice, garlic, onion, parsley, salt, pepper and thyme in a large bowl. Stir in lamb cubes. Marinate at least 2 hours or overnight, stirring occasionally.

Drain lamb thoroughly. Alternate lamb cubes and vegetable pieces on 4 bamboo skewers. Place skewers on microwave oven-proof rack which fits inside a glass baking dish. Place dish in microwave oven and cook on high setting 10 minutes or until lamb is done.

Conventional Directions Marinate meat as described in basic recipe. Drain and arrange with vegetables on metal skewers. Broil or grill about 4 inches (10 cm) from a flame about 15 minutes, turning once.

YIELD: 4 servings

The birth of the State of Israel welded together the eastern and western Jewish worlds in many ways, one of which is culinary tradition. Today, in Israel, Jews from Arab-speaking countries have become familiar with chopped herring and gefilte fish, unknown to them until Israel's establishment. Similarly, thousands of European Jews have now become familiar with traditional Middle Eastern recipes, such as Kibbee, a delicious blend of lamb, bulghor and pine nuts.

Kibbee   F L E I S H I G

KIBBEE

2 to 2½ lbs/1 kilo lean lamb,   2 cups/500 ml fine bulghor
  cut in cubes   1 tsp/5 ml salt, or to taste
1 small onion   ¼ tsp/1 ml *each* allspice and pepper

FILLING

½ lb/250 grams lean lamb, cubed   ¾ cup/175 ml pine nuts
1 large onion   Salt, pepper and allspice
4 Tbsp/50 ml pareve margarine   to taste

Food Processor Directions   Insert steel blade in food processor. Lamb for kibbee must be chopped very fine. Place ½ pound (250 grams) lamb cubes at a time in container and process, at first with rapid on-off bursts of energy, then with continuous processing, until lamb is finely processed. Transfer lamb to large mixing bowl and repeat procedure with remaining lamb.

Peel onion, cut into chunks and place in container. Process until finely chopped. Combine with lamb until well mixed.

Return the lamb-onion mixture to food processor container, about 1½ cupfuls (375 ml) at a time, and process until the mixture is very finely blended. Return to mixing bowl.

Place bulghor in a strainer and rinse with cold water. Combine bulghor, salt and spices with lamb mixture, mixing well. Set aside.

To make filling: Insert steel blade in food processor. Place the lamb cubes in container and process until chopped. Transfer to a mixing bowl. Peel onion, cut in chunks and place in container. Process until coarsely chopped. In a hot frying pan, melt pareve margarine. Add pine nuts and cook until golden, stirring constantly. Add chopped lamb and onion, cooking until lamb is lightly browned. Season to taste.

To assemble Kibbee: Grease a large baking dish. Pat half the kibbee mixture evenly into dish. Sprinkle filling evenly over the bottom layer. Pat the remaining kibbee mixture into a top layer over the filling and smooth the surface. Cut through the meat into diamond shapes. Bake at 475° F (250° C) for 30 minutes. Reduce oven temperature to 350° F (180° C) and cook 15 minutes longer.   YIELD: 6 to 8 servings

POULTRY

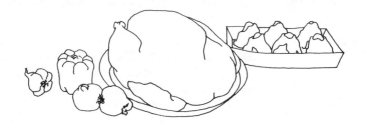

"When a poor man eats a chicken, it's a sign one of them is sick," says Tevye the Dairyman in *Fiddler on the Roof.* For generations, chicken, in fact all poultry, has been an important food in Jewish homes, almost synonymous with Shabbat, holidays and aspirations to good health and wealth.

"Will the chicken brown?" is perhaps the most often expressed doubt about cooking poultry in the microwave oven. Any food with some natural fat will begin to brown in 8 to 10 minutes in the microwave oven, however a variety of ideas are presented which can be used to enhance the appearance of the poultry.

You may wish to add color to poultry cooked in the crock pot, also. In addition to any of the above tricks, try transferring the cooked poultry to a baking dish and placing it in a 400° F (200° C) oven for 10 to 15 minutes, or until the skin is brown and crispy.

When cooking chicken and vegetables together in the crock pot, the vegetables may take longer to cook than the chicken. This can be corrected, in part, by cutting the vegetables in even-sized pieces, placing them under the chicken and making sure the vegetables are covered with liquid.

Although most recipes in this chapter give the main crock pot cooking time on low setting, the time can be cut nearly in half by using the high setting.

The food processor is featured in one recipe, Chicken Croquettes, which calls for chopping leftover poultry fine and then blending ingredients for a velvety smooth wine sauce. However, the food processor can be used in almost any recipe which calls for chopping, dicing or slicing ingredients.

POULTRY—MICROWAVE OVEN GUIDE

This chapter presents many favorite recipes adapted to the microwave oven. Poultry cooks in 7 minutes per pound (500 grams) in the microwave oven on a high setting.

151

Stuffing the Poultry

Fill the body and neck cavities of poultry with prepared stuffing and close securely using toothpicks or tie with thread. Do not use metal skewers. If the poultry is stuffed with an uncooked stuffing, such as those made with bread crumbs, croutons or matzah, additional cooking time of 2½ minutes per cup (250 ml) of stuffing must be allowed. A cooked stuffing such as rice placed in the fowl does not require additional cooking time.

Use a Rack

Poultry that is to be roasted or cooked without a sauce should be placed on a microwave-proof rack or an inverted saucer which fits inside a glass baking dish. As liquid collects under the rack, it should be removed or basted off, as it will slow down the cooking time. Poultry cooked in a sauce does not require a rack.

Cover

When cooking poultry, cover the baking dish with wax paper or a glass casserole lid. Poultry with a crumb or dry coating, such as Oven-"Fried" Chicken, may be left uncovered or covered with a paper towel to absorb excess moisture.

Turn Poultry

When cooking a whole bird, place it in the dish breast side down, then halfway through the cooking time turn it breast side up. Cut-up poultry should be started skin side down and halfway through turned skin side up. Also, the baking dish should be rotated a quarter turn once or twice during the cooking time, unless the oven has a carousel or turntable.

Browning

Here are some garnishing suggestions and browning aids to use to add color when cooking poultry in the microwave oven:

· Dry soup mixes, especially onion, lend color. The time to sprinkle them on top is just after the poultry pieces have been turned skin side up. Dry products such as these do not affect the total cooking time.
· Thick sauces, tomatoes and dark-colored condensed soups add color to poultry. Allow an extra 2½ to 3 minutes per cup (250 ml) or 10¾-oz (305 ml) can of condensed soup to the total cooking time to allow this extra liquid to boil.
· Parsley, paprika, oregano and other spices. Dry products such as these do not affect the total cooking time.
· Liquid gravy coloring, Worcestershire sauce, soy sauce, etc. These dark-colored liquids can be used as bastes in appropriate recipes.
· Bread crumbs or packaged coating mixes help to give a golden-brown color to poultry. Poultry cooked this way, such as Oven-"Fried" Chicken, should be started skin side up. The pieces should not be turned, as the effect of the coating mix would be lost.

Aftercooking

After the poultry has completed the microwave cooking time, remove it from the oven and cover it with a piece of foil. Wait 5 to 10 minutes before serving (15 minutes for a stuffed turkey). During this "standing time" or "aftercooking," the poultry finishes cooking and, in fact, gets hotter.

A small turkey breast, or half breast, makes a lovely meal in itself or can be cooked and used in any recipe which calls for leftover chicken or turkey.

Mini Roast Turkey Breast   F L E I S H I G

3-lb/1½ kilos half turkey breast
1 tsp/5 ml liquid gravy coloring
1 Tbsp/15 ml dry white wine

Salt and pepper to taste
2 Tbsp/25 ml oil
(for Conventional Directions)

Microwave Oven Directions   Place the turkey, skin side down, in a glass dish. Combine the gravy coloring and wine to form a baste and brush half of this mixture over turkey. Cook on high setting 10 minutes.

Turn turkey and brush with remaining marinade. Cook on high setting 10 to 12 minutes longer. To serve, season to taste with salt and pepper.

Conventional Directions   Add oil to marinade mixture. Place turkey on a rack in a baking dish, skin side down, and brush with marinade. Bake at 350° F (180° C) 1½ to 2 hours, turning breast side up when half done. Baste frequently with pan drippings. Season to taste.   YIELD: 4 servings

---

Saucy Cranberry Turkey Roll   F L E I S H I G

2 Tbsp/25 ml cornstarch
¼ cup/50 ml apple juice
¼ cup/50 ml honey
¾ cup/175 ml orange marmalade

1 cup/250 ml fresh cranberries,
   finely chopped
1 frozen turkey roll
   (about 2½ lbs, 1 kilo),
   partially thawed
Salt and pepper to taste

Crock Pot Directions   Dissolve cornstarch in the apple juice and place in a saucepan. Add honey, marmalade and cranberries. Cook, stirring constantly, until mixture is bubbly and slightly thickened.

Place turkey roll in crock pot. Sprinkle lightly with salt and pepper. Pour cranberry sauce over turkey. Cover crock pot and cook on low setting 9 to 10 hours.

To help determine when turkey roll is done, lift crock pot lid and insert a meat thermometer into center of the roll during the last 2 or 3 hours of cooking. Re-cover crock pot and cook until temperature reaches 185° to 190° F (87° C). Slice turkey and serve in sauce.   YIELD: 4 to 6 servings

A turkey is moist and flavorful when cooked by microwaves. Most ovens will easily accommodate a 10- to 12-pound (5-kilo) bird. The cooking time is determined by the weight of the turkey—7 minutes per pound (500 grams) at high setting, plus an additional 2½ minutes cooking time for each cup (250 ml) of uncooked stuffing.

Holiday Roast Turkey   FLEISHIG

10- to 12-lb/5 kilos turkey
Salt and pepper
8 cups/2 liters Traditional
   Bread Stuffing (see recipe
   in Savory Stuffings chapter)
¼ cup/50 ml dry white wine

1 Tbsp/15 ml paprika
1 tsp/5 ml garlic powder
½ tsp/2 ml pepper
¼ cup/50 ml oil
   (for Conventional Directions)

Microwave Oven Directions   Sprinkle inside of turkey with salt and pepper. Fill the body and neck cavities with stuffing and close securely with toothpicks or tie with thread (do not use metal skewers). Place turkey, breast side down, on a plastic or microwave oven-proof rack which fits inside a glass baking dish.

Combine wine and seasonings and baste the turkey with half of this mixture. Place turkey in microwave oven and cook on high setting 45 minutes. About halfway through this cooking time, drain off or remove with a baster the liquid which has collected in the bottom of the dish. Save to use as gravy.

Turn the turkey breast side up, and remove any additional liquid which has collected in the dish. Baste the turkey with the remaining marinade mixture and return to microwave oven. Cook on high setting an additional 45 to 60 minutes (longer time for larger bird).

About a half hour before the turkey has finished cooking, use a small, sharp knife to gently prick the skin of the turkey at the points where the legs and the wings meet the body. Liquid collects under the skin at these points and, if not allowed to drain off, can result in four small raw points on the turkey. At the same time, drain off the liquid which has collected in the dish.

After the microwave oven cooking time is completed, allow the turkey to stand, covered with foil, 15 minutes before carving.

Conventional Directions   Add ¼ cup (50 ml) oil to marinade mixture. Prepare turkey as in basic recipe. Brush with marinade mixture and place breast side down on a cooking rack in a large roasting pan. Bake at 325° F (160° C) 2 to 3 hours for a small bird (6 to 10 pounds or 3 to 4 kilos) and 4 to 4½ hours for a medium-size bird (11 to 14 pounds, 5 to 6 kilos). Baste turkey frequently. About halfway through the cooking time, turn turkey breast side up.

YIELD: 12 to 15 servings

Shabbat Roast Chicken

4-lb/2 kilos roasting chicken
Salt and pepper to taste
4 cups/1 liter stuffing
  (see recipes in
   Savory Stuffings chapter)

1 tsp/5 ml paprika
2 Tbsp/25 ml oil
  (for Conventional Directions)
½ cup/125 ml water
  (for Crock Pot Directions)

Microwave Oven Directions   Sprinkle body and neck cavity of chicken lightly with salt and pepper, then fill with stuffing. Use toothpicks to close securely, or tie cavities closed with string (do not use metal skewers). Place chicken, breast side down, on a plastic or microwave oven-proof rack which fits inside a glass baking dish. Sprinkle chicken with half the paprika. Cook on high setting 20 minutes. Drain off, or remove with a baster, the liquid which has collected in the dish. Reserve this liquid for gravy.

Turn the chicken breast side up. Sprinkle with remaining paprika, baste with pan juices, and cook on high setting an additional 18 to 20 minutes, or until tender. Brush with pan drippings. Season to taste with salt and pepper

Crock Pot Directions   Stuff the chicken, sprinkle with salt, pepper and paprika, and place in crockpot. Add ½ cup water (125 ml). Cover pot and cook at low setting 6 to 8 hours or until chicken is tender. If desired, chicken may be transferred to a roasting pan after cooking, and placed in a 400° F (200° C) oven 15 minutes, or until skin is crispy and brown.

Conventional Directions   Place stuffed chicken on a rack in an open roasting pan, breast side down. Brush with oil and sprinkle with salt, pepper and paprika. Bake at 350° F (180° C) 2 hours or until browned and tender, basting frequently with pan drippings. About halfway through cooking time, turn chicken breast side up and finish baking.   YIELD: 6 servings

Oven-"Fried" Chicken   F L E I S H I G

SINGLE SERVING

8-oz/250 grams chicken breast   2 Tbsp/25 ml packaged coating mix
                                        or crushed cereal crumbs

Microwave Oven Directions   Rinse chicken breast in water, then roll in coating mix. Place chicken, skin side up, on a paper plate. Cover with a paper towel. Cook on high setting 3½ minutes.   YIELD: 1 serving

FAMILY SERVING

2½- to 3-lb/1 kilo fryer, cut up   ½ cup/125 ml packaged coating mix
                                        or crushed cereal crumbs

Microwave Oven Directions   Rinse chicken pieces in water, then roll in coating mix. In a glass baking dish arrange chicken with the thicker portions to the outer edge of the dish and the wings in the center. Cover chicken with a paper towel. Cook on high setting 18 to 20 minutes. Do not turn.

Conventional Directions   Place chicken pieces, coated as above, in baking pan. Bake at 350° F (180° C) 1 hour or until chicken is hot and crispy.

                                                            YIELD: 4 servings

Barbecued Chicken   F L E I S H I G

2½- to 3-lb/1 kilo fryer, cut up   1 envelope onion soup mix
1 cup/250 ml Barbecue Sauce
  (see Gravy and Savory Sauces
  chapter)

Microwave Oven Directions   Place chicken, skin side down, in a glass baking dish. Arrange pieces so that the thicker portions are to the outer edge of the dish and the thinner portions, such as the wings, are in the center.
   Pour Barbecue Sauce over chicken. Cover dish with wax paper and cook on high setting 15 minutes. Turn chicken skin side up, and spoon sauce over top. Sprinkle envelope of onion soup mix over top of chicken. Cover with wax paper and cook on high setting 10 to 12 minutes longer or until tender.

Crock Pot Directions   Place chicken in crock pot and pour Barbecue Sauce over top. Sprinkle on onion soup mix. Cover and cook on low setting 5 to 7 hours.

Conventional Directions   Place chicken, skin side down, in a baking dish and bake at 350° F (180° C) 1 to 1½ hours. Halfway through cooking time, turn chicken skin side up and spoon sauce over top. Sprinkle on onion soup mix.
   Chicken may also be cooked by broiling over hot coals or under broiler. Turn chicken at least once and baste frequently with Barbecue Sauce. Total cooking time is about 30 to 45 minutes.   YIELD: 4 servings

This recipe makes a great sauce. Use sauce as a gravy, or as a topping for rice or spaghetti to serve as a side dish.

Chicken Cacciatore
FLEISHIG

4 Tbsp/50 ml flour
Salt, pepper and oregano to taste
2½- to 3-lb/1 kilo fryer, cut up
2 cups/500 ml Marinara Sauce
   (see recipe in Gravy and Savory
   Sauces chapter)

½ cup/125 ml dry red wine
1 (4-oz)/(113.5 grams) can
   sliced mushrooms, drained
4 Tbsp/50 ml olive oil (for Crock
   Pot or Conventional Directions)

Microwave Oven Directions   Combine flour and seasonings in a paper or plastic bag. Place chicken pieces in bag and shake to coat lightly with flour mixture.

Place chicken, skin side down, in a glass baking dish, arranging pieces so that the thicker portions are to the outer edge of the dish and the thinner pieces, such as the wings, are in the center. Combine the sauce and wine and pour over chicken. Cover dish with wax paper and cook on high setting 20 minutes.

Turn the chicken skin side up, and spoon sauce over top. Arrange mushroom pieces on top of chicken. Cover dish with wax paper and cook on high setting 10 to 15 minutes longer or until chicken is tender. Taste to correct seasonings.

Crock Pot Directions   Coat chicken lightly with flour mixture as described in basic recipe. In a frying pan, heat olive oil and brown chicken pieces on all sides. Transfer to crock pot. Combine remaining ingredients and pour over chicken. Cover and cook on low setting 5 to 7 hours.

Conventional Directions   Coat chicken lightly with flour mixture as described in basic recipe. In a large frying pan, heat olive oil and brown chicken pieces on all sides. Add remaining ingredients, cover tightly and simmer until chicken is tender, about 45 minutes.   YIELD: 4 servings

Chicken and Mashed-Potato Dumplings   FLEISHIG

1 onion	Salt to taste
2½- to 3-lb/1 kilo fryer, cut up	½ cup/125 ml hot water
1 tsp/5 ml paprika	(for Crock Pot Directions)
¼ tsp/1 ml *each* pepper,	2 cups/500 ml water
marjoram and thyme	(for Conventional Directions)
4 Tbsp/50 ml flour, optional	

DUMPLINGS

1 Tbsp/15 ml chicken fat	1 egg
or pareve margarine	¾ cup/175 ml matzah meal or flour
2 cups/500 ml mashed potatoes	1 tsp/5 ml salt, or to taste
1 Tbsp/15 ml minced onion	½ tsp/2 ml pepper

Microwave Oven Directions Slice onion and arrange slices in a glass baking dish. Sprinkle chicken with seasonings and, if a thickened gravy is desired, with flour. Place chicken skin side down in a dish, arranging thicker portions to the outer edge of the dish and thinner pieces, such as wings, toward the center. Cover dish with wax paper and cook on high setting 15 minutes. Turn chicken skin side up, and return to microwave oven. Cook on high setting 5 to 10 minutes longer, or until chicken is tender.

To prepare dumplings, add melted fat to mashed potatoes and begin stirring. Add onion and egg, blending well, then add remaining ingredients. Shape potato mixture into 12 balls. Place dumplings over chicken, around the sides of the baking dish, and cook on high setting 6 to 7 minutes or until dumplings are no longer sticky. Season chicken with salt, to taste.

Crock Pot Directions Slice onion and place in crock pot. Sprinkle chicken with seasonings and place in crock pot. Add ½ cup hot water. Cover and cook on low setting 5 to 7 hours. Prepare dumplings as directed in basic recipe. Place dumplings over chicken. Turn control to high setting. Cover and cook on high 15 to 30 minutes, until dumplings are done.

Conventional Directions Slice onion and place with chicken sprinkled with seasonings in a large pot with a tight-fitting lid. Add about 2 cups (500 ml) water. Cover, bring to a boil, then reduce heat. Simmer slowly until chicken is tender, about 3 hours. Prepare dumplings as directed in basic recipe. Place dumplings over chicken. Cook, covered, 10 to 12 minutes longer.

YIELD: 4 servings

Glazed Chicken   FLEISHIG

2½- to 3-lb/1 kilo fryer, cut up	1 Tbsp/15 ml chili sauce
1 Tbsp/15 ml orange marmalade	1 Tbsp/15 ml mayonnaise
1 Tbsp/15 ml lemon juice	1 package dry onion soup mix

Microwave Oven Directions Arrange chicken pieces in a glass baking dish skin side down, placing the thicker portions to the outer edge of the dish and the thinner portions, such as the wings, in the center. Cover dish with wax paper and cook on high setting 10 minutes. Turn chicken skin side up.

Combine marmalade, lemon juice, chili sauce and mayonnaise in a small glass bowl. Stir until smooth. Cook mixture on high setting 1 minute or until bubbly. Pour sauce mixture over chicken and sprinkle top with onion soup mix. Cover dish with wax paper and cook on high setting 10 to 12 minutes longer, or until chicken is tender.

Conventional Directions Arrange chicken in a baking dish skin side up. Combine remaining ingredients and spoon over chicken pieces. Bake, uncovered, at 350° F (180° C) 1 to 1½ hours or until chicken is tender. YIELD: 4 servings

---

Sweet and tangy citrus flavors combine with Middle Eastern spices to make this special chicken dish.

Israeli Chicken   F L E I S H I G

2½- to 3-lb/1 kilo fryer, cut up
1 tsp/5 ml garlic powder
½ tsp/2 ml crushed tarragon
2 tsp/10 ml paprika
¼ tsp/1 ml pepper
½ tsp/2 ml cumin
½ tsp/2 ml grated lemon peel

½ tsp/2 ml grated orange peel
¼ cup/50 ml lemon juice
½ cup/125 ml orange juice
1 tsp/5 ml salt
1 Tbsp/15 ml cornstarch
¼ cup/50 ml water

Microwave Oven Directions Arrange chicken in a glass baking dish, skin side down. Combine garlic powder, tarragon and spices and sprinkle half the mixture over chicken. Reserve remaining half. Combine grated peels and juices and pour over chicken. Cover dish with wax paper and place in microwave oven. Cook on high setting 12 minutes.

Turn chicken skin side up. Sprinkle with remaining spice mixture and spoon juices on top of chicken. Cover with wax paper and return to microwave oven. Cook 12 to 15 minutes longer or until chicken is tender.

Sprinkle chicken with salt. Transfer to a serving dish and cover with foil. Thicken pan juices with cornstarch dissolved in water. Cook on high setting 2 minutes, or until sauce is thickened and bubbly. Pour sauce over chicken to serve.

Conventional Directions Combine salt with remaining seasonings and sprinkle over chicken. Arrange chicken, skin side down, in a baking dish. Combine peels and juices and pour over chicken. Bake, uncovered, at 375° F (190° C) 45 minutes. Turn chicken skin side up, and continue baking 30 minutes longer, basting frequently with pan juices.   YIELD: 4 servings

Chicken Paprikash is a delicious Hungarian dish, traditionally served with hot noodles. A lower-calorie version can be made by omitting the chicken fat and the flour from this basic recipe.

Chicken Paprikash   F L E I S H I G

2 onions
1 green pepper
2 stalks celery
4 Tbsp/50 ml chicken fat
    or pareve margarine
4 Tbsp/50 ml flour
2 tsp/10 ml paprika
½ tsp/2 ml pepper

2½- to 3-lb/1 kilo fryer, cut up
1 (8-oz)/(227 grams) can
    tomato sauce
½ cup/125 ml dry white wine
1 envelope onion soup mix
½ tsp/2 ml salt, or to taste
¼ cup/50 ml water
    (for Crock Pot Directions)

Microwave Oven Directions   Peel onions and remove seeds from green pepper. Finely chop the onion, celery and green pepper and place in a glass baking dish. Add chicken fat. Cover dish with plastic wrap and cook on high setting for 10 minutes or until vegetables are soft. Set aside.

Combine flour, paprika and pepper, and sprinkle lightly over chicken pieces until evenly coated. Arrange chicken pieces on top of vegetables in baking dish, skin side down. Place chicken so that the thicker portions are toward the outer edge of the dish and the thinner pieces, such as the wings, are in the center. Cover dish with wax paper and cook on high setting 10 minutes.

Turn chicken skin side up. Combine tomato sauce, wine and soup mix and pour over chicken. Cover dish with wax paper and cook on high setting 15 to 20 minutes longer or until chicken is tender. Salt to taste.

Crock Pot Directions   Place all ingredients except flour in crock pot. Stir to blend. Cover pot and cook on low setting 5 to 7 hours or until chicken is tender. Transfer chicken pieces to a serving dish. Skim fat from sauce. Turn control to high setting. Blend flour with ¼ cup (50 ml) water and mix into sauce, stirring until thickened. Pour sauce over chicken or serve separately in a gravy dish.

Conventional Directions   In a large, heavy frying pan, fry onions, green pepper and celery in hot fat until golden brown. Coat the chicken with flour and seasonings and sauté until brown. Combine remaining ingredients and pour over chicken. Cover and simmer gently until the chicken is tender, 1½ to 2 hours. Turn occasionally.   YIELD: 4 servings

The olives give the rice an appearance and flavor somewhat similar to wild rice, but at a much lower cost. This dish is a good choice for a company dinner.

Chicken and Rice

F L E I S H I G

1 (10¾-oz)/(305 grams) can
   condensed clear chicken soup
¾ cup/175 ml dry white wine
1½ teaspoon/7 ml paprika
2 Tbsp/25 ml pareve margarine
1 cup/250 ml rice

¼ cup/50 ml black olives, chopped
¼ tsp/1 ml pepper
¼ tsp/1 ml garlic powder
4 Tbsp/50 ml olive oil
2½- to 3-lb/1 kilo fryer, cut up
½ tsp/2 ml salt, or to taste

Microwave Oven Directions In a large glass casserole combine condensed soup, wine, ½ teaspoon (2 ml) paprika and margarine. Cover dish with plastic wrap and cook on high setting 5 minutes, or until boiling. Stir in rice and olives. Cover with plastic wrap and cook on high setting 3 minutes, then reduce setting to medium and cook 10 minutes longer.

While the rice is cooking, prepare chicken pieces. Combine 1 teaspoon (5 ml) paprika, the pepper and garlic powder, and sprinkle evenly over chicken. In a frying pan, heat the oil and sauté the chicken until brown.

Arrange chicken pieces over rice. Place chicken skin side down, with thickest portions near the outer edge of the dish and thinner pieces, such as wings, in the center. Cover with a casserole lid and cook on high setting 15 minutes. Turn chicken skin side up, replace cover and cook on high setting 5 to 10 minutes longer or until chicken is tender. If desired, sprinkle chicken with salt. Cover and let stand 5 to 10 minutes before serving.

Crock Pot Directions Sprinkle chicken pieces with salt, 1 teaspoon (5 ml) paprika, pepper and garlic powder. Brown in hot oil in a large frying pan. Set aside. Place chicken, condensed soup, wine and margarine in crock pot. Cover and cook on low setting 5 to 7 hours. Stir in rice, ½ teaspoon (2 ml) paprika and olives. Cover and cook on high setting 30 minutes or more, or until rice is tender. Stir occasionally.

Conventional Directions Sprinkle chicken pieces with salt, 1 teaspoon (5 ml) paprika, pepper and garlic powder. Brown in hot oil in a large frying pan. Set aside. In saucepan, melt margarine, then stir in ½ teaspoon (2 ml) paprika and rice. Add wine and chicken stock. Bring mixture to a boil, reduce heat and simmer, covered, 15 minutes. Add olives and place in a large baking dish. Arrange chicken pieces on top. Cover with foil or casserole lid and bake at 350° F (180° C) 45 minutes, or until chicken is tender.

YIELD: 4 servings

Chicken and Vegetables   FLEISHIG

1 onion
2 Tbsp/25 ml chicken fat
   or pareve margarine
1 (10-oz)/(283 grams) carton
   frozen succotash
   (corn and lima beans)

1 lb/500 grams carrots
1 (16-oz)/(454 grams) can tomatoes
2 tsp/10 ml Worcestershire sauce
¼ tsp/1 ml pepper
2½- to 3-lb/1 kilo fryer, cut up
½ tsp/2 ml salt, or to taste

Microwave Oven Directions Peel onion, slice thin and place in a large glass baking dish. Add chicken fat. Cover dish with plastic wrap and place in microwave oven. Cook on high setting 3 minutes or until onion is soft.

Place carton of frozen succotash on a paper towel in microwave oven. Cook on high setting 2½ to 3 minutes or until vegetables are defrosted. Transfer vegetables to baking dish with the onions.

Peel carrots, slice thin and add to dish with vegetables. Add tomatoes, Worcestershire sauce and pepper, mixing well. Place chicken pieces in dish, arranging thicker portions toward the outer edges of dish and thinner pieces, such as the wings, in the center. Place chicken skin side down and spoon some of the sauce on top.

Cover dish with wax paper and cook on high setting 20 minutes. Turn chicken skin side up and spoon sauce over top. Cook on high setting 15 minutes longer or until chicken is tender and sauce is bubbly. Salt to taste.

Crock Pot Directions In crock pot place chicken, onion and ½ cup (125 ml) hot water. Cover and cook on low setting 5 to 7 hours, or until chicken is tender. Stir in remaining ingredients. Turn control to high setting. Cover and cook on high 1 hour longer.

Conventional Directions In a large pan with a tight-fitting lid melt the chicken fat. Sauté the onion and chicken until brown. Add remaining ingredients and bring to a boil. Reduce heat, cover pan and simmer until chicken is tender, about 1½ hours.   YIELD: 4 servings

Duck in Wine Sauce   FLEISHIG

1 duck/(2 kilos) (about 5 lbs)
2 Tbsp/25 ml pareve margarine
2 Tbsp/25 ml minced onion
1 garlic clove, minced

½ tsp/2 ml crushed tarragon
2 Tbsp/25 ml flour
2 cups/500 ml dry red wine

Crock Pot Directions With a fork, prick the skin of the duck all over at about 2-inch (5-cm) intervals. Place duck, breast side up, on a rack in crock pot.

In a saucepan, melt margarine and sauté onion, garlic and tarragon. Add flour, stirring to form a paste. Gradually add wine, stirring constantly. Cook over medium heat until sauce is thickened. Brush half of sauce mixture over duck. Cover crock pot and cook on low setting 7 to 9 hours. Drain off fat from sauce before serving.   YIELD: 4 servings

---

Orange-Glazed Duck   F L E I S H I G

1 duck/(2 kilos) (about 5 lbs)   2 Tbsp/25 ml dry white wine
Salt   1 Tbsp/15 ml soy sauce
2 oranges, quartered
½ cup/125 ml orange marmalade

Microwave Oven Directions   Sprinkle cavity of duck with salt. Fill cavity with orange quarters and close opening with toothpicks. Tie legs together and tie wings to the body with string. Place duck, breast side down, on a plastic or microwave oven-proof rack which fits inside a glass baking dish.

Combine marmalade, wine and soy sauce and brush one-third of the mixture over duck. Cook on high setting 15 minutes. Drain fat from dish or remove fat with a baster. Turn duck breast side up and brush with marmalade mixture. Cook on high setting 20 minutes longer, or until duck is tender. Transfer duck to a serving platter and cover with foil. Skim fat from pan drippings. Combine pan drippings with remaining marmalade mixture and serve as a sauce with the duck.

Conventional Directions   Prepare duck for cooking as described in basic recipe. Place on a rack in an open roasting pan and cook at 450° F (230° C) 1 to 1½ hours, or until duck is tender. Baste frequently with marmalade mixture. Skim fat from sauce and serve with duck.   YIELD: 4 servings

---

Simple Rock Cornish Hens   F L E I S H I G

2 Rock Cornish hens   2 Tbsp/25 ml dry white wine
  (about 1¼ lbs each/500 grams   1 Tbsp/15 ml oil
  each)   (for Conventional Directions)
1 Tbsp/15 ml liquid gravy coloring

Microwave Oven Directions   Place hens breast side down, on a plastic or microwave oven-proof rack which fits inside a glass baking dish. Brush hens with a mixture of gravy coloring and wine. Cook on high setting 10 minutes. Turn hens breast side up and brush with remaining wine mixture. Cook on high setting 10 to 12 minutes longer or until tender. Cover with foil and allow to stand 5 minutes before serving.

Conventional Directions   Add 1 tablespoon (15 ml) oil to marinade mixture and brush over hens. Place hens in a baking dish and cook at 350° F (180° C) 45 minutes or until tender.   YIELD: 2 servings

Lemon-Glazed Rock Cornish Hens   FLEISHIG

4 Rock Cornish hens (about 1¼ lbs each/500 grams each)
2 cups or more/500 ml Wild Rice and Mushroom Stuffing (see recipe in Savory Stuffings chapter)

¼ cup/50 ml melted pareve margarine
2 Tbsp/25 ml honey
2 Tbsp/25 ml lemon juice
2 Tbsp/25 ml dry white wine
2 tsp/10 ml soy sauce

Crock Pot Directions   Stuff hens with rice stuffing and close cavity securely. Mix remaining ingredients to form a sauce and brush each hen until well coated. Place rack in bottom of crock pot. Arrange birds in pot, neck end down. Pour remaining sauce over top. Cover crock pot and cook on low setting 5 to 7 hours, or until hens are tender.   YIELD: 4 servings

---

A velvety-smooth, rich wine sauce gives Chicken Croquettes a touch of elegance.

Chicken Croquettes   FLEISHIG

3 cups/750 ml cooked chicken, finely chopped
1 cup/250 ml cooked rice
Salt and pepper to taste
1 egg, beaten

¾ cup/175 ml dry pareve crumbs (bread, cracker, matzah)
½ cup/125 ml or more hot oil for frying

SAUCE

⅓ cup/75 ml dry white wine
1 Tbsp/15 ml tarragon-flavored vinegar
1 Tbsp/15 ml chopped green onion or chives
1 Tbsp/15 ml chopped parsley

Dash salt
½ cup/125 ml (1 stick) pareve margarine
3 egg yolks
½ cup/125 ml mayonnaise

Food Processor Directions   To prepare croquettes: Use the steel blade attachment on the food processor to chop cooked chicken fine to yield 3 cups. Combine with rice and seasonings. Chill mixture in refrigerator for easier handling.

To prepare sauce: While croquette mixture is chilling, prepare sauce. Combine wine, vinegar, onion, parsley and salt in a saucepan. Bring to a boil, lower heat and simmer 5 minutes. Add margarine and stir until melted. Insert plastic disc in food processor. Place egg yolks in container and begin processing. With motor running, slowly add hot liquid in a fine stream through feed tube, processing until mixture is smooth. Return mixture to saucepan and cook, stirring constantly, until thickened. Remove from heat, and stir in mayonnaise. Cover pan to keep sauce hot.

To fry croquettes: Use a spatula or 2 spoons to form chilled croquette mixture into balls. Roll in dry crumbs, dip in beaten egg and roll in crumbs again. Fry in hot oil until brown.

Serve croquettes with sauce. YIELD: 4 to 6 servings

For a real treat, serve Chicken à la King over biscuits, rice or noodles.

Chicken à La King   F L E I S H I G

4 Tbsp/50 ml chicken fat
  or pareve margarine
4 Tbsp/50 ml flour
2 cups/500 ml chicken stock
1½ cups/375 ml cooked chicken,
  cut in chunks

1 (4-oz)/(125 grams) can
  sliced mushrooms, drained
1 cup/250 ml cooked peas and
  carrots
Salt and pepper to taste

Microwave Oven Directions Prepare a white sauce: Place chicken fat in a large glass dish. Place in microwave oven and cook on high setting 30 seconds or until melted. Stir in flour until well blended. Slowly pour in chicken stock, stirring constantly. Return to microwave oven and cook on high setting 5 to 6 minutes, stirring once every minute, until sauce is thick and bubbly.

Add chicken, mushrooms and peas and carrots. Cover dish with wax paper and cook on high setting 4 to 5 minutes, or until chicken is heated through. Season to taste with salt and pepper.

Conventional Directions In a saucepan, melt fat. Blend in flour and slowly add stock. Cook over medium heat, stirring constantly, until sauce is smooth and bubbly. Add remaining ingredients and cook, over low heat, until hot.

YIELD: 4 servings

Nutty Chicken Casserole   F L E I S H I G

2 cups/500 ml cooked chicken,
  cut in chunks
2 cups/500 ml cooked rice or kasha
¼ cup/50 ml chicken broth
2 beaten eggs

1 cup/250 ml chopped nuts
  (pistachios, almonds,
  walnuts or pecans)
Salt and pepper to taste

Microwave Oven Directions Combine all ingredients and spoon into a glass ring mold (or form mixture into a circle shape on a glass baking dish). Cover with wax paper and cook on high setting 10 to 15 minutes or until heated through.

Conventional Directions Combine all ingredients and place in a greased loaf pan. Bake, uncovered, at 350° F (180° C) about 30 minutes.

YIELD: 4 to 6 servings

SAVORY STUFFINGS

Stuffings are a delicious addition to any dinner, whether cooked inside meat or poultry or baked separately in a casserole. Each stuffing recipe in this chapter yields about 4 to 5 cups (1000 to 1250 ml), which is enough for 1 large or 2 medium-sized chickens. Recipes may be doubled for turkey.

Before stuffing poultry, wash the cavity with cold water and sprinkle with salt. Pack the stuffing lightly because it expands during cooking as it absorbs liquid. Any leftover stuffing may be cooked in a casserole. Stuffing cooked in this manner requires some additional liquid to keep from drying out.

Use the microwave oven for precooking rice and vegetables for stuffing mixtures. The stuffing itself may be cooked in a covered glass casserole about 8 minutes, or leftover stuffing may be cooked in individual glass custard cups, covered with wax paper, until hot.

Use the food processor to chop and shred dried fruit and vegetables. The blender is used to prepare crumbs for stuffing and to chop vegetables in liquid.

Challah Stuffing   PAREVE

4 cups/1 liter day-old Challah, cut
   into cubes
2 cups/500 ml water
1 bunch green onions
1 carrot and 1 stalk celery

4 sprigs parsley
1 egg, beaten
½ tsp/2 ml garlic powder
Salt and pepper to taste
¼ cup/50 ml pareve margarine

Food Processor Directions Insert steel blade in food processor. Place Challah cubes, in container and process until Challah is reduced to crumbs. Transfer crumbs to large mixing bowl. Soak in water for 5 minutes. Drain well, then squeeze out excess water.

Cut green onions, carrot, celery and parsley into small pieces. Place in container and use steel blade to chop fine. Place vegetables in bowl along with Challah. Add beaten egg, garlic powder, salt and pepper. Melt margarine and combine with Challah mixture, mixing well.

Allow ¾ cup (175 ml) stuffing for each poultry.

YIELD: About 5 cups (1250 ml)

This stuffing is delicious cooked inside poultry, fish or meat. However, it is equally good cooked separately in a casserole because stuffing cooked in a microwave oven stays moist and tasty.

Traditional Bread Stuffing   P A R E V E

¼ cup/50 ml chopped onion
½ cup/125 ml melted
  pareve margarine
4 cups/1 liter pareve croutons
  or dry bread cubes
1 tsp/5 ml poultry seasoning

½ tsp/2 ml thyme or marjoram
⅓ to ½ cup/75 to 125 ml hot water
  or vegetable stock
2 Tbsp/25 ml chopped parsley
1 tsp/5 ml salt, or to taste
½ tsp/2 ml pepper

Microwave Oven Directions Place onion and margarine in a glass dish. Cover with plastic wrap and cook on high setting 2 minutes. Combine with remaining ingredients and mix well.

To stuff poultry: Allow about ¾ cup (175 ml) stuffing for each pound of poultry. Stuffing expands as it cooks and should not be tightly packed into the cavity.

To cook separately: Put stuffing into a 1½-quart (1½-liter) casserole, or into 8 small glass custard cups. Cover with wax paper and cook on high setting 8 minutes, or until hot.

Conventional Directions Melt margarine in a large frying pan. Sauté onion and parsley. Combine with croutons and seasonings. Add liquid and mix well.   YIELD: About 4 cups (1 liter)

Variations Make the following changes in basic stuffing recipe:

Celery Stuffing   P A R E V E

1 cup/250 ml chopped celery   Add to basic recipe.

Cornbread Stuffing   P A R E V E or D A I R Y

4 cups/1 liter cornbread crumbs

Substitute cornbread crumbs for bread crumbs.

Giblet Stuffing   F L E I S H I G

Giblets from 1 turkey
  or 2 chickens

2 cups/500 ml water
1 tsp/5 ml salt

Cook giblets in boiling salted water until tender, 1 to 2 hours. Chop fine and add to stuffing. Use ½ cup (125 ml) giblet stock to moisten stuffing.

Mushroom Stuffing   P A R E V E

8 oz/250 grams fresh mushrooms

Chop mushrooms and cook along with onion and margarine before combining with other ingredients.

Fresh Fruit Stuffing is excellent with duck and poultry.

Fresh Fruit Stuffing   P A R E V E

8 slices day-old bread
1 apple
⅔ cup/150 ml orange juice

¼ cup/50 ml melted pareve
  margarine
Salt and paper to taste
⅓ cup/75 ml pine nuts, optional

Blender Directions Cut each slice of bread into 8 pieces. Place in blender goblet and blend at high speed until reduced to fine crumbs. Transfer to mixing bowl. Quarter and core apple and cut into 8 pieces. In blender goblet put orange juice and apple pieces. Blend at medium speed until apple is coarsely chopped. Add to crumbs in mixing bowl. Combine all ingredients well.   YIELD: About 4 cups (1 liter)

Dried-Fruit Stuffing   P A R E V E

¼ lb/125 grams dried pitted prunes
¼ lb/125 grams dried apricots
1 cup/250 ml water
2 stalks celery

½ small onion
2 Tbsp/25 ml pareve margarine
½ cup/125 ml chopped pecans
3 cups/750 ml croutons

Food Processor Directions Insert steel blade in food processor. Place prunes and apricots in container and process until fruit is coarsely chopped. Place chopped fruit in a saucepan, add water, and simmer 5 minutes. Drain and reserve the liquid. Set fruit aside to cool.

Cut celery into chunks and place in container. Peel the onion, cut into chunks, and add to container. Process the celery and onion until finely chopped. In a frying pan melt the margarine and sauté the onion and celery until tender. Transfer to a large mixing bowl. Add cooked fruit, pecans and croutons, and combine well. If stuffing is to be cooked inside meat or poultry, add ⅓ cup (75 ml) of the reserved liquid to moisten stuffing. If stuffing is to be cooked separately, add up to 1 cup (250 ml) liquid.

Stuff mixture lightly into poultry cavity or into lamb breast. Secure the closing and roast as directed in meat or poultry recipe.

Stuffing may be cooked separately in a greased 1½-quart (1½-liter) casserole at 350° F (180° C) for 1 hour.   YIELD: About 5 cups (1250 ml)

Potato Stuffing goes very well with beef or with roast breast of veal.

Potato Stuffing PAREVE

4 medium potatoes
1 onion
2 carrots
2 eggs
½ cup/125 ml flour

1 tsp/5 ml salt
½ tsp/2 ml pepper
⅓ cup/75 ml melted
  pareve margarine

Food Processor Directions Wash potatoes and cut into chunks (it is not necessary to peel the potatoes). Insert shredding disc in food processor. Use the pusher to guide potato chunks through the feed tube to the cutting disc. As container becomes full, empty contents into a large mixing bowl, then continue processing. Squeeze shredded potatoes to remove excess liquid.

Insert steel blade in food processor. Peel onion and cut in chunks, then place in the container. Cut the carrot into chunks and place in container. Process until vegetables are finely chopped and add to potatoes.

Beat the eggs and add to vegetable mixture along with remaining ingredients.   YIELD: About 5 cups (1250 ml)

Rice and Vegetable Stuffing goes well with poultry or lamb.

Rice and Vegetable Stuffing PAREVE

1 cup/250 ml brown rice
2 cups/500 ml boiling water
¼ tsp/1 ml salt
1 to 4 Tbsp/15 to 50 ml oil,
  as needed
2 onions, chopped

1 green pepper, chopped
2 carrots, thinly sliced
1 stalk celery, chopped
1 cup/250 ml mushrooms, sliced
2 Tbsp/25 ml soy sauce
½ cup/125 ml dry white wine

Microwave Oven Directions Wash rice and place in a large glass bowl with boiling water and salt. Cover bowl with plastic wrap and cook on high setting 3 minutes, then reduce setting to medium and cook 35 minutes longer, or until rice is soft. Set aside.

In glass mixing bowl combine 1 tablespoon (15 ml) oil and vegetables. Cover with plastic wrap and cook on high setting 7 minutes or until vegetables are soft. Combine vegetables and rice and add soy sauce and wine. Cover with plastic wrap and cook in microwave oven 2 minutes on high setting.

Conventional Directions Wash rice and place in a saucepan with water and salt. Cover and simmer rice 40 minutes, or until tender. Set aside.

In a large frying pan heat 4 tablespoons (50 ml) oil. Sauté vegetables until soft. Add cooked rice and remaining ingredients.

YIELD: About 4 to 5 cups (1000 to 1250 ml)

Wild rice requires a long time to soften. It should be prepared several hours in advance. This stuffing is delicious with poultry.

Wild Rice and Mushroom Stuffing   P A R E V E

½ cup/125 ml (95 grams) wild rice   1 small onion, chopped
 (about 3 oz)   1 cup/250 ml sliced mushrooms
2 cups/500 ml water   ½ tsp/2 ml poultry seasoning
½ tsp/2 ml salt   Dash nutmeg
2 Tbsp/25 ml pareve margarine   Salt and pepper to taste

Microwave Oven Directions   Combine wild rice, water and salt in a glass bowl. Cover with plastic wrap and place in microwave oven. Cook on high setting until mixture boils, about 5 or 6 minutes. Let stand, tightly covered, at least 3 hours.

Place margarine, onion and mushrooms in a glass bowl. Cover with plastic wrap and cook on high setting in microwave oven until vegetables are tender, about 4 minutes. Combine cooked vegetables with wild rice. Add remaining ingredients and blend well.

Conventional Directions   Wash wild rice and place in a saucepan with 2 cups (500 ml) boiling water and salt. Cover pan and simmer, without stirring, until tender, about 40 minutes.

Melt margarine in a large frying pan and sauté vegetables until tender. Combine with rice, add remaining ingredients and blend well.

YIELD: About 4 cups (1 liter)

Variation   Make the following changes in basic recipe:

Chestnut and Wild Rice Stuffing   P A R E V E

½ lb/250 grams chestnuts

Omit mushrooms and add chopped chestnuts to basic stuffing recipe.

Prepare chestnuts in the microwave oven by slashing a crisscross on each nut. Place nuts in a shallow glass dish and cook on high setting until nuts pop out of the skins, about 3 to 4 minutes. Cool nuts, then peel and chop.

YIELD: About 4 cups (1 liter)

This chapter contains recipes for gravy and savory sauces to be served with meat, poultry, fish, vegetables and eggs. Some of these recipes, such as Schmaltz and Horseradish, are used rather extensively in Jewish cooking. Others like Barbecue Sauce or Chili Sauce are American favorites, while another recipe, Hollandaise Sauce, adds a gourmet touch to food.

The microwave oven is a great aid in making gravies and sauces because it reduces the amount of stirring and close watching often associated with gravy making. Also, gravies do not have a tendency to lump in the microwave oven as they do when cooked conventionally.

Use the crock pot to develop flavors made possible through slow coooking.

The blender and food processor combine ingredients to produce smooth, creamy sauces.

Barbecue Sauce improves in flavor if refrigerated overnight before serving.

Barbecue Sauce   P A R E V E

2 cups/500 ml ketchup
4 Tbsp/50 ml Worcestershire sauce
2 tsp/10 ml chili powder
1 cup/250 ml water
4 Tbsp/50 ml cider vinegar

2 Tbsp/25 ml brown sugar
1 tsp/5 ml salt, or to taste
½ tsp/2 ml pepper
2 Tbsp/25 ml minced onion

Microwave Oven Directions Combine all ingredients in a glass bowl and cover with plastic wrap. Place in microwave oven and cook on high setting 10 minutes. Lower setting to medium and cook an additional 10 minutes.

Crock Pot Directions Combine all ingredients in crock pot and stir well. Cover and cook on low 4 to 5 hours.   YIELD: 4 cups (1 liter)

Brown Gravy   P A R E V E or F L E I S H I G

4 Tbsp/50 ml pareve margarine   ½ tsp/2 ml salt, or to taste
4 Tbsp/50 ml flour   Dash pepper
2 cups/500 ml chicken, vegetable   1 tsp/5 ml gravy coloring
   or meat stock (or 2 cups water   or Worcestershire sauce
   plus 2 tsp pareve soup mix, beef-
   flavored)

Microwave Oven Directions   Place margarine in a glass mixing bowl and cook in microwave oven until melted, about 30 seconds on high setting. Stir in flour, blending until smooth. Add remaining ingredients, stirring constantly. Place in microwave oven and cook on high setting 4 to 6 minutes, until sauce is bubbly and thickened. Stir once every minute. Taste to correct seasonings.

Conventional Directions   Melt margarine in a small saucepan. Blend in flour and cook until browned, stirring constantly. Gradually add stock and remaining ingredients, stirring constantly until mixture boils and thickens. Reduce heat to allow gravy to simmer 3 to 5 minutes longer. Taste to correct seasonings.   YIELD: 2 cups (500 ml)

Variations   Make the following changes in basic Brown Gravy recipe:

Giblet Gravy   F L E I S H I G

Giblets from chicken or turkey   1 tsp/5 ml salt
2 cups/500 ml water

Cook giblets in boiling salted water until tender, 1 to 2 hours. Chop fine and add to gravy.

Mushroom Gravy   P A R E V E or F L E I S H I G

½ cup/125 ml sliced mushrooms
1 tsp/5 ml chopped onion

Microwave Oven Directions   Put sliced mushrooms and chopped onion in a small glass dish. Cover with plastic wrap and place in microwave oven. Cook on high setting 1 minute, until soft. Drain and add to gravy.

                                          YIELD: 2 cups (500 ml)

The long, slow cooking provided by the crock pot brings out the rich and spicy flavors of this chili sauce.

Chili Sauce   P A R E V E

1 (16-oz)/(454 grams) can tomatoes
2 (8-oz)/(227-grams) cans
  tomato sauce
1 onion, chopped
1 green pepper, chopped
1 garlic clove, minced
4 Tbsp/50 ml vinegar
3 Tbsp/45 ml brown sugar

1 tsp/5 ml chili powder
  or to taste
1 tsp/5 ml salt, or to taste
½ tsp/2 ml pepper
½ tsp/2 ml dry mustard
¼ tsp/1 ml cayenne pepper
Dash *each* of cumin,
  celery seed and allspice

Crock Pot Directions Combine all ingredients in crock pot, stirring well. Cover and cook on low setting 5 to 6 hours, or overnight. Store, covered, in the refrigerator.

For a smoother consistency, sauce may be forced through a sieve or pureed in a blender.   YIELD: 4 cups (1 liter)

Hollandaise Sauce is a good accompaniment for baked fish, vegetables and eggs.

Hollandaise Sauce   D A I R Y or P A R E V E

4 Tbsp/50 ml butter or
  pareve margarine
2 Tbsp/25 ml cream
  or nondairy creamer
2 egg yolks, well beaten

1 Tbsp/15 ml lemon juice
¼ tsp/1 ml salt
Dash dry mustard or cayenne
  pepper

Microwave Oven Directions Place butter in a glass bowl and cook in microwave oven until melted, about 30 seconds on high setting. Add remaining ingredients and mix well. Return to microwave oven and cook on medium setting 1 to 1½ minutes or until thickened, stirring twice. Beat with a wire whisk or beater until fluffy. Serve with eggs, fish or vegetables.

Conventional Directions In top of a double boiler, over boiling water, place egg yolks, lemon juice and half the butter. Cook, stirring constantly, until mixture begins to thicken. Remove from heat and add remaining butter and seasonings, stirring well. Return to top of double boiler and continue cooking until thickened. Serve at once.   YIELD: About ½ cup (125 ml)

Variations   Make the following changes in basic Hollandaise Sauce recipe:

Béarnaise Sauce

DAIRY or PAREVE

1 tsp *each*/5 ml crushed tarragon   1 Tbsp/15 ml vinegar
   and chopped parsley   1 tsp/5 ml minced onion

Reduce lemon juice to 1½ teaspoons (7 ml). Add tarragon, parsley, vinegar and onion with other seasonings.

Dill Hollandaise Sauce

DAIRY or PAREVE

1 Tbsp/15 ml dill weed   YIELD: About ½ cup (125 ml)

Easy Hollandaise Sauce

PAREVE

3 egg yolks   Dash of cayenne pepper
½ tsp/2 ml salt   ½ cup/125 ml (1 stick)
½ tsp/2 ml dry mustard   pareve margarine, melted
2 Tbsp/25 ml lemon juice

Food Processor Directions   Insert plastic blade in food processor. Place all ingredients except melted margarine in container. Begin processing and slowly add margarine through feed tube, processing until thick.

Blender Directions   Combine all ingredients except margarine in blender goblet. Blend on medium speed. With motor running, slowly pour in melted margarine in a steady stream until mixture is thick. Serve immediately.

YIELD: About ¾ cup (175 ml)

Horseradish

PAREVE

1 cup/250 ml horseradish root,   1½ Tbsp/20 ml sugar, or to taste
   peeled and cut into chunks   Dash salt
¾ cup/175 ml white vinegar

Food Processor Directions   Insert shredding disc in food processor and push horseradish chunks through feed tube to shred. If a finer consistency is desired, use steel blade to chop finely. Mix well with vinegar and sugar. Cover tightly and store in refrigerator.

Blender Directions   Cut horseradish into ½-inch (2 cm) cubes. Place all ingredients in blender goblet. Blend on medium speed until finely grated.

YIELD: About 1½ cups (375 ml)

Variation   Make the following changes in Horseradish recipe:

Pink Horseradish   PAREVE

2 to 4 Tbsp/25 to 50 ml beet juice

Add beet juice along with white vinegar to grated horseradish.

YIELD: About 1½ cups (375 ml)

To peel fresh tomatoes: Dip each tomato in boiling water for about 45 seconds to loosen skin, then rinse under cold, running water. If skin does not come off easily, repeat process.

Marinara Sauce   PAREVE

12 fresh tomatoes, peeled and chopped or 5 cups/1250 ml canned tomatoes	1 bay leaf
	1 tsp/5 ml sweet basil
	1 tsp/5 ml oregano
3 Tbsp/45 ml olive oil	1 Tbsp/15 ml chopped parsley
3 garlic cloves, minced	¾ tsp/4 ml salt, or to taste
1 onion, chopped	

Microwave Oven Directions   In a large glass bowl, place olive oil, garlic and onion. Cover with plastic wrap and cook on high setting 3 minutes or until onion is soft. Stir in remaining ingredients, cover with plastic wrap and return to microwave oven. Cook on high setting 10 to 15 minutes or until bubbly.

Crock Pot Directions   In a large frying pan, heat oil and sauté garlic and onion until soft. Transfer to crock pot. Stir in remaining ingredients. Cover and cook on low setting 4 to 5 hours.

Conventional Directions   In a large frying pan, heat oil and sauté garlic and onion until soft. Stir in remaining ingredients. Bring to a boil, cover, reduce heat and simmer gently 1 hour.   YIELD: About 5½ cups (1375 ml)

Schmaltz (Rendered Chicken Fat)   FLEISHIG

8 oz/250 grams unrendered chicken fat
  and skin

Microwave Oven Directions   Remove fat and skin from poultry and place in a
glass dish. Cover dish with wax paper and place in microwave oven. Cook on
high setting until liquid fat accumulates in dish and skin pieces (grebenes)
are brown and crisp, about 6 to 8 minutes. Remove grebenes, drain on paper
towel and save to use in kugels, stuffings, kasha or rice dishes. Store chicken
fat in a covered jar in the refrigerator.

Conventional Directions   Place fat pieces in a frying pan. Cook over low heat
until liquid fat is rendered and grebenes are brown and crisp. Remove grebenes and drain on paper towel. Continue cooking fat 5 to 10 minutes longer
to evaporate water. Pour into a jar, cover and refrigerate.

Variations   Sliced onion or garlic may be added to the fat during rendering.
Strain the fat and discard the onion or garlic before refrigerating.

YIELD: About ¾ cup (175 ml)

A sauce synonymous with fish.

Tartar Sauce   PAREVE

1 cup/250 ml mayonnaise   1 Tbsp/15 ml chopped green onions
2 tsp/10 ml vinegar   or chives
2 Tbsp/25 ml chopped   ½ tsp/2 ml paprika
  sweet pickles   2 hard-cooked egg yolks
1 Tbsp/15 ml chopped parsley   4 pitted green olives, chopped

Food Processor Directions   Insert plastic blade in food processor. Place all ingredients in container and process until well combined.

Blender Directions   Place all ingredients in blender goblet. Blend on high
speed until well combined. Serve with fish.

YIELD: About 1½ cups (375 ml)

White Sauce   DAIRY or PAREVE

	THIN	MEDIUM	THICK
Butter or			
pareve margarine	1 Tbsp (15 ml)	2 Tbsp (25 ml)	2½–3 Tbsp (40 ml)
Flour	1 Tbsp (15 ml)	2 Tbsp (25 ml)	2½–3 Tbsp (40 ml)
Salt	½ tsp (2 ml)	½ tsp (2 ml)	½ tsp (2 ml)
Milk or			
nondairy creamer	1 cup (250 ml)	1 cup (250 ml)	1 cup (250 ml)

Microwave Oven Directions Put butter in glass dish and cook on high setting until melted, about 30 seconds. Add flour and salt, stirring until smooth. Cook on high setting 30 seconds, until very hot. Add milk, stirring constantly until smooth. Cook on high setting 4 minutes, stirring once every minute, until sauce is thick and bubbly.

Conventional Directions In a small saucepan, melt butter over medium heat. Stir in flour and salt. Cook until mixture bubbles, stirring constantly, but do not allow to brown. Remove from heat. Add milk and stir until smooth. Return to heat and cook until mixture thickens, stirring constantly.

YIELD: 1 cup (250 ml)

Variations Make the following changes to basic White Sauce recipe:

Cheese Sauce

DAIRY

1 cup/250 ml grated yellow cheese   Dash paprika
½ tsp/2 ml Worcestershire sauce

Stir cheese, Worcestershire sauce and paprika into prepared White Sauce. Return sauce to microwave oven and cook on high setting until cheese is melted, about 1 minute. Serve with eggs, macaroni, rice, fish or vegetables.

Curry Sauce

DAIRY

½ tsp/2 ml curry powder

Stir curry powder into prepared White Sauce. Serve with rice, fish or eggs. Use nondairy creamer and pareve margarine to make a pareve sauce to serve with lamb or chicken.

Horseradish Sauce

DAIRY

¼ cup/50 ml prepared horseradish
½ tsp/2 ml prepared mustard

Add horseradish and mustard to prepared White Sauce. Use nondairy creamer and pareve margarine to make a pareve sauce to serve with corned beef or flanken.

Mushroom Sauce

DAIRY

1 (4-oz)/(113 grams) can sliced mushrooms,
   drained

Add mushrooms to prepared White Sauce. Serve with eggs or vegetables.

YIELD: 1 cup (250 ml)

VEGETABLES

One of the best appliances ever designed for cooking vegetables is the microwave oven. Fresh vegetables seem to cook faster and more easily in the microwave oven and come out tastier and more colorful than if cooked conventionally. Frozen vegetables can be cooked directly in the freezer carton or cooking pouch. Canned vegetables, also, are easily reheated. Vegetables can be cooked directly on a serving platter or dish.

Although the crock pot is probably not one of the first applicances to come to mind when you think of cooking vegetables, its use should not be overlooked. Many vegetables develop a lovely, interesting flavor and texture when slow-cooked. Particularly suitable for crock pot cookery are squash, cabbage, potatoes, carrots, turnips and casserole combinations.

The blender is used in this chapter to mix batters for croquettes, patties and filling mixtures.

The food processor is featured for vegetable recipes which require fancy cutting, such as shredded cabbage or carrots or "French-cut" green beans. The food processor, however, could be used extensively in almost every recipe for routine chopping and mincing of onions, garlic, etc.

The mixer is featured in only 1 recipe—Mashed Potatoes; however, without a mixer it is one recipe that would need to be prepared by hand.

MICROWAVE OVEN TECHNIQUES
FOR FRESH VEGETABLES

Three guidelines should be followed when cooking fresh vegetables in the microwave oven:

1. Cook vegetables on high setting.
2. Use plastic wrap as a covering to seal in moisture.
3. Cooking time is determined by the weight
   of the vegetables. Always use a kitchen scale.

The tight cover that plastic wrap provides (far more effectively than a casserole lid) allows vegetables to steam in their own moisture, and in most cases no additional liquid is needed for cooking.

Always vent the plastic wrap covering by puncturing 1 or 2 small holes in it. This acts as a pressure valve, allowing some of the steam to escape, and prevents the plastic wrap from tearing. When removing the covering, be very careful because there is a buildup of *very hot* steam under the plastic wrap.

If a thick-skinned vegetable is cooked unpeeled, the skin serves the same function as plastic wrap (creates a tight seal) and does not need to be covered again. The skin, however, should be vented by poking a small hole in it with a fork or knife.

TIMING GUIDE FOR FRESH VEGETABLES
IN MICROWAVE OVEN

The weight of the vegetable should be used as a guide for determining how long to cook. The following times produce a crisp-textured, Japanese-style vegetable (all vegetables cook on high setting):

1 oz = 30 grams   1 lb = 500 grams

Artichokes	1 min per oz
Asparagus	10 min per lb
Bean sprouts	3½ min per lb
Beets	7 min per lb
Broccoli	7 min per lb
Brussels sprouts	6 min per lb
Cabbage	5 min per lb
Carrots	7 min per lb
Cauliflower	7 min per lb
Corn	2½ min per ear
Eggplant	5 min per lb
Green beans	12 min per lb *
Green pepper	10 min per lb
Lima beans	12 min per lb *
Mushrooms	3½ min per lb
Peas	6 min per lb *
Potato	1 min per oz
Sweet potato	1 min per oz
Spinach	4 min per lb
Squash, soft-texture	8 min per lb
Turnips	7 min per lb
Zucchini, crisp-texture	6 min per lb

* Add 2 Tbsp (25 ml) liquid for each pound (500 grams) of vegetable.

FROZEN VEGETABLES IN THE MICROWAVE OVEN

There are two ways to buy frozen vegetables today—in a cardboard carton and in a plastic pouch. Many frozen food manufacturers now give microwave oven cooking instructions and times on the backs of the packages.

Timing guides for cooking frozen vegetables in the microwave oven can only be approximated, because food is "frozen" in a temperature range of 32° F (0° C) down to 0° F (–18° C) or even below. Vegetables frozen at the lower temperature may take a little longer to thaw and cook in the microwave oven.

A carton of frozen vegetables weighs 10 ounces (283 grams) and contains approximately 1½ cups (375 ml) frozen vegetables, or enough for 2 to 4 servings. The vegetables may be cooked directly in the carton: punch 1 or 2 holes in the carton (to allow steam to escape), place the carton on a paper towel in the microwave oven and cook on high setting 5 minutes. If desired, the frozen vegetables may instead be transferred to a glass serving dish, covered with plastic wrap, and then cooked 5 minutes on high.

Vegetables frozen in a pouch, sometimes called "boil-in-the-bag" vegetables, may also be cooked in the microwave oven directly in the pouch (vegetables from the larger, family-size bags should be transferred to a glass dish and covered with plastic wrap before cooking). The technique for cooking vegetables directly in the pouch is to punch a hole in the middle of the pouch, place the pouch on a paper towel in the microwave oven and cook on high setting 6 to 8 minutes or until hot.

CANNED VEGETABLES IN THE MICROWAVE OVEN

Canned vegetables should be well drained and transferred to a glass dish or serving bowl before being cooked in the microwave oven. Cover the bowl with plastic wrap and place in the oven.

Canned vegetables are precooked and therefore need only to be reheated before serving. A 16-ounce (500-gram) can of vegetables cooks on high setting in about 2½ to 3 minutes.

VEGETABLE PLATTERS IN THE MICROWAVE OVEN

Vegetable platters are a delicious idea for entertaining. Fresh, frozen or canned vegetables can be attractively arranged on a large glass dish or platter, covered with plastic wrap, cooked in the microwave oven and then served as a beautiful side dish or edible centerpiece.

Microwave oven cooking produces vegetables with a brilliant, natural color. When arranging vegetables on a platter, be creative with colors, placing different-colored vegetables side by side for contrast.

As the vegetables cook, excess juices will gather. These can be drained off without disturbing the vegetable arrangement by lifting a small section of the plastic wrap and tilting the platter to one side. Collect these vegetable juices to use later in sauces or gravies.

Vegetable platters can be arranged ahead of time and kept in the refrigerator, covered with plastic wrap, until time to cook. When arranging vegetable platters, leave space for a small bowl, if a sauce or dip is to be added later (this, however, will cook separately).

After cooking, vegetable platters will retain their heat up to 15 or 20 minutes if kept tightly covered with plastic wrap and then covered again with a sheet of foil, shiny side toward the food.

Fresh Vegetable Platter   P A R E V E

Microwave Oven Directions   Select vegetables with similar cooking times (see "Timing Guide for Fresh Vegetables in Microwave Oven"). If one vegetable requires a longer cooking time than the rest, it may be partially cooked before the platter is assembled. Season vegetables to taste before serving.

Cooking times are determined by carefully weighing the vegetables and adding together the various cooking times. For example, broccoli, carrots and cauliflower each cook in 7 minutes per pound (500 grams). If the platter has 1 pound (500 grams) of each vegetable, for a total weight of 3 pounds (1500 grams), the cooking time is about 21 minutes (all vegetables cook on high setting).

Some suggestions for attractive fresh vegetable platters are:

BROCCOLI, CARROTS AND CAULIFLOWER
Place a whole head of cauliflower in the center of a dish. Surround with broccoli flowerets. Cut the carrots into sticks and arrange like spokes on a wheel, radiating out from the center. Cover dish with plastic wrap before cooking.

GREEN PEAS AND BEETS
Peel uncooked beets and cut into slices. Border the edges of the glass dish with beet slices and pile fresh peas in the center. Cover the dish with plastic wrap before cooking.

SUMMER SQUASH AND ZUCCHINI
Wash and trim the vegetables. Cut into circles and arrange overlapping slices on platter. Cover with plastic wrap and cook.

CORN, SPINACH AND MUSHROOMS

Cook corn on the cob separately and cut each piece in thirds. On a glass serving dish, arrange raw spinach and mushrooms. Cover with plastic wrap and cook. To serve, place the corn pieces so that they border the edge of the dish.

Frozen Vegetable Platter   PAREVE

Microwave Oven Directions Place cartons of frozen vegetables on a paper towel in the microwave oven. Cook on high setting 2½ minutes per carton, or until vegetables are thawed and will separate easily. Arrange the vegetables on a glass dish or platter and cover securely with plastic wrap (the platter may be refrigerated at this point for later cooking). Vent the plastic wrap by puncturing 1 or 2 small holes to allow steam to escape. Cook on high setting in microwave oven until plastic wrap covering billows and forms a balloon around the vegetables. This means that the plastic wrap has filled with steam and the vegetables are hot. Allow to stand a few minutes before serving.

Frozen vegetables are partially cooked before freezing. Since they need only to be defrosted and reheated when cooking, any combination of frozen vegetables works well. Some suggestions are:

> Whole baby carrots, asparagus spears
> Beets and French-cut green beans
> Broccoli and corn
> Mixed vegetables surrounded by whole green beans
> Diced carrots and peas surrounded by Brussels sprouts

Frozen vegetables are one of the few foods that can be cooked in the microwave oven directly from the freezer, without prior defrosting.

Creamed sauces are a good way to add a little extra zip and spice to cooked vegetables—fresh, frozen, canned or even leftover.

Creamed Vegetables   DAIRY

2 cups/500 ml drained cooked vegetables	¼ to 1 tsp/1 to 5 ml seasoning, if desired
1 cup/250 ml sauce	¼ cup/50 ml cheese or other garnish, if desired

Microwave Oven Directions Combine vegetables and sauce, mixing well. Add flavoring, if desired. Place mixture in a glass serving bowl. Cook in microwave oven on high setting 2 minutes, or until sauce is hot and bubbly. A cheese garnish or other topping should be added after the mixture is cooked.

If the steam from the vegetables is not hot enough to melt the cheese, return dish to microwave oven for a few seconds on high setting until the cheese begins to melt.

Conventional Directions Drain cooked vegetables, combine with sauce, flavoring and garnish. Heat in 350° F (180° C) oven until sauce is hot and bubbly.

Sauce suggestions: Medium white sauce; ¾ cup (175 ml) condensed creamed soup (celery, mushroom, onion) diluted with ¼ cup (50 ml) milk; ½ cup (125 ml) white sauce and ½ cup (125 ml) sour cream, or a cheese sauce.

Seasoning suggestions: 1 tsp (5 ml) chili powder, curry powder or horseradish; ½ tsp (2 ml) prepared mustard, dill weed or soy sauce; ¼ tsp (1 ml) onion salt, garlic salt, celery salt, thyme, marjoram, basil or oregano.

Garnish or topping suggestions: ¼ cup (50 ml) grated cheese; 1 tsp (5 ml) chopped parsley, chives or green onion; ½ tsp (2 ml) paprika; or ¼ cup (50 ml) bread crumbs or croutons.   YIELD: 4 servings

---

A variety of vegetables can be used to make croquettes. Some suggestions are eggplant, mushrooms, potatoes, parsnips, spinach or zucchini. A traditional croquette is made by blending a pureed cooked vegetable with a heavy white sauce, forming into balls, breading and then frying in oil.

Vegetable Croquettes   DAIRY or PAREVE

2 cups/500 ml cooked
   vegetable puree
1 cup/250 ml thickened white
   or brown sauce
   (see Gravy and Savory Sauces
   chapter)
2 egg yolks
Seasonings to taste (salt and pepper,
   curry powder, chili powder,

cayenne pepper, Worcestershire
   sauce, dried herbs, lemon juice,
   paprika or parsley)
¼ cup or more/50 ml breading
   (use crumbs made from bread,
   crackers, cornflakes
   or other cereal or potato chips;
   matzah meal; or seasoned flour)
¼ cup or more/50 ml hot oil

Blender Directions Puree vegetables in blender: Cut the cooked vegetables into chunks, place in the goblet and cover with water. Blend at low speed until finely chopped. Drain, pressing the vegetables to remove as much of the liquid as possible (reserve to use for soups or the croquette sauce).

Prepare sauce (see Gravy and Savory Sauces chapter). Allow to cool slightly and stir in egg yolks and seasonings.

Combine vegetable puree, sauce and enough breading to make a thick batter. Chill mixture for 1 hour. Using a spoon or spatula, form mixture into 12 balls. Fry in hot oil about 5 minutes, until golden brown. After cooking, croquettes may be kept warm, briefly, in a 350° F (180° C) oven.

YIELD: 12 croquettes

Variation

Broiled Croquettes   DAIRY or PAREVE

Broil the croquettes at 550° F (285° C) 12 to 15 minutes on the first side, turn and broil 5 to 7 minutes longer.   YIELD: 12 croquettes

Canned Vegetable Platters   PAREVE

Microwave Oven Directions   Open vegetable cans and drain well. Arrange 2 or more vegetables in combination on a glass dish or platter. Cover with plastic wrap. Cook on high setting, allowing about 2 minutes cooking time for each 1-pound (500-gram) can of vegetables. The vegetables are hot when the plastic wrap covering fills with steam and billows. Some vegetable combinations might be:

> Green and wax beans surrounded by beet slices
> Corn surrounded by whole green beans

Asparagus, broccoli, cauliflower, carrots, mushrooms and spinach are some of the vegetables that can be used to make a delicious custard dish.

Vegetable Custard   DAIRY

1 small onion
1 to 2 cups/250 to 500 ml
   cooked vegetables
4 eggs
½ tsp/2 ml salt, or to taste
½ tsp/2 ml paprika

1½ cups/375 ml hot liquid
   (milk, cream, yogurt,
   sour cream or combination)
2 oz (½ cup)/125 ml
   shredded cheese, optional

Food Processor Directions for Preparing Custard   Insert steel blade in food processor. Peel onion and cut into chunks. Place in container and process until finely chopped. Place well-drained vegetable pieces in container and process, along with onion, until mixture is finely chopped. Add eggs, salt and paprika, and process until smooth. Combine mixture with hot liquid and cheese. Pour into a well-greased large mold or into 6 small individual molds. Bake at 350° F (180° C) 45 minutes for large mold and 30 minutes for individual ones. Custard is done when knife inserted near center comes out clean.

Microwave Oven Directions for Cooking Custard   Place in microwave oven and cook on medium setting 10 minutes.   YIELD: 6 servings

FRESH VEGETABLES

Artichokes   P A R E V E

Microwave Oven Directions   Wash artichokes, but do not trim. Carefully check weight. Place one upside down in glass measuring cup or arrange several in a glass bowl. Cover with plastic wrap. Cook on high setting 1 minute per ounce (30 grams). Allow to stand a few minutes after cooking, then uncover and turn measuring cup over to remove artichoke to serving dish. Trim. Serve hot or cold.

Conventional Directions   Cut off stem of the artichoke. Pull off bottom row of tough leaves and cut off sharp tips from remaining leaves, using a knife or scissors. Place artichoke in a saucepan with 1 inch (2.5 cm) boiling salted water. Cook, covered, for 35 to 45 minutes or until leaves pull out easily. Drain and serve.   YIELD: Allow 1 artichoke per serving

---

Asparagus   P A R E V E

Microwave Oven Directions   Wash asparagus and break away hard, fibrous part of the stalk. Weigh asparagus. Wrap in plastic wrap and place on paper (or place asparagus in a glass dish and cover top of dish with plastic wrap). Cook in microwave oven 10 minutes per pound (500 grams) on high setting. Allow to stand a few minutes before serving.

Conventional Directions   Wash asparagus and break away hard, fibrous part of stalk (may be used in soup). Tie asparagus in serving bunches with thread or string. Place, standing upright, in a deep saucepan with 1 inch (2.5 cm) boiling salted water. Cover and cook over medium heat 12 to 15 minutes, or until tender.   YIELD: Allow 3 to 5 spears per serving

---

Beets   P A R E V E

Microwave Oven Directions   Weigh beets on a kitchen scale. Place in glass dish and cover with plastic wrap. Cook beets 7 minutes per pound (500 grams). After cooking, the beets may be easily peeled, then sliced, quartered, chopped or cut into julienne strips for serving. Serve hot or cold.

Conventional Directions   Cut tops from beets, leaving short stems. Wash well. Place beets in a saucepan with 1 inch (2.5 cm) of boiling salted water. Cover pot and cook until beets are tender, about 1 hour. When beets are done, cool slightly and slip off the skins. Serve as in basic recipe.

YIELD: 3 servings per pound (500 grams)

Pickled Beets   PAREVE

2 to 2½ lbs/1 kilo beets   1 tsp/5 ml mustard seed
1 cup/250 ml cider vinegar   ½ tsp/2 ml whole allspice
1 cup/250 ml water   ½ tsp/2 ml whole cloves
1 cup/250 ml sugar   1 small stick cinnamon
½ tsp/2 ml salt

Microwave Oven Directions Wash beets and place in glass baking dish. Cover dish with plastic wrap and cook on high setting 15 to 18 minutes, or until tender. Set aside to cool.

In large glass mixing bowl, combine vinegar and water. Cover and place in microwave oven. Bring to a boil on high setting. Stir in sugar, salt and spices. Cook on high setting 1 minute, or until sugar is dissolved.

Peel cooled beets, slice and add to hot liquid. Refrigerate 12 hours or overnight to blend flavors.

Conventional Directions Cut tops from beets, leaving short stems, but do not peel. Wash well. Place beets in a saucepan with 1 inch (2.5 cm) boiling salted water. Cover pot and cook until beets are tender, about 1 hour. Cool slightly, then peel.

In saucepan, combine vinegar, water, salt, sugar and spices. Bring to a boil and boil for 5 minutes. Add sliced, cooked beets and simmer for 15 minutes. Chill beets and liquid in refrigerator overnight.   YIELD: 6 servings

---

Broccoli   PAREVE

Microwave Oven Directions Wash broccoli well and weigh on kitchen scale. Cut slashes in bottom of stalks. Wrap in plastic wrap and place on paper plate (or arrange broccoli in glass serving dish and cover with plastic wrap). Cook on high setting 7 minutes per pound (500 grams). After cooking, the tough part of the stem may be used in a puree or diced and used in a salad. Season to taste. Serve broccoli hot or cold.

Conventional Directions Trim broccoli by removing large leaves and tough part of stalk. Cut slashes in bottom of stalk. Place broccoli in a saucepan with 1 inch (2.5 cm) boiling salted water. Cook, covered, until barely tender, about 10 to 12 minutes. Broccoli tastes best when steamed to the tender-crisp stage. Drain and serve.   YIELD: 3 or 4 servings per pound (500 grams)

Brussels Sprouts   P A R E V E

Microwave Oven Directions   Wash Brussels sprouts, cut off stem ends and weigh on a kitchen scale. Place in a glass dish and cover dish with plastic wrap. Cook on high setting in microwave oven 6 minutes per pound (500 grams). Season to taste before serving.

Conventional Directions   Wash and trim Brussels sprouts. Steam in about 1 inch (2.5 cm) boiling salted water. Cook, covered, until barely tender, about 10 minutes. Drain and serve.   YIELD: 4 or 5 servings per pound (500 grams)

Cabbage   P A R E V E

Microwave Oven Directions   Remove outer leaves from a head of cabbage. Wash cabbage and weigh. Cabbage may be cooked whole, quartered or shredded. Place in a deep glass bowl and cover top of bowl with plastic wrap. Cook on high setting 5 minutes per pound. Serve hot or cold.

Conventional Directions   Remove outer leaves from a head of cabbage and wash well. Cut head in half. Boil a large pot of water and cook cabbage, uncovered, until tender crisp, about 15 minutes. Drain. Serve hot or cold.

YIELD: 4 or 5 servings per pound (500 grams)

Cabbage with Sweet and Sour Sauce   P A R E V E

1 medium head red cabbage   ⅓ cup/75 ml brown sugar
3 tart apples   1 tsp/5 ml salt
1 cup/250 ml boiling water   1 tsp/5 ml cornstarch
⅓ cup/75 ml lemon juice

Crock Pot Directions   Shred cabbage and place in crock pot. Quarter and core unpeeled apples, cut in thin slices and add to cabbage. Combine remaining ingredients, except cornstarch, and pour over cabbage. Cover and cook on low setting 5 to 6 hours or longer. Turn setting to high. Dissolve cornstarch in a small amount of cold water and stir into cabbage mixture. Cook 10 minutes longer or until mixture is thickened.   YIELD: 6 servings

Cabbage with Tomato Sauce   PAREVE

1 medium head cabbage	Salt and pepper to taste
2 onions	1 (16-oz)/(454 grams) can
2 Tbsp/25 ml oil	stewed tomatoes
1 Tbsp/15 ml paprika	

Food Processor Directions   Insert shredding disc in food processor. Cut cabbage into wedges and remove core. Guide wedges through feed tube to shred fine. Transfer to mixing bowl. Insert slicing disc in food processor. Peel onions, cut into pieces, and guide through feed tube to slice fine.

Heat oil in a large frying pan and sauté onions and cabbage. Season to taste with paprika, salt and pepper. Add tomatoes. Cover and simmer 20 minutes.   YIELD: 4 to 6 servings

Carrots   PAREVE

Microwave Oven Directions   Wash, peel and trim carrots. Check weight on a kitchen scale. Carrots may be left whole or cut into circles, sticks or dice. Place carrots in a glass dish and cover top of dish with plastic wrap. Cook to a tender-crisp stage on high setting in microwave oven 7 minutes per pound (500 grams). For soft-cooked carrots, cook on a high setting 2 minutes, lower setting to medium and cook 10 minutes longer.

Conventional Directions   Prepare carrots as directed above. Place carrots in a saucepan with 1 inch (2.5 cm) boiling salted water. Cook, covered, until tender, about 30 minutes or more. Drain and serve.

                              YIELD: 5 servings per pound (500 grams)

Orange-Glazed Carrot Coins   PAREVE

1 lb/500 grams carrots, peeled	3 Tbsp/45 ml pareve margarine
2 cups/500 ml water	3 Tbsp/45 ml orange marmalade
¼ tsp/1 ml salt	

Crock Pot Directions   Slice carrots crosswise into thin circles. Combine carrots, water and salt in crock pot. Cover and cook on high setting 2 to 3 hours, until carrots are tender. Drain well.

Stir in remaining ingredients. Cover and cook on high setting 20 to 30 minutes.   YIELD: 5 or 6 servings

Glazed Carrots   PAREVE

1 lb/500 grams carrots, peeled	1 Tbsp/15 ml water
½ cup/125 ml brown sugar	¼ cup/50 ml water (for
2 Tbsp/25 ml pareve margarine	Conventional Directions)

Microwave Oven Directions   Cut carrots lengthwise into long, thin strips. Place carrot strips in a glass dish. Cover with plastic wrap. Cook on high setting 7 minutes.

In glass measuring cup, combine sugar, margarine and water. Cook on high setting until sugar is dissolved and sauce is bubbly, about 1 minute. Pour sauce over carrots. Cover dish with plastic wrap. Return to microwave oven and cook on medium setting 10 minutes or until carrots are glazed.

Conventional Directions   In a saucepan, cook carrots in 1 inch (2.5 cm) boiling salted water until carrots are tender-crisp. Transfer to baking dish. In saucepan, combine sugar, margarine and liquid from carrots. Cook until sugar is dissolved and sauce is bubbly. Pour over carrots. Bake at 350° F (180° C) about 20 minutes, until carrots are glazed.   YIELD: 5 to 6 servings

---

Carrot-Kasha Bake   D A I R Y

2 cups/500 ml carrot chunks
1 large onion, cut in eighths
4 oz/125 grams yellow cheese,
    cut in chunks
4 oz/125 grams white cheese,
    cut in chunks
3 eggs

1 tsp/5 ml salt
½ tsp/2 ml thyme
2 cups/500 ml cooked kasha
1 cup/250 ml fresh mushrooms,
    sliced
2 cups/500 ml water
    (for Blender Directions)

Food Processor Directions   Insert steel blade in food processor. Coarsely chop carrot chunks and onion pieces. Set vegetables aside in mixing bowl. Insert shredding disc and shred cheeses. Add to vegetables. Make a well in center of mixture. Break eggs into well and beat with a fork, then combine with vegetables. Add salt, thyme, kasha and mushrooms, mixing well with fork or spoon. Pour mixture into greased casserole and bake at 350° F (180° C) 45 minutes.

Blender Directions   Place carrot chunks in blender goblet. Cover with water and blend on high setting until carrots are chopped. Drain, saving the water. Transfer carrots to mixing bowl. Place onion pieces in blender goblet along with water from the carrots. Blend on high setting until onion is chopped. Drain (liquid may be saved for soup or gravy). Put onion in mixing bowl with carrots.

Break eggs into blender goblet and add salt and thyme. Start the motor at high speed and drop the cheese chunks, one at a time, into egg mixture. Blend until cheese is grated fine. Pour the cheese-egg mixture into the mixing bowl with the vegetables. Add the kasha and mushrooms and stir well. Pour mixture into a greased casserole. Bake at 350° F (180° C) for 45 minutes.

                                                  YIELD: 6 to 8 servings

Cauliflower   P A R E V E

Microwave Oven Directions   Wash cauliflower and check weight on a kitchen scale. Cauliflower may be cooked whole, with outer leaves left on, or else trimmed and broken into flowerets. Completely cover whole cauliflower with plastic wrap and place on a paper plate. Cook flowerets in a glass bowl covered with plastic wrap. Cook on high setting in microwave oven 7 minutes per pound (500 grams).

Conventional Directions   In a saucepan boil 1 inch (2.5 cm) water with 1 tablespoon (15 ml) lemon juice. Place cauliflower, head up, in boiling liquid. Cook, partially covered, until tender-crisp, about 15 minutes.

YIELD: 1 large head serves 4 to 6

Chick Peas (Nahit)   P A R E V E

1 lb/500 grams chick peas   2 quarts/2 liters or more water
  (garbanzos)   Pepper to taste
2 tsp/10 ml salt

Crock Pot Directions   Soak dried peas overnight in cold water. The next morning drain well. Place in crock pot with salt and water to cover. Cook on low setting 4 to 6 hours or until beans are soft and skin begins to peel.

Drain well. Dry between layers of paper towels. Sprinkle lightly with pepper. Refrigerate several hours. Serve chilled.   YIELD: 10 servings

Succotash   P A R E V E

1½ cups/375 ml corn kernels   ½ tsp/2 ml salt
  (fresh, frozen or canned)   Dash paprika
1½ cups/375 ml cooked lima beans   ¼ cup/50 ml water
  (frozen or canned)   (for Conventional Directions)
2 Tbsp/25 ml pareve margarine

Microwave Oven Directions   In a glass dish combine all ingredients except water. Cover with plastic wrap and cook on high setting in microwave oven until vegetables are hot and margarine is melted, about 5 minutes.

Conventional Directions   Combine all ingredients in a saucepan. Cook over low heat until heated through.   YIELD: 6 servings

If you live in the country, or have access to a fresh-vegetable stand, perhaps you have treated yourself to steaming hot corn, buttered and salted. The sweet taste and tender texture of fresh corn are best when it is cooked within a few hours of being picked.

Corn on the Cob   P A R E V E or D A I R Y

Microwave Oven Directions   Remove the husks and silk from each ear of corn. Wrap each ear in plastic wrap and place in microwave oven. Cook on high setting 2½ minutes per ear. Serve plain or buttered.

Conventional Directions   Place corn in a large saucepan with 1 inch (2.5 cm) boiling water. Cover pan, return to a boil and cook corn 4 to 10 minutes, depending on maturity, or until tender. Corn may also be cooked in a large pot filled with boiling water. Cover pot and cook corn about 5 minutes.

YIELD: Allow 1 ear per serving

Corn Pudding   D A I R Y

1 (16-oz)/(454 grams) can
   corn kernels
2 eggs, slightly beaten
2 Tbsp/25 ml melted butter
1 cup/250 ml hot milk

½ cup/125 ml sour cream
¼ cup/50 ml chopped green pepper
Salt and pepper to taste
4 cups/1 liter hot water

Crock Pot Directions   Combine all ingredients except water. Pour into a greased casserole. Place a metal rack or trivet in bottom of crock pot. Cover casserole securely with foil and place on rack in crock pot. Pour 4 cups (1 liter) hot water around dish. Cover crock pot and cook on high setting 2 to 2½ hours or until pudding is firm.   YIELD: 6 servings

Variation   Make following changes in basic recipe:

Tomato-Corn Pudding   D A I R Y

1 (16-oz)/(454 grams) can
   tomatoes, cut up

1 small onion, minced

Omit milk and sour cream. Add tomatoes and onion when preparing basic recipe.   YIELD: 6 servings

Eggplant   PAREVE

Microwave Oven Directions   Eggplant may be cooked whole, sliced or cubed. Eggplant cooks on high setting in microwave oven, 5 minutes per pound (500 grams).

If eggplant is left whole, prick the outside skin with a fork to allow steam to escape. Place on a paper plate in microwave oven.

If eggplant is to be cooked sliced or cubed, place pieces in a glass baking dish and cover with plastic wrap before placing in microwave oven.

After cooking, eggplant may be mashed and chilled for use in an appetizer or salad (see Chatzelim in Appetizer chapter). Eggplant slices may be fried in oil and served in a sauce. Cubed eggplant may be scalloped or served sprinkled with salt, pepper and bread crumbs (see following recipe) and whole eggplant may be stuffed before cooking.

Conventional Directions   Preheat oven to 400° F (200° C). Wash and dry eggplant and then cut into halves, lengthwise. Season and brush cut portions with melted pareve margarine. Place in a baking dish and cook until tender, about 30 minutes.   YIELD: 1 large eggplant serves 4 to 6

Eggplant Parmesan   DAIRY

2 medium eggplants	½ tsp/2 ml sweet basil
1 Tbsp/15 ml salt	Salt and pepper to taste
1 onion	⅓ cup/75 ml dry red wine,
3 garlic cloves	optional
8 sprigs parsley	2 Tbsp/25 ml flour
2 Tbsp/25 ml oil	4 Tbsp/50 ml oil
2 (16-oz)/(454-gram) cans	1 cup/250 ml shredded
tomatoes	white cheese
2 tsp/10 ml oregano	1 cup/250 ml grated hard cheese

Food Processor Directions   Peel and slice eggplants. Sprinkle lightly with salt and allow to stand 30 minutes.

To prepare the sauce: Insert steel blade in food processor. Peel onion and garlic, cut into chunks and place in the container. Add the parsley. Process until mixture is finely chopped. Heat 2 tablespoons (25 ml) oil in a frying pan. Add onion mixture and sauté until golden. Drain the tomatoes (reserve liquid for soup or beverage) and place in food processor, using steel blade. Process until pureed. Add to frying pan, along with seasonings and wine. Simmer sauce for 25 to 30 minutes.

Rinse the salt from the eggplant and pat dry. Coat the eggplant slices with flour and fry in 4 tablespoons (50 ml) oil until crisp and brown.

Grease a large casserole. Place in it a layer of eggplant slices, cover with tomato sauce and top with some of the cheeses. Continue to layer, using all ingredients and ending with a layer of cheese. Bake at 350° F (180° C) 25 to 30 minutes.   YIELD: 6 servings

---

Israeli Eggplant Casserole   P A R E V E

1 large eggplant/1 kilo	2 Tbsp/25 ml flour
(about 2 lbs)	¼ cup/50 ml oil
1½ tsp/7 ml salt	1 (8-oz)/(227 grams) can
1 large onion	tomato sauce
2 cloves garlic	Salt and pepper, to taste
1 green pepper	Dash cinnamon or allspice

Microwave Oven Directions Peel and slice eggplant. Sprinkle with salt and allow to stand 25 to 30 minutes.

Chop the onion, garlic and green pepper fine and place in a glass mixing bowl. Cover bowl with plastic wrap and place in microwave oven. Cook on high setting 5 minutes or until vegetables are soft.

Rinse the eggplant and pat dry. Coat eggplant slices with flour and fry in hot oil until crisp and brown. Set aside.

Combine tomato sauce, salt, pepper and cinnamon. In a large glass casserole place half the eggplant slices. Cover with onion mixture. Arrange remaining eggplant slices on top and pour tomato sauce over the vegetables. Cover with plastic wrap. Place in microwave oven and cook on high setting 8 minutes, or until eggplant is tender and sauce is bubbly.

Conventional Directions Sauté onion, garlic and green pepper in hot oil. Set aside, then fry eggplant. Assemble casserole as described in basic recipe. Bake in a 350° F (180° C) oven about 30 minutes.   YIELD: 4 to 6 servings

Variations Make the following changes in basic casserole recipe:

Eggplant with Meat   F L E I S H I G

1 lb/500 grams ground beef or lamb

Place ground beef or lamb in glass mixing bowl, along with onion, garlic and green pepper. Cover with wax paper. Place in microwave oven and cook on high setting 7 minutes for beef and 10 minutes for lamb. Crumble meat and drain off excess fat. Assemble casserole as described in basic recipe. Cover with wax paper. Cook on high setting in microwave oven 12 minutes for a beef casserole and 15 minutes for lamb.

Eggplant with Cheese   DAIRY

2 beaten eggs   ½ cup/125 ml cottage cheese
2 tsp/15 ml water   ½ cup/125 ml unflavored yogurt
½ cup/125 ml grated hard cheese   or sour cream

Before frying eggplant slices, dip them in a batter of beaten eggs, water and grated hard cheese. Assemble casserole as described in basic recipe. Top with a mixture of cottage cheese and yogurt. Cover with wax paper and place in microwave oven. Cook on medium setting 10 minutes, or until sauce is bubbly.

YIELD: 4 to 6 servings

Ratatouille is a famous mixed-vegetable dish from France. The vegetable combination (eggplant, green pepper, zucchini, onion and tomatoes) may seem a bit unusual at first, but this dish is delicious and worth a try.

Ratatouille   PAREVE

4 Tbsp/50 ml oil   2½ cups/625 ml peeled
1 cup/250 ml coarsely chopped   diced eggplant
  onions   3 medium zucchini, sliced
2 large garlic cloves, minced   1 (16-oz)/(454 grams) can tomatoes,
2 Tbsp/25 ml chopped parsley   cut up
2 green peppers, coarsely chopped   Salt and pepper to taste

Microwave Oven Directions In a large glass casserole combine oil, onions, garlic, parsley and green peppers. Cover with plastic wrap and place in microwave oven. Cook on high setting 5 minutes or until vegetables are soft. Add eggplant and zucchini. Cover with plastic wrap and return dish to microwave oven. Cook on high setting 8 minutes or until zucchini has softened.

Add remaining ingredients. Cover with plastic wrap. Cook in microwave oven 5 minutes on high setting, until sauce boils. Reduce setting to medium and cook 10 minutes longer or until vegetables are tender.

Crock Pot Directions In a frying pan heat oil. Sauté onions and garlic. Add parsley and cook until vegetables are soft. Combine all ingredients in crock pot. Cover and cook on low setting 6 to 8 hours.

Conventional Directions In a very large frying pan, heat oil. Sauté onions and garlic. In the frying pan arrange vegetables in layers, first onion mixture, then green peppers, eggplant, zucchini, tomatoes, salt, pepper and parsley. Cook, covered, over low heat for 30 to 45 minutes, until vegetables are tender. Remove cover the last 15 minutes to reduce the sauce to desired thickness. Serve hot or cold.   YIELD: 6 to 8 servings

Cooked green beans may be mixed with any of the following to serve: cooked chopped onion, sautéed sliced mushrooms, toasted slivered almonds or sliced water chestnuts.

Green Beans   P A R E V E

Microwave Oven Directions Wash and trim green beans and weigh on a kitchen scale. Young green beans may be cooked whole; older ones may be cut in 1-inch (2.5 cm) pieces crosswise, or cut through the center lengthwise (French style). Place beans in a glass dish, adding 2 tablespoons (25 ml) water for each pound (500 grams) of beans. Cover with plastic wrap. Place in microwave oven and cook on high setting 12 minutes per pound (500 grams). Season with salt and pepper to serve.

Conventional Directions Wash and trim green beans. Place in a saucepan, add ½ cup (125 ml) boiling salted water and cover tightly. Simmer until barely tender, about 20 minutes. Drain.

YIELD: 5 or 6 servings per pound (500 grams)

French-Style Green Beans with Mushrooms   P A R E V E

1 lb/500 grams green beans
¼ lb/125 grams (or more)
   fresh mushrooms
2 cups/500 ml water

Salt and pepper to taste
2 Tbsp/25 ml olive oil
Dash vinegar

Food Processor Directions To slice green beans in the "French cut": Trim the green beans and cut into 2-inch (5-cm) slices (to fit width of food processor feed tube). Insert the slicing disc in food processor. Arrange green beans sideways to fill the feed tube. Start the motor and use the pusher to gently guide the green beans through the feed tube to slice thin.

To slice mushrooms: Insert slicing disc in food processor. Pack the feed tube with mushrooms, laying the mushrooms straight down for round slices or laying sideways for "hammerhead" slices. When the mushrooms are arranged in place, start the motor and use the pusher to gently guide the mushrooms through the feed tube to slice thin.

To cook green beans in the French manner, cook sliced green beans in boiling salted water until tender-crisp. Beans may be refrigerated at this point for later cooking.

Just before serving, sauté the mushrooms in olive oil. When mushrooms are soft, season with salt and pepper. Add green beans and sauté with mushrooms until beans are hot. Add a few drops of vinegar before serving.

YIELD: 5 to 6 servings

Italian-Style Green Beans   PAREVE

1 small onion, chopped
2 Tbsp/25 ml olive oil
1 lb/500 grams cooked green beans,
   cut in 1-inch (2.5-cm) pieces

1 (8-oz)/(227 grams) can tomato
   sauce
2 garlic cloves, minced
Salt and pepper to taste
½ tsp/2 ml oregano

Microwave Oven Directions   In glass baking dish combine chopped onion and olive oil. Cover with plastic wrap and place in microwave oven. Cook on high setting 3 minutes, or until onion is soft.

Add remaining ingredients to cooked onion and stir well. Cover dish with plastic wrap. Cook in microwave oven on high setting 3 minutes, or until sauce boils and green beans are hot.

Conventional Directions   Sauté onion in olive oil, add green beans and cook until beans are hot. Add remaining ingredients and simmer 10 minutes longer.   YIELD: 5 to 6 servings

Green Peas   PAREVE

Microwave Oven Directions   Shell and wash fresh peas. Check weight on a kitchen scale. Place peas in a baking dish with 2 tablespoons (25 ml) water per pound (500 grams) of peas. Cover with plastic wrap and place in microwave oven. Cook on high setting 6 minutes per pound (500 grams).

Conventional Directions   Place peas in a saucepan with ¼ inch (1 cm) boiling water. Add ½ teaspoon (2 ml) lemon juice and a pinch of sugar. Simmer 10 to 15 minutes, until tender.   YIELD: 1 lb (500 grams) serves 4

Green Pepper   PAREVE

Microwave Oven Directions   Wash green pepper, remove stem, seeds and fibrous portions. Check weight on a kitchen scale. Pepper may further be cut into strips or chopped to use in recipes. Place in a glass dish, cover with plastic wrap and place in microwave oven. Cook on high setting 10 minutes per pound (500 grams). Serve hot.

Conventional Directions   Wash green pepper, remove seeds and membranes and cut into desired shapes. Boil 1 inch (2.5 cm) water in a saucepan. Drop pepper into boiling water and cook until tender.

                                      YIELD: 1 large green pepper serves 2

Lima Beans   P A R E V E

Microwave Oven Directions   Shell and wash fresh lima beans. Check weight on
a kitchen scale. Place in a glass dish with 2 tablespoons (25 ml) water for
each pound (500 grams) of beans. Cover with plastic wrap. Cook on high
setting in microwave oven 12 minutes per pound (500 grams). Serve plain or
with sauce.

Conventional Directions   Place shelled lima beans in a saucepan. Add 1 inch
(2.5 cm) boiling salted water. Cook covered, until beans are tender, about 35
minutes.   YIELD: 1 pound (500 grams) serves 4

Onions require a relatively longer amount of cooking time than most other
vegetables when cooking in the microwave oven. For this reason, they are
often precooked before being combined with other ingredients in a recipe.

Onions   P A R E V E

Microwave Oven Directions   To sauté onions: Chop or slice the desired amount
of onion and place in a glass dish. Oil or margarine may be added for flavor.
Cover dish with plastic wrap and place in microwave oven. Cook on high
setting about 3 to 4 minutes per onion.

To cook whole onions: Peel onions and check weight on a kitchen scale.
With a knife, make a slash in the side of each onion, to allow steam to
escape. Place in a glass dish. cover with plastic wrap and place in microwave
oven. Cook on high setting 10 minutes per pound (500 grams).

Crock Pot Directions   Place onions in crock pot. Add 1 cup (250 ml) water and
cook on low setting 4 to 5 hours. Onions have a lovely texture and flavor
when cooked this way.

Conventional Directions   Boil onions by placing in a pot of boiling salted
water. Cover and cook 30 to 40 minutes for whole onions, or 20 minutes for
smaller or quartered onions.   YIELD: 1 large onion serves 1 to 2

Baked Potatoes   PAREVE

Microwave Oven Directions   Wash and dry potatoes and carefully check weight on a kitchen scale. Pierce the skin with a fork to allow steam to escape. Place potatoes on a paper towel in microwave oven. If cooking just a few potatoes, allow 1 minute per ounce (30 grams) cooking time at high setting. If total weight of potatoes is between 1 and 2 pounds (500 and 1000 grams), allow about 45 seconds cooking time per ounce. If total weight exceeds 2 pounds (1 kilo), allow 30 seconds per ounce.

Crock Pot Directions   Scrub potatoes but do not dry. Place in crock pot, cover and cook on low setting 6 to 8 hours or until potatoes are tender. There is no need to add liquid.

Conventional Directions   Wash and dry potatoes. Rub surface lightly with oil or pareve margarine. Bake at 425° F (220° C) 45 minutes to 1 hour, or until potatoes are soft. Halfway through cooking time, pierce the skins with a fork to allow steam to escape.   YIELD: Allow 1 potato per serving

---

Mashed Potatoes   PAREVE, DAIRY or
                                                  FLEISHIG

5 large cooked potatoes   2 Tbsp/25 ml pareve margarine
⅓ cup/75 ml hot liquid (vegetable   or butter or chicken fat
   or chicken broth, milk   1 tsp/5 ml salt, or to taste
   or nondairy creamer)   ¼ tsp/1 ml pepper, or to taste

Mixer Directions   Peel cooked potatoes and, while still very hot, break into chunks and place in mixer bowl. Attach beaters and begin mixing at low speed. As potatoes become smooth, gradually increase to medium speed and add remaining ingredients. Continue mixing until liquid is absorbed and potatoes are fluffy.   YIELD: 4 to 6 servings

Variations   Make the following changes in basic Mashed Potato recipe:

Cheese Potatoes   DAIRY

½ cup/125 ml grated cheese

Add grated cheese to mashed potatoes. Sprinkle additional cheese over the top. Bake at 350° F (180° C) until cheese is melted.

Potato Puffs   PAREVE

2 eggs, separated   ½ tsp/2 ml paprika
Salt and pepper to taste   2 Tbsp/25 ml melted margarine
1 Tbsp/15 ml grated onion

Add egg yolks to Mashed Potatoes. Season to taste with salt, pepper, grated
onion, and paprika. Beat 2 or more egg whites until stiff and fold into potato
mixture. Drop mixture by spoonfuls onto a greased baking sheet. Brush tops
with melted margarine. Bake at 350° F (180° C) about 20 minutes or until
puffed and browned.

Potato Patties   PAREVE

1 egg   ¼ cup/50 ml pareve margarine

Beat one egg and combine with seasoned Mashed Potatoes. Shape mixture
into 4 patties. Melt pareve margarine in hot frying pan and brown patties on
both sides.   YIELD: 4 to 6 servings

Scalloped Potatoes   DAIRY

6 potatoes, peeled   ¼ cup/50 ml milk
1 medium onion or 2 green onions   ¼ cup/50 ml fine, dry bread
1 (10¾-oz)/(305 grams) can   crumbs
   cream of mushroom soup

Food Processor Directions Trim potatoes or cut in halves so that potatoes will
fit through feed tube in cover of food processor. Insert slicing disc. Use the
pusher to guide the potato pieces through the feed tube to slice thin. Set
potatoes aside. Insert steel blade. Cut the onion into chunks and place in
container, processing until finely chopped.

Microwave Oven Directions In a 3-quart (3-liter) glass casserole layer potatoes
and onions. (Use an extra-large dish to allow room for the milk to boil.)
Combine soup and milk and pour over vegetables. Cover dish with plastic
wrap and place in microwave oven. Cook on high setting 15 minutes or until
potatoes are soft and sauce is bubbly. Sprinkle crumbs over top. Cook on
high setting 30 seconds or until crumbs are hot.

Crock Pot Directions Slice potatoes, chop onion and combine in crock pot.
Pour soup and milk over top. Sprinkle with bread crumbs. Cover and cook
on low setting 7 to 9 hours.

Conventional Directions Grease a large casserole. Arrange ingredients as described in basic recipe. Sprinkle with bread crumbs. Bake at 350° F (180° C)
for 1½ hours.   YIELD: 6 servings

Baked Sweet Potatoes   PAREVE

Microwave Oven Directions   Wash and dry potatoes, then check weight on a kitchen scale. Pierce skin with a fork to allow steam to escape. Place potatoes on a paper towel in microwave oven. Cook on high setting 1 minute per ounce (30 grams). After cooking, wrap potatoes in foil and allow to stand 5 to 10 minutes.

Crock Pot Directions   Scrub potatoes but do not dry. Pierce skin and place in crock pot, cover and cook on low setting 5 to 6 hours or until tender. There is no need to add liquid.

Conventional Directions   Wash and dry potatoes. Rub surface lightly with oil or pareve margarine. Bake at 425° F (220° C) 45 minutes to 1 hour, or until potatoes are soft. Halfway through cooking time, pierce the skins with a fork to allow steam to escape.   YIELD: 1 potato per serving

---

Candied Sweet Potatoes   PAREVE

6 sweet potatoes, cooked	2 Tbsp/25 ml orange juice
Salt and pepper to taste	1 Tbsp/15 ml grated orange peel
4 Tbsp/50 ml pareve margarine	¼ tsp/1 ml nutmeg
⅓ cup/75 ml brown sugar	¼ tsp/1 ml cinnamon

Microwave Oven Directions   Peel and slice potatoes. Arrange slices in a glass baking dish. Sprinkle with salt and pepper. Set aside.

Place margarine and brown sugar in a small glass bowl. Place in microwave oven and cook on high setting 1 minute or until melted. Stir in remaining ingredients, blending well. Pour sugar mixture over potatoes. Cover dish with plastic wrap. Place in microwave oven and cook on high setting 3 minutes. Reduce setting to medium and cook 12 minutes longer.

Crock Pot Directions   Peel and slice potatoes and arrange slices in crock pot. Melt margarine. Combine with remaining ingredients and pour over top. Cover and cook on high setting 30 to 45 minutes.

Conventional Directions   Peel and slice potatoes and arrange slices in a greased baking dish. Melt margarine and combine with remaining ingredients. Pour over top of potatoes. Bake at 375° F (190° C) 20 minutes.   YIELD: 6 servings

Sauerkraut Special   P A R E V E

2 (16-oz)/(454-gram) cans   2 Tbsp/25 ml pareve margarine
  sauerkraut   2 tsp/10 ml sugar
1 small head cabbage, shredded   1 Tbsp/15 ml vinegar
3 tart apples, sliced and cored   Salt and pepper to taste

Crock Pot Directions Combine all ingredients in crock pot. Cover and cook
on low setting 3 to 5 hours.   YIELD: 8 servings

Variation Make the following changes in basic Sauerkraut Special recipe:

Sauerkraut with Onions   P A R E V E

1 onion, minced
1 Tbsp/15 ml caraway seeds

Omit apples. Add onion when preparing basic recipe. Sprinkle with caraway
seeds before serving.   YIELD: 8 servings

Spinach (Other Greens)   P A R E V E

Microwave Oven Directions Trim and wash spinach leaves. Put into a glass
bowl, cover top of bowl with plastic wrap and place in microwave oven.
Cook on high setting 4 minutes per pound (500 grams).

    Other greens, such as beet greens, collards and kale, are cooked in the
same manner and for the same length of time. Cook mustard greens and
Swiss chard 5 minutes per pound.

Conventional Directions Wash and trim spinach or other greens. Shake off
excess water, but do not dry. Place in a saucepan with 1 tablespoon (15 ml)
pareve margarine. Cook over high heat until steam appears. Reduce heat,
cover and simmer 5 to 6 minutes or until tender.

YIELD: 1 pound (500 grams) serves 3

Stuffed Acorn Squash

1 large acorn squash
1 cup/250 ml cooked rice
1 Tbsp/15 ml chopped parsley
1 (4-oz)/(113 grams) can mushroom
  pieces, drained

Salt and pepper to taste
1 Tbsp/15 ml pareve margarine
  (for Crock Pot Directions)

Microwave Oven Directions   Weigh squash on a kitchen scale. Pierce with a knife to allow an escape for steam. Place on a paper towel in microwave oven. Cook on high setting 8 minutes per pound (500 grams).

After cooking, the squash may be kept warm for as long as 30 to 45 minutes by wrapping in foil. Cut and stuff when ready to serve.

To stuff squash: Cut in half and remove seeds. Combine rice with parsley, mushrooms, salt and pepper, and stuff into cavity. Place stuffed squash on a glass dish and return to microwave oven. Cover with wax paper and cook on high setting 3 minutes or until filling is hot.

Crock Pot Directions   Cut squash in half and remove seeds. Sprinkle cavity with salt and pepper. Place squash in crock pot, cover and cook on low setting 3 to 5 hours or until tender. Remove squash from crock pot and place, cavity side up, on an oven-proof platter. Brush inside of squash with melted pareve margarine. Stuff cavity with rice mixture. Bake at 400° F (200° C) 15 minutes or until rice is hot.

Conventional Directions   Cut squash in half and remove seeds. Bake at 375° F (190° C) 1 hour or until soft. Brush cavity with melted pareve margarine and stuff with rice mixture. Return to oven 15 minutes, or until rice is hot.

YIELD: 2 to 4 servings

Summer Squash

2 to 2½ lbs/1 kilo summer squash
  (any variety)
1 large onion, chopped

4 Tbsp/50 ml butter
  or pareve margarine
Salt and pepper to taste

SAUCE

1 (10¾-oz)/(305 grams) can cream
  of celery soup
½ cup/125 ml liquid
  (from cooking squash)

½ cup/125 ml finely
  chopped celery
2 Tbsp/25 ml butter
Salt and pepper to taste
2 Tbsp/25 ml grated hard cheese

Crock Pot Directions Slice squash and place in bottom of crock pot. Sprinkle the chopped onion over squash. Dot with butter and season with salt and pepper. Cover and cook on low setting 3 to 5 hours or until squash is tender. Drain and reserve excess liquid for sauce.

To make sauce: Sauté celery in butter, combine with soup, ½ cup (125 ml) liquid from squash and seasonings. Pour sauce mixture over squash. Cover and cook on high setting 15 to 30 minutes or until sauce is hot. To serve, sprinkle with grated cheese. YIELD: 6 servings

---

Glazed Butternut Squash P A R E V E

1 medium-size butternut squash
¼ cup/50 ml melted
   pareve margarine
⅓ cup/75 ml brown sugar
¼ tsp/1 ml nutmeg

Dash salt
1 tsp/5 ml water
1 cup/250 ml hot water
   (for Crock Pot Directions)

Microwave Oven Directions Weigh squash on a kitchen scale. Pierce with a knife to allow steam to escape. Place on a paper towel in microwave oven and cook 8 minutes per pound (500 grams) on high setting.

In a small glass bowl combine margarine and sugar. Cook on high setting in microwave oven 1 minute or until melted; stir until well blended. Add nutmeg, salt and 1 teaspoon (5 ml) water.

Cut squash in half and remove seeds. Brush sugar mixture over cavity side of squash. Return to microwave oven. Cook on high setting 2 to 3 minutes or until glaze is bubbly.

Crock Pot Directions Cut squash in half and remove seeds. Place a metal rack or trivet in bottom of crock pot. Pour in 1 cup (250 ml) hot water and place squash on rack. Cover pot and cook on high setting 2 to 3 hours or until squash is tender. In a small bowl, combine remaining ingredients. Place squash on broiler pan and brush cavity side with glaze. Place under broiler several minutes, until glaze is bubbly.

Conventional Directions Cut squash in half and remove seeds. Place in a casserole, add glaze mixture and cover tightly with casserole lid. Bake at 375° F (190° C) 1 hour or until squash is tender. YIELD: 6 servings

Turnips   PAREVE

2 to 2½ lb/1 kilo turnips,   4 Tbsp/50 ml pareve margarine
  peeled and quartered   3 cups or more/750 ml water
2 Tbsp/25 ml minced onion   (for Crock Pot or
1 tsp/5 ml salt   Conventional Directions)
¼ tsp/1 ml pepper

Microwave Oven Directions Place turnips and onion in a glass bowl. Cover
with plastic wrap and cook on high setting in microwave oven 15 to 18
minutes, or until turnips are tender. Allow to stand a few minutes. Mash
well and season with salt, pepper and margarine. Whip until fluffy.

Crock Pot Directions Place turnips, onion and salt in crock pot. Cover with
water. Cover crock pot and cook on low setting 6 to 8 hours, or until turnips
are tender. Drain. Mash the turnips, adding margarine and salt and pepper
to taste. Whip until fluffy.

Conventional Directions Place turnips in a pot with 2 cups (500 ml) boiling
salted water. Cover and cook for 30 minutes or until tender. Drain well.
Mash and add remaining ingredients. Whip until fluffy.

YIELD: 4 to 6 servings

Zucchini   PAREVE

3 lbs/1500 grams or 1½ kilos   ¼ tsp/1 ml paprika
  zucchini   ¼ tsp/1 ml pepper
3 Tbsp/45 ml pareve margarine   Dash dry mustard
1 tsp//5 ml garlic salt   ½ tsp/2 ml Worcestershire sauce
                                    3 Tbsp/45 ml dry pareve bread
                                      crumbs

Microwave Oven Directions Cut zucchini into 1-inch (2.5-cm) chunks and
place in a large glass casserole. Dot with pareve margarine. Combine garlic
salt, spices and Worcestershire sauce and sprinkle over zucchini. Cover with
plastic wrap and cook on high setting in microwave oven 18 to 20 minutes or
until zucchini is tender. To serve, sprinkle with bread crumbs.

Crock Pot Directions Cut zucchini into 1-inch (2.5-cm) chunks and place in
crock pot. Add remaining ingredients, cover and cook on high setting 2 to 3
hours, or until zucchini is tender.

Conventional Directions Cut zucchini into 1-inch (2.5-cm) chunks. Combine
all ingredients and bake in a covered casserole at 350° F (180° C) 50 to 60
minutes or until zucchini is tender.   YIELD: 6 servings

Cheesy Zucchini   DAIRY

2 lbs/1 kilo zucchini
3 Tbsp/45 ml butter
4 eggs
1 cup/250 ml shredded cheese

¼ cup/50 ml grated hard cheese
1 cup/250 ml crisp croutons
(see recipe in Soup Mates
chapter)

Microwave Oven Directions Wash zucchini and cut into 1-inch (2.5-cm) chunks. Place in a glass casserole. Add butter. Cover with plastic wrap and place in microwave oven. Cook on high setting 5 minutes.

Beat together the eggs and cheeses and combine with zucchini. Cover with plastic wrap and return to microwave oven. Cook on medium setting 10 minutes.

Uncover, and sprinkle croutons evenly over top. Cook, uncovered, in microwave oven on medium setting 2 minutes or until croutons are hot.

YIELD: 6 servings

Israeli-Style Zucchini in Tomato Sauce   PAREVE

1 large onion, chopped
2 garlic cloves, minced
3 Tbsp/45 ml olive oil
2 lbs/1 kilo zucchini

2 (8-oz)/(227-gram) cans tomato
sauce
1 tsp/5 ml salt, or to taste
¼ tsp/1 ml pepper
¼ tsp/1 ml cumin

Microwave Oven Directions In a glass casserole, place onion, garlic and oil. Cover with plastic wrap and place in microwave oven. Cook on high setting 3 minutes.

Cut zucchini into 1-inch (2.5-cm) chunks and add to onion mixture. Combine remaining ingredients and pour over vegetables. Cover with plastic wrap, place in microwave oven, and cook on high setting 18 minutes or until zucchini is tender.

Crock Pot Directions Heat olive oil in a frying pan and sauté onion and garlic. Place onion mixture in crock pot. Cut zucchini into 1-inch (2.5-cm) chunks and place in crock pot along with remaining ingredients. Stir to combine. Cover and cook on high setting 2 or 3 hours, until zucchini is tender.

Conventional Directions Heat olive oil in a frying pan and sauté onion and garlic. Cut zucchini into 1-inch (2.5-cm) chunks and add to onion mixture in frying pan. Sauté lightly. Add remaining ingredients. Bring to a boil, reduce heat. Cover pan and simmer very gently 1 hour.   YIELD: 6 servings

PREPARING VEGETABLES FOR STUFFING

Stuffed vegetables make a very nourishing and tasty main course. Following are suggestions for preparing 7 different vegetables for stuffing as well as 2 recipes for a stuffing mixture, one made with cheese and the other made with vegetables. Any of the recipes in the Savory Stuffings chapter can be used for vegetable stuffing, and almost any pareve recipe can be made fleishig with 1 pound (500 grams) ground beef or lamb added to the stuffing mixture and cooked inside the vegetable.

Stuffed Artichokes   P A R E V E

Conventional Directions   Remove stem from artichoke. Cut artichoke in half crosswise, about 2 inches (5 cm) from the base. With a sharp knife scrape out and remove the choke, the inner hairlike part of the artichoke. Pack the prepared filling mixture tightly into the hollowed-out artichoke. Place stuffed artichokes in a baking dish with ½ cup (125 ml) water or sauce, and cook in a 350° F (180° C) oven 45 minutes or until artichoke is softened and leaves pull out easily. Allow 1 artichoke per serving.

Stuffed Cabbage   P A R E V E

(See additional Stuffed Cabbage recipes in Meat chapter.)
Conventional Directions   Remove core from a large head of cabbage. Place the cabbage in a large pot of boiling water until the outer leaves are softened and pliable. Place a spoonful of prepared filling mixture on each cabbage leaf. Roll the leaf from the stem end, tucking in the sides. Place in a baking dish with ½ cup (125 ml) water or sauce. Cover and cook at 350° F (180° C) 45 minutes or until filling is cooked. One large cabbage yields about 10 to 12 cabbage rolls (4 to 6 servings).

Stuffed Eggplant   P A R E V E

Cut the eggplant in half lengthwise and scoop out the fleshy pulp, leaving a ½-inch (2-cm) shell. If desired, the eggplant pulp may be finely chopped and added to filling mixture. Pack the prepared filling mixture tightly into eggplant cavity. Place eggplant in a baking dish with ½ cup (125 ml) water or sauce. Bake at 350°F (180° C) 45 minutes or until eggplant is tender and filling is cooked. One large stuffed eggplant serves 4 to 6.

Stuffed Onion   P A R E V E

Cook whole peeled onions in boiling water until softened but not completely cooked. Allow to cool, then remove the centers, leaving about 3 rings of onion forming a hollow shell. Pack the prepared filling mixture tightly into the onion cavity. Place onion in a baking dish with ½ cup (125 ml) water or sauce. Bake at 350° F (180° C) 45 minutes or until filling is cooked. Allow 2 onions per serving.

Stuffed Tomatoes   P A R E V E

Cut tomatoes in half crosswise. Carefully remove the pulp and seeds, leaving ½ inch (2 cm) of tomato shell. Pack the prepared filling mixture tightly into the tomato cavity. Place the tomato halves in a baking dish with ½ cup (125 ml) water or sauce. Bake at 350° F (180° C) 45 minutes or until filling is cooked. Allow 1 large tomato per serving.

Stuffed Green Pepper   P A R E V E

Cut green pepper in half lengthwise and remove seeds and membranes. Pack the prepared filling mixture tightly into the cavity. Place in a baking dish with ½ cup (125 ml) water or sauce. Bake at 350° F (180° C) 45 minutes or until pepper is soft. Allow 1 green pepper per serving.

Stuffed Zucchini   P A R E V E

Cut zucchini in halves lengthwise. Scoop out the centers and cook zucchini in boiling water 10 minutes, until softened but not cooked. If desired, zucchini pulp may be chopped fine and added to filling mixture. Pack filling mixture tightly into zucchini cavity. Place zucchini in a baking dish with ½ cup (125 ml) water or sauce. Bake at 350° F (180° C) 45 minutes or until zucchini is tender and filling is cooked. Allow 2 zucchini halves per serving.

Vegetables Stuffed with Cheese   DAIRY

2 oz/60 grams white cheese,   ½ cup/125 ml cottage cheese
  cut into chunks   ½ tsp/2 ml oregano
4 sprigs fresh parsley   Salt and pepper to taste
¾ cup/175 ml fine dry bread   3 fresh tomatoes, coarsely chopped
  crumbs   Vegetables for stuffing
1 egg   (see previous explanation)

Blender Directions Start blender motor running on high speed. Drop in cheese chunks and blend until cheese is grated. Add fresh parsley and blend until finely chopped. Reduce speed to low. Add bread crumbs, egg, cottage cheese and seasonings, blending until mixture is smooth and thick.

Place chopped tomatoes in bottom of a shallow baking dish. Tightly pack filling mixture into prepared vegetables and place vegetables on top of tomatoes. Cover tightly and bake at 350° F (180° C) 45 minutes, or until vegetables are soft and filling is hot.   YIELD: 4 servings

---

Vegetables Stuffed with Vegetables   PAREVE

FILLING

1 to 2 cups/250 to 500 grams   1 tomato
  cooked rice, kasha or barley   1 (16-oz)/(454 grams) can corn
1 onion   kernels, drained
2 stalks celery   2 eggs, beaten
1 green pepper   Salt and pepper to taste
6 mushrooms   Vegetables for stuffing
      (see previous explanation)

SAUCE

2 (4-oz)/(227-gram) cans   ½ tsp/2 ml black pepper,
  tomato sauce   or to taste
½ tsp/2 ml cumin   Dash cinnamon
      Dash salt

Food Processor Directions To prepare filling: Cook rice and set aside to cool. Insert steel blade in food processor. Peel onion and cut in chunks. Cut celery into chunks. Remove stem and seeds from green pepper and cut into chunks. Place vegetables in container and process until coarsely chopped. Add to rice.

Insert slicing disc in food processor. Fill feed tube with mushrooms and use the pusher to guide onto slicing disc to slice thin. Cut tomato into quarters and guide through the feed tube to slice fine. Add to rice and vegetable mixture. Add corn and beaten eggs to vegetables. Blend well and season to taste. Tightly pack filling mixture into prepared vegetables. Place in a baking dish and set aside.

To prepare sauce: Combine all ingredients, tasting to correct seasonings. Pour sauce over stuffed vegetables. Cover baking dish tightly and bake at 350° F (180° C) 45 minutes or until vegetables are tender.

YIELD: 6 servings

For some reason, known only to a 5-year-old, my middle child decided that this dish is a "vegetable hamburger," and he insists on eating his between two pieces of bread with a pickle and lots of ketchup.

Vegetarian Patties   P A R E V E

4 eggs
1 (10-oz)/(283 grams) package
    frozen vegetables
    (corn, peas, peas and carrots,
    mixed vegetables, etc.)
1 cup/250 ml pareve bread crumbs
    or matzah meal

½ cup/125 ml onion,
    finely chopped
¼ cup/50 ml celery, finely chopped
½ tsp/2 ml garlic powder
2 Tbsp/25 ml parsley
Salt and pepper to taste
4 Tbsp or more/50 ml oil

Blender Directions Break eggs into blender goblet and blend on low to mix. Add frozen vegetables (yes, frozen!) and blend on low until finely chopped, stopping the blender to stir contents with a rubber scraper as needed. Pour mixture into a serving bowl and add remaining ingredients, mixing until mixture forms a very thick batter. Fry by tablespoonfuls in oil until golden brown on both sides.

YIELD: 4 servings

Variation

Vegetable Kugel   P A R E V E

Prepare batter as described in basic recipe. Pour into a greased 1½-quart baking dish. Bake at 350° F (180° C) 30 minutes or until lightly browned.

YIELD: 4 servings

SALADS

A variety of salad recipes are featured in this chapter, including egg, fruit, imitation-jel, poultry and vegetable salads. In addition, there is a section on quantity salads which serve 25 or more.

The food processor is the outstanding appliance in this chapter because it can make the preparation of almost any salad easier and faster. Prepare food for the food processor by trimming, peeling or seeding and then cutting into chunks. Use the steel blade for chopping and mincing or to guide vegetables through the feed tube onto the slicing or shredding disc. Cabbage for cole slaw may be cut either with the slicing or shredding disc. As the container of the food processor becomes full, empty the contents into a mixing bowl, reassemble, then continue processing. The plastic disc attachment is used for combining salad dressing ingredients.

Imitation-jel dessert is a kosher, all-vegetable product used in gelatin-type recipes. The microwave oven cooks and dissolves the jel mixture. After flavorings are added the mixture is chilled until slightly thickened, and then fruits and vegetables are folded in.

The mixer and the blender are also featured in recipes to whip or blend salad dressing ingredients.

Waldorf Salad   PAREVE

3 red apples   1 stalk celery
½ cup/125 ml pitted dates   ½ cup/125 ml mayonnaise
½ cup/125 ml pecans

Food Processor Directions Core the apples, but do not peel. Cut into chunks. Insert steel blade in food processor. Place apple chunks in container and process until very coarsely chopped. Transfer to mixing bowl. Place dates in food processor. Process until chopped and add to apple mixture. Place pecans in food processor container. Process until chopped and add to apples. Cut celery into chunks. Insert slicing disc in food processor. Guide celery through feed tube to slice thin. Add celery and mayonnaise to apple mixture and mix well.   YIELD: 4 to 6 servings

Variation   Make the following changes in basic Waldorf Salad recipe:

Tuna-Waldorf Salad   P A R E V E

1 (7-oz)/(200 grams) can tuna
¾ cup/175 ml mayonnaise

Add tuna fish, drained and flaked, to prepared salad. Increase mayonnaise to ¾ cup (175 ml) when preparing basic recipe.   YIELD: 4 to 6 servings

---

A lovely pink salad to serve with a holiday turkey

Cranberry Fruit Mold   P A R E V E

½ lb/250 grams fresh cranberries
1 small lemon
¾ cup/175 ml sugar
1 package kosher imitation-jel
   dessert, pineapple-,
   lemon- or orange-flavored

1½ cups/375 ml boiling water
½ cup/125 ml mayonnaise
1 (8-oz)/(227 grams) can
   pineapple tidbits, drained
⅓ cup/75 ml chopped walnuts

Food Processor Directions   Insert steel blade in food processor. Place cranberries in container and process until coarsely chopped. Transfer cranberries to mixing bowl. Cut lemon in quarters and remove seeds. Place lemon in container along with sugar. Process until lemon is very finely chopped. Add sugar-lemon mixture to cranberries, mixing well. Set aside.

In bowl, stir jel dessert and water until thoroughly dissolved. Insert plastic disc in food processor. Place jel mixture and mayonnaise in container and process until smooth and well blended. Pour mixture into a shallow dish and place in freezer 15 to 20 minutes, until firm at edge but soft in center.

Return jel mixture to food processor and whip until fluffy, using plastic disc attachment. Fold in cranberries, pineapple and nuts. Pour into lightly greased mold and chill until firm. To serve, unmold on serving plate.

YIELD: 6 servings

Garnish this pretty jel mold with salad greens and plump strawberries.

Fruity Jel Salad   PAREVE

1 (10-oz)/(283 grams) package   ¼ cup/50 ml water
  frozen strawberries   8 whole cloves
1 package kosher imitation-jel   1 Tbsp/15 ml lemon juice
  dessert, strawberry flavor   2 bananas
1 (12-oz)/(325 ml) can
  apricot nectar

Microwave Oven Directions   Place pouch of frozen strawberries on paper plate in microwave oven. Cook on high setting 30 seconds. Rearrange fruit in pouch and return to microwave oven. Cook on medium setting 30 seconds longer. Set aside.

In glass bowl, thoroughly combine jel dessert, nectar, water and cloves. Cook on high setting 4 minutes, or until jel is dissolved, stirring twice. Remove cloves and stir in lemon juice. Chill jel mixture until consistency of unbeaten egg white.

Peel bananas and cut into small chunks. Fold bananas and drained strawberries into jel mixture. Pour into a lightly greased mold and chill until firm. To serve, unmold onto a platter.

Conventional Directions   Remove pouch of strawberries from freezer and allow to defrost at room temperature. In small saucepan, combine jel, nectar, water and cloves. Cook over low heat, stirring constantly, until jel is dissolved. Proceed as in basic recipe.   YIELD: 6 servings

Sliced tomatoes and whole olives make an attractive garnish for . . .

Green Garden Salad   PAREVE

1 package unflavored   2 Tbsp/25 ml cider vinegar
  kosher imitation-jel dessert   or lemon juice
1 Tbsp/15 ml sugar   1 cucumber
1 tsp/5 ml salt   1 large stalk celery
Dash pepper   2 green onions
1¾ cups/425 ml water   1 green pepper
                                       1 carrot

Food Processor Directions   In small saucepan, combine jel dessert, sugar, salt, pepper and half the water. Place over low heat and cook, stirring constantly, until jel is dissolved. Remove from heat and stir in remaining water and vinegar. Chill mixture to unbeaten-egg-white consistency.

Cut cucumber in half lengthwise and remove seeds. Insert slicing disc in food processor and guide cucumber through feed tube to slice thin. Cut celery in large chunks and guide through feed tube to slice thin. Transfer to mixing bowl. Insert steel blade in food processor. Trim onions and cut in quarters. Remove seeds and membranes from green pepper, then cut in chunks. Place onions and green pepper in container, and process until coarsely chopped. Transfer to mixing bowl with cucumber mixture. Peel carrot and cut in chunks. Insert shredding disc in food processor and guide carrot through feed tube to shred. Add to vegetable mixture and stir well.

Fold vegetables into jel mixture. Lightly grease a mold and spoon in mixture. Chill until firm. To serve, unmold onto serving dish.

YIELD: 6 servings

Leftover roast chicken or chicken from a soup recipe may be used for a salad. However, if you are making a large salad, buy a half turkey breast. Roast in microwave oven 7 minutes a pound (500 grams) on high setting. Allow to cool and use in the salad.

Chicken Salad   FLEISHIG

2 cups/500 ml diced cooked
   chicken or turkey
1 celery stalk
2 eggs, hard-cooked

Salt and pepper to taste
¼ cup/50 ml
   mayonnaise, or to taste

Food Processor Directions Best results are obtained if the chicken is diced by hand; however, the food processor may be used if desired. Insert steel blade in food processor. Place chunks of chicken in container and coarsely chop, using pulse button or quick on-off motion. If chicken is overprocessed it will form a pâté (which is also delicious). Place diced chicken in mixing bowl.

Insert steel blade in food processor. Cut celery into large chunks and place in container. Process until coarsely chopped. Add to diced chicken in mixing bowl. Peel eggs and cut into quarters. Place eggs in container and process until finely chopped. Combine with chicken mixture. Season to taste and add mayonnaise until salad reaches desired consistency. YIELD: 4 servings

Variations Make the following changes in basic Chicken Salad recipe:

Avocado-Chicken Salad   FLEISHIG

1 large avocado
¼ cup/50 ml Russian Dressing (see recipe in Salad Dressings chapter)

Peel 1 large avocado and remove pit. Dice by hand and add to chicken mixture. Omit mayonnaise and moisten salad with Russian Dressing.

Chicken and Fruit Salad   FLEISHIG

1 red apple

Decrease celery to ½ stalk. Quarter, core and dice 1 red apple and fold into prepared salad.

Gourmet Chicken Salad   FLEISHIG

½ cup/125 ml French Dressing
    (see recipe in Salad Dressings chapter)
2 Tbsp/25 ml sliced black olives
½ cup/125 ml slivered almonds

Marinate chicken in French Dressing several hours. Combine with chopped celery and eggs. Add black olives (slice in food processor using slicing disc) and almonds.   YIELD: 4 servings

Cabbage Fruit Salad   DAIRY

1 small head of cabbage   1 orange
1 red apple   1 (8-oz)/(227 grams) carton
1 (8-oz)/(227 grams) can crushed   yogurt, lemon-flavored
    pineapple, reserve liquid   ½ cup/(125 ml) mayonnaise
1 banana   1 Tbsp/15 ml honey

Food Processor Directions   Cut cabbage into quarters and remove core. Cut apple into quarters and remove core. Insert slicing disc in food processor. Guide cabbage and apple through feed tube, then transfer to mixing bowl. Add pineapple. Peel banana and slice. Peel orange, remove seeds and cut into chunks. Add to cabbage mixture.

Insert plastic disc in food processor. In container combine yogurt, mayonnaise, honey and juice from pineapple. Process until smooth. Pour over cabbage mixture and combine well.   YIELD: 4 to 6 servings

Variation   Make the following changes in basic Cabbage Fruit Salad recipe:

Pareve Cabbage Fruit Salad   PAREVE

1 cup/250 ml mayonnaise
2 tsp/10 ml lemon juice

Omit yogurt. Increase mayonnaise to 1 cup (250 ml) and add 2 teaspoons (10 ml) lemon juice.   YIELD: 4 to 6 servings

Dairy Cole Slaw   D A I R Y

1 small head cabbage   1 small green pepper, seeded
2 large carrots, peeled   ¼ small onion

DRESSING

1 cup/250 ml mayonnaise   2 tsp/10 ml sugar
½ cup/125 ml sour cream   1 tsp/5 ml salt
½ cup/125 ml buttermilk   ¼ tsp/1 ml dry mustard
2 Tbsp/25 ml lemon juice   ¼ tsp/1 ml pepper

Blender Directions Coarsely chop the cabbage, thickly slice the carrots and cut the green pepper into chunks. Half fill the blender goblet with water and add one-third of the vegetables. Blend on high speed until vegetables are finely chopped. Pour mixture into a colander and drain well. Repeat 2 more times, until all vegetables are finely chopped.

Put dressing ingredients into blender goblet. Blend on low speed a few seconds until well combined. Pour dressing into a large serving bowl. Add vegetables and toss to blend well. Refrigerate before serving.

YIELD: 6 servings

Hot Slaw   P A R E V E

2 egg yolks, slightly beaten   1 Tbsp/15 ml honey
¼ cup/50 ml cold water   ½ tsp/2 ml salt
¼ cup/50 ml vinegar   Dash pepper
1 Tbsp/15 ml oil   3 cups/750 ml shredded cabbage

Microwave Oven Directions In glass bowl, combine all ingredients except cabbage. Cook on high setting about 1 minute, or until mixture thickens. Pour over shredded cabbage in a glass bowl, tossing well to combine. Place slaw in microwave oven and heat on high setting 2 minutes, or until slaw is hot.

Conventional Directions In a medium saucepan, combine all ingredients except cabbage. Cook on low heat, stirring constantly, until mixture thickens. Add cabbage and toss to blend well. Continue cooking until slaw is hot.

YIELD: 4 to 6 servings

Old-Fashioned Cole Slaw   PAREVE

1 small head cabbage
1 carrot, peeled
1 stalk celery, cut in chunks

½ green pepper, quartered
¼ small onion

DRESSING

½ cup/125 ml mayonnaise
2 Tbsp/25 ml vinegar
½ tsp/2 ml salt

½ tsp/2 ml sugar
Dash pepper
¼ tsp/1 ml paprika

Food Processor Directions   Insert the slicing disc to cut cabbage into long, thin strips. (Or the shredding disc may be used for smaller pieces of cabbage.) Cut the cabbage into chunks and guide through feed tube to cutting blade. Remove cabbage from food processor container and place in serving bowl. Insert shredding disc to grate carrot fine. Insert steel blade and chop fine the celery, green pepper and onion. Combine with cabbage.

Combine dressing ingredients in food processor, using plastic blade, or by hand, and toss gently with cabbage mixture. Refrigerate before serving.

YIELD: 6 servings

Rainbow Red Cabbage Salad   PAREVE

1 medium head red cabbage
1 lb/500 grams carrots
1 bunch red radishes

½ small red Bermuda onion
1 stalk celery
1 cucumber

DRESSING

¾ cup/175 ml salad oil
¼ cup/50 ml vinegar
1 Tbsp/15 ml minced onion

1 tsp/5 ml salt
¼ tsp/1 ml dry mustard
¼ tsp/1 ml sugar

Food Processor Directions   Cut cabbage into wedges and remove core. Peel carrots and cut into chunks. Insert shredding disc in food processor. Guide cabbage and carrots through feed tube to shred, emptying container into mixing bowl as it becomes full.

Trim radishes. Cut onion and celery into chunks. Slice cucumber lengthwise and remove seeds, then cut into chunks. Insert slicing disc in food processor. Guide vegetables through feed tube to slice fine. Combine with cabbage mixture.

Insert plastic disc in food processor. Combine all dressing ingredients in container and process until blended. Pour dressing over vegetables and toss together.   YIELD: 10 servings

Carrot and Raisin Salad   P A R E V E

1 lb/500 grams carrots   ½ cup/125 ml mayonnaise
1 cup/250 ml seedless raisins   ¼ tsp/1 ml salt, or to taste

Food Processor Directions Wash carrots and cut into chunks. Insert shredding
disc in food processor. Guide carrots through feed tube to shred fine, emptying container as it becomes full. Combine raisins, mayonnaise and salt with
carrots in salad bowl.   YIELD: 6 servings

Variations Make the following changes in basic Carrot and Raisin Salad
recipe:

Carrot-Fruit Salad

3 apples
1 (8-oz)/(227 grams) can crushed pineapple

Cut apple into quarters and remove core. Shred in food processor using
shredding disc. Add, along with pineapple (well drained), to prepared salad.

Dairy Carrot Salad   D A I R Y

½ cup/125 ml sour cream

Omit mayonnaise and substitute sour cream.

French Carrot-Raisin Salad   P A R E V E

½ cup/125 ml French Dressing (see recipe
   in Salad Dressings chapter)

Omit mayonnaise and substitute French Dressing.   YIELD: 6 servings

Use whatever amounts or whatever combinations you like in this do-it-your-self salad.

Farmer's Chop Suey   DAIRY

Carrots   Green pepper   Cucumber
Celery   Radishes   Tomatoes

DRESSING

Cottage cheese, 1 part   Buttermilk, 1 part

Food Processor Directions Trim vegetables and cut all except tomatoes into chunks. Insert slicing disc in food processor and guide vegetables through feed tube. Use a knife to cut tomato into wedges. Place vegetables in serving bowl.

Insert plastic disc in food processor. Combine equal amounts of cottage cheese and buttermilk in container. Process until smooth. Pour dressing over vegetables to serve.   YIELD: Allow 2 cups (500 ml) vegetables and ½ cup (125 ml) dressing per serving

Variation

Sour Cream Chop Suey   DAIRY

Omit cottage cheese and buttermilk and substitute sour cream.

Israeli Salad   PAREVE

2 cucumbers   2 pickles
1 green pepper   2 green onions
½ bunch radishes   ¼ cup/50 ml
2 carrots   chopped fresh parsley
½ head lettuce   1 large tomato

DRESSING

4 Tbsp/50 ml olive oil   1 tsp/5 ml salt, or to taste
2 Tbsp/25 ml lemon juice   ¼ tsp/1 ml pepper

Food Processor Directions Slice cucumbers lengthwise, remove seeds from cucumbers and green pepper and cut into chunks. Trim radishes. Peel carrots and cut into chunks. Insert shredding disc in food processor. Guide these vegetables through feed tube to shred, emptying contents into large mixing bowl as container becomes full.

Cut lettuce into wedges. Insert slicing disc in food processor. Guide lettuce through feed tube to slice. Empty container into mixing bowl with other vegetables. Guide pickles through feed tube to slice.

Trim green onions and cut into chunks. Insert steel blade in food processor. Process green onion and parsley until finely chopped, and add to vegetable mixture. Use a knife to dice the tomato into salad mixture. Combine the vegetables and mix well.

Sprinkle oil over vegetables and toss to coat well. Add lemon juice and seasonings and toss again.   YIELD: 4 to 6 servings

---

Macaroni Salad   PAREVE

2 cups/500 ml elbow macaroni	2 Tbsp/25 ml minced onion
1 quart/1 liter boiling water	½ cup/125 ml chopped celery
1 tsp/5 ml salt	⅓ cup/75 ml French Dressing (see
1 tsp/5 ml oil	Salad Dressings chapter)
4 eggs	⅓ cup/75 ml mayonnaise, or to
¼ cup/50 ml minced green pepper	taste

Microwave Oven Directions   Place macaroni in 3-quart glass dish. Pour boiling water over macaroni. Add salt and oil. Cover with plastic wrap and place in microwave oven. Cook on high setting 6 to 8 minutes. Let stand, covered, 10 minutes after cooking. Drain.

Break eggs into 4 individual custard cups and place in microwave oven. Cook on medium setting 4 to 5 minutes or until yolk is "hard." Allow to cool, then chop fine.

Combine all ingredients except mayonnaise in large serving bowl. Chill well. Just before serving, fold in desired amount of mayonnaise.

Conventional Directions   Cook macaroni in boiling salted water until tender; drain. Boil eggs and chop fine. Combine all ingredients except mayonnaise. Chill. Fold in mayonnaise before serving.   YIELD: 6 servings

Variations   Make the following changes to basic Macaroni Salad recipe:

Tuna-Macaroni Salad   PAREVE

1 (7-oz)/(200 grams) can tuna	½ cup/125 ml mayonnaise, optional
1 tsp/5 ml lemon juice	

Add tuna, drained and flaked, to basic recipe. Add lemon juice, and additional mayonnaise if desired.

Vegetable-Macaroni Salad   PAREVE

1 (10-oz)/(283 grams) carton frozen vegetables

Poke a vent hole in carton of frozen vegetables (peas, carrots, string beans, mixed, etc.). Place carton on paper towel in microwave oven and cook on high setting 5 minutes. Drain, cool and add to prepared salad.

YIELD: 6 servings

Nuts-for-Your-Health Vegetable Salad   DAIRY

½ head cauliflower   1 small green pepper
½ lb/250 grams carrots   1 bunch radishes
1 small head iceberg lettuce   1 cup chopped walnuts

DRESSING

½ cup/125 ml honey   ½ cup/125 ml evaporated milk
⅓ cup/75 ml lemon juice   ½ tsp/2 ml salt

Food Processor Directions Cut cauliflower and carrots into chunks. Cut lettuce
into wedges. Remove stem, seeds and membranes from green pepper and cut
into quarters. Trim radishes. Insert slicing disc in food processor and guide
vegetables through feed tube to slice fine. As container becomes full, transfer
vegetables to large serving bowl. Add walnuts.

To make dressing, insert plastic disc in food processor. Place honey and
lemon juice in container and begin processing. Pour milk slowly through
feed tube, processing until well blended. Add salt.

Pour dressing over salad ingredients and toss to combine.

YIELD: 8 servings

Variation Substitute the following in basic salad recipe:

Sour Cream Dressing   DAIRY

½ cup/125 ml sour cream

Omit evaporated milk and substitute sour cream.   YIELD: 8 servings

Potato Salad   PAREVE

4 medium potatoes, cooked   3 Tbsp/45 ml French Dressing
3 eggs, hard-cooked   (see recipe in Salad Dressings
1 pickle   chapter)
½ onion   ½ tsp/2 ml dry mustard
1 stalk celery   ⅓ cup/75 ml mayonnaise
                                      Salt and pepper to taste

Food Processor Directions Peel potatoes and cut each into 4 slices lengthwise.
Insert slicing disc in food processor. Guide potato slices through feed tube to
slice thin. Peel eggs and cut into quarters. Guide egg quarters and then
pickle through feed tube to slice. Transfer to serving bowl.

Peel onion and cut into chunks. Cut celery into chunks. Insert steel blade
in food processor. Place onion and celery in container and process until
finely chopped. Add to potato mixture. Sprinkle with French Dressing and
mustard and toss to coat well. Just before serving fold in mayonnaise and
season to taste.   YIELD: 6 servings

Variations   Add the following to basic Potato Salad recipe:

Potato-Carrot Salad   P A R E V E

1½ cups/375 ml shredded carrots

Add shredded carrots to basic recipe. Use shredding disc to shred carrots.

Potato-Cabbage Salad   P A R E V E

1 cup/250 ml shredded cabbage

Add 1 shredded cabbage to basic recipe. Use shredding disc.

Potato-Cucumber Salad   P A R E V E

1 cucumber

Use steel blade to dice cucumber to add to potato mixture.

YIELD: 6 servings

Hot Potato Salad   F L E I S H I G

3 lbs/1500 grams potatoes	¼ lb/125 grams pastrami, sliced thin
1 large onion	½ cup/125 ml beef stock
1 garlic clove	¼ cup/50 ml vinegar
3 Tbsp/45 ml chopped parsley	Salt and pepper to taste

Microwave Oven Directions   Scrub potatoes, prick skin and cook on high setting 20 minutes, or until done. Allow potatoes to stand for 5 minutes, then peel and slice. Chop onion, garlic and parsley, and place in a glass bowl. Cover with plastic wrap. Cook on high setting 4 minutes, or until soft. Add to potatoes.

Cut pastrami slices into small pieces and arrange between paper towels. Place in microwave oven and cook on high setting 1½ minutes, or until hot. Add to potato mixture.

In a glass bowl, combine beef stock, vinegar, salt and pepper. Cook on high setting until boiling, about 2 minutes. Pour over hot vegetables. Toss well before serving.

Conventional Directions   Boil potatoes in their jackets. Peel and slice while still hot. Cut pastrami into small pieces and fry until brown. Add finely chopped onion, garlic and parsley. Continue to cook until vegetables are soft. Add the stock, vinegar, salt and pepper, and bring mixture to a boil. Pour over hot potatoes and serve.   YIELD: 6 to 8 servings

SIMCHA SALADS

A simcha is a very special, happy occasion which is frequently celebrated with a kiddush luncheon after Shabbat services.

Here are 5 salad recipes—all pareve—which can be used for a simcha celebration. These are all designed to serve 25 people, but can easily be doubled for 50, tripled for 75 or quadrupled to serve 100.

Modern appliances can greatly reduce the preparation time and ease the labor involved in fixing a feast for a crowd.

All of these salads can easily be prepared before Shabbat begins and need no last-minute preparation.

Simcha Salad: Cole Slaw   P A R E V E

3 heads/2500 ml cabbage
 (to yield 10 cups shredded)
1 lb/500 grams carrots
3 stalks celery
1 onion
1 green pepper

2 Tbsp/25 ml minced parsley
2 cups/500 ml mayonnaise
2 Tbsp/25 ml
 lemon juice or vinegar
Salt and pepper to taste

Food Processor Directions   Cut cabbages into chunks and core. Peel carrots and cut into chunks. Insert shredding disc in food processor. Guide chunks of cabbage and carrots through feed tube to shred fine. As container becomes full transfer contents to a large mixing bowl. To cut cabbage into longer pieces, use the slicing disc.

Cut celery into chunks. Insert slicing disc and guide celery through feed tube to slice fine. Add to cabbage mixture.

Peel onion and cut into eighths. Remove seeds from green pepper and cut into pieces. Insert steel blade in food processor. Process the onion and green pepper until finely chopped. Add to cabbage along with remaining ingredients and mix well. Chill before serving.   YIELD: 25 servings

---

Simcha Salad: Fruit Salad   P A R E V E

4 quarts/4 liters cut-up fruit
½ lb/250 grams slivered almonds
¼ cup/50 ml honey
¼ cup/50 ml lemon juice

¼ cup/50 ml orange juice
2 (10-oz)/(253-gram) cartons
 pareve dessert whip
4 Tbsp/50 ml sugar

Mixer Directions Any combination of fresh, canned or frozen fruit may be used, but try to select ones with color contrast. Some suggestions are cherries (halved and pitted), pineapple (diced), orange sections, banana slices, apple slices (unpeeled), peach slices, pear slices and strawberries.

Combine fruit with nuts, tossing to blend well. Combine honey and fruit juices and pour over fruit mixture.

Pour dessert whip into mixer. Attach beaters and mix on high speed until stiff, then beat in sugar. Fold whipped topping into fruit mixture and chill overnight.   YIELD: 25 servings

---

Simcha Salad: Fruit Cider Mold   P A R E V E

4 packages kosher imitation-jel
   dessert, lemon-flavored
2½ cups/625 ml hot water
1 quart/1 liter apple cider

1 cup/250 ml chopped celery
½ cup/125 ml raisins
½ cup/125 ml chopped nuts
3 cups/750 ml chopped apples

Microwave Oven Directions In a large glass dish combine jel dessert and hot water and place in microwave oven. Cook on high setting, uncovered, about 5 minutes, until mixture boils. Stir to dissolve jel. Stir in cider and allow mixture to cool.

Chill jel mixture until consistency of unbeaten egg whites. Add celery, raisins, nuts and apples. Pour mixture into a large greased mold and chill until firm. To serve, unmold onto serving platter.   YIELD: 25 servings

---

Simcha Salad: Orange-Carrot Mold   P A R E V E

3 packages kosher imitation-jel
   dessert, orange-flavored
1 cup/250 ml cold water
1 quart/1 liter pineapple juice
1 tsp/5 ml salt

⅓ cup/75 ml vinegar
2 (16-oz)/(454-gram) cans
   orange sections, well drained
1 lb/500 grams carrots

Microwave Oven Directions Place jel dessert and water in a large mixing bowl for 10 minutes or until jel is softened.

In a glass bowl heat pineapple juice in microwave oven until very hot, about 5 minutes. Add hot pineapple juice to jel mixture and stir to dissolve. Add salt and vinegar and chill until jel is consistency of unbeaten egg white.

Drain can of orange sections and set aside. Peel carrots and shred fine (or use shredding disc attachment in food processor). Fold oranges and carrots into jel mixture. Pour into lightly greased mold and chill until firm. To serve, unmold onto serving platter.   YIELD: 25 servings

Simcha Salad: Salmon-Potato Salad PAREVE

5 lbs/2 kilos potatoes
3 (16 oz)/(454-gram) cans
 red salmon
3 bunches green onions
3 cucumbers
3 celery stalks

6 sprigs parsley
1 Tbsp/15 ml dried dill weed
6 cups/1500 ml mayonnaise
⅓ cup/75 ml lemon juice
2 tsp/10 ml salt, or to taste
½ tsp/2 ml pepper

Food Processor Directions   Cook potatoes conventionally by boiling, or by baking in a 425° F (220° C) oven about 1 hour. Peel and dice. Set aside in a large bowl.

Drain salmon, reserving liquid. Remove skin and bones and discard. Flake salmon with a fork, then add to potatoes.

Insert steel blade in food processor. Remove roots from green onions and slice crosswise into 6 chunks. Place half the onions in food processor container and process until finely chopped. Remove and process other half. You should have 1½ cups (375 ml) chopped green onions. Add to potatoes.

Peel cucumbers, cut into quarters lengthwise and remove seeds. Place in food processor container and process until diced. Add to potatoes. Cut celery stalks into chunks. Place in container, in 2 loads, and process until chopped. Place parsley sprigs in container and mince. Add vegetables to potato mixture along with dill weed. Gently combine.

In mixing bowl, combine remaining ingredients, including reserved salmon liquid. Pour over potato mixture, combining thoroughly but gently. Pack salad into a large rounded bowl or mold and chill. YIELD: 25 servings

SALAD DRESSINGS

The blender and food processor can both be used to great advantage in preparing salad dressings. Although salad dressings are generally prepared uncooked, one recipe for a cooked dairy dressing is given, using the microwave oven.

In making salad dressings you might try experimenting or substituting ingredients for new flavors or fewer calories. A recipe for pareve "Sour Cream" is given in the Appetizers chapter. It can be substituted for dairy sour cream in any salad dressing recipe. Mayonnaise, which is pareve, is also a frequent substitute for either sour cream or yogurt.

Avocado Dressing   PAREVE or DAIRY

1 large avocado
½ cup/125 ml fruit juice
  (orange, pineapple or tomato)
2 tsp/10 ml lemon juice

1 tsp/5 ml grated lemon peel
2 tsp/10 ml mayonnaise,
  sour cream or yogurt
Salt and pepper to taste

Food Processor Directions Peel avocado and remove pit. Cut avocado into chunks. Insert steel blade in food processor. Place avocado chunks in container with remaining ingredients. Process until smooth.

Blender Directions Peel avocado, remove pit and cut into chunks. Place chunks in blender goblet with remaining ingredients. Blend on high speed until smooth and creamy. Serve on tossed green salads.

YIELD: About 1 cup (250 ml)

Cheese Dressing   DAIRY

¼ cup/50 ml grated hard cheese   ¼ cup/50 ml lemon juice
1 cup/250 ml sour cream   1 garlic clove, peeled
½ cup/125 ml salad oil   ½ tsp/2 ml salt, or to taste

Food Processor Directions   Insert plastic disc in food processor. Place all ingredients in container and process until smooth and creamy.

Blender Directions   Put all ingredients into blender goblet. Blend on high speed until smooth and creamy. Serve on lettuce salad.

YIELD: About 2 cups (500 ml)

Dairy Dressing   DAIRY

¼ tsp/1 ml salt   2 Tbsp/25 ml butter, melted
2 Tbsp/25 ml sugar   1 cup/250 ml light cream
1 Tbsp/15 ml flour   ¼ cup/50 ml vinegar
½ tsp/2 ml dry mustard   or lemon juice
1 egg, slightly beaten

Microwave Oven Directions   In a glass bowl combine dry ingredients. Mix remaining ingredients and add slowly, stirring constantly. Cook on medium setting 3 or 4 minutes, until thickened, stirring once every minute. Strain and cool.

Conventional Directions   In top of a double boiler, combine dry ingredients. Mix remaining ingredients and add very slowly, stirring constantly. Cook, over boiling water, stirring constantly, until mixture begins to thicken. Strain and cool.   YIELD: 1½ cups (375 ml)

Variations   Make the following changes in basic Dairy Dressing recipe:

Cucumber Dressing   DAIRY

½ cup/125 ml diced cucumber

Add cucumber to prepared dressing. This is an excellent accompaniment to fish.

Fruit Dressing   DAIRY

1 cup/250 ml orange juice   ¼ cup/50 ml slivered almonds
1 banana, diced

Omit light cream and substitute orange juice. After straining, add banana
and almonds. Serve with fruit salads.

Honey Dressing   DAIRY

2 to 4 Tbsp/25 to 50 ml
   honey (to taste)

Omit sugar and substitute honey.

Sour Cream Dressing   DAIRY

1 cup/250 ml sour cream

Allow prepared dressing to cool, then fold in sour cream.

Whipped Cream Dressing   DAIRY

1 cup/250 ml whipped cream

Allow prepared dressing to cool, then fold in whipped cream.

YIELD: 1½ cups (375 ml)

French Dressing   PAREVE

¾ cup/175 ml salad oil   ¼ tsp/1 ml dry mustard
¼ cup/50 ml vinegar   ½ tsp/2 ml salt, or to taste
   or lemon juice   ¼ tsp/1 ml pepper
1 garlic clove, peeled

Food Processor Directions Insert plastic disc in food processor. Combine all
ingredients in container and process until well mixed.

Blender Directions Combine all ingredients in blender goblet. Blend on low
speed until well mixed.   YIELD: 1 to 1½ cups (250 to 375 ml)

Variations Add the following to basic French Dressing recipe:

Creamy French Dressing   DAIRY

2 Tbsp/25 ml sour cream

Spicy French Dressing   PAREVE

1 tsp/5 ml sugar   2 tsp/10 ml Worcestershire sauce
½ tsp/2 ml *each* cumin
   and coriander seed

Tomato French Dressing   PAREVE

⅓ cup/75 ml ketchup   1 Tbsp/15 ml sugar
¼ cup/50 ml chopped onion   1 tsp/5 ml Worcestershire sauce

                                    YIELD: 1 to 1½ cups (250 to 375 ml)

Honey Fruit Dressing   DAIRY

2 Tbsp/25 ml honey   ½ tsp/2 ml grated lemon peel
1 cup/250 ml sour cream   ¼ tsp/1 ml cinnamon
¼ cup/50 ml pineapple juice   Dash salt

Food Processor Directions Insert plastic disc in food processor. Combine all ingredients in container and process until smooth and creamy.

Blender Directions Combine all ingredients in blender goblet. Blend on high speed until smooth and creamy. Serve on fresh fruit.

                                    YIELD: About 1⅓ cups (325 ml)

Italian Dressing   PAREVE

½ cup/125 ml olive oil   ½ tsp/2 ml salt
¼ cup/50 ml vinegar   ½ tsp/2 ml oregano
1 garlic clove, peeled   ¼ tsp/1 ml sweet basil
½ tsp/2 ml dry mustard

Food Processor Directions Insert plastic disc in food processor. Combine all ingredients in container and process until well mixed.

Blender Directions In blender goblet combine all ingredients. Blend on low speed until dressing is well mixed. Serve on tossed green or mixed vegetable salads.   YIELD: About ¾ cup (175 ml)

Variation

Cheesy-Italian Dressing   D A I R Y

2 oz/60 grams grated hard cheese

Add before blending.   YIELD: About ¾ cup (175 ml)

Low-Calorie Dressing   D A I R Y

½ cup/125 ml buttermilk
½ cup/125 ml cottage cheese
  or yogurt
2 Tbsp/25 ml lemon juice
2 Tbsp/25 ml chopped onion

1 large cucumber,
  peeled and diced
½ celery stalk, cubed
4 sprigs parsley
½ tsp/2 ml oregano
½ tsp/2 ml salt, or to taste

Food Processor Directions Insert steel blade in food processor. Place onion, cucumber, celery and parsley in container. Process until finely chopped. Add buttermilk, cottage cheese and lemon juice. Process until smooth. Add remaining ingredients and process until mixture is smooth and creamy.

Blender Directions In blender goblet, place buttermilk, cottage cheese and lemon juice. Blend at high speed 30 seconds or until creamy. Add onion, celery and cucumber. Blend at high speed 1 minute or until smooth. Add remaining ingredients and blend at high speed until vegetables are finely chopped and dressing is smooth.   YIELD: About 2 cups (500 ml)

Mayonnaise   P A R E V E

1 egg
1 tsp/5 ml salt
½ tsp/2 ml dry mustard
2 Tbsp/25 ml lemon juice

1 tsp/5 ml sugar, if desired
Dash cayenne pepper, if desired
1 cup/250 ml oil (about)

Food Processor Directions Insert plastic disc attachment in food processor. Place egg, salt, mustard, lemon juice and, if desired, sugar and pepper in container. Process until well combined. With motor running, slowly pour oil through feed tube. Mixture will thicken and turn light colored. Continue adding oil until it no longer blends in but sits in drops on top of mixture. Cover and store in refrigerator.

Blender Directions Drop egg into blender goblet. Add salt, mustard, lemon juice and sugar and pepper, if desired. Blend on high speed. With motor running, very slowly pour oil into egg mixture. Mixture will thicken and turn light colored. Continue adding oil until it no longer blends in but sits in drops on top of mixture. Cover and store in refrigerator.
                          YIELD: 1 to 1½ cups (250 to 375 ml)

Variations   Add the following ingredients to basic Mayonnaise recipe:

Green Goddess Dressing   DAIRY

1 Tbsp/15 ml minced parsley   ½ tsp/2 ml salt
2 Tbsp/25 ml minced green onion   Dash pepper
¼ tsp/1 ml garlic powder   ½ cup/125 ml sour cream

Mix ingredients with Mayonnaise until smooth and creamy.

Russian Dressing   PAREVE

1 Tbsp/15 ml   1 tsp/5 ml grated onion
  prepared horseradish   1 Tbsp/15 ml minced green pepper
½ cup/125 ml chili sauce   1 hard-cooked egg, chopped

Mix ingredients with Mayonnaise until smooth and creamy.

Thousand Island Dressing   PAREVE

¼ cup/50 ml chili sauce   1 Tbsp/15 ml
  or ketchup   chopped green pepper
2 Tbsp/25 ml sweet pickle relish   1 Tbsp/15 ml chopped green onion

Mix ingredients with Mayonnaise until smooth and creamy.

YIELD: 1 to 1½ cups (250 to 375 ml)

Poppy Seed Dressing   PAREVE

1 Tbsp/15 ml poppy seeds   ⅓ cup/75 ml lemon juice
⅓ cup/75 ml light corn syrup   1 Tbsp/15 ml minced onion
1 tsp/5 ml dry mustard   1 cup/250 ml salad oil
1 tsp/5 ml salt, or to taste

Food Processor Directions   Insert plastic blade in food processor. Put all ingredients except oil and poppy seeds into container. Process until smooth. With motor running, gradually add oil through feed tube, processing until mixture thickens. Add poppy seeds and process until well mixed.

Blender Directions   In blender goblet, combine everything except salad oil. Blend on high speed a few seconds until well mixed. With blender running, gradually add oil until mixture thickens. Chill well. Serve over cold asparagus, avocado or broccoli or with crisp lettuce salad.

YIELD: About 2 cups (500 ml)

DAIRY MAIN DISHES

Dairy dishes are an important and delicious part of Jewish cuisine, both for holidays and every day. It is traditional to eat such foods as Cheese Blintzes on Shavuot and Cheese or Potato Latkes on Hanukah.

Each appliance has its own specialty recipe in this chapter. The blender produces the smooth batters needed for blintzes and crêpes. Use the microwave oven to try a new dish—a versatile Quiche, ready in just 17 minutes (unless your microwave oven has a carousel or turntable, remember to rotate the baking dish every 4 to 5 minutes). The mixer is featured in a recipe for a light, golden Cheese Soufflé. The food processor is used to shred cheese and slice vegetables as toppings for homemade Pizza. Finally, the crock pot is featured in casserole-type recipes, such as Macaroni and Cheese and Cheesy Noodle-Vegetable Bake.

Dairy main dishes are comprised primarily of cheeses, milk, eggs, vegetables and pastas. They are very nutritious—high in calcium and protein—and provide a nice change-of-pace dinner during the week.

Serve these sweet Blintzes hot with sour cream or jam.

Blintzes
DAIRY

3 eggs
1½ cups/375 ml milk
1 cup/250 ml flour
3 Tbsp/45 ml oil
1 tsp/5 ml salt

2 Tbsp/25 ml sugar, optional
2 cups/500 ml Blintz filling
  (see following recipes)
2 Tbsp/25 ml butter

Blender Directions Combine first 6 ingredients in blender goblet. Blend on high speed 1½ minutes, scraping sides of goblet with rubber spatula as necessary.

To Cook Blintzes   Preheat and grease lightly a 6-inch (15-cm) frying pan. Pour Blintz batter into pan to form a thin pancake, tilting pan and swirling batter to patch up holes. It is sometimes easier to pour in extra batter, then quickly pour off the excess. When first side of Blintz is lightly browned, turn and cook the other side. Turn Blintz out of the pan onto a plate or cloth. Allow to cool before filling.

Place a tablespoon of filling in the center of each Blintz. Fold over edges to form an envelope. Just before serving, fry the Blintzes in butter, turning to brown both sides.   YIELD: 12 to 15 Blintzes

---

Cheese Filling for Blintzes   DAIRY

1 cup/250 ml dry cottage cheese   1 tsp/5 ml vanilla
1 cup/250 ml cream cheese   Dash salt
1 egg   1 tsp/5 ml cinnamon
1 tsp/5 ml sugar

Food Processor Directions   Insert plastic disc into food processor and place all ingredients in container. Process until smooth and creamy. Use as filling for Blintzes.

Blender Directions   Combine all ingredients in blender goblet. Blend at high speed until smooth and creamy. Use as filling for Blintzes.

YIELD: 2 cups (500 ml) or filling for 12 to 15 Blintzes

Apple Filling for Blintzes   PAREVE

3 apples, peeled and chopped   1 Tbsp/15 ml powdered sugar,
   or shredded   or to taste
½ tsp/2 ml almond extract   ½ tsp/2 ml cinnamon

Food Processor Directions   Use shredding disc to shred apples, or use the steel blade to chop apples fine. Combine with remaining ingredients. Use as a filling for Blintzes.   YIELD: 2 cups (500 ml) or filling for 12 to 15 Blintzes

---

Blueberry Filling for Blintzes   PAREVE

2 cups/500 ml blueberries,   1 Tbsp/15 ml sugar, or to taste
   drained (fresh, canned or frozen) ½ tsp/2 ml cinnamon
2 Tbsp/25 ml flour

Conventional Directions   Combine all ingredients. Taste to correct sweetness. Use as a filling for Blintzes.

YIELD: 2 cups (500 ml) or filling for 12 to 15 Blintzes

Jam Filling for Blintzes   PAREVE

1 to 1½ cups/250 to 375 ml jam

Use any fruit jam, such as strawberry, blackberry or cherry, as a filling for
Blintzes. Use 1 to 1½ tablespoons (15 to 20 ml) to fill each Blintz.

YIELD: 1 to 1½ cups (250 to 375 ml) or filling for 12 to 15 Blintzes

---

Crêpes have a fancy reputation that might intimidate someone trying them
for the first time, but a crêpe is really just a tender, thin pancake that holds
various fillings. It can be an appetizer, an entree, a side dish or a dessert. The
crêpe is a good party dish because it can be made ahead.

Crêpes   DAIRY or PAREVE

3 eggs

½ cup/125 ml milk (or nondairy
  creamer)

½ cup/125 ml water

3 Tbsp/45 ml
  pareve margarine, melted

¾ cup/175 ml flour

½ tsp/2 ml salt

1 Tbsp/15 ml oil

1½ to 2 cups/375 to 500 ml
  prepared crêpe filling (see
  following recipes)

½ cup/125 ml
  white sauce, optional

½ cup/125 ml
  shredded cheese, optional

Blender Directions Combine first 6 ingredients in blender goblet and blend
on medium speed until smooth. Refrigerate batter 1 hour.

To Make Crêpes Over medium-high heat, heat frying pan (or special omelet
or crêpe pan). Pour oil on a paper towel and rub towel over inside of pan.
Pour a generous amount of batter into hot pan, swirl pan to distribute
batter, then pour excess back into blender goblet. Use paper towel or fork to
remove any batter clinging to edge of pan. When crêpe is lightly browned
around edges, use spatula to turn crêpe to briefly cook the other side. As soon
as one crêpe is finished, start another. It is not necessary to regrease pan
unless crêpes start to stick. As crêpes are finished, stack on a plate.

To Store Crêpes If crêpes are to be refrigerated for a day or two, place sheets
of wax paper between them, cover tightly and seal in a plastic bag. Keep
crêpes lying flat on a refrigerator shelf. They may be kept frozen for several
weeks, wrapped in heavy-duty foil or freezer wrap.

To fill and fold crêpes: Place a spoonful of prepared filling in the center of
each crêpe (see following recipes). Fold one side toward the center, then the
other side. Then fold one end toward the center, then the other end, forming
a square or "pocket" shape.

To Cook Filled Crêpes

Microwave Oven Directions   Arrange 4 filled crêpes on a serving dish. Cover with sauce and cook on high setting 3 minutes or until hot. Shredded cheese may be sprinkled on top for a garnish; return to microwave oven for about 30 seconds on high setting, until cheese is melted.

Conventional Directions   Arrange filled crêpes in a greased baking dish. Crêpes may be covered with white sauce or shredded cheese. Bake at 400° F (200° C) 5 to 10 minutes, or until filling is hot.

YIELD: About 2 cups (500 ml) batter or approximately 12 crêpes

Variations   Prepare the following mixtures to use as crêpe fillings:

Mexican Crêpes   DAIRY

1 (16-oz)/(454 grams) can
  vegetarian baked beans
¼ cup/50 ml minced onion

1 tsp/5 ml chili powder
¼ cup/50 ml shredded
  yellow cheese

Drain liquid from can of beans and mash beans. Add remaining ingredients. Place 1 heaping spoonful of mixture in center of each crêpe. Fold and cook as directed in basic recipe.

Sea Salad Crêpes   DAIRY

2 (7-oz)/(200-gram) cans tuna,
  drained and flaked
½ cup/125 ml mayonnaise
1 Tbsp/15 ml minced onion
1 Tbsp/15 ml minced celery

⅓ cup/75 ml canned condensed
  cream of mushroom soup
2 Tbsp/25 ml milk
½ cup/125 ml
  shredded yellow cheese

Combine tuna, mayonnaise, onion and celery. Place 1 heaping tablespoonful of mixture in center of each crêpe. Fold as directed in basic recipe and place in baking dish. Combine condensed soup and milk and pour over crêpes. Sprinkle with cheese. Bake as in basic recipe.

Vegetable Crêpes   DAIRY

1½ cup/375 ml creamed vegetable
  (see recipe in
  Vegetables chapter)

½ cup/125 ml shredded cheese

Place 1 heaping tablespoonful (15 ml) of vegetable in center of each crêpe. Sprinkle with cheese. Fold and cook as directed.   YIELD: 12 crêpes

A crock pot is so convenient to use when making fondue. It not only doubles as a serving container but also keeps the fondue warm.

Swiss Cheese Fondue   DAIRY

1 lb/500 grams shredded Swiss
  cheese
1½ tsp/7 ml cornstarch
1½ cups/375 ml dry white wine
¼ tsp/1 ml salt

Dash garlic powder
Dash pepper
¼ tsp/1 ml nutmeg
½ loaf French bread
  cut into bite-size chunks

Microwave Oven Directions   In a large glass bowl combine all ingredients except bread. Cover bowl with plastic wrap and place in microwave oven. Cook on high setting 5 to 7 minutes or until cheese is melted. If fondue becomes cold while serving, reheat 1 to 2 minutes on high setting.

Crock Pot Directions   Combine Swiss cheese with cornstarch and set aside. Pour wine into crock pot and cook on high setting 20 to 30 minutes, or until wine is very hot. Gradually add cheese, one handful at a time, stirring well after each addition. Add remaining ingredients except bread. Stir and cook until cheese is completely melted. Turn control to low to keep warm.

Use long-handled fondue forks to dip pieces of French bread into cheese mixture.

YIELD: 4 servings

Cheese Latkes are sweet and delicious served with butter, confectioners' sugar, and jam.

Cheese Latkes   DAIRY

6 eggs
1 lb/500 grams
  dry cottage cheese
¼ cup/50 ml milk

½ cup/125 ml flour
1 tsp/5 ml salt
½ tsp/2 ml cinnamon
2 Tbsp/25 ml butter, or as needed

Blender Directions   Combine all ingredients except butter in blender goblet and blend on high speed until smooth. Melt butter in a hot frying pan. Drop batter by spoonfuls and fry until brown, turning once to fry the other side.

YIELD: 6 servings

Potato Latkes served hot with applesauce or sour cream are an annual Hanukah treat and, in the not-so-distant days when the potatoes and onions had to be hand grated, that was about as often as most housewives felt up to making them. Hanukah may still be an annual event, but the food processor has made it easy to enjoy potato latkes any time.

Potato Latkes   PAREVE

6 potatoes	½ tsp/2 ml baking powder
1 onion	1 tsp/5 ml salt
2 eggs, beaten	¼ tsp/1 ml pepper
¼ cup/50 ml flour or matzah meal	About ½ cup/125 ml oil for frying

Food Processor Directions Insert shredding disc in food processor. Peel potatoes and cut into eighths. Use pusher to guide potato pieces through the feed tube to shred fine. As the container becomes filled, transfer potatoes to a mixing bowl. Potatoes give off a lot of liquid after shredding. Allow to stand a few minutes, then drain off liquid before adding remaining ingredients.

Insert steel blade in food processor. Peel onion and cut in eighths. Place onion in the container and process until finely chopped. Add to potatoes, along with remaining ingredients, and stir until well blended.

Pour oil to about ¼ inch (.6 cm) depth in a large frying pan. Drop latke batter by spoonfuls into hot oil. Fry until golden brown, then turn once to fry other side. Drain on paper towels.   YIELD: 6 servings

Spinach-Cheese Latkes   DAIRY

1 (10-oz)/(283 grams) carton frozen chopped spinach	2 cups/500 ml shredded cheddar cheese
6 eggs	1 cup/250 ml flour
1 cup/250 ml milk	4 Tbsp/50 ml oil, or as needed

Blender Directions Defrost package of spinach and squeeze well to remove excess liquid. Place spinach in blender goblet and add remaining ingredients except oil. Blend on low speed until well combined.

Fry latkes in hot oil until brown, turning once to brown the other side.

YIELD: 4 to 6 servings

Macaroni and Cheese DAIRY

2 cups/500 ml white sauce
  (see recipe in Gravy and Savory
  Sauces chapter)
2 cups/500 ml
  shredded yellow cheese
3 Tbsp/45 ml minced onion

¼ tsp/1 ml dry mustard
Dash cayenne pepper
1 Tbsp/15 ml butter
3 cups/750 ml cooked macaroni
  (1½ cups uncooked)

Crock Pot Directions In crock pot combine everything except macaroni. Stir well. Cover and cook on high setting 1 hour. Add cooked macaroni. Reduce setting to low, cover pot and cook 3 to 4 hours longer.   YIELD: 4 servings

Variation Add following to basic Macaroni and Cheese recipe:

Tuna Macaroni and Cheese DAIRY

1 (7-oz)/(200 grams) can tuna

Add tuna, drained and flaked, to the cheese mixture, and proceed with basic recipe.   YIELD: 4 servings

Preparing macaroni, spaghetti or noodle dishes with uncooked pasta is a great time- and labor-saving idea, made possible by the use of the microwave oven. In addition to the prepared sauce, extra liquid must be added so that the pasta product will soften. The dish must be kept tightly covered.

One-Dish Macaroni and Cheese DAIRY

1½ cups/375 ml elbow macaroni
1 (10¾-oz)/(305 ml) can
  condensed cream of mushroom
  soup

1½ cups/375 ml water
¼ cup/50 ml minced onion
1 cup/250 ml shredded
  yellow cheese

Microwave Oven Directions In a large glass dish combine macaroni, soup, water and onion. Cover with plastic wrap and place in microwave oven. Cook on high setting 5 or 6 minutes, or until the mixture boils. Let stand 5 minutes.

Stir in cheese. Re-cover with plastic wrap. Cook on high setting 5 minutes longer. Stir well and allow to stand 5 minutes before serving.

YIELD: 4 to 6 servings

This is a recipe to admire! First, it is absolutely delicious. Second, it can be easily stretched to accommodate extra guests. Third, it is durable enough to thrive in a warm conventional oven several hours until serving, or in a freezer for several weeks before the next serving.

Manicotti   PAREVE or DAIRY

10 to 12 manicotti shells
2 quarts/2 liters salted water
1 (15½-oz)/(439 grams) jar
  pareve spaghetti sauce
  with mushrooms

3 to 3½ cups/750 to 875 ml
  prepared filling
  (see following recipe)
1½ cups/125 ml shredded cheese,
  optional

Microwave Oven Directions   Cook manicotti shells in 2 quarts (2 liters) boiling salted water for 5 to 8 minutes, or until slightly softened but still firm enough to handle and stuff. Carefully drain and rinse in cold water.

Pour about ½ cup (125 ml) sauce into an oblong glass baking dish and spread sauce to cover bottom of dish. Stuff each shell with prepared filling mixture and arrange in baking dish. Pour remaining sauce over shells.

Cook on high setting 10 to 12 minutes or until filling is hot and sauce is bubbly. If desired, shredded cheese may be sprinkled on top. Return dish to microwave oven and cook on high setting 1 minute or until cheese is melted.

Conventional Directions   Prepare manicotti as described above. Cheese may be sprinkled over uncooked manicotti. Bake uncovered in a 375° F (190° C) oven 30 minutes, or until filling is hot and sauce is bubbly.

                                         YIELD: 4 to 6 servings

Lasagna   DAIRY

1 package lasagna noodles, cooked
3 cups/750 ml Spinach Filling
  (see following recipe)

3½ cups/875 ml Cheese Filling
  (see below)
2 (15½-oz)/(439-gram) jars
  pareve spaghetti sauce

Microwave Oven Directions   In a large glass baking dish pour ½ cup (125 ml) spaghetti sauce and spread to cover bottom of dish. Cover with some of the spinach filling. Arrange a layer of noodles over the spinach. Spoon on more sauce and cover with a layer of cheese filling. Top with another layer of noodles and more sauce. Continue layering until all ingredients are used, ending with a layer of sauce and a layer of filling.

Cook on a high setting 12 to 15 minutes or until hot and bubbly.

Conventional Directions   Prepare Lasagna as above and bake at 375° F (190° C) 30 minutes or until bubbly.   YIELD: 6 to 8 servings

Spinach Filling for Pasta

2 (10-oz)/(283-gram) cartons
  frozen chopped spinach
2 eggs, beaten
1 (4-oz)/(113 grams) can
  mushroom pieces, drained

1 Tbsp/15 ml chopped parsley
1 tsp/5 ml oregano
¼ tsp/1 ml garlic powder

Microwave Oven Directions   Place carton of frozen spinach on a paper towel in microwave oven. Cook on high setting 3 minutes or until spinach is defrosted but not cooked. Squeeze spinach to drain out excess liquid. Combine with remaining ingredients and use as a filling for Manicotti or Lasagna.

Conventional Directions   Allow frozen spinach to thaw at room temperature 1 hour. Squeeze out excess liquid and combine with remaining ingredients. Use as a filling for pasta.   YIELD: About 3 cups (750 ml)

Cheese Filling for Pasta   DAIRY

1 lb/500 grams dry cottage cheese
1 cup/250 ml shredded
  white cheese
⅓ cup/75 ml grated hard cheese
2 eggs

½ tsp/2 ml salt
½ tsp/2 ml sugar
Dash pepper
1 Tbsp/15 ml chopped parsley,
  optional

Blender Directions   Combine all ingredients in blender goblet and blend on low speed until smooth and creamy. Use as a filling for Manicotti or Lasagna.
                              YIELD: About 3½ cups (875 ml)

This recipe is a good example of the "fix-it-and-leave-it" advantages of crock pot cooking. Once this cheese, noodle and vegetable dish is in the crock pot, it needs no more attention until serving time, 4 or 5 hours later.

Cheesy Noodle-Vegetable Bake   DAIRY

2 cups/500 ml noodles
2 quarts/2 liters salted water
2 (10-oz)/(283-gram) cartons
  frozen broccoli,
  thawed and drained
1 (10¾-oz)/(305 grams) can condensed cream of mushroom soup

1 cup/250 ml shredded yellow
  cheese
½ cup/125 ml minced onion
¼ cup/50 ml chopped celery
¼ cup/50 ml pareve margarine,
  melted

Crock Pot Directions Cook noodles in boiling salted water 4 to 5 minutes, until slightly tender. Drain. Cut broccoli into large chunks. Mix with noodles and remaining ingredients. Spoon noodle mixture into a baking dish which fits comfortably into crock pot. Place dish in crock pot and cover pot. Cook on low setting 4 to 5 hours, stirring occasionally.   YIELD: 4 servings

Vegetarian Spaghetti   PAREVE

2 Tbsp/25 ml olive oil
2 garlic cloves, minced
2 celery stalks, chopped
1 large green pepper, chopped
2 large onions, chopped
2 small zucchini,
  cut in small chunks
1 (4-oz)/(113 grams) can mushroom
  pieces; plus liquid

2 (16-oz)/(454-gram) cans tomatoes
1 (6-oz)/(170 grams) can tomato
  paste
½ cup/125 ml dry red wine
1 tsp/5 ml oregano
1 tsp/5 ml sweet basil
1 bay leaf
Salt and pepper to taste
1 lb/500 grams spaghetti

Microwave Oven Directions In a 4-quart glass bowl, place oil, garlic, celery, green pepper, onions and zucchini. Cover with plastic wrap and cook on high setting 10 to 12 minutes or until vegetables are soft. Stir in remaining ingredients except spaghetti. Cover with plastic wrap and return to microwave oven. Cook on high setting 10 to 12 minutes or until sauce is bubbly. Serve over cooked spaghetti.

Crock Pot Directions Heat oil in a large frying pan and sauté the garlic, celery, green pepper and onions until soft. Transfer vegetables to crock pot. Add remaining ingredients except spaghetti, and stir well. Cover crock pot and cook on low setting 4 to 6 hours or until vegetables are tender. Cook spaghetti according to package directions and drain well. When ready to serve, top each portion of spaghetti with vegetable-sauce mixture.

Conventional Directions   Heat oil in a very large frying pan and sauté garlic, celery, green pepper, and onions until soft. Add remaining ingredients except spaghetti. Cover pan and simmer sauce 1½ to 2 hours. Serve over cooked spaghetti.   YIELD: 6 to 8 servings

---

Use the food processor to prepare the vegetable and cheese toppings for Pizza quickly and conveniently. The uncooked Pizza may be tightly wrapped in freezer foil and frozen for up to one week.

Pizza   D A I R Y

Dough for 12-inch (30-cm) pizza
   pan (see Pizza Dough in Yeast
   Breads chapter).
⅔ cup/150 ml Marinara Sauce
   (see recipe in Gravy and
   Savory Sauces chapter)
   or ⅔ cup/150 ml pareve
   spaghetti sauce from a jar

2 to 3 cups/500 to 750 ml
   vegetables, sliced or chopped
   (see below)
1 cup or more/250 ml shredded
   cheese

Food Processor Directions   Pat and stretch the dough to fit into a 12-inch (30-cm) pizza pan. Spread the Marinara Sauce evenly over the dough. Arrange vegetables over sauce and sprinkle cheese thick to cover the topping. Bake at 400° F (200° C) 25 minutes or until crust is brown and sauce is bubbly.

Topping Suggestions   Prepare any of the following toppings, using the recommended blade attachments on the food processor:

VEGETABLES

Green pepper. Use slicing disc.
Mushrooms (fresh or canned).
   Use slicing disc.
Olives (pitted). Use slicing disc.

Onions, sliced. Use slicing disc.
Onions, chopped. Use steel blade.
Parsley, chopped. Use steel blade.

CHEESES

White or yellow cheese. Use shredding disc.
Hard cheese, grated. Use steel blade.   YIELD: 12-inch (30-cm) Pizza

A quiche is an all-occasion, all-purpose dish. It can be dressed up, with a green salad and chilled white wine, for an elegant midnight supper, or dressed down, a handy, make-ahead dish for a pot-luck supper. A quiche refrigerates well. To reheat, place in microwave oven and cook on high setting 4 minutes, then let stand another 4 minutes before serving.

Onion-Cheese Quiche   DAIRY

3 eggs
½ cup/125 ml milk
½ cup/125 ml cream
1 cup/250 ml shredded Swiss cheese

1 cup/250 ml shredded cheddar cheese
1 green onion, chopped
1 (3-oz)/(87 grams) can french-fried onion rings
9-inch (23-cm) baked pie shell

Microwave Oven Directions   Beat the eggs and blend with milk, cream, cheeses and onion. Pour into baked pie shell and top with french-fried onion rings. Cook on medium setting 17 minutes. Let stand 5 minutes before serving.

Conventional Directions   Mix ingredients as above and pour into unbaked pie shell. Bake at 375° F (190° C) about 45 minutes, or until knife inserted near the center comes out clean. Let stand 5 minutes before serving.

YIELD: 6 servings

Variations   Add the following to basic Quiche filling. Pour prepared mixture into a baked 10-inch (24-cm) pie shell or into a glass baking dish. (The basic microwave oven cooking time, 17 minutes on medium setting, remains the same in all variations.)

Asparagus Quiche   DAIRY

1 cup/250 ml cooked chopped asparagus

Broccoli Bake   DAIRY

1 (10-oz)/(283 grams) carton frozen chopped broccoli

Defrost broccoli by placing carton on a paper towel in microwave oven. Cook on high setting 3 minutes. Drain well and combine with egg mixture. Pour into a large glass baking dish and cook as directed in basic recipe.

Spinach Bake   DAIRY

1 (10-oz)/(283 grams) carton frozen chopped spinach

Defrost spinach by placing carton on a paper towel in microwave oven. Cook on high setting 3 minutes. Drain well and combine with egg mixture. Pour into a large glass baking dish and cook as directed in basic recipe.

Tuna-Olive Quiche   D A I R Y

1 (7-oz)/(200 grams) can tuna,   2 Tbsp/25 ml sliced olives
    drained and flaked   YIELD: 6 servings

A combination of appliances can be used to make a cheese soufflé. Use the
food processor to grate or shred cheese and vegetables. Use the microwave
oven to cook the white sauce which is the basis of a soufflé. Actually a
microwave oven can also be used to cook the soufflé, but best results are
obtained when the soufflé is cooked in the conventional oven (a soufflé depends on beaten egg whites to give it shape and egg whites need the dry heat
of a hot oven to set properly). In this recipe, the mixer is used to beat the
egg-yolk mixture, then to beat the egg whites stiff.

Cheese Soufflé   D A I R Y

1 cup/250 ml white sauce   ½ tsp/2 ml oregano
    (see recipe in Gravy and Savory   ¼ tsp/1 ml dry mustard
    Sauces chapter)   Dash pepper
1 cup/250 ml shredded yellow   4 eggs, separated
    cheese   ¼ tsp/1 ml cream of tartar
½ tsp/2 ml salt

Mixer Directions Butter a 2- or 2½-quart (2- or 2½-liter) soufflé dish or casserole and dust surface with grated hard cheese. Set aside.

In a saucepan, heat the white sauce. Add cheese and seasonings, stirring
until cheese is melted and mixture is smooth. Set aside to cool slightly.

Place egg yolks in mixer bowl and attach beaters. Mix on medium speed
until yolks are thick and lemon-colored, about 5 minutes. Blend a little of
the cooled cheese-sauce mixture into yolks, mixing constantly. Gradually
pour yolks into cheese-sauce mixture, stirring to blend well. Set aside.

Add cream of tartar to egg whites and beat on high mixer speed until stiff
but not dry. Gently fold cheese-sauce mixture into whites.

Carefully pour mixture into prepared soufflé dish. For an attractive appearance, use a spoon to completely circle the soufflé mixture, about 1 inch
(2.5 cm) from the sides of the dish and about 1 inch (2.5 cm) deep. This
indentation causes the soufflé to bake in a crown shape.

Conventional Directions Bake in a preheated 350° F (180° C) oven 40 to 45
minutes, or until puffy and delicately browned. Serve immediately.

Microwave Oven Directions Prepare mixture as described in basic recipe and
pour into a large ungreased 2-quart (2-liter) glass soufflé dish. Cook on low
setting 10 minutes. Increase setting to medium and cook 10 to 12 minutes
longer, or until surface is dry.   YIELD: 4 to 6 servings

Variations   Make the following changes in basic Cheese Soufflé recipe:

Green Cheese Soufflé   DAIRY

1 Tbsp/15 ml minced green onion
1 Tbsp/15 ml minced parsley

Add to mixture along with stiffly beaten egg whites.

Mushroom Cheese Soufflé   DAIRY

½ cup/125 ml chopped mushrooms
1 Tbsp/15 ml butter

Sauté mushrooms in butter for a few minutes. Add to mixture along with
stiffly beaten egg whites.

Salmon Soufflé   DAIRY

1 cup/250 ml   ¼ cup/50 ml milk
   flaked cooked salmon
1 (10¾-oz)/(305 grams) can cream
   of mushroom soup

Omit cheese and add salmon. Combine soup and milk and cook until hot
but not boiling. Use soup mixture as a sauce when serving salmon soufflé.

Vegetable Soufflé   DAIRY

1 cup/250 ml cooked vegetables,
   finely chopped

Omit cheese. Add vegetables to soufflé mixture along with stiffly beaten egg
whites.   YIELD: 4 to 6 servings

KUGELS AND SIDE DISHES

The recipes in this chapter are for kugels and side dishes, foods to eat along with fish, chicken or meat, although it is easy enough to get carried away over the sweet, creamy Noodle Kugel and not have room left for the rest of the meal.

Almost all of the recipes in this chapter can be made in the microwave oven. Barley, kasha and rice need to cook as long as if made on top of the stove, but the results from the microwave oven are light, fluffy and evenly cooked. Kugels can be made in the microwave oven in 15 minutes, instead of the usual 1 hour of conventional cooking. The microwave oven kugels are light and creamy. If a brown or crisp top is desired, either add a cornflake topping or put the cooked kugel under the broiler or in a very hot 400° F (200° C) oven for a few minutes.

Use the blender or food processor to speed preparation of a Potato Kugel. The mixer whips up egg whites for a fluffy kugel.

Spanish Rice develops a delicious, slow-cooked flavor when made in the crock pot.

My mother-in-Law, Gussie London, used to make the sweetest, most luscious kugel I have ever tasted. I say "used to" because the kugel gradually and with much regret disappeared from our holiday dinners. First, the raisins went, to cut back on calories a little. Next, the sugar took leave and was replaced by the contents of little pink packets of artificial sweetener. The margarine was then reduced to a teaspoon of "butter flavoring." And finally what was left was eliminated altogether because rice, noodles or matzah are "too starchy." But, if you backtrack and start adding everything that was left out, you too can make a memorable kugel your mother-in-law will envy.

Basic Sweet Kugel   PAREVE

3 eggs
½ cup/125 ml sugar
¼ cup/50 ml
   pareve margarine, melted
½ tsp/2 ml salt, or to taste
1 tsp/5 ml cinnamon

2 cups/500 ml cooked rice
or 8 oz/250 grams noodles,
   cooked and drained
or 3 cakes matzah, crumbled
   and soaked in warm water,
   then well drained

Microwave Oven Directions   Beat eggs and sugar together. Add margarine, salt
and cinnamon. Fold in rice or noodles or matzah. Pour mixture into a glass
baking dish, cover with plastic wrap, and place in microwave oven. Cook on
high setting 15 minutes.

Conventional Directions   Pour prepared mixture into a greased baking dish
and bake at 350° F (180° C) 1 hour, or until browned. YIELD: 4 to 6 servings

Variation   Add the following to Basic Sweet Kugel recipe:

Fruit Kugel   PAREVE

⅓ cup/75 ml raisins

1 large apple, sliced

YIELD: 4 to 6 servings

Noodle Kugel   DAIRY

½ lb/250 grams broad noodles
4 eggs, separated
¼ cup/50 ml butter
½ cup/125 ml sugar
2 cups/500 ml cottage cheese
1 cup/250 ml sour cream

1 (3-oz)/(87 grams) package
   cream cheese, softened
½ cup/125 ml milk
½ tsp/2 ml vanilla
½ tsp/2 ml cinnamon
½ cup/125 ml
   golden raisins, optional

TOPPING

½ cup/125 ml cornflakes, crushed
1 tsp/5 ml cinnamon

1 tsp/5 ml sugar

Mixer Directions   Cook noodles according to package directions. Drain and
set aside to cool.

    Place egg whites in mixer bowl and attach beaters. Beat until whites are
stiff but not dry. Set aside.

    Place butter and sugar in a separate bowl. Mix on medium mixer speed
until mixture is creamy. Add egg yolks and continue mixing. Add cottage
cheese, sour cream, cream cheese, milk, vanilla and cinnamon, mixing until
well blended. Fold in raisins, noodles and beaten egg whites by hand.

Microwave Oven Directions   Pour into an ungreased glass baking dish and cover with topping. Place in microwave oven and cook on medium setting 20 minutes, or until set.

Conventional Directions   Pour mixture from basic recipe into a greased baking dish. Combine topping ingredients and sprinkle on top. Bake at 350° F (180° C) 1 to 1½ hours, until golden brown.   YIELD: 6 to 8 servings

---

Noodle Kugel with Fruit   P A R E V E

½ lb/250 grams noodles
1 quart/1 liter water
1 tsp/5 ml vegetable oil
1 tsp/5 ml salt
3 eggs, well beaten
½ to ¾ cup/125 to 175 ml
   sugar (according to taste)

½ tsp/2 ml salt
1 tsp/5 ml cinnamon
3 apples
⅓ cup/75 ml raisins

Microwave Oven Directions   In a large glass casserole add noodles to boiling water. Add oil and 1 teaspon (5 ml) salt. Cover with plastic wrap and cook on high setting 6 to 8 minutes, stirring halfway through cooking time. Let stand, covered, 10 minutes. Drain well.

When noodles are drained and slightly cooled, make a well in center of noodles. Add eggs, sugar, ½ teaspoon (2 ml) salt and cinnamon. Blend well. Peel, slice apples thin and remove core. Fold apples and raisins into noodle mixture.

Cover with plastic wrap and cook on high setting 15 to 20 minutes, or until top of kugel is firm.

Conventional Directions   In a large pot, cook noodles in rapidly boiling water with oil and 1 teaspoon (5 ml) salt until tender. Drain. Combine eggs, sugar, ½ teaspoon (2 ml) salt and cinnamon in large mixing bowl. Slice apples thin and remove core. Fold into egg mixture with noodles and raisins. Transfer mixture to greased baking dish. Bake in a 350° F (180° C) oven 45 minutes.

YIELD: 4 to 6 servings

Variations   Make the following changes in basic Noodle Kugel with Fruit:

Kugel with Dried Fruit   P A R E V E

½ cup/125 ml
   chopped dried apricots or prunes

1 Tbsp/15 ml lemon juice
¼ tsp/1 ml grated lemon peel

Omit raisins. Add apricots or prunes, lemon juice and peel when preparing basic Kugel recipe.

Nutty Noodle Kugel   P A R E V E

¼ cup/50 ml raisins
¼ cup/50 ml chopped almonds, walnuts or pecans

Reduce raisins to ¼ cup (50 ml). Add chopped nuts when preparing basic recipe.

Pineapple Noodle Kugel   P A R E V E

1 (8-oz)/(227 grams) can   ¼ cup/50 ml brown sugar
   pineapple tidbits   ¼ cup/50 ml sugar

Omit apples and raisins. Substitute ¼ cup (50 ml) brown sugar for ¼ cup (50 ml) sugar when preparing basic kugel recipe. Stir pineapple tidbits into prepared mixture.   YIELD: 4 to 6 servings

Potato Kugel   P A R E V E or F L E I S H I G

4 cups/1 liter potatoes,   1 tsp/5 ml salt, or to taste
   peeled and cubed   ½ tsp/2 ml pepper
1 carrot   ¼ cup/50 ml chicken fat
1 large onion   or pareve margarine, melted
3 eggs   ⅓ cup/75 ml matzah meal

Food Processor Directions   Use shredding disc of food processor for coarsely grated potatoes or use steel blade for finely grated. Transfer potatoes to mixing bowl. Use steel blade to chop carrot and onion fine. Add, along with remaining ingredients, to well-drained potatoes.

Blender Directions   Put half of potato pieces into blender goblet. Cover with water and blend at medium speed until chopped. Pour into a strainer, drain well, reserving liquid, then place potatoes in a large mixing bowl. Repeat procedure with remaining potatoes. As potatoes stand, they continue to give off liquid. If necessary, drain once again before adding other ingredients.

Peel onion and carrot and cut into chunks. Place in blender goblet, cover with water from potatoes and blend at medium speed until vegetables are chopped. Strain off excess liquid (may be saved for soup or stew) and add vegetables to potatoes. Add remaining ingredients and mix thoroughly.

Microwave Oven Directions   Pour potato mixture into an ungreased glass baking dish and cover with plastic wrap. Place in microwave oven and cook on high setting 15 minutes.

Conventional Directions   Pour mixture into a greased casserole. Bake at 350° F (180° C) 1 hour or until browned.   YIELD: 4 to 6 servings

Serve barley as a side dish, or as a soup mate, floating in a bowl of chicken or beef soup.

Barley FLEISHIG

1 onion	Dash pepper
1 cup/250 ml barley	2 Tbsp/25 ml chicken fat
2 cups/500 ml hot chicken stock	or pareve margarine
½ tsp/2 ml salt, or to taste	(for Conventional Directions)

Microwave Oven Directions Peel the onion, chop fine and place in a glass bowl. Cover with plastic wrap and place in microwave oven. Cook on high setting 3 minutes or until onion is soft. Add remaining ingredients and re-cover bowl with plastic wrap. Return to microwave oven and cook on high setting 3 minutes, or until mixture is boiling. Reduce setting to simmer and cook 35 minutes longer, or until barley is tender.

Conventional Directions In a large frying pan, melt 2 tablespoons (25 ml) chicken fat or pareve margarine. Add onion and fry until lightly browned. Add barley and cook 5 minutes longer. Add remaining ingredients, cover pan and simmer 40 minutes, or until barley is tender. YIELD: 4 servings

Kasha from the microwave oven is surprisingly lighter and fluffier than when cooked conventionally.

Kasha PAREVE

1 egg	1 tsp/5 ml salt
1 cup/250 ml kasha	½ tsp/2 ml pepper
(buckwheat groats)	1 Tbsp/15 ml
2 cups/500 ml boiling water	minced onion, optional
2 Tbsp/25 ml pareve margarine	

Microwave Oven Directions In a glass bowl, stir slightly beaten egg into kasha. Place in microwave oven and cook on high setting 1 minute, stirring after 30 seconds to separate the grains. Add boiling water and remaining ingredients. Cover with plastic wrap and return to microwave oven. Cook on high setting 2 minutes, reduce setting to medium and cook 10 minutes longer.

Conventional Directions Stir slightly beaten egg into kasha. Place mixture in a very hot frying pan and cook, stirring constantly, until each grain is dry and separated, about 2 to 3 minutes. Add remaining ingredients, cover tightly and simmer 15 to 20 minutes, or until liquid is absorbed and kasha is tender. YIELD: 4 servings

Variation Add the following to basic Kasha recipe:

Kasha Varnishkas

½ lb/250 grams noodle bow ties
2 quarts/2 liters salted water

Cook noodle bow ties in boiling salted water until tender. Drain and add to
hot cooked kasha, mixing well.   YIELD: 4 servings

Rice is a dry ingredient and must absorb liquid to soften. For this reason,
not much cooking time is saved by using the microwave oven. However, rice
can be cooked directly in the serving dish, and microwave oven rice always
comes out light and fluffy—never burns.

Rice   P A R E V E

1 cup/250 ml rice   1 tsp/5 ml salt
2 cups/500 ml boiling water   2 tsp/10 ml pareve margarine

Microwave Oven Directions In a large glass bowl or serving dish, add rice to
boiling salted water. Stir in margarine. Cover bowl with plastic wrap and
place in microwave oven. Cook on high setting 3 minutes, then reduce setting to medium and cook 14 minutes longer. Allow rice to stand 5 minutes.
Fluff with a fork before serving.

Conventional Directions Add rice to boiling water in a saucepan. Add salt and
pareve margarine. Cover tightly, reduce heat and simmer 20 minutes. Fluff
with a fork.   YIELD: 4 servings

Rice Pilaf   F L E I S H I G or P A R E V E

2 cups/500 ml chicken stock   2 tsp/10 ml chopped parsley
  (or 2 cups water and 2 tsp/10 ml   Dash garlic powder
  pareve soup mix, chicken-   ½ tsp/2 ml salt, or to taste
  flavored)   Dash paprika
2 Tbsp/25 ml   1 Tbsp/15 ml olive oil
  instant minced onion   1 cup/250 ml rice

Microwave Oven Directions In a large glass mixing bowl, combine stock,
onion, parsley, garlic powder, salt, paprika and oil. Cover with plastic wrap
and place in microwave oven. Cook on high setting 5 minutes or until boiling. Add rice, re-cover with plastic wrap and cook on high setting 3 minutes.
Reduce setting to medium and cook 15 minutes longer, or until rice is
tender. Fluff with a fork.

Conventional Directions In a large frying pan, place rice and olive oil. Cook over medium heat, stirring constantly, until rice is lightly browned. Add remaining ingredients. Bring to a boil, reduce heat to low, cover pan and simmer gently 20 minutes or until rice is tender.   YIELD: 4 servings

Variation Add the following when preparing basic Rice Pilaf recipe:

Curried Rice   F L E I S H I G or P A R E V E

2 tsp/10 ml curry powder

Add curry powder along with seasonings.   YIELD: 4 servings

Spanish Rice   P A R E V E

2 Tbsp/25 ml pareve margarine
1 cup/250 ml rice
¼ cup/50 ml minced onion
¼ cup/50 ml chopped celery

¼ cup/50 ml chopped green pepper
1 tsp/5 ml salt
2 cups/500 ml tomato juice

Crock Pot Directions In hot frying pan, melt margarine. Add rice and sauté until golden brown. Add onion and cook until soft. Transfer to crock pot. Combine remaining ingredients and add to rice. Stir well. Cover and cook on low setting 4 to 6 hours.   YIELD: 4 servings

The brown sugar in this recipe forms a sauce to serve with the pudding—fancy as well as delicious.

Rice Pudding   D A I R Y

¾ cup/175 ml dark brown sugar
½ tsp/2 ml cinnamon
2 cups/500 ml cooked rice
2 Tbsp/25 ml butter
½ cup/125 ml raisins

3 eggs, beaten
1 (13-oz)/(384 ml) can
   evaporated milk
¼ tsp/1 ml salt
1 tsp/5 ml vanilla

Microwave Oven Directions In a glass casserole, combine brown sugar, cinnamon, rice, butter and raisins. In a separate bowl, combine eggs, milk, salt and vanilla, beating well. Pour over rice mixture and very lightly blend to mix ingredients. Place dish in microwave oven.

Cook on medium setting 8 to 10 minutes, or until mixture just reaches the boiling point. Do not allow to boil. Serve warm or cold.

Conventional Directions Prepare mixture as described and pour into a greased casserole. Bake at 325° F (160° C) until pudding is set, about 50 minutes.

YIELD: 6 servings

SWEET SAUCES AND FILLINGS

The microwave oven is featured in many recipes for sweet sauces and fillings, not only because of the time saving, but because it reduces much of the stirring and watching involved in conventional preparation. Instead of cooking sauces in the top of a double boiler, over boiling water, and stirring constantly, microwave oven sauces are cooked in a glass mixing bowl and need to be stirred only once or twice. Best of all, there is no danger of the sauces' scorching when cooked in microwave oven.

The blender is used to mix sauce or filling ingredients before cooking.

The crock pot can be used to cook slowly and develop a special flavor in chocolate sauce.

The mixer is the best appliance to use for whipped cream and can also be used to mix smooth and creamy sauces.

Butterscotch Sauce   D A I R Y

2 Tbsp/25 ml butter
¾ cup/175 ml evaporated milk
½ cup/125 ml water
⅔ cup/150 ml light-brown sugar

1 Tbsp/15 ml light corn syrup
2 Tbsp/25 ml flour
½ tsp/2 ml vanilla

Blender Directions Melt butter in a saucepan. Put remaining ingredients, except vanilla, into blender goblet. Blend on high speed until smooth. Pour mixture into saucepan with melted butter. Cook, stirring constantly, until mixture boils. Cook 1 minute longer. Stir in vanilla. Serve hot or cold.

YIELD: About 1½ cups (375 ml)

Caramel Sauce   D A I R Y

½ lb/250 grams   ½ cup/125 ml milk
  caramel candy chews   ½ cup/125 ml cream

Microwave Oven Directions   Place caramel chews in a large glass bowl. Cook in microwave oven on high setting 3 to 4 minutes, or until melted. Stir in milk and cream. Return to microwave oven and cook on high setting until sauce is bubbly, about 2 to 3 minutes longer.

Conventional Directions   Combine caramel chews, milk and cream in the top of a double boiler. Cook over boiling water, stirring constantly, until caramels melt and mixture is well blended.   YIELD: About 2½ cups (625 ml)

Cherry Sauce   P A R E V E

1 (16-oz)/(454 grams)   ¼ tsp/1 ml salt
  can cherries, packed in water   ½ cup/125 ml water
3 Tbsp/45 ml cornstarch   ¼ tsp/1 ml
½ cup/125 ml sugar, or to taste   red food coloring, optional

Microwave Oven Directions   Drain liquid from cherries into a glass mixing bowl. Combine with cornstarch to make a smooth paste. Add sugar, salt, water and, if desired, red food coloring. Place in microwave oven and cook on high setting 3 minutes, or until mixture thickens, stirring once. Add cherries. Return to microwave oven and cook 1 minute longer on high setting, or until cherries are warm. Serve warm over pound cake or ice cream.

Conventional Directions   In top of a double boiler combine ingredients as described in basic recipe. Cook over boiling water, stirring constantly until sauce thickens. Add cherries, and cook until they are warm. Serve warm over pound cake or ice cream.   YIELD: About 3 cups (750 ml) or 4 servings

Variation   Add the following ingredient to basic Cherry Sauce recipe:

Flaming Cherries   P A R E V E

¼ cup/50 ml brandy

Add 2 tablespoons (25 ml) brandy along with the cherries and cook as directed. When ready to serve, warm remaining brandy in a large spoon or ladle over a candle or flame. Ignite and pour flaming liquid over cherries. Serve at once, alone or over ice cream.

YIELD: About 3 cups (750 ml) or 4 servings

Chocolate Sauce   DAIRY

3 squares (3 oz)/(90 grams)   ½ cup/125 ml light corn syrup
  unsweetened chocolate   1 cup/250 ml heavy cream
½ cup/125 ml water   1 tsp/5 ml vanilla
1 cup/250 ml sugar

Microwave Oven Directions In a glass mixing bowl combine chocolate and
water. Place in microwave oven and cook on high setting 2 minutes or until
chocolate is melted. Stir in sugar and corn syrup. Return to microwave oven
and cook 2 minutes longer, or until a spoonful dropped in a glass of cold
water forms a soft ball, or sauce measures 240° F (115° C) on a candy thermometer. (*Do not* put candy thermometer in the microwave oven. Remove
sauce from oven, insert thermometer and take a reading, then remove thermometer before returning sauce to the oven.)

When the soft stage is reached, gradually stir in cream and vanilla. Serve
warm or cold, on ice cream or cake.

Conventional Directions Cook syrup, sugar and water to the soft-ball stage
(240° F or 115° C). Remove from heat and stir in chocolate, blending well.
Add vanilla. Slowly add cream, stirring constantly. Serve warm or cold.

YIELD: About 3 cups (750 ml)

Chocolate Mint Sauce   PAREVE

2 squares (2 oz)/(60 grams)   ⅓ cup/75 ml warm water
  unsweetened chocolate   ½ tsp/2 ml mint flavoring
½ to ⅔ cup/125 to 150 ml sugar   Dash salt
  (depending upon sweetness
  desired)

Blender Directions Break chocolate into chunks. Place all ingredients in
blender goblet. Blend on medium speed until well combined. Pour mixture
into a saucepan and cook, stirring constantly, until chocolate and sugar are
dissolved. Serve warm or cool.   YIELD: About 1 cup (250 ml)

Dairy Chocolate Sauce   DAIRY

1 (16-oz)/(454 grams)   ½ cup/125 ml cream
  milk chocolate candy bar   ⅓ cup/75 ml butter
½ cup/125 ml milk   1 tsp/5 ml vanilla

Crock Pot Directions Break chocolate bar into small pieces and place in crock
pot. Add milk, cream and butter. Cover and cook on low setting for 2 to 2½
hours. Stir in vanilla and beat until smooth. Serve warm over cake or ice
cream.   YIELD: 3 cups (750 ml)

Serve this sauce well chilled, on cold cake or pudding.

Hard Sauce   P A R E V E

¼ cup/50 ml pareve margarine   1 tsp/5 ml vanilla
1 cup/250 ml confectioners' sugar   Dash salt

Mixer Directions   Insert beater attachment in mixer. On medium speed, cream margarine, gradually adding sugar until mixture is fluffy. Mix in vanilla and salt. When well blended pile lightly into serving dish. Chill until cold but not hard.   YIELD: ¾ cup (175 ml)

Variations   Make the following changes in basic Hard Sauce recipe:

Apricot Hard Sauce   P A R E V E

1 Tbsp/15 ml apricot brandy
½ cup/125 ml apricot puree

Omit vanilla. Add apricot brandy and puree along with sugar and proceed as in basic recipe.

Brandy Hard Sauce   P A R E V E

2 Tbsp/25 ml brandy

Omit vanilla and substitute brandy.

Butterscotch Hard Sauce   D A I R Y

½ cup/125 ml   ¼ cup/50 ml butter
  confectioners' sugar   1 Tbsp/15 ml evaporated milk
½ cup/125 ml brown sugar

Reduce confectioners' sugar to ½ cup (125 ml) and add ½ cup (125 ml) brown sugar. Use butter instead of margarine. Add evaporated milk along with vanilla.

Fluffy Hard Sauce   P A R E V E

1 egg white, stiffly beaten

Fold egg white into prepared sauce before chilling.

Orange Hard Sauce   PAREVE

1 Tbsp/15 ml liqueur
2 tsp/10 ml grated orange peel

Omit vanilla and substitute liqueur and peel.

Spicy Hard Sauce   PAREVE

½ tsp/2 ml *each* cinnamon,
  cloves and lemon juice

Add with sugar.   YIELD: ¾ cup (175 ml)

Favorite Hot Fudge Sauce   PAREVE

6 Tbsp/75 ml cocoa   1 cup/250 ml sugar
3 Tbsp/45 ml pareve margarine   2 Tbsp/25 ml corn syrup
⅓ cup/75 ml boiling water   1 tsp/5 ml vanilla

Microwave Oven Directions Place cocoa and margarine in a 4-cup (1-liter) glass measure. Cook on high setting until margarine is melted, about 30 to 45 seconds. Stir well. Add boiling water, sugar and corn syrup, stirring well. Cook on high setting until mixture comes to a boil, about 2 minutes.

On medium setting allow sauce to boil for 5 minutes. Add vanilla and stir well. This sauce becomes very thick when cold. Store in refrigerator. Reheat in microwave oven before serving.

Conventional Directions Melt margarine in top half of double boiler, over water. Add cocoa and blend well. Stirring constantly, add water, sugar and syrup. Bring to a boil and allow to boil, without stirring, for 5 to 8 minutes. The longer cooking time produces a sauce which hardens over ice cream. Add vanilla and stir well. Serve hot.   YIELD: 1½ cups (375 ml)

Lemon Sauce

PAREVE

½ cup (1 stick)/125 ml
  pareve margarine
3 eggs

½ cup/125 ml lemon juice
1 cup/250 ml sugar
1 Tbsp/15 ml grated lemon peel

Microwave Oven Directions   Place margarine in a small glass bowl and place in microwave oven. Cook on high setting 45 seconds or until melted. In another glass mixing bowl, beat eggs. Add melted margarine, lemon juice, sugar and lemon peel. Place in microwave oven and cook on high setting 3 minutes. Beat until smooth, then cook 1 minute longer on high setting, until mixture is thickened. Serve over cake or fruit.

Conventional Directions   Combine beaten eggs, lemon juice, sugar and grated peel in top of a double boiler. Place over boiling water. Add margarine and cook, stirring constantly, until margarine is melted and sauce is thickened.

YIELD: About 2 cups (500 ml)

Custard Sauce

DAIRY

2 cups/500 ml milk
3 eggs
⅓ cup/75 ml sugar

Dash salt
½ tsp/2 ml vanilla

Microwave Oven Directions   Pour milk into a glass bowl and place in microwave oven. Cook on high setting 3 minutes or until very hot. In a separate bowl beat eggs with sugar, salt and vanilla. Pour a small amount of milk into egg mixture, stirring well. Pour egg mixture back into hot milk. Stirring well. Cook on medium setting 10 minutes, or until sauce thickens and coats a spoon. Serve over cake or ice cream.

Conventional Directions   Scald milk. Beat eggs and blend in sugar, salt and vanilla. Combine with milk as described in basic recipe. Pour mixture into top of a double boiler and cook, over boiling water, until sauce is thickened, stirring constantly.   YIELD: About 2 cups (500 ml)

Variation   Add the following to basic Custard Sauce recipe:

Chocolate Custard Sauce

DAIRY

1 square (1 oz)/(30 grams)
  unsweetened chocolate

3 Tbsp/45 ml honey

Melt chocolate and blend with honey. Add with beaten eggs to hot milk. Proceed as directed in basic recipe.   YIELD: About 2 cups (500 ml)

Perfect Custard   D A I R Y

1¾ cups/425 ml milk
3 eggs
⅓ cup/75 ml sugar
Dash salt

1 tsp/5 ml vanilla
½ tsp/2 ml nutmeg
2 cups/500 ml water
　　(for Conventional Directions)

Microwave Oven Directions   Pour milk into a glass bowl and place in microwave oven. Cook on high setting 3 minutes, until milk is very hot but not boiling. In another bowl, beat eggs. Add sugar, salt and vanilla, mixing well. Pour a small amount of hot milk into egg mixture and blend well. Pour egg mixture back into hot milk, stirring well. Strain egg mixture into 5 glass custard cups. Sprinkle with nutmeg. Arrange cups in a circle in microwave oven. Cook on medium setting 10 to 12 minutes, or until custard just starts to boil. Remove custard from oven and allow to stand 10 minutes. Custard will thicken as it cooks.

Conventional Directions   Prepare custard mixture as described in basic recipe. Custard may be cooked in the top of a double boiler, over boiling water. Stir constantly until thickened. Or pour the egg mixture into individual custard cups. Place cups in a shallow pan with 2 cups (500 ml) warm water. Cook in a preheated 300° F (150° C) oven 1 hour, or until a knife inserted in the custard mixture comes out clean.   YIELD: 5 servings

Instant Pudding   D A I R Y

2 cups/500 ml cold milk
1 package (4-serving size)
　　instant pudding mix, any flavor

Blender Directions   Put milk and pudding mix into blender goblet. Blend at medium speed about 15 seconds, until the mix is dissolved. Scrape sides of goblet with rubber spatula and blend 15 seconds longer. Pour into four serving dishes. Mixture sets and thickens in a few minutes. May be served chilled.   YIELD: 4 servings

Packaged Pudding   D A I R Y

1 package (4-serving size)   2 cups/500 ml milk
  pudding, any flavor
  (*not* instant pudding)

Microwave Oven Directions   In a glass mixing bowl combine pudding mix and
milk. Stir well and place in microwave oven. Cook on high setting 4 minutes.
Stir well and return to microwave oven. Cook on high setting 2 minutes
longer, or until mixture just comes to a boil. Remove from oven and allow to
stand 10 minutes before serving. Pudding continues to thicken as it cools.
Stir and pour into individual dishes. Serve warm or cold.   YIELD: 4 servings

---

There are three appliances to choose from when whipping cream. The most
preferable, by far, is the mixer. In addition to mixing at a very fast speed, the
beaters aerate the cream, causing it to rise considerably in volume. Although
both the blender and food processor can whip cream, not enough air is
incorporated into the cream to give it a high volume. Whipped cream may
be sweetened to taste with sugar or powdered sugar and flavored with vanilla, brandy or liqueurs.

Whipped Cream   D A I R Y

1 cup/250 ml whipping cream

Mixer Directions   For best results, chill mixer bowl and beaters before whipping cream. Pour cream into mixer bowl. Begin mixing on low speed and
gradually work up to the highest speed. Whipped cream is ready when it is
thick and beaters leave an impression on cream when removed.

Blender Directions   Chill blender goblet in refrigerator for 15 minutes before
whipping cream. Pour cream and sugar and/or flavorings into goblet. Blend
on low speed 5 to 10 seconds. Stop blender. Using rubber spatula, stir cream,
turning and lifting to mix air through cream. Blend another 5 to 10 seconds
and repeat process to give cream extra air as it whips. Cream will whip in
about 20 seconds.

Food Processor Directions   Insert S-shaped plastic blade. Pour cream into container. Keep feed tube open to allow air to be incorporated into cream.
Cream will whip in about 20 to 30 seconds.   YIELD: 2 cups (500 ml)

CAKES

A good cake recipe is a nice thing to have, but a good pareve cake recipe is a treasure. With the exception of the basic butter cake, cheesecake and a chocolate sourdough cake that is absolutely stunning, all of the cake recipes in this chapter are pareve. The icings, too, can all be made pareve.

The mixer is the real workhorse appliance of this chapter. Both a portable hand mixer and the heavier table model do beautiful jobs of mixing cakes and beating icings and frostings.

The microwave oven produces homemade or package cakes that are lighter and rise higher than if baked conventionally. These cakes do not form a dark crust, and frostings will be easier to apply if the cakes are first chilled in the refrigerator.

Cakes in a crock pot "bake" best on a high setting. Place any cake pan that fits comfortably and is easy to remove in the bottom of the crock pot. Place several layers of paper towels over the top of the cake pan to absorb excess moisture, then cover the crock pot.

Use the blender for mixing single or one-layer cakes. In making frostings, the blender technique is to combine all liquid ingredients with a small amount of confectioners' sugar in blender goblet. Blend until smooth, then pour this mixture into the remaining sugar and stir by hand until smooth.

Each frosting recipe in this chapter yields at least 2 cups, which is the amount needed for covering the top and sides of an 8- or 9-inch (20- or 23-cm) layer cake, a 9-by-13-inch (23-by-33-cm) flat cake, a 10-inch (25-cm) tube cake or 24 cupcakes. The glaze recipes make enough to drizzle a decorative glaze over the top of a tube cake.

The standard procedure for making most cakes in a mixer is first to cream together shortening and sugar until the mixture is fluffy, using the beater attachment and medium mixer speed; add the eggs and mix well, sift flour before mixing, then add the dry and liquid ingredients alternately in the following manner:

⅓ dry ingredients   ½ liquid ingredients
½ liquid ingredients   ⅓ dry ingredients
⅓ dry ingredients

When using the mixer to beat icing, frosting and candies, insert the beater attachment. Combine the ingredients on a low mixer speed, then beat until creamy on medium speed. Boiled frostings are whipped at high speed.

In the microwave oven, cakes bake best in a circular pan with a tube in the center. If the pan is plastic, it need not be greased (greasing the pan may produce a tough cake). If the pan is glass or ceramic, it may be sprayed with an aerosol vegetable coating.

Use the medium-high setting for microwave oven cakes. The following guide can be used to estimate the timing of both packaged cake mixes and homemade cakes.

ITEM	SETTING	TIME
8- or 9-inch layer cake		
time required for *each* layer	medium-high	7–8 min
10-inch tube cake	medium-high	12–14 min
Cupcakes: 1	medium-high	45 sec
2	medium-high	1–1½ min
4	medium-high	2–2½ min
6	medium-high	2½–3 min

When baking cakes in the microwave oven, it is necessary to rotate the baking dish several times while the cake is cooking. A good system is to give the dish a one-third turn after each of the first 3 quarters of the cooking time, so that if a recipe calls for 12 minutes of microwave oven cooking, the dish should be rotated after 3, 6 and 9 minutes of cooking. A carousel or turntable eliminates the need for rotating the cake.

Although almost any cake can be baked in the microwave oven, conventional baking produces much better results for those cakes that use beaten egg whites for leavening and shape.

Packaged Cake Mix   DAIRY or PAREVE

Blender Directions Put half the liquid, half the eggs and half the package of cake mix into the blender goblet. Cover and blend on medium speed a few seconds until batter is smooth. If necessary, use a rubber spatula to help blend dry mix with the liquid. Do not overblend. Pour batter into prepared, greased and floured cake pan and repeat procedure with remaining ingredients. Bake as directed on package.

Basic Butter Cake   D A I R Y

3 cups/750 ml cake flour   1½ cups/375 ml sugar
3 tsp/15 ml baking powder   2 eggs
1 tsp/5 ml salt   1¼ cups/300 ml milk
½ cup/125 ml butter or margarine   1 tsp/5 ml vanilla

Mixer Directions Sift together dry ingredients except sugar. Place butter and
sugar in mixer bowl and attach beaters. On medium speed cream butter and
sugar until mixture is fluffy. Add eggs one at a time, beating well after each
addition.

Add dry ingredients alternately with milk and vanilla to creamed mixture, beating after each addition until batter is smooth. Scrape sides of bowl
as needed.

Pour batter into 2 greased and floured 9-inch (23-cm) cake pans. Bake at
350° F (180° C) 35 to 40 minutes. Cool in pans 10 minutes before turning
cakes onto a wire rack to finish cooling. Spread with frosting to serve.

YIELD: 2-layer-cake

Variations Add the following to Basic Butter Cake recipe:

Marble Cake   D A I R Y

1½ squares (1½ oz)/(45 grams)   ½ tsp/2 ml cinnamon
   unsweetened chocolate, melted   1 Tbsp/15 ml milk

Divide prepared batter into two parts. To one part of the batter add chocolate, cinnamon and milk. Drop batter by spoonfuls into greased pan,
alternating yellow and chocolate. Swirl with a knife for a marbled effect.

Spice Cake   D A I R Y

½ tsp/2 ml ground cloves   1 tsp/5 ml nutmeg
1 tsp/5 ml cinnamon

To basic batter add cloves, cinnamon and nutmeg.

White Cake   D A I R Y

4 egg whites

Use 4 egg whites instead of 2 whole eggs in basic recipe. After creaming
sugar and butter, add dry and liquid ingredients alternately. Whip egg
whites on high speed of mixer until stiff but not dry. Fold egg whites lightly
into cake batter.

Yellow Cake   DAIRY

4 tsp/20 ml baking powder   4 egg yolks

Increase baking powder to 4 teaspoons (20 ml) in basic recipe and use 4 egg
yolks instead of 2 whole eggs.   YIELD: 2-layer cake

Pareve Layer Cake   PAREVE

2¼ cups/550 ml cake flour   2 eggs
2½ tsp/12 ml baking powder   1 cup/250 ml liquid (any fruit
1 tsp/5 ml salt   juice or drink, or ½ cup/125 ml
½ cup/125 ml vegetable   nondairy creamer
   shortening or pareve margarine   and ½ cup/125 ml water)
1½ cups/375 ml sugar   1 tsp/5 ml vanilla

Mixer Directions Sift together flour, baking powder and salt. Set aside dry
ingredients. Place shortening and sugar in mixer bowl and attach beaters.
On medium speed, cream until mixture is fluffy. Add eggs one at a time,
beating well after each addition.

Add dry ingredients alternately with liquid and vanilla to creamed mixture, beating after each addition until batter is smooth.

Pour batter into 2 greased and floured 9-inch (23-cm) cake pans. Bake at
375° F (190° C) 25 minutes, or until toothpick inserted near the center
comes out clean. Cool in pans 10 minutes before turning cakes onto a wire
rack. Cool thoroughly before frosting.   YIELD: 2-layer cake

An Angel Food Cake contains no fat or shortening. Even the cake pan needs no grease.

Angel Food Cake   PAREVE

1 cup/250 ml cake flour   1¼ tsp/6 ml cream of tartar
1⅓ cups/325 ml sugar   ½ tsp/2 ml salt
1¼ cups/300 ml egg whites   1 tsp/5 ml vanilla
   (about 10 to 12 egg whites)   ¼ tsp/1 ml almond extract

Mixer Directions Sift flour and ½ cup (125 ml) sugar together. Set aside.

Place egg whites in mixer bowl and add cream of tartar and salt. On high speed, whip the egg whites until stiff but not dry (about 2 to 3 minutes).

Reduce mixer speed to low. Sift remaining sugar (not sugar-flour mixture) into egg whites gradually. Manually fold the sugar-flour mixture into egg whites, very gently lifting and turning the batter with a spatula. Fold in vanilla and almond extract.

Spoon batter into an ungreased 10-inch (25-cm) tube pan. Bake at 300° F (150° C) about 1 hour. Invert cake pan on wire rack. Allow to stand until cool, about 1 hour.   YIELD: 10-inch (25-cm) tube cake

Variations Make the following changes in basic Angel Food Cake recipe:

Chocolate Angel Food Cake   PAREVE

¾ cup/175 ml flour
¼ cup/50 ml cocoa

Reduce flour to ¾ cup (175 ml) and add cocoa. Sift flour and cocoa with half the sugar. Proceed as in basic recipe.

Orange Angel Food Cake   PAREVE

1½ tsp/7 ml grated orange peel
2 oranges

Omit vanilla and almond extract and substitute orange peel. Peel and section 2 oranges and cut into small pieces. Pour a small portion of batter into tube pan. Sprinkle on some of the orange pieces. Continue layering batter and orange sections, ending with batter. Bake as in basic recipe.

YIELD: 10-inch (25-cm) tube cake

Holiday Apple Cake   PAREVE

5 apples
2 tsp/10 ml cinnamon
5 Tbsp/65 ml sugar
1 cup (2 sticks)/250 ml
   pareve margarine
2 cups/500 ml sugar
4 eggs

3 cups/750 ml sifted flour
3 tsp/15 ml baking powder
½ tsp/2 ml salt
⅓ cup/75 ml orange juice
1½ tsp/7 ml vanilla
1 tsp/5 ml almond extract
¾ cup/175 ml White Glaze

Mixer Directions Peel and quarter apples, core and slice. In mixing bowl combine apple slices, cinnamon and 5 tablespoons (65 ml) sugar. Set aside.

In mixer bowl combine margarine and 2 cups (500 ml) sugar. Cream at medium speed until fluffy. Add eggs one at a time, mixing well after each addition. Sift flour, baking powder and salt together and add to batter. Add juice and flavorings. Continue mixing until batter is smooth (it will be thick).

Grease and flour a 10-inch (25-cm) tube pan. Place a small amount of batter in prepared pan. Arrange a layer of apple slices on top of batter. Continue layering, ending with a layer of batter.

Bake in a preheated 350° F (180° C) oven 1½ hours or until cake tests done. Cool on a wire rack. Drizzle with White Glaze. (See under Frostings.)

YIELD: 10-inch (25-cm) tube cake

New England Applesauce Cake   PAREVE

½ cup (1 stick)/125 ml
   pareve margarine
1 cup/250 ml sugar
½ cup/125 ml brown sugar
2 eggs
3 cups/750 ml sifted flour
1 tsp/5 ml salt

2 tsp/10 ml baking soda
1 tsp/5 ml cinnamon
1 tsp/5 ml ground cloves
½ tsp/2 ml nutmeg
1 (16-oz)/(454 grams)
   can unsweetened applesauce
½ cup chopped nuts

Crock Pot Directions In mixing bowl cream shortening and white and brown sugars. Beat in eggs and mix thoroughly. Sift together flour, salt, baking soda and spices and add alternately with applesauce to the creamed mixture. Stir in nuts. Pour mixture into a greased and floured 8-cup (2-liter) mold or spring-form pan.

Place mold or pan in crock pot. Lay 4 or 5 paper towels on top of cake mold to absorb excess moisture. Cover crock pot and cook on high setting 3 to 4½ hours or until toothpick inserted in cake comes out clean. Cool 15 minutes, then unmold cake. To serve, sprinkle top with powdered sugar or frost with confectioners' sugar frosting.   YIELD: Large 1-layer cake

This recipe is designed for pure indulgence. It will expand everything from your morale and reputation as a hostess to your waistline and cholesterol count.

Cheesecake

¼ cup/50 ml sugar
1 tsp/5 ml grated lemon peel
1 cup/250 ml sifted flour
½ tsp/2 ml vanilla

1 egg yolk
¼ cup/50 ml
   butter or pareve margarine

FILLING

4 (8-oz)/(227-gram)
  packages cream cheese, softened
1¼ cups/300 ml sugar
½ cup/125 ml heavy cream

3 Tbsp/45 ml flour
1 tsp/5 ml vanilla
5 eggs, separated
1 cup/250 ml fruit, optional

Mixer Directions Place sugar, lemon peel and flour in mixer bowl. Attach beaters and mix a few seconds on low speed until well combined. Add vanilla, egg yolk and butter. Mix on medium speed until mixture forms into a dough and ingredients are well combined. Press half the dough mixture onto the bottom of a 9-inch (23-cm) spring-form pan. Bake at 400° F (200° C) 6 to 8 minutes. When the pan is cool, press the remaining crust mixture onto the sides. Set aside.

Place softened cream cheese in mixer bowl. Using beater attachment, mix in sugar, cream, flour, vanilla and egg yolks. Continue mixing until mixture is smooth and creamy.

In another mixer bowl place egg whites. Using whisk or beater attachment, mix on high speed until egg whites are stiff but not dry. Gently fold egg whites into cheese mixture.

Pour filling into crust. Bake at 350° F (180° C) 1 hour. Allow cheesecake to cool in pan at least 2 hours before serving. If desired, canned or fresh fruit, well drained (cherries, blueberries or pineapple) may be spooned over the top.   YIELD: 1 large cheesecake, 16 servings

Variation

Lower-Calorie Cheesecake

4 cups/1 liter dry cottage cheese

Dry cottage cheese may be substituted for all or part of the cream cheese. Using the beater attachment, whip cottage cheese in mixer on high speed until smooth and creamy before adding.

YIELD: 1 large cheesecake, 16 servings

Basic Chocolate Cake   PAREVE or DAIRY

2 cups/500 ml sifted flour
1 tsp/5 ml baking powder
½ tsp/2 ml baking soda
1 tsp/5 ml salt
1⅓ cups/325 ml sugar
½ cup/125 ml pareve margarine
2 eggs

3 squares (3 oz)/(90 grams)
  unsweetened chocolate, melted
1 cup/250 ml liquid
  (milk, buttermilk, coffee or
  ½ cup/125 ml nondairy creamer
  and ½ cup/125 ml water)
1 tsp/5 ml vanilla
½ tsp/2 ml almond extract

Mixer Directions Sift together dry ingredients except sugar and set aside. Place sugar and shortening in mixer bowl. Attach beaters and mix at medium speed until creamy. Add eggs and mix 2 minutes longer. Add chocolate. Combine liquid, vanilla and almond extract, and add alternately with dry ingredients, mixing well after each addition.

Pour batter into 2 greased and floured cake pans. Bake at 375° F (190° C) 25 minutes or until done. Remove from pans and allow to cool thoroughly before frosting.   YIELD: 2-layer cake

Chocolate Blender Cake   PAREVE

1¼ cups/300 ml sifted flour
1 tsp/5 ml baking powder
½ tsp/2 ml baking soda
¼ tsp/1 ml salt
½ tsp/2 ml cinnamon
2 eggs

½ cup/125 ml cocoa
1½ tsp/7 ml almond extract
1½ cups/375 ml brown sugar
¾ cup/175 ml pareve margarine
¾ cup/175 ml hot coffee
¾ cup/175 ml Coffee Glaze icing

Blender Directions Sift flour, baking powder, baking soda, salt and cinnamon into a mixing bowl. Put the remaining ingredients into the blender goblet, cover and blend on low setting until smooth. Pour into flour mixture. Stir quickly just until smooth. Pour batter into a greased cake pan. Bake in a 350° F (180° C) oven 35 to 40 minutes. Drizzle cake with Coffee Glaze (see under Frostings) before serving.   YIELD: 1-layer cake

This is an outstanding and unusual cake—a real specialty item.

Sourdough Chocolate Cake   DAIRY

3 squares (3 oz)/(30 grams)
   semi-sweet chocolate
1 cup/250 ml sugar
½ cup/125 ml butter
2 eggs
1 cup/250 ml Sourdough Batter
   (see recipe in Yeast Breads
   chapter)

1 cup/250 ml evaporated milk
1 tsp/5 ml vanilla
1 tsp/5 ml cinnamon
½ tsp/2 ml salt
1½ tsp/7 ml soda
2 cups/500 ml flour

Microwave Oven Directions In a small glass measuring cup place chocolate squares. Cook on high setting until melted. Set aside.

In mixing bowl, cream sugar and butter until light and fluffy. Beat in eggs, one at a time. Stir in Sourdough Batter, milk, vanilla, cinnamon and melted chocolate. If using mixer, beat batter at medium speed for 2 minutes, or beat 200 strokes by hand.

Blend salt and soda together. Sprinkle over batter and fold in gently. Fold in flour, mixing until batter is smooth.

Cut wax-paper circles to fit into bottom of two 8-inch (20-cm) round glass baking pans. Pour batter into pans. Cook, one at a time, on medium-high setting for 7 minutes, or until top is dry and toothpick, inserted near edge, comes out clean. Cool 10 minutes before turning out onto cake rack. Cool thoroughly before frosting.

Conventional Directions Pour cake batter into greased and floured cake pans. Bake in a 350° F (180° C) oven for 40 minutes. Cool before frosting.

YIELD: Two 8-inch (20-cm) cake layers

I have a friend, Anne Griggs, who was developing recipes and cooking with a microwave oven about a decade before most consumers even realized that such an item was on the market. She really should write her own cookbook, but until she finds the time I am delighted to borrow one of her specialty recipes.

Anne's Microwave Fruitcake Miniatures   PAREVE

2 eggs
¾ cup/175 ml firmly packed brown
  sugar
2 Tbsp/25 ml unsulfured molasses
⅓ cup/75 ml cooking oil
¾ cup/175 ml flour
1 tsp/5 ml baking powder
½ tsp/2 ml salt
¼ tsp/1 ml *each* nutmeg,
  cinnamon and cloves
½ cup/125 ml grape juice or orange
  juice

½ lb/250 grams candied fruits
  (about 1 cup)
½ lb/250 grams candied cherries
  (about 1 cup)
½ lb/250 grams pitted dates (about
  1 cup)
1 cup/250 ml chopped walnuts
¾ cup/175 ml flour
1 cup/250 ml water
2 Tbsp/25 ml brandy, optional

Microwave Oven Directions   In a very large mixing bowl, combine eggs, sugar and molasses. Beat in the oil until well blended. Sift together ¾ cup/(175 ml) flour, baking powder, salt and spices. Stirring constantly, add dry ingredients and juice alternately to egg mixture.

Chop candied fruit, cherries and dates. Coat fruits and nuts with the remaining ¾ cup (175 ml) flour and stir into batter.

Line five 10-ounce (25-cm) custard cups with wax paper, extending about ¼ inch (.6 cm) up the sides. Fill cups three-quarters full with the fruitcake batter. Arrange the filled cups in a circle in microwave oven.

Fill another custard cup or similar-sized glass with 1 cup (250 ml) water and put in center of fruitcakes. Cover fruitcakes and water loosely with wax paper.

Cook on medium setting 25 minutes, turning each cup of fruitcake batter halfway around about halfway through cooking. Uncover fruitcakes and cook 5 minutes longer on medium setting.

Remove fruitcakes from oven and let cool on wire rack. Remove from cups, peeling off wax paper.

Wrap fruitcakes in cheesecloth moistened with brandy or rum, then wrap in foil and store in container with tight-fitting lid. Moisten cheesecloth with liquor every day. Store fruitcakes 4 to 6 weeks. Slice thin to serve.

Conventional Directions   Prepare individual fruitcakes as in basic recipe. Bake in 350° F (180° C) oven 45 minutes to 1 hour, or until toothpick inserted in the center comes out dry.   YIELD: 5 miniature fruitcakes

Honey Cake   P A R E V E

2 eggs
¾ cup/175 ml sugar
2 Tbsp/25 ml vegetable oil
½ cup/125 ml honey
½ cup/125 ml strong, hot coffee
1½ cups/375 ml sifted flour
1 tsp/5 ml baking soda
1 tsp/5 ml baking powder
½ tsp/2 ml cinnamon

¼ tsp/1 ml *each* ginger, nutmeg,
   cloves and allspice
½ cup/125 ml finely chopped nuts
¼ cup/50 ml raisins
1 tsp/5 ml lemon juice
½ tsp/2 ml grated lemon peel
1 Tbsp/15 ml brandy, optional
¼ cup/50 ml confectioners' sugar

Mixer Directions   Place eggs, sugar and oil in mixer bowl. Attach beaters and mix on medium speed until smooth and creamy. Combine honey and hot coffee and stir until honey is dissolved. Sift dry ingredients and add alternately to batter with coffee-honey mixture, mixing well after each addition. Add nuts, raisins, lemon juice and peel and brandy, and mix well.

Pour batter into a greased and wax-paper-lined 9-by-13-inch (23-by-33-cm) cake pan. Bake at 350° F (180° C) 1 hour. Turn out of pan and remove wax paper. Turn upright. To serve, sprinkle top with confectioners' sugar.

YIELD: 9-by-13-inch (23-by-33-cm) cake

A jelly roll is a magnificent dessert that looks and tastes as if it takes more work that it actually does. Even a noncook can usually make a pretty good jelly roll and find that it is easier than assembling and frosting a layer cake.

Easy Jelly Roll   P A R E V E

1 cup/250 ml sifted flour
1 tsp/5 ml baking powder
½ tsp/2 ml salt
4 eggs, separated
1 cup/250 ml sugar
1 tsp/5 ml grated lemon peel
1 tsp/5 ml vanilla

2 Tbsp/25 ml lemon juice
2 Tbsp/25 ml hot water
¼ cup/50 ml confectioners' sugar
2 cups/500 ml prepared
   Jelly-Roll Filling
   (see following recipe)

Mixer Directions   Sift flour, baking powder and salt, and set aside. Break egg yolks into mixer bowl, attach beaters and mix on medium speed until lemon-colored. Gradually add sugar, lemon peel and vanilla, beating well. Add dry ingredients and beat just until blended. Add lemon juice and hot water and beat to a smooth batter.

In another mixer bowl place egg whites. Using whisk or beater attachments, mix on high speed until egg whites are stiff but not dry. Gently fold egg whites into prepared batter.

Grease and line with wax paper a 15½-by-10½-by-1-inch (39-by-25-by-2.5-cm) jelly-roll pan. Spread batter evenly in pan and bake at 375° F (190° C) 12 to 15 minutes. Cake is done when it springs back when touched.

Remove cake from oven and immediately run a sharp knife carefully around all edges to loosen cake from pan. Sift confectioners' sugar lightly over top of cake. Quickly cover cake with a towel and invert on counter (towel is now on the bottom and cake on top of towel). Remove wax paper from bottom of cake and trim all sides of cake to remove crisp edges.

Beginning on short side, roll cake and towel together until cake is a complete roll. Cool on rack. Unroll and remove towel. Spread jam or filling on cake. Reroll and sprinkle with confectioners' sugar. Refrigerate until serving time.   YIELD: 1 Jelly Roll 10 servings

Variation   Make the following changes in basic Jelly Roll recipe:

Chocolate Jelly-Roll   PAREVE

¼ cup/75 ml cup cocoa

Omit lemon peel and juice from basic recipe. Add cocoa along with dry ingredients. Proceed as in basic recipe.   YIELD: 10 servings, 1 Jelly Roll

---

Many of the recipes in the Sweet Sauces and Fillings chapter can be used to fill a Jelly Roll, as well as jelly, jam or preserves. Another filling idea is a classic flavored whipped cream.

Jelly-Roll Filling   PAREVE or DAIRY

1 (10-oz/(296 ml) carton   4 Tbsp/50 ml sugar, or to taste
  pareve dessert whip or   2 Tbsp/25 ml cocoa, optional
1 (8-oz/(237 ml) carton
  whipping cream

Pour dessert whip or whipping cream into mixer bowl and attach beaters. On high speed whip until stiff. Gradually add sugar, or, for chocolate filling, mix sugar and cocoa together and beat into whipped topping. Spread filling on cooled Jelly Roll.   YIELD: About 2 cups (500 ml), filling for 1 Jelly Roll

Pound cake gets its name from the fact that each of the major ingredients—butter, sugar, flour and eggs—weighs one pound. This cake is traditionally baked in a bread loaf pan and this recipe makes enough for two loaves.

Pound Cake   P A R E V E

4 cups/1 liter sifted flour
1 tsp/5 ml salt
3 tsp/15 ml baking powder
½ tsp/2 ml mace
2 cups/500 ml pareve margarine

2 cups/500 ml sugar
1 tsp/5 ml grated lemon peel
9 eggs
2 tsp/10 ml vanilla
½ cup/125 ml confectioners' sugar

Mixer Directions Sift dry ingredients except sugar together and set aside.

Place margarine in mixer bowl, attach beaters, and cream on medium speed until soft. Add sugar and lemon peel and beat until mixture is fluffy. Add eggs, one at a time, beating well after each addition. Add flour mixture, beating until batter is smooth. Add vanilla.

Pour batter into 2 greased and floured loaf pans. Bake at 325° F (160° C) 1 hour, or until toothpick inserted in the center comes out clean. To serve, sprinkle top with confectioners' sugar.   YIELD: 2 loaf cakes

Sponge Cake   P A R E V E

5 to 8 eggs, separated
1⅓ cup/325 ml sugar
1 tsp/5 ml grated lemon peel
1 tsp/5 ml vanilla

3 Tbsp/45 ml water
1 cup/250 ml sifted flour
½ tsp/2 ml salt

Mixer Directions Place egg yolks in mixer bowl and attach beaters. Mix on medium speed until yolks are very thick and lemon-colored. Gradually beat in 1 cup (250 ml) of the sugar, the lemon peel, vanilla and water. Combine flour and salt and gradually add to the batter, mixing well. Set aside.

Whip egg whites on high mixer speed until stiff. Beat in remaining ⅓ cup (125 ml) sugar gradually. Gently fold egg whites into batter. Pour batter into lightly greased tube pan, or wax-paper-lined 9-by-13-inch (23-by-33-cm) cake pan. Bake at 350° F (180° C) 50 minutes. Turn cake onto a rack to cool.
                                                              YIELD: 1 large tube cake

FROSTINGS

This is a rich, but not overly sweet, frosting often favored by bakery shops because of its durability. It holds its shape (seemingly forever) and freezes well. It is very fluffy, good for filling in cracks and uneven spaces and for covering large areas on a cake.

Bakery-Shop Frosting   P A R E V E

2 Tbsp/25 ml flour
½ cup/125 ml nondairy creamer
½ cup/125 ml water
2 cups/500 ml sifted confectioners'
  sugar

½ cup (1 stick)/125 ml
  pareve margarine
2 tsp/10 ml vanilla

Mixer Directions Place flour in a saucepan. Slowly add creamer and water, stirring to eliminate lumps. Cook over low heat until thickened, stirring constantly. Cool in the refrigerator about 1 hour.

In mixer bowl combine sugar, margarine and vanilla. Beat at high speed at least 10 minutes. Gradually add the cooled flour mixture and beat until fluffy.   YIELD: 3 cups (750 ml)

Basic Butter Frosting   D A I R Y or P A R E V E

¾ cup/175 ml
  butter or pareve margarine
2½ cups/625 ml
  sifted confectioners' sugar

Dash salt
1 tsp/5 ml vanilla
⅓ cup/75 ml liquid (milk,
  coffee, juice, nondairy creamer)

Mixer Directions On medium mixer speed, cream butter with half the sugar. Add the remaining sugar, salt, vanilla and liquid. Continue mixing until icing is smooth and creamy.   YIELD: About 2 cups (500 ml)

Variations Make the following changes in Basic Butter Frosting recipe:

Chocolate Butter Frosting   D A I R Y or P A R E V E

2 Tbsp/25 ml cocoa   Add to butter and sugar mixture in basic recipe.

Lemon Butter Frosting   D A I R Y or P A R E V E

2 Tbsp/25 ml lemon juice
1 tsp/5 ml grated lemon peel

Dash yellow food coloring,
  optional

Omit vanilla. Add lemon juice, lemon peel and yellow food coloring to prepared frosting.

Mocha Butter Frosting   DAIRY or PAREVE

1 Tbsp/15 ml cocoa
½ tsp/2 ml instant coffee powder

Add to basic recipe.

Orange Butter Frosting   DAIRY or PAREVE

⅓ cup/75 ml orange juice   Dash orange food coloring,
2 Tbsp/25 ml lemon juice   optional
1 tsp/5 ml grated orange peel

Omit vanilla. Use orange juice for the liquid. Add lemon juice, orange peel
and orange food coloring when preparing basic recipe.

Peanut-Butter Frosting   DAIRY or PAREVE

¼ cup/50 ml butter
½ cup/125 ml creamy peanut butter

Reduce butter to ¼ cup (50 ml) and add peanut butter to basic recipe.
                                    YIELD: About 2 cups (500 ml)

Brown Sugar Frosting   PAREVE

1 cup/250 ml   2½ cups/625 ml
   firmly packed brown sugar   sifted confectioners' sugar
½ cup/125 ml pareve margarine
¼ cup/50 ml liquid (nondairy
   creamer or apple juice)

Microwave Oven Directions In glass bowl combine brown sugar and margarine. Place in microwave oven and cook on high setting 2 minutes or until
mixture boils. Stir until thoroughly combined. Add liquid. Cook on high
setting 1 minute longer or until mixture returns to a boil. Stir, then allow
mixture to cool.

Slowly stir sugar into cooled mixture, then beat until frosting reaches
spreading consistency.

Conventional Directions In a saucepan melt margarine over medium heat. Stir
in brown sugar and cook, stirring constantly, until mixture comes to a boil.
Add liquid and return mixture to a boil. Remove from heat and let stand to
cool. Slowly beat in confectioners' sugar, beating until frosting reaches a
spreading consistency.   YIELD: 2 cups (500 ml)

Chocolate Icing   PAREVE

1 (6-oz/(168 grams) package   4 Tbsp/50 ml liquid (water,
  chocolate chips   coffee or nondairy creamer)
4 Tbsp/50 ml pareve margarine   2½ cups/625 ml confectioners' sugar
                                     1 tsp/5 ml vanilla

Microwave Oven Directions   In a glass bowl combine chocolate chips, margarine and liquid. Place in microwave oven and cook on high setting 2 minutes, or until chocolate and margarine are melted. Stir in sugar and vanilla. Beat until smooth.

Conventional Directions   In a saucepan combine chocolate chips, margarine and liquid, cook slowly, stirring constantly, until chocolate and margarine are melted. Stir in sugar and vanilla. Beat until smooth.

YIELD: 2 cups (500 ml)

Variation   Make the following changes in Chocolate Icing recipe:

Chocolate Mint Icing   PAREVE

1 tsp/5 ml mint extract   Omit vanilla and substitute mint extract, following basic recipe.

YIELD: 2 cups (500 ml)

Confectioners' Sugar Frosting   PAREVE

4 Tbsp/50 ml pareve margarine   ¼ tsp/1 ml salt
1 egg yolk   3½ cups (1 lb)/875 ml sifted
1 tsp/5 ml vanilla   confectioners' sugar
4 Tbsp/50 ml liquid (nondairy
  creamer, juice, coffee)

Mixer Directions   Place margarine and egg yolk in mixer bowl and attach beaters. Beat on medium speed until light and fluffy. Add vanilla, liquid and salt and beat about 2 minutes longer.

Reduce mixer speed to low. Add about 1 cup (250 ml) sugar and mix until combined. Increase speed to medium and beat until smooth. Continue adding sugar in the same manner until frosting reaches proper consistency.

YIELD: 2 cups (500 ml)

Variations   Make the following changes in basic Confectioners' Sugar Frosting recipe:

Chocolate Frosting   PAREVE

6 Tbsp/75 ml liquid   ½ cup/125 ml cocoa
Omit egg and increase liquid to 6 tablespoons (75 ml). Add cocoa.

Lemon Frosting   PAREVE

1 tsp/5 ml grated lemon peel   Dash yellow food coloring,
2 Tbsp/25 ml lemon juice   optional
2 Tbsp/25 ml water

Omit vanilla and substitute grated lemon peel. For liquid use lemon juice
and water. If desired, add a few drops of yellow food coloring.

Pineapple Frosting   PAREVE

½ cup/125 ml crushed pineapple

Omit liquid. Add crushed pineapple, undrained, to basic recipe.

YIELD: 2 cups (500 ml)

This snowy-white, candy-sweet icing is made by folding a cooked sugar
syrup into stiffly beaten egg whites. Do not attempt to put a candy thermometer in the microwave oven. Remove the bowl of syrup from the oven,
test with a candy thermometer, then remove the thermometer before returning the mixture to the microwave oven.

Cooked Icing   PAREVE

1½ cups/375 ml granulated sugar   2 egg whites
¼ cup/50 ml light corn syrup   Dash of salt
½ cup/125 ml water   1½ tsp/7 ml vanilla

Microwave Oven Directions   In a large glass bowl combine sugar, corn syrup
and water. Place in microwave oven and cook on high setting 5 minutes or
until mixture is clear. Stir well. Cook on high setting 6 to 8 minutes longer or
until syrup measures 240° F (115° C) on a candy thermometer. (Do not use
candy thermometer in microwave oven.) Allow syrup to cool.

Beat egg whites with salt until stiff but not dry. Pour syrup slowly over egg
whites, beating constantly. Add vanilla and continue beating until mixture
is thickened. Spread on cake while icing is still warm. If icing hardens, add a
few drops of hot water to regain spreading consistency.

Conventional Directions   In a saucepan combine sugar, corn syrup, water and
salt. Cook over medium heat to the soft-ball stage (240° F or 115° C). Beat
egg whites until stiff and gradually beat in cooled syrup mixture. Add vanilla and beat until icing reaches spreading consistency.

YIELD: 2 cups (500 ml)

Variations Add the following ingredients to basic Cooked Icing recipe:

Birthday Icing   PAREVE

¼ tsp/1 ml food coloring   1½ tsp/7 ml extract

Add food coloring to prepared icing. Various flavors of extract, such as orange, banana, lemon, strawberry and peppermint, may be substituted for the vanilla.

Chocolate Icing   PAREVE

2 squares (2 oz)/(60 grams) unsweetened chocolate, melted

Stir melted chocolate into prepared icing.

Coconut Icing   PAREVE

½ cup/125 ml shredded coconut   Fold coconut into prepared icing.

YIELD: 2 cups (500 ml)

Marshmallow Frosting   PAREVE

½ cup/125 ml   2 Tbsp/25 ml
  vegetable shortening   hot water, or as needed
2½ cups/625 ml   ¾ cup/175 ml
  sifted confectioners' sugar   marshmallow topping
½ tsp/2 ml salt   ½ tsp/2 ml vanilla

Mixer Directions Combine shortening, sugar and salt in mixer bowl. Attach beaters and begin mixing on medium speed. Add water, more if necessary, mixing until frosting reaches a spreading consistency. Add marshmallow topping and vanilla and beat until smooth and creamy.

YIELD: 2 cups (500 ml)

Simple Pareve Frosting   PAREVE

3 cups/750 ml   1 egg
  sifted confectioners' sugar   1 tsp/5 ml vanilla
4 Tbsp/50 ml pareve margarine, softened

Blender Directions Place 2 cups (500 ml) of sugar in a mixing bowl. Set aside. In blender goblet, combine remaining sugar, margarine, egg and vanilla. Blend at medium speed until smooth. Add to sugar in mixing bowl and stir until well blended.

YIELD: 2 cups (500 ml)

Walnut Frosting   PAREVE

1 cup/250 ml
  pareve margarine, softened
½ cup/125 ml brown sugar
2 cups/500 ml confectioners' sugar

½ cup/125 ml apple juice
1 cup/250 ml walnuts, ground
  (or very finely chopped)
1 tsp/5 ml vanilla

Mixer Directions In mixer bowl, place margarine and brown sugar. Cream at medium speed until well blended and fluffy. With motor running, add confectioners' sugar and mix until smooth. Add juice, walnuts and vanilla. Beat until fluffy.   YIELD: 2 cups (500 ml)

GLAZES

See Passover chapter for Chocolate Glaze Topping recipe.

Coffee Glaze   PAREVE

1½ Tbsp/20 ml pareve margarine
1 Tbsp/15 ml hot coffee

½ tsp/2 ml vanilla
1 cup/250 ml confectioners' sugar

Microwave Oven Directions In small glass mixing bowl heat margarine on high setting until melted, about 30 seconds. Add coffee and vanilla. Gradually stir in sugar, by hand, to make a smooth glaze. Drizzle over cake.

Conventional Directions Melt margarine in small saucepan. Add remaining ingredients, stirring to make a smooth glaze. YIELD: About ¾ cup (175 ml)

White Glaze   PAREVE or DAIRY

1½ to 2 cups/375 to 500 ml
  confectioners' sugar
Dash salt

4 Tbsp/50 ml liquid (see below),
  or as needed
½ tsp/2 ml vanilla

Conventional Directions Place sugar and salt in mixing bowl. Add enough liquid to form an icing of spreading consistency. A variety of liquids can be used, such as milk, nondairy creamer, orange or lemon juice, brandy or liqueur, etc. Flavor icing with vanilla. Drizzle over baked cake, coffee cake or rolls.   YIELD: About ¾ cup (175 ml)

DESSERTS

There is certainly more than one way to do something well. Many types of desserts can easily be made with one, another, or even a third kitchen appliance.

The microwave oven can be used to cook pie crusts, fillings and fondue. Although it is faster to cook cookies conventionally, since 2 or 3 dozen can be baked at once, the microwave oven can be used to cook delicious bars and brownies.

Use the mixer for heavy mixtures, such as strudel and cookie doughs, as well as for any recipe that calls for beating egg whites or dessert whip, such as the frozen desserts.

The blender can be used to make crumb crusts for pies, to blend jel mixtures for pie fillings or frozen desserts and to blend the liquid ingredients for cookies.

The food processor, also, is used for cookies only to combine liquid ingredients, which are then stirred by hand into a flour mixture. The food processor makes short work of grinding poppy and sesame seeds for cookie fillings and candy. This appliance is the number-one choice for making pastry dough.

Many of these dessert recipes call for chocolate. If you are out of one kind and want to substitute another, the following guide will be helpful:

For 1 oz (30 grams) unsweetened chocolate use:

    1 square (1 oz, 30 grams) chocolate, or
    3 Tbsp (45 ml) cocoa *plus* 1 Tbsp (15 ml) shortening or oil

For 6 oz (180 grams) semi-sweet chocolate use:

    1 cup (250 ml) semi-sweet chocolate chips, or
    6 squares semi-sweet chocolate, or

6 Tbsp (75 ml) cocoa plus 7 Tbsp (100 ml) sugar plus ¼ cup (50 ml) shortening

For 4 oz (125 grams) sweet cooking chocolate use:

4 squares sweet chocolate, or
4 Tbsp (50 ml) cocoa plus 4⅔ Tbsp (60 ml) sugar plus 2⅔ Tbsp (35 ml) shortening

---

Plan to set aside an entire morning or afternoon for rolling strudel dough, when you can work leisurely and uninterrupted. Although some cooks feel that "many hands make light work" and welcome assistance in pulling and shaping the strudel dough, I have come to the conclusion that, at least for me, strudel rolling work is much lighter when my "many hands" go to the movies with their daddy.

Old-Fashioned Stretched Strudel Dough   PAREVE

3 cups or more/750 ml flour
½ tsp/2 ml baking powder
½ tsp/2 ml salt
1 egg
1 Tbsp/15 ml oil
1 Tbsp/15 ml sugar

1 cup/250 ml warm water (about)
4 Tbsp/50 ml
   pareve margarine, melted
Prepared strudel filling
   (see page 282)
¼ cup/50 ml confectioners' sugar

Mixer Directions Sift flour, baking powder and salt into mixer bowl. Attach dough hook and begin mixing on low speed. Add egg, oil and sugar, mixing well. Gradually add water and continue mixing to form a soft dough. If necessary, add more flour until proper consistency is reached. Knead the dough, on low speed, 15 minutes or until it is very pliable and silky. Place dough in a greased bowl and allow to rest in a warm place 20 minutes.

To roll strudel dough: Prepare the kitchen table or large, flat surface with a lightly floured cloth. Put dough in center of cloth and roll as thin as possible, keeping the rolling pin and surface well floured.

Now it is necessary to stretch the strudel dough to make it even thinner. Put your hands under the dough, palms down and stretch and pull the dough gently, with slightly raised knuckles. Gently and steadily pull and stretch the dough, walking around the table to keep the dough thickness even. This dough recipe can stretch over an ordinary-size kitchen table to semi-transparent thickness.

To fill strudel dough: Brush dough with melted pareve margarine. Sprinkle the prepared filling evenly over the dough surface. Trim off the hanging edges of the dough. Gently lift the tablecloth from one end and the strudel dough will roll itself up. This will result in one long roll, 3 or 4 inches (8 to

10 cm) in diameter. Gently transfer the strudel to a greased cookie sheet and bend it to make a horseshoe shape. Brush the top with melted pareve margarine.

Bake the strudel at 400° F (200° C) 35 to 45 minutes or until golden brown. Sprinkle with confectioners' sugar and cut into 2-inch (5-cm) slices. Serve warm or cold.

YIELD: 1 very large strudel
3 dozen 2-inch (5-cm) pieces

My good friend Marshall Gollub has many reasons to be content with life. He has a beautiful wife, Lois, who is a great cook, four lively children, success in his chosen profession—even a reliable auto mechanic. So what's missing? Marshall expresses it in a rather incomplete sentence, "If my wife could only learn to make strudel like my aunt Sadie . . ."

The following recipe for Dairy Dough is good for those learning to make strudel because this soft, pliable dough is easy to handle and, unlike the old-fashioned kind, does not need to be stretched.

Dairy Dough for Strudel   D A I R Y

4½ cups/1125 ml sifted flour
½ tsp/2 ml salt
1 lb (4 sticks)/500 grams
  butter or margarine, melted
1 pint (2 cups)/500 ml sour
  cream or vanilla
  ice cream, softened

4 Tbsp/50 ml butter or
  pareve margarine, melted
Prepared strudel filling
  (see following recipes)
¼ cup/50 ml confectioners' sugar

Mixer Directions Combine flour and salt in mixer bowl. Attach beaters and begin mixing on low speed. Add melted butter and sour cream, mixing until smooth. Add more flour, if necessary, until dough is firm enough to hold together. Divide dough into quarters and refrigerate at least 2 hours, or overnight.

Lightly flour working surface and rolling pin. Roll each section of dough to about ⅛-inch (.5-cm) thickness. Brush top of dough with melted butter. Sprinkle filling mixture (see following two recipes) evenly over surface. Roll dough jelly-roll style. Place roll on ungreased baking sheet. Repeat procedure with remaining pieces of dough. Bake at 400° F (200° C) 1 hour. Sprinkle with confectioners' sugar and slice while still warm.

YIELD: 4 dozen slices

Apple Filling for Strudel   PAREVE

1 lemon
½ cup/125 ml sugar
1 cup/250 ml walnuts
8 apples,
    peeled, quartered and cored

1 cup/250 ml raisins
¾ cup/175 ml
    pareve dry bread crumbs
2 tsp/10 ml cinnamon

Food Processor Directions   Peel off the thin outer portion of the lemon peel, using a paring knife or vegetable peeler, and set aside. Squeeze the juice from the lemon, strain and set aside.

Insert steel blade in food processor. Place outer peel of lemon and sugar in the container and process until peel is finely chopped. Transfer to a mixing bowl.

Place walnuts in container and process, using pulse button or quick on-off motion, until coarsely chopped. Add to sugar mixture.

Insert shredding disc in food processor. Cut the apple into chunks and guide through feed tube to shred. As container becomes full, empty contents into mixing bowl. Add remaining ingredients and mix well. Use as a filling for prepared strudel dough.

YIELD: Filling for large strudel (about 8 cups or 2 liters)

Mohn (Poppy Seed) Filling for Strudel   PAREVE

1 lb/500 grams poppy seeds
1 lemon
½ cup/125 ml sugar

½ cup/125 ml honey
1 cup/250 ml raisins, optional
1 cup/250 ml nuts, optional

Food Processor Directions   Rinse poppy seeds thoroughly in boiling water and drain. Spread thin on a clean cloth and allow to dry overnight.

Insert steel blade in food processor. Place 1 cup (250 ml) of the poppy seeds in container and process until finely ground. Transfer to mixing bowl and continue processing remaining poppy seeds.

Slice off the thin outer portion of the lemon peel, using a paring knife or vegetable peeler, and set aside. Squeeze the juice from the lemon, strain and add to poppy seeds in mixing bowl.

Place lemon peel and sugar in food processor container and process until peel is finely ground. Add to poppy-seed mixture. Add remaining ingredients and stir until well combined. Use as a filling for prepared strudel dough.   YIELD: Filling for large strudel

Cream puffs are a luscious, fancy dessert, perfect for big celebrations (such as *finally* reaching Weight Watchers' goal!). Both the food processor and the mixer can be used to simplify the mixing process, but the initial cooking of the dough must be done conventionally.

Cream Puffs   PAREVE

1 cup/250 ml water
½ cup/125 ml pareve margarine
¼ tsp/1 ml salt
1 cup/250 ml sifted flour

4 large eggs
2 cups/500 ml filling
(see Sweet Sauces
and Fillings chapter)

Conventional Directions   Step 1. Combine water, margarine and salt in a saucepan and heat to a full, rolling boil. Remove saucepan from the heat and add all the flour at once. Stir flour until the mixture forms a ball and pulls away from sides of pan. Let mixture stand 5 minutes.

Step 2. Add unbeaten eggs, one at a time, beating thoroughly after each addition.

Step 3. To form cream puffs, drop spoonfuls of dough onto greased cookie sheet. Place puffs about 2 to 3 inches apart. Bake in preheated 400° F (200° C) oven 35 to 40 minutes, or until light brown. Cool the puffs completely on a wire rack. Cut off the tops and pull out any filaments of soft dough. Fill each puff with about 2 tablespoons (25 ml) desired filling (see Sweet Sauces and Fillings chapter).

Food Processor Directions   Follow Step 1 under Conventional Directions. Insert steel blade in food processor. Place cooked dough in container. Begin processing and add eggs, one at a time, through feed tube. Process well after each addition. Follow Step 3, shaping and cooking as directed.

Mixer Directions   Follow Step 1 under Conventional Directions. Place cooked dough in mixer bowl and attach dough hook. On low speed add the eggs, one at a time, beating about 30 seconds after each addition. Shape as directed.   YIELD: 16 cream puffs

Variation

Eclairs

Shape finished dough into 16 rectangles, 1 inch by 4 inches (2.5 cm by 10 cm). Bake and fill as for Cream Puffs.   YIELD: 16 eclairs

PIE CRUSTS

Pie crust dough is often chilled before rolling for easier handling. The dough is then rolled in a large circle, 1½ inches (4 cm) larger than the inverted pie dish and about ⅛ inch (.3 cm) thick. Gently ease the rolled dough into the dish.

For single-crust pies, trim the dough ½ inch (2 cm) beyond the edge of the dish, fold under to make a double thickness of dough around the rim and flute with fingers or fork. If the pie is to be filled before baking, bake according to the time and temperature recommended for the filling. For a single crust baked without filling, prick the bottom and sides thoroughly with a fork before baking. This crust is usually baked in a very hot oven, 400° to 450° F (200° to 230° C) 10 to 15 minutes, or until lightly browned.

For a double-crust pie, trim the dough edge even with the edge of the pie dish, then add desired filling. Roll top crust and lift onto filled pie. Fold top edge under bottom crust and flute with fingers. Slit top crust to allow steam to escape. Bake according to time and temperature recommended for filling.

PIE CRUSTS IN THE MICROWAVE OVEN

The following tips and timing guide will result in tender, flaky pie crusts from the microwave oven:
· Place the rolled dough in a glass pie dish.
· Use a fork to prick the sides and bottom of the crust.
· Rotate the dish once or twice during cooking time.
· Always precook the bottom crust before adding the filling.
· A frozen crust should be completely defrosted before cooking.
· Crust is done when it flakes easily and no longer looks doughy.
 The pie does not brown in the microwave oven.

MICROWAVE OVEN TIMING GUIDE FOR PIE CRUSTS

Basic Pie Crust	4–5 min	High setting
Coconut Macaroon Crust	2 min	High setting
(Passover chapter)		
Cookie Crumb Crust	2 min	High setting
Fancy Pie Crust	4–5 min	High setting
Graham Cracker Crust	2 min	High setting
Matzah Meal Pie Crust	4 min	High setting
(Passover chapter)		
Passover Nut Pie Crust	2 min	High setting
(Passover chapter)		

Basic Pie Crust   P A R E V E

SINGLE CRUST	DOUBLE CRUST
1⅓ cups/325 ml flour	2½ cups/625 ml flour
½ tsp/2 ml salt	1 tsp/5 ml salt
½ cup/125 ml vegetable shortening	1 cup/250 ml vegetable shortening
¼ cup/50 ml ice water	⅓ to ½ cup/75 to 125 ml ice water

Food Processor Directions Insert steel blade in food processor. Sift together flour and salt and place in container. Add shortening and process until mixture resembles cornmeal (about 5 seconds). Slowly pour water through feed tube and process until dough forms a ball (about 5 to 10 seconds).

Chill dough for easier handling. Roll into a circle ⅛ inch (.5 cm) thick and place in pie dish. Flute edges. Bake at 450° F (230° C) 12 to 15 minutes. Cook crust before adding filling.   YIELD: Single or double pie crust

Variations Add the following ingredients to Basic Pie Crust recipe:

Lemon Pie Shell   P A R E V E

1 tsp/5 ml grated lemon peel	2 Tbsp/25 ml water
1½ tsp/7 ml sugar	1 egg yolk, optional
2 Tbsp/25 ml lemon juice	

Add lemon peel and sugar to dry ingredients. For liquid use lemon juice and 2 tablespoons (25 ml) or more water. One beaten egg yolk may be added, along with the liquid, for added color.

Nut Pie Shell   P A R E V E

⅔ cup/150 ml finely chopped nuts

Use steel blade of food processor to chop nut meats fine. Add with flour when preparing basic recipe.

Spiced Pie Shell   P A R E V E

2 Tbsp/15 ml	¼ tsp/1 ml
confectioners' sugar	*each* cinnamon and nutmeg

YIELD: Single or double pie crust

Fancy Pie Crust   DAIRY or PAREVE

2 cups/500 ml flour
½ tsp/2 ml salt
1 cup (2 sticks)/250 grams frozen
   butter or pareve margarine

2 egg yolks
About ⅓ cup/75 ml ice water

Food Processor Directions Insert steel blade in food processor. Sift together flour and salt and place in container. Cut each stick of butter into 8 pieces and place in container. Process until mixture resembles cornmeal (5 seconds). Lightly beat the 2 egg yolks in measuring cup and add enough ice water to make ½ cup (125 ml). Start the motor and pour water mixture in a steady stream through the feed tube. Dough is ready when it forms a ball (5 to 10 seconds).

Divide dough in half. Roll each out on a pastry board and fit into 9-inch (23-cm) pie dishes. Bake in 400° F (200° C) oven 15 minutes.

YIELD: Two 9-inch (23-cm) pie shells

Variations Make the following changes in basic Fancy Pie Crust recipe

Cream Cheese Pie Shell   DAIRY

½ cup/125 ml butter

½ cup/125 ml cream cheese

Reduce butter to ½ cup (125 ml) and add ½ cup (125 ml) cream cheese. This makes a light, soft, delicate dough.

Yogurt Pie Shell   DAIRY

¼ tsp/1 ml baking soda

⅓ cup/75 ml unflavored yogurt

Add baking soda with sifted dry ingredients. Substitute yogurt for water, using just enough to hold the dough together.

YIELD: Two 9-inch (23-cm) pie shells

Cookie Crumb Crust   PAREVE

12 to 15 cookies, or enough to yield
   1 cup (250 ml) crumbs
⅓ cup/75 ml
   melted pareve margarine

2 Tbsp/25 ml sugar
½ tsp/2 ml cinnamon

Blender Directions Break cookies into blender goblet and process on low setting until mixture is reduced to crumbs. Add remaining ingredients and blend thoroughly on low speed. Press mixture onto the bottom and sides of a 9-inch (23-cm) pie dish. Bake at 350° F (180° C) 10 minutes.

YIELD: One 9-inch (23-cm) pie crust

Graham Cracker Crust   P A R E V E

12 graham crackers,   ¼ cup/50 ml sugar
  broken into quarters   ½ tsp/2 ml cinnamon, optional
6 Tbsp/75 ml pareve margarine

Food Processor Directions   Insert steel blade in food processor. Place graham
cracker pieces in container and process until reduced to fine crumbs. Cut the
margarine into chunks and place in container. Add sugar and process until
mixture is well combined. Press mixture into a 9-inch (23-cm) pie dish. Bake
at 375° F (190° C) for 8 minutes.   YIELD: 9-inch (23-cm) pie crust

PIE FILLINGS

Following are recipes for fruit pies (from fresh, canned and dried fruit),
chiffon pies using imitation-jel dessert, a nut pie and luscious, rich lemon
and chocolate pies. For tips on adapting these filling recipes for Passover use
see Passover chapter.

Apple Streusel Pie   P A R E V E

6 cups/1500 ml apple slices   ½ tsp/2 ml nutmeg
¾ cup/175 ml sugar   9-inch (23-cm) pie shell
Dash salt   1¾ cups/425 ml
2 tsp/10 ml lemon juice   Streusel Topping, optional
1 tsp/5 ml cinnamon   (see following recipe)

Microwave Oven Directions   Mix apple slices with sugar, salt, lemon juice and
spices and arrange mixture in baked pie shell. Sprinkle with Streusel Topping, if desired (see following recipe) and place in microwave oven. Cook on
high setting 8 minutes.

Conventional Directions   Combine apples, sugar, salt, lemon juice and spices,
and spoon into unbaked pie shell. Sprinkle on Streusel Topping, if desired.
Bake at 400° F (200° C) 45 minutes.   YIELD: 9-inch (23-cm) pie

Streusel Topping   P A R E V E

1 cup/250 ml   1 tsp/5 ml cinnamon
  flour or matzah meal   ⅓ cup/75 ml pareve margarine
½ cup/125 ml brown sugar

Conventional Directions   Combine flour, brown sugar and cinnamon. Cut in
margarine until crumbly. Spoon evenly over pie filling and bake according
to filling directions.   YIELD: About 1¾ cup (425 ml)

Dried Apricot Pie   PAREVE

1½ cups/375 ml (½ lb)
  dried apricots, coarsely chopped
1 cup/250 ml raisins
¾ cup/175 ml apricot nectar
2 Tbsp/25 ml lemon juice
1 tsp/5 ml lemon peel

1 cup/250 ml water, or as needed
3 Tbsp/45 ml cornstarch
¼ cup/50 ml water
1 cup/250 ml chopped nuts
9-inch (23-cm) baked pie shell

Crock Pot Directions Place apricots in crock pot. Add raisins, nectar, lemon juice and peel. Add water to barely cover apricots. Place cover on crock pot and cook on low setting 2 to 3 hours. Turn control to high. Mix cornstarch in ¼ cup (50 ml) water and stir into apricot mixture. Cook on high setting 10 minutes or until mixture is thickened. Add nuts and stir. Pour into baked pie shell. Serve warm or cold.   YIELD: 9-inch (23-cm) pie

Blueberry "Can-Do" Pie   PAREVE

1 Basic Pie Crust recipe,
  dough for double crust
1 tsp/5 ml lemon juice

1 (21-oz/588-gram) can
  blueberry pie filling
½ tsp/2 ml sugar
¼ tsp/1 ml cinnamon

Microwave Oven Directions Roll half of the Basic Pie Crust dough into a circle ⅛ inch (.5 cm) thick and place in a glass pie dish. Flute edges. Use a fork to prick the sides and bottom of the crust. Cook on high setting 4 to 5 minutes until crust flakes easily and no longer looks doughy.

Add lemon juice to blueberry pie filling. Stir well and pour into baked pie shell. Cook on high setting in microwave oven for 8 minutes or until filling is hot and bubbly. Set aside to cool.

Roll the pie-crust dough on a floured surface into a 9-inch (23-cm) circle. Place pastry circle on a paper towel. Fold under ½ inch (1.25 cm) around edge of dough and flute to form a rim. Cut circle into 6 wedges. Sprinkle surface with a mixture of sugar and cinnamon. Cook, uncovered, on high setting 4 minutes or until pastry is flaky. Remove wedges from paper towel while still warm and arrange on finished pie. Serve warm or cool.

Conventional Directions Prepare bottom crust as described above, but do not bake. Spoon pie filling into crust. Roll top crust and place over filling. Sprinkle surface with mixture of sugar and cinnamon. Flute edges together. Bake at 350° F (180° C) 40 to 45 minutes.   YIELD: 9-inch (23-cm) pie

Cherry Sour-Cream Pie   P A R E V E

FILLING

2 cans (1 lb 4 oz/567 grams)
   cherries, drained
1 cup/250 ml sugar, or to taste
Dash salt

2 Tbsp/25 ml flour
¼ tsp/1 ml almond extract
9-inch (23-cm) baked pie shell

TOPPING

1 cup/250 ml sour cream
¼ cup/50 ml sugar

½ tsp/2 ml almond extract

Microwave Oven Directions Combine drained cherries, sugar, salt, flour and almond extract. Pour into baked pie shell and place in microwave oven. Cook on high setting 8 minutes, until mixture boils and thickens.

Combine topping ingredients and spread over hot filling. Return to microwave oven and cook on high setting 1½ to 2½ minutes, or until topping is hot.

Conventional Directions Combine all filling ingredients and pour into unbaked pie shell. Bake in a 400° F (200° C) oven 45 minutes. Remove from oven. Reduce heat to 350° F (180° C). Spread topping over pie filling and bake 10 minutes.   YIELD: 9-inch (23-cm) pie

---

Sabra Chocolate Pie   P A R E V E

6 oz/180 grams
   semi-sweet chocolate
⅓ cup/75 ml sugar
2 Tbsp/25 ml water

2 Tbsp/25 ml Sabra liqueur
6 eggs, separated
9-inch (23-cm) baked pie shell

Microwave Oven Directions In a glass mixing bowl combine chocolate, 2 tablespoons (25 ml) sugar and water. Cook on high setting in microwave oven 2 minutes, or until chocolate is melted. Stir until mixture is smooth. Allow to cool slightly. Stir in liqueur.

Beat egg yolks until thick and lemon-colored and add to chocolate mixture, beating well. Beat egg whites until stiff but not dry. Add remaining sugar gradually. Gently fold egg whites into chocolate mixture. Pour into prepared pie shell and freeze until firm. Serve plain or garnished with pareve dessert whip.

Conventional Directions In a saucepan, combine chocolate, 2 tablespoons (25 ml) sugar and water. Cook over low heat, stirring constantly, until chocolate is melted and mixture is smooth. Proceed as in basic recipe.

YIELD: 9-inch (23-cm) pie or 6 cups

Variation

Chocolate Mousse   P A R E V E

Pour prepared mixture into 6 individual cups. Chill in refrigerator several
hours.   YIELD: 9-inch (23-cm) pie or 6 cups

Cottage Cheese—Pineapple Pie   D A I R Y

1 package kosher imitation-jel
  dessert, pineapple-flavored
½ cup/125 ml
  pineapple juice, very hot
2 Tbsp/25 ml lemon juice
1 egg
2 cups/500 ml
  creamed cottage cheese

9-inch (23-cm)
  Graham Cracker Crust
  (see recipe in this chapter)
1 (8-oz/227-gram) can
  pineapple tidbits, drained

Blender Directions   Place jel, pineapple juice and lemon juice in blender goblet. Blend on low speed until jel is dissolved. Add egg and blend until
smooth. Add cottage cheese and blend on high speed until mixture is smooth
and creamy. Pour into prepared Graham Cracker Crust. Chill until set. To
serve, spoon pineapple tidbits over top of pie.   YIELD: 9-inch (23-cm) pie

---

Orange Chiffon Pie   P A R E V E

1 package kosher imitation-jel
  dessert, orange-flavored
½ cup/125 ml orange juice
1 Tbsp/15 ml grated orange peel

½ cup/125 ml boiling water
4 eggs, separated
¼ cup/50 ml sugar
9-inch (23-cm) baked pie shell

Blender Directions   Place jel, orange juice and grated peel in blender goblet.
Blend on low speed until jel is softened. Add boiling water and blend until
jel is dissolved. Increase to high speed and add egg yolks, one at a time. Pour
mixture into a shallow dish and chill until mixture thickens to consistency of
unbeaten egg whites.

Beat egg whites until stiff but not dry. Gradually beat sugar into egg
whites, adding 1 tablespoon (15 ml) at a time. Fold chilled jel mixture into
egg whites. Pour into prepared pie shell and chill until firm.

YIELD: 9-inch (23-cm) pie

This fabulous lemon filling called "lemon curd" in England, is a thicker variation of the recipe for Lemon Sauce found in the Sweet Sauce chapter.

Lemon Meringue Pie   PAREVE

3 whole eggs
3 egg yolks
1 cup/250 ml sugar
2 Tbsp/25 ml grated lemon peel
½ cup/125 ml lemon juice

½ cup/125 ml
   pareve margarine, melted
9-inch (23-cm) baked pie shell
Meringue Topping (see following
   recipe)

Microwave Oven Directions In a glass mixing bowl beat eggs and egg yolks until thick and lemon-colored. Add sugar, lemon peel and lemon juice, and beat until mixture is smooth. Add melted margarine.

Place lemon mixture in microwave oven and cook on high setting 4 minutes, or until mixture is thick and bubbly, stirring each minute. Pour into baked pie shell and chill thoroughly. Prepare Meringue Topping (see following recipe) and spread over filling, bringing it well out onto the edge of the crust, completely covering filling. Bake at 325° F (160° C) 12 to 15 minutes or until browned.

Conventional Directions Combine beaten eggs and yolks, sugar, lemon peel and juice in top of a double boiler. Place over boiling water. Add margarine and cook, stirring constantly, until margarine is melted and sauce is thickened. Prepare Meringue Topping and bake as directed.

YIELD: 9-inch (23-cm) pie.

Meringue Topping   PAREVE

3 egg whites
¼ tsp/1 ml salt

6 Tbsp/75 ml sugar
1 tsp/5 ml vanilla

Mixer Directions Place egg whites in mixer bowl and attach beaters. Beat on high speed until egg whites are stiff but not dry. With mixer running, gradually add salt and sugar. Continue mixing until sugar is well blended and mixture is fluffy. Mix in vanilla.

Spread meringue over cooked pie filling, bringing it well out onto the edge of the crust and completely covering filling. Bake at 325° F (160° C) 12 to 15 minutes or until browned. Chill before serving.

YIELD: Topping for 9-inch (23-cm) pie

This is among the easiest of all pies to make in the microwave oven.

Pecan Pie
P A R E V E

3 Tbsp/45 ml pareve margarine
3 eggs
1 cup/250 ml dark corn syrup
¼ cup/50 ml dark brown sugar

1 tsp/5 ml vanilla
½ cup (4-oz)/(125 grams)
 chopped pecans
9-inch/23-cm baked pie shell

Microwave Oven Directions   Place margarine in small custard cup. Cook on high setting 30 seconds or until melted. In mixing bowl, beat eggs. Add corn syrup, sugar and vanilla, and stir until well blended. Add melted margarine and pecans and mix well. Pour mixture into baked pie shell. Use a spoon or spatula to distribute pecans evenly over the top. Cook, uncovered, on medium setting 17 minutes. Allow to cool before serving.

Conventional Directions   Melt margarine in small pan on stove. Beat eggs and mix ingredients as described above. Pour mixture into unbaked pie shell. Bake in a 450° F (230° C) oven about 40 minutes, or until knife inserted in the center comes out clean.   YIELD: 9-inch (23-cm) pie

Pumpkin Pie
D A I R Y

2 eggs
⅔ cup/150 ml brown sugar
⅓ cup/75 ml sugar
1 Tbsp/15 ml flour
2 tsp/10 ml pumpkin pie spice
½ tsp/2 ml salt

½ tsp/2 ml vanilla
1 (16-oz)/(454 grams) can
 cooked pumpkin
1 (13-oz)/(384 ml)
 can evaporated milk
9-inch/23-cm pie shell

Microwave Oven Directions   Beat eggs in a large mixing bowl. Add remaining ingredients except pie shell, and blend thoroughly. Pour mixture into baked pie shell and place in microwave oven. Cook on medium setting 5 minutes, or until edges begin to set. Carefully stir to move the cooked portions toward the center. Continue cooking on medium setting 10 to 12 minutes longer or until knife inserted in the center comes out clean. Cool before serving.

Conventional Directions   Prepare filling as in basic recipe and pour mixture into unbaked pie shell. Bake at 425° F (220° C) 20 minutes, then reduce to 325° F (160° C) and bake 35 to 45 minutes longer. YIELD: 9-inch (23-cm) pie

A layer of creamy vanilla filling, topped with fresh, plump strawberries and drizzled with a sweetened glaze—luscious!!!

Strawberry Pie
D A I R Y

1 quart/1 liter fresh strawberries   ½ cup/125 ml confectioners' sugar

1¼ cups/300 ml milk
¼ cup/50 ml sugar
Dash salt
3 eggs

1 Tbsp/15 ml butter
1 tsp/5 ml vanilla
9-inch/23-cm baked pie shell

½ cup/125 ml water
½ cup/125 ml sugar, or to taste
1 Tbsp/15 ml cornstarch
2 Tbsp/25 ml water

¼ tsp/1 ml red food coloring,
   optional
Whipped cream

Wash and hull strawberries. Set aside 1 cup (250 ml) of the smaller berries to use in glaze. Mix remaining berries with confectioners' sugar. Let stand at least 1 hour.

Microwave Oven Directions   Pour milk into a glass measuring cup and cook on high setting 2 minutes, or until very hot.

In a glass mixing bowl, combine sugar, salt and eggs, and beat well. Slowly pour in hot milk, stirring constantly. Stir in butter and vanilla. Cook on medium setting 3 minutes, or until mixture boils. Stir well and allow to cool slightly.

Pour vanilla filling into baked pie shell. Arrange strawberries mixed with confectioners' sugar over filling. Chill thuroughly.

Prepare glaze by thoroughly mashing or blending the 1 cup (250 ml) reserved strawberries. Combine with ½ cup (125 ml) water and sugar in a glass mixing bowl. Place in microwave oven and cook on high setting 3 minutes, or until mixture boils. Dissolve cornstarch in 2 tablespoons cold water and add to mixture. Cook on high setting 1 minute longer or until mixture thickens. If desired, a few drops of red food coloring may be added for a more intense red color. Pour hot glaze over top of pie. Chill in refrigerator. To serve, garnish with whipped cream.

Conventional Directions   To prepare filling, combine milk, sugar and salt in top of a double boiler. When mixture is hot, add beaten eggs and cook, stirring constantly, until mixture is thickened. Stir in butter and vanilla. Cool before pouring into pie shell. Arrange strawberries mixed with confectioners' sugar on top. Chill.

To prepare glaze, place set-aside strawberries, water and sugar in a saucepan. Mash strawberries and cook until mixture is hot. Mix cornstarch in 2 tablespoons water and add to strawberry mixture. Cook, stirring constantly, until mixture is thickened. Pour hot glaze over top of pie. Chill before serving. To serve, garnish with whipped cream.   YIELD: 9-inch (23-cm) pie

Fondue is a perfect party food and the crock pot can be used for both preparation and serving. You will find the crock pot ideal for keeping food hot at a serving table or buffet.

Chocolate Fondue   DAIRY

6 squares (6 oz)/(180 grams)   Dash salt
   unsweetened chocolate   3 Tbsp/45 ml brandy or liqueur,
1½ cups/375 ml sugar   optional
1 cup/250 ml half and half   Angel Food Cake chunks or fruit for
½ cup/125 ml butter   dipping

Crock Pot Directions   Place chocolate squares in crock pot. Cover and cook on high setting about 30 minutes or until chocolate is melted. Stir in remaining ingredients, except brandy. Cook on high setting, stirring constantly, for about 10 minutes, until sugar is dissolved and mixture is hot. Add brandy. Reduce setting to low. Serve fondue directly from crock pot.

Items for dipping: Cut Angel Food Cake into bite-size chunks. Also cut-up fruit, such as pineapple, strawberries or bananas, may be used. Arrange dunking items in a bowl or tray next to crock pot. Use fondue forks to spear cake or fruit and dip into chocolate mixture.   YIELD: 6 to 8 servings

---

For a simple dessert add well-drained fresh or canned fruit when jel has chilled to the consistency of unbeaten egg whites. Chill until firm, then garnish with whipped cream.

Blender Jel   PAREVE

1 package kosher imitation-jel   ½ cup/125 ml boiling water
   dessert, any flavor   1½ cups/375 ml crushed ice

Blender Directions   Place jel and boiling water in blender goblet. Blend on low speed until jel is dissolved. Increase to high speed and, with motor running, add crushed ice. Continue blending until ice is liquefied and jel begins to thicken. Pour into a mold or into individual serving dishes and chill until firm, about 15 minutes.   YIELD: 4 servings

Pareve Peach Whip   P A R E V E

1 package kosher imitation-jel
  dessert, orange-flavored
1 cup/250 ml boiling water

1 (10-oz)/(296 grams) carton pareve
  dessert whip
1 (16-oz)/(454 grams) can peaches,
  well drained

Mixer Directions In small bowl, combine jel and boiling water. Stir until jel is dissolved, then pour into a shallow dish and refrigerate until jel is consistency of unbeaten egg whites.

Insert beater attachment in mixer. Pour dessert whip into mixer bowl and whip at high speed until thick and fluffy. Reduce speed to low and add thickened jel. Mix only until swirled effect is created. Dice peaches and fold into gelatin mixture.

Pour mixture into lightly greased mold and refrigerate until firm. To serve, unmold onto serving dish.   YIELD: 4 to 6 servings

FROZEN DESSERTS

The 3 recipes which follow are examples of different types of frozen desserts—a pareve "ice cream," made from pareve dessert whip, eggs and flavorings; a "sherbet," made from whipped jel-dessert and fruit; and a "freeze" made from fruit-juice concentrate and ice. Variations of these basic recipes can be used to make a variety of pareve frozen desserts.

Rocky Road "Ice Cream"   P A R E V E

1 (10-oz)/(296 ml) carton pareve
  dessert whip
2 Tbsp/25 ml sugar
2 eggs, separated

1 (6-oz)/(168 grams) package
  chocolate chips, melted
½ cup/125 ml marshmallow cream
1 cup/250 ml chopped nuts

Mixer Directions Empty carton of dessert whip into mixer bowl. Attach beaters and beat on high speed until stiff. Gradually beat in sugar. Set aside.

Beat egg yolks until thick and lemon-colored. Slowly beat in melted chocolate and marshmallow cream. Set aside.

Beat egg whites until stiff but not dry. Fold all 3 mixtures—egg whites, dessert whip and egg yolks—together and blend well. Fold in chopped nuts. Pour mixture into a freezer container and freeze until firm. To serve, scoop out with an ice cream spoon and serve in individual bowls or on top of cake.

YIELD: 6 servings

Strawberry Sherbet PAREVE

1 package kosher imitation-jel
   dessert, strawberry-flavored
½ cup/125 ml cold water

1 cup/250 ml boiling water
2 Tbsp/25 ml lemon juice
3 cups/750 fresh strawberries

Put jel dessert and cold water into blender goblet. Blend on low speed until jel is softened. Add boiling water and blend on low until jel is dissolved. Add lemon juice.

Wash strawberries and remove stems. Place strawberries in blender goblet along with jel mixture. Blend on high speed until mixture is smooth. Pour mixture into a shallow dish and place in freezer. Freeze until ice crystals have formed around edges but center is still soft.

Return partially frozen mixture to blender goblet and blend on low speed until mixture is fluffy. Pour into a freezer container, cover and freeze until firm.
    YIELD: 6 servings

Juicy-Fruity Freeze PAREVE

1 (6-oz)/(177 ml) can frozen
   fruit-juice concentrate

4 Tbsp/15 ml sugar, or to taste
3 cups/750 ml crushed ice

Blender Directions Place all ingredients in blender goblet. Blend on high speed for 30 seconds. Stop motor and stir contents with a rubber scraper. Blend again on high speed for 30 seconds. Spoon into dessert dishes and serve immediately.
    YIELD: 4 servings

COOKIES

Almond Cookies PAREVE

1½ cups/375 ml almonds
1 cup/250 ml sifted flour
2 Tbsp/25 ml sugar
½ cup/125 ml vegetable shortening

¼ tsp/1 ml salt
1 tsp/5 ml almond extract
1 cup/250 ml confectioners' sugar,
   or as needed

Blender Directions Place almonds in blender goblet. Blend at medium speed until almonds are very finely ground. Empty into mixing bowl. Add everything except confectioners' sugar and mix thoroughly. Refrigerate dough at least 1 hour for easier handling.

Use your hands to form dough into 1-inch (2.5-cm) balls. Place balls on ungreased cookie sheet and bake at 375° F (190° C) 15 to 20 minutes, until set but not brown. Transfer cookies to a wire rack.

While cookies are still warm, roll in confectioners' sugar. Roll again in sugar before serving.
    YIELD: 2 dozen cookies

Brownies   PAREVE

¾ cup/175 ml pareve margarine
4 squares (4 oz)/(120 grams)
  unsweetened chocolate
2 cups/500 ml sugar
4 eggs

1 tsp/5 ml vanilla
1 cup/250 ml flour
½ tsp/2 ml salt
1 cup/250 ml chopped nuts,
  optional

Microwave Oven Directions   Place half margarine and all the chocolate in a small glass bowl. Cook on high setting in microwave oven for 1½ minutes or until chocolate is melted. Stir until mixture is smooth and allow to cool.

Cream remaining margarine and the sugar together. Add eggs, one at a time, beating well after each addition. Add vanilla and cooled chocolate mixture and mix well. Add remaining ingredients.

Pour mixture into a glass baking dish which has been lined with wax paper. A 9-by-13-inch (23-by-33-cm) pan makes Brownies which are chewy, while a smaller 9-by-9-inch (23-by-23-cm) pan makes cakelike Brownies.

Cover dish with wax paper and place in microwave oven. Cook on medium high setting 7 to 9 minutes, or until top is dry.

Conventional Technique   Prepare Brownies as described above, using a small saucepan and low heat to melt the chocolate. Bake Brownies at 350° F (180° C) 30 to 40 minutes. Cool in pan and cut into small squares.

YIELD: 2 dozen small squares

Chocolate Cookies   PAREVE

1¼ cups/300 ml flour
1½ tsp/7 ml baking powder
½ tsp/2 ml salt
½ cup/125 ml vegetable shortening
1 cup/250 ml sugar
2 eggs, beaten

3 squares (3 oz)/(90 ml) chocolate,
  melted
½ cup/125 ml nondairy creamer
  (or coffee)
1 tsp/5 ml vanilla
¾ cup/175 ml chopped nuts, and/
  or raisins, optional

Mixer Directions   Sift together flour, baking powder and salt, and set aside.

Place shortening in mixer bowl and attach beaters. Begin mixing on medium speed until shortening is fluffy. Gradually add sugar and continue beating until light and creamy. Add eggs and chocolate, beating until mixture is smooth. Reduce speed to low. Add half the dry ingredients. When fully incorporated add the creamer and vanilla. Add remaining dry ingredients, mixing until smooth. If desired, add nuts and raisins.

Drop dough by teaspoonfuls onto greased baking sheet. For crisp cookies, flatten dough with a fork or with the bottom of a glass dipped in sugar or flour to prevent sticking. Bake at 350° F (180° C) 12 to 15 minutes. Cool on racks.

YIELD: About 4 dozen cookies

Variation   Make the following changes in basic Chocolate Cookie recipe:

Double Chocolate Cookies   P A R E V E

1 (6-oz)/(168 grams) package chocolate chips

Add chocolate chips along with nuts and raisins. Bake as in basic recipe.

YIELD: About 4 dozen cookies

Pinwheel Cookies   P A R E V E

1 recipe Chocolate Cookie dough   1 recipe Sugar Cut-out Cookie dough
                                        (see recipe later in chapter)

Prepare dough for Chocolate Cookies and dough for Sugar Cut-outs. Roll
each batch of dough into a thin rectangle and place chocolate rectangle over
vanilla. Roll up the two doughs together, lengthwise, as for jelly roll. Slice
thin, placing slices on greased baking sheet. Bake as for Chocolate Cookies.

YIELD: About 4 dozen cookies

Chocolate Chip Cookies   P A R E V E

1¼ cups/300 ml flour   1 egg
¼ tsp/1 ml salt   ½ tsp/2 ml vanilla
1 tsp/5 ml baking powder   1 (6-oz)/(168 grams) package
½ cup/125 vegetable shortening   chocolate chips
½ cup/125 ml sugar   ½ cup/125 ml chopped nuts,
½ cup/125 ml brown sugar   optional

Mixer Directions   Sift together flour, salt and baking powder, and set aside.
    Place shortening in mixer bowl and attach beaters. Begin mixing at me-
dium speed until shortening is fluffy. Gradually add sugars and continue
beating until light and creamy. Add egg and vanilla and mix until well
blended. On low speed slowly add dry ingredients until thoroughly mixed.
Add chocolate chips and nuts, mixing well.
    Drop dough by teaspoonfuls onto greased baking sheet. Bake at 375° F
(190° C) 10 to 12 minutes. Cool on racks.   YIELD: 3 to 4 dozen cookies

Chocolate-Almond Bars   P A R E V E

2 cups/500 ml flour   1 cup/250 ml brown sugar
1 egg   1 (6-oz)/(168 grams) package
1 tsp/5 ml almond extract   chocolate chips
1 cup (2 sticks)/250 ml soft   1 cup/250 ml almonds
  pareve margarine

Blender Directions   Sift flour into a large mixing bowl and set aside.

Place egg, almond extract, margarine and brown sugar in blender goblet. Blend on high speed until smooth. Add to flour and mix well. Spread batter in greased 9-by-13-inch (23-by-33-cm) pan. Bake at 350° F (180° C) 25 minutes.

Remove pan from oven. Sprinkle chocolate chips evenly over the top. Return pan to oven for a few minutes to melt chocolate. When the chocolate chips have melted, spread the chocolate evenly, like an icing.

Place almonds in blender goblet. Grind nuts on low speed. Sprinkle nuts over warm chocolate. Cut into bars while warm, and cool in pan.

YIELD: 3 dozen small bars

Two types of dough are traditionally used to form Hamentaschen, the triangular filled cookies eaten on Purim. Use the Sweet Dough recipe with your mixer (recipe is found in Yeast Breads chapter) for a soft cookie. This recipe, using the food processor, is for a cookie dough, sweet and crisp.

Hamentaschen Dough   P A R E V E

2½ cups/625 ml flour
3 tsp/15 ml baking powder
1 tsp/5 ml salt
½ cup/125 ml sugar, or to taste
½ cup/125 ml vegetable shortening
1 egg

½ to ¾ cup/125 to 175 ml orange juice
2½ cups/625 ml prepared Hamentaschen filling (following recipes), or as needed

LEMON GLAZE

2 Tbsp/25 ml confectioners' sugar, or as needed

2 tsp/10 ml lemon juice

Food Processor Directions   Insert steel blade in food processor. Sift dry ingredients and place in container along with the sugar. Add shortening and process, using the pulse button or quick on-off motion, until shortening is incorporated into flour. Add egg and process until well mixed. With motor running, slowly pour orange juice through feed tube. Process until dough forms a ball and clears the sides of the container.

Remove dough to a floured surface and knead 5 or 6 times. Roll dough to ¼-inch (1-cm) thickness. Cut into circles with the open end of a glass. Place a spoonful of filling (see following recipes) in center of each circle. Pinch sides together, forming a closed triangle over filling. Bake on ungreased cookie sheet at 400° F (200° C) 10 to 15 minutes or until lightly browned. Brush cookies with lemon glaze while still warm.

To prepare lemon glaze: Add lemon juice to confectioners' sugar to form a thin syrup. Brush over warm cookies. Vanilla or almond extract may be substituted for the lemon juice.   YIELD: 2 to 3 dozen Hamentaschen

Mohn (Poppy Seed) Filling   DAIRY

1 cup/250 ml poppy seeds
½ cup/125 ml milk
¼ cup/50 ml honey
2 Tbsp/25 ml sugar
Dash salt

1 egg, beaten
1 tsp/5 ml grated lemon peel
¼ tsp/1 ml cinnamon
¼ cup/50 ml raisins
½ cup/125 ml finely ground
  almonds

Food Processor Directions Insert steel blade in food processor. Place poppy seeds in container and process until finely ground.

In a saucepan, combine ground seeds, milk, honey, sugar and salt. Cook over low heat, stirring frequently, until thickened, about 10 to 15 minutes.

Add a little of the hot mixture to beaten egg and then stir egg back into hot mixture. Stir in remaining ingredients, mixing well. Allow to cool and use as a filling for Hamentaschen.

Microwave Oven Directions Grind poppy seeds in food processor or grinder and combine in glass mixing bowl with milk, honey, sugar and salt. Cook on high setting 3 to 4 minutes, until mixture thickens. Proceed as in basic recipe.

YIELD: About 2½ cups (625 ml), filling for 2 to 3 dozen Hamentaschen

Prune Filling   PAREVE

1 lb/500 grams pitted prunes
½ cup/or more 125 ml sugar
1 or 2 cups/250 or 500 ml water

1 lemon
½ cup/125 ml finely chopped nuts

Microwave Oven Directions In glass mixing bowl, combine prunes, sugar and 1 cup (250 ml) water. Cover with plastic wrap and cook on high setting in microwave oven 8 to 10 minutxes, until prunes are tender. Allow to cool.

Drain liquid from prunes and mash (or use food processor with steel blade attachment or use blender). Add juice and grated peel of lemon and chopped nuts. Taste mixture and sweeten with additional sugar, if desired. Use as a filling for Hamentaschen.

Conventional Directions Combine prunes, sugar and 2 cups (500 ml) water in a saucepan. Cover, bring to a boil and simmer 30 to 35 minutes, until prunes are tender. Drain and press through a sieve. Combine with juice and grated peel of lemon and chopped nuts. Use as a filling for Hamentaschen.

YIELD: About 2½ cups (625 ml), filling for 2 to 3 dozen Hamentaschen

Mandelbrot   P A R E V E

½ cup/125 ml salad oil   3½ cups/875 ml flour
1 cup/250 ml sugar   1½ tsp/7 ml baking powder
4 eggs   ½ tsp/2 ml salt
1 tsp/5 ml grated lemon peel   1 cup/250 ml slivered almonds
1 tsp/5 ml almond extract   1 egg white, slightly beaten

Mixer Directions In mixer bowl combine salad oil, sugar, eggs, lemon peel and almond extract. Attach beaters and mix thoroughly on medium speed. Sift together dry ingredients and add with almonds to batter. The dough should be soft.

On a greased cookie sheet form two loaves of dough. Brush tops with beaten egg white. Bake at 375° F (190° C) 20 to 30 minutes, until top is lightly browned. Remove from oven, slice, and place slices flat on greased cookie sheet. Return to oven and bake until slices are golden brown, about 10 minutes. Remove from pan and cool on a rack.   YIELD: About 40 slices

Oatmeal Cookies   P A R E V E

1 cup/250 ml vegetable shortening   1½ tsp/7 ml cinnamon
1 cup/250 ml sugar   1 tsp/5 ml ground cloves
½ cup/125 ml brown sugar   ½ tsp/2 ml ground ginger
1 egg   1½ cups/375 ml quick rolled oats
1 tsp/5 ml vanilla   ½ cup/125 ml chopped nuts,
1½ cups/375 ml flour   optional
1 tsp/5 ml baking soda   ½ cup/125 ml raisins, optional
½ tsp/2 ml salt

Food Processor Directions Insert steel blade in food processor. In container combine shortening, sugars and egg. Process until mixture is light and fluffy. Sift flour, soda, salt and spices into a large mixing bowl and add the creamed mixture, stirring by hand until well mixed. Add oats, nuts and raisins, mixing well.

Drop dough by teaspoonfuls onto a greased baking sheet. For a crisp cookie, flatten the dough with a fork or with the bottom of a glass which has been dipped in flour or sugar. Bake at 350° F (180° C) 10 to 12 minutes, or until lightly browned.   YIELD: 4 dozen cookies

Orange Juice Cookies   P A R E V E

3 cups/750 ml sifted flour   ½ cup/125 ml sugar, or to taste
1 tsp/5 ml baking soda   1 (6-oz)/(177 ml) can frozen
2 eggs   orange juice concentrate, thawed
1 cup/250 ml vegetable shortening

Blender Directions   Sift flour and soda into a large mixing bowl and set aside.
Place eggs, shortening, sugar, and ½ cup (125 ml) of the orange juice concentrate in blender goblet. Blend on high speed until smooth. Pour into flour and stir until well mixed.

Drop by spoonfuls onto ungreased baking sheet. Bake at 400° F (200° C) 8 minutes or until lightly browned around the edges.

Brush hot cookies lightly with remaining orange juice concentrate. Remove cookies to cooling rack.   YIELD: 4 dozen cookies

Variation   Make the following changes in basic Orange Juice Cookie recipe:

Pink-Lemonade Cookies   P A R E V E

1 (6-oz)/(177 ml) can pink-lemonade concentrate

Omit orange juice and substitute pink-lemonade concentrate.
                                                        YIELD: 4 dozen cookies

Peanut Butter Cookies   P A R E V E

½ cup/125 ml vegetable shortening   1¾ cups/425 ml flour
1 cup/250 ml peanut butter   1 tsp/5 ml baking soda
½ cup/125 ml sugar   ½ tsp/2 ml salt
½ cup/125 brown sugar   1 tsp/5 ml water, as needed
1 egg   1 cup/250 ml unsalted peanuts,
1 tsp/5 ml vanilla   coarsely chopped

Food Processor Directions   Insert steel blade in food processor. Place shortening, peanut butter, sugars and egg in container. Process until light and fluffy. Add vanilla and process until mixed.

Sift the flour, baking soda and salt into a large mixing bowl. Add creamed mixture and stir by hand until well combined. If necessary add a teaspoon (5 ml) of water until a soft dough is formed. Fold in peanuts.

Drop the dough by rounded teaspoonfuls onto a lightly greased baking sheet. Press cookies down with a fork to flatten. Bake at 375° F (190° C) 10 to 12 minutes, or until lightly browned. Transfer the cookies to a wire rack to cool.   YIELD: About 4 dozen cookies

Sesame Nut Bars   P A R E V E

2 cups/500 ml flour
½ tsp/2 ml salt
1½ tsp/7 ml baking powder
1 egg, separated
1 cup (2 sticks)/250 ml
   pareve margarine

1 cup/250 ml sugar
1 tsp/5 ml vanilla
⅓ cup/75 ml toasted sesame seeds
1 cup/250 ml chopped nuts

Blender Directions Sift flour, salt and baking powder in a large mixing bowl, and set aside.

In blender goblet, place egg yolk and ½ cup (1 stick, 125 ml) margarine. Blend on medium speed until mixture is fluffy. With motor running, gradually add remaining margarine and sugar. Add vanilla and sesame seeds, blending until mixture is well combined.

Add blender mixture to dry ingredients and mix well. Spread dough evenly in a lightly greased 15-by-10-by-1-inch (39-by-25-by-2.5-cm) jelly-roll pan. Press to make a smooth surface. Beat egg white slightly and brush over dough. Sprinkle nuts evenly over top and press into dough.

Bake at 300° F (150° C) 45 minutes to 1 hour. While hot cut into 1½-inch (4-cm) squares. Cool before serving.   YIELD: 48 squares

---

Sugar Cut-outs   P A R E V E

2 cups/500 ml sifted flour
1 tsp/5 ml baking powder
¼ tsp/1 ml salt
⅔ cup/150 ml vegetable
   shortening, or pareve margarine

¾ cup/175 ml sugar
1 egg
1 tsp/5 ml vanilla
White Glaze (see recipe in
   Cakes chapter)

Mixer Directions Sift flour, baking powder and salt together and set aside.

Place shortening in mixer bowl. Attach beaters and mix on medium speed until creamy. Add sugar and mix until fluffy. Beat in egg and vanilla. When mixture is smooth add dry ingredients, mixing until a dough is formed. Refrigerate for at least 1 hour, for easier handling.

Roll dough ⅛ inch (.5 cm) thick on a lightly floured board and cut into shapes with floured cookie cutters. Place cookies on an ungreased cookie sheet and bake at 400° F (200° C) 8 to 10 minutes. Cool cookies on a wire rack. Decorate with White Glaze. To keep glaze hard, store cookies in the refrigerator or freezer.   YIELD: 4 to 5 dozen cookies

CANDY

See Children's Chapter for additional candy recipes.

Do not use a candy thermometer in microwave oven. Remove the syrup mixture from the oven to take a temperature reading.

Peanut Brittle   P A R E V E

1½ cups/375 ml sugar	¼ tsp/1 ml salt
¾ cup/175 ml light corn syrup	2 tsp/10 ml pareve margarine
¾ cup/175 ml water	1 tsp/5 ml baking soda
2 cups/500 ml raw peanuts	½ tsp/2 ml vanilla or lemon extract

Microwave Oven Directions In a large glass bowl, combine sugar, corn syrup and water. Place in microwave oven and cook on high setting 5 minutes, until sugar is dissolved. Stir. Add peanuts. Continue cooking on high setting about 15 to 20 minutes longer or until a small amount of syrup dropped into very cold water separates into hard, brittle threads (290° F or 145° C).

Stir in margarine, soda and vanilla, mixing well. Pour mixture onto a buttered cookie sheet. Break into pieces when cool. Store in a covered container.

Conventional Directions In a large, heavy pot, bring to a boil sugar, syrup and water. Add peanuts and salt. Cook, stirring occasionally, until syrup measures 290° F (145° C) on a candy thermometer. Remove from heat. Stir in margarine, soda and vanilla. Pour mixture onto a buttered cookie sheet. Break into pieces when cool.   YIELD: About 1⅓ lbs (600 grams)

Poppy-Nut Candy   P A R E V E

1 cup/250 ml poppy seeds	¼ cup/50 ml honey
1 cup/250 ml nuts	1 Tbsp/15 ml lemon juice
¼ tsp/1 ml cinnamon	

Food Processor Directions Insert steel blade in food processor. Place poppy seeds in container and process until finely ground. Transfer to a mixing bowl. Place nuts in container and process until finely chopped. Add half the nuts to the poppy seeds, along with cinnamon, honey and lemon juice. Blend mixture well and form into small balls. Roll balls in the remaining nuts to form a coating.   YIELD: 15 to 20 candy pieces

This recipe started out to be halvah—a favorite candy of Middle Eastern origin—made from a doubtful collection of ingredients, one of which is sesame seeds. I set out, with great enthusiasm and energy, to duplicate a halvah recipe in the food processor. After I had made several attempts mixing sesame seeds, sugar, vanilla and other things, my husband, who knows about such things, finally said, "Well, it's good, but it's not quite halvah." The local authority, Rabbi Goldman, who spent his formative years in the land of blue-and-white flags, Mediterranean breezes and halvah candy, was brought in as a consultant. Several attempts later, after juggling various consistencies of sesame seeds and adding a bit of chocolate, the same verdict reared its ugly head, "Well, it's good, but it's not halvah." I tried again, using honey, egg, corn syrup, more vanilla, less chocolate. . . . More tasting, but the same comment, "It's very good, but . . ." I tried changing sugar to a powdered form. I briefly considered changing to more sympathetic tasters. Finally, a brilliant idea struck. If I had a good recipe, why not just change the name? So here I present my latest version of . . . "It's not halvah, but it's . . ."

Very Good Sesame-Seed Candy   P A R E V E

1 cup/250 ml sesame seeds	½ tsp/2 ml cocoa
2 Tbsp/25 ml sesame paste	1 tsp/5 ml corn syrup
(see recipe in Appetizers chapter)	¼ tsp/1 ml vanilla
2 Tbsp/25 ml sugar, or to taste	1 Tbsp/15 ml water (about)

Food Processor Directions Insert steel blade in food processor and place sesame seeds in container. Process until fine and powdery, about 1 minute. Add sesame paste, sugar and cocoa, processing until mixed well. With motor running add corn syrup and vanilla. Slowly add water until mixture holds together.

On a piece of wax paper, mold the mixture into a rectangular shape, about 5 by 2 inches (13 by 5 cm). Chill before cutting into small pieces.

YIELD: ¼ lb (125 grams)

JAMS, PRESERVES, RELISHES

Four appliances are featured in this chapter and each, in a unique way, simplifies the job of making jams, preserves and relishes.

The use of the crock pot to make Old-Fashioned Apple Butter eliminates much of the stirring and fear of scorching found in conventional cooking.

Chopping fruits and vegetables for Chutney, a tangy relish, is greatly simplified when using a food processor.

A combination of dried and canned fruit is used in making Pineapple-Peach Marmalade, a blender specialty.

Two microwave oven recipes, Classic Apricot Jam and Raspberry Refrigerator Jam, require added pectin. This is a natural substance which has the ability to absorb water and form a jel. It is added in powdered or liquid form to produce perfect jam, which cooks in just 15 minutes in the microwave oven.

Several of these recipes specify pouring foods into sterilized jars. To sterilize glass jars, immerse them in boiling water for several minutes and then drain. Pour the jam or marmalade mixture into the hot jar, filling it to within ¼ inch of the top. Seal by pouring a thin layer of melted paraffin on the top and tilting the jar to be sure the paraffin completely covers the marmalade, sealing out all air. Other foods such as Chutney may be sealed by using vacuum-seal lids. For these, carefully follow manufacturer's instructions.

Old-Fashioned Apple Butter   PAREVE

4½ lbs/2 kilos cooking apples
2 cups/500 ml apple cider
2½ cups/625 ml sugar

2 tsp/10 ml cinnamon
¼ tsp/1 ml *each* nutmeg, allspice
   and cloves

Crock Pot Directions Wash, quarter and core apples but do not peel. Chop or shred apples (the food processor is great for this step).

Combine apples and cider in crock pot. Cover and cook on low setting 6 to 8 hours or overnight, until apples are mushy. Puree apples (the blender is great for this step). Return pureed mixture to crock pot. Add sugar, cinnamon and spices. Cover and cook on low setting 1 hour.

This may be stored in the refrigerator for several weeks, or it may be kept in the freezer. YIELD: 2 quarts (2 liters)

Chutney   P A R E V E

1 cup/250 ml pitted prunes
2 cups/500 ml water
1 cup/250 ml seedless raisins
4 green apples, cut into 8 pieces
  and core
2 green pears, cut into 8 pieces
  and core
1 onion, peeled

1 small clove garlic, peeled
2 cups/500 ml cherry tomatoes,
  quartered
3 cups/750 ml brown sugar
1½ tsp/7 ml salt
½ cup/125 ml red currant jelly
2 tsp/10 ml ground ginger
Dash cayenne pepper

Food Processor Directions In a large saucepan cover the prunes with water and cook about 10 minutes. Drain. Insert steel blade in food processor and chop prunes. Return prunes to saucepan and add raisins.

Insert shredding disc in food processor and shred apples. Add to mixture in saucepan. Insert slicing disc and slice pears thin, then add to saucepan. Insert steel blade and chop onion and garlic very fine. Add to saucepan, along with remaining ingredients.

Stir mixture well. Bring to a boil over high heat, then simmer and reduce until thick, about 3 hours. Pour into sterilized jars while hot and seal.

YIELD: 2½ quarts (2½ liters)

Pineapple-Peach Marmalade   P A R E V E

1 (1-lb 4-oz)/(567 grams) can
  crushed pineapple, with syrup
2 cups/500 ml dried peaches

1 (1¾-oz)/(49 grams) package
  powdered fruit pectin
3 cups/750 ml sugar

Blender Directions Put half the pineapple and syrup and 1 cup (250 ml) peaches into blender goblet. Cover and blend on low setting, using pulse button or short on-off bursts of energy, until peach is coarsely chopped. Empty into a saucepan and repeat with remaining fruit. Add pectin.

Bring to a boil and boil for 5 minutes, stirring constantly. Add sugar and continue to boil until mixture is thick and clear, about 10 minutes. If using a thermometer, boil until a temperature of 212° F (100° C) is reached. Pour into sterilized jars and seal. YIELD: 2 pints (1 liter)

The beauty of this jam, a microwave oven favorite, is that it can be kept in the refrigerator in any pretty jars, goblets or cups. No fuss with sterilizing.

Classic Apricot Jam   P A R E V E

2 cups/500 ml apricots   1 tsp/5 ml lemon juice
1¾ cups/425 ml sugar   3 tsp/15 ml powdered fruit pectin

Microwave Oven Directions Prepare apricots by washing, peeling, removing pits and slicing thin. The easiest way to peel the apricots is to dip them, briefly, in boiling water before removing the skins.

Into a glass bowl slice apricots (the food processor is great for this step). Stir in sugar, lemon juice and pectin and combine thoroughly. Cook on high setting 3 to 4 minutes, or until mixture comes to a full rolling boil.

Reduce setting to medium and cook 6 minutes more, or until jam is slightly thickened. It will thicken more as it cools. Pour into glasses. Cover with plastic wrap and store in refrigerator.

Conventional Directions Combine lemon juice, pectin and sugar in saucepan. Cook and stir until mixture boils and sugar is dissolved, about 5 minutes. Add the fruit and simmer until fruit is soft and syrup is thick and clear, about 10 minutes. Pour into glasses, cover with plastic wrap and store in refrigerator.   YIELD: 1 pint (500 ml)

Variations Omit apricots and substitute the following ingredients when preparing Classic Jam recipe.

Blueberry Jam   P A R E V E

2 cups/500 ml blueberries

Peach Jam   P A R E V E

2 cups/500 ml peeled, sliced peaches
½ tsp/5 ml cinnamon

Strawberry Jam   P A R E V E

2 cups/500 ml mashed strawberries   YIELD: 1 pint (500 ml)

Raspberry Refrigerator Jam   P A R E V E

1 (16-oz)/(454 grams) package   1½ cups/375 ml sugar
  frozen sweetened raspberries   2 tsp/10 ml lemon juice, or to taste
1 Tbsp/15 ml powdered fruit pectin

Microwave Oven Directions In a large glass bowl place package containing
frozen raspberries. Cook on high setting 2 minutes. Open package and pour
berries into mixing bowl. Add pectin and stir well.

Cook on high setting 3 to 4 minutes. Stir and cook 1 to 2 minutes longer or
until mixture boils. Stir in sugar and lemon juice. Cook on medium setting 5
minutes, stirring once.

Pour into glasses, cover with plastic wrap and store in refrigerator.

Conventional Directions Thaw frozen fruit. In a saucepan combine fruit,
sugar, pectin and lemon juice. Cook and stir until mixture boils and sugar is
dissolved, about 5 minutes. Pour into glasses, cover with plastic wrap and
store in refrigerator.   YIELD: About 2½ cups (625 ml)

Variations Omit raspberries and substitute the following ingredients in Refrigerator Jam recipe:

Peach Refrigerator Jam   P A R E V E

1 (16-oz)/(454 grams) package frozen peaches

Strawberry Refrigerator Jam   P A R E V E

1 (16-oz)/(454 grams) package frozen strawberries
                    YIELD: About 2½ cups (625 ml)

BEVERAGES

The blender is featured in the majority of recipes in this chapter, both for its ability to liquefy solid foods (see recipe for Vegetable-Fruit Combo) and for its capacity to aerate mixtures to a frothy consistency.

With the crock pot, beverages can be prepared and cooked slowly hours in advance of serving. This slow cooking helps to develop a special delicious flavor. The crock pot is especially convenient to use for entertaining because hot beverages can be served directly from the pot. The crock pot can be placed attractively at a buffet or party table.

The microwave oven is featured primarily in single-serving beverage recipes, where drinks are heated directly in cups or mugs. Only glass or microwave-proof cups should be used in the microwave oven. Be especially careful to avoid cups with metal parts or metal trim.

How to Grind Coffee Beans   P A R E V E

Blender Directions   Most blenders will accommodate 1 cup (250 ml) coffee beans at a time. Place beans in blender goblet. For regular grind, blend at medium speed approximately 10 seconds. For a fine grind, blend at medium speed 10 seconds, then increase speed to high and blend 5 to 10 seconds longer.

Grind only as much coffee as you will use in one day, as freshly ground coffee loses flavor rapidly.   YIELD: 1 cup (250 ml)

How to Brew Coffee   P A R E V E

FOR EACH CUP USE

2 level Tbsp/45 ml coffee   ¾ to 1 cup/175 to 250 ml water

Drip Method   Measure finely ground coffee into the filter section of a coffee pot. Pour boiling water into upper section of pot. When all of the water has dripped through, remove coffee grounds. Serve at once.

Percolator Method   Measure water into coffee pot. Measure regular-grind coffee into the basket. Place basket in percolator and cover. Bring to a boil and percolate slowly 6 to 8 minutes. Remove basket and serve.

YIELD: 1 (or more) servings

Percolator Method   Coffee for a large group:
   Allow 1 pound (500 grams) medium-ground coffee to 7 quarts (7 liters) water.

YIELD: About 40 servings

Instant Coffee   P A R E V E

¾ to 1 cup/175 to 250 ml water
1 rounded tsp/6 ml instant coffee

Microwave Oven Directions   Pour water into a cup or mug. Add coffee and stir. Place cup in microwave oven and cook on high setting 1½ minutes or until hot.

YIELD: 1 serving

To Reheat Coffee   P A R E V E

Microwave Oven Directions   To have fresh-tasting coffee all day long, brew a pot of coffee in the morning, using whatever method is most convenient. Refrigerate coffee. To serve, pour 1 cup (250 ml) coffee directly into cup or mug. Place in microwave oven and cook on high setting about 2 minutes or until hot.

If you have a temperature probe and wish to use it to determine if coffee is heated to exactly the right temperature, insert the jack-end of probe in oven. Place the probe point in coffee mug. Cook on high setting until a temperature of 170° F (75° C) is reached. Stir before serving.

YIELD: 1 serving

Café au Lait   D A I R Y

⅓ cup/75 ml double-strength coffee
⅓ cup/75 ml milk or cream

¼ cup/50 ml whipped cream, for garnish

Microwave Oven Directions   Combine coffee and milk in coffee cup or mug and place in microwave oven. Cook on high setting 1½ to 2 minutes or until hot. Stir and serve topped with whipped cream.

YIELD: 1 serving

Special-Occasion Coffee   DAIRY

2 quarts/2 liters strong   1 tsp/5 ml whole cloves
   hot coffee   ½ tsp/2 ml whole allspice
¼ cup/50 ml chocolate syrup   1 cup/250 ml whipped cream,
⅓ cup/75 ml honey   for garnish
4 cinnamon sticks

Crock Pot Directions Combine coffee, chocolate syrup, honey and spices in crock pot. Cover and cook on low setting 2 to 3 hours. Serve garnished with dollops of whipped cream.   YIELD: 12 servings

---

Sweeten tea with sugar, honey or fruit preserves. Flavor tea with cream or milk; lemon, orange or lime slices; mint leaves; crystallized ginger, whole cloves or stick cinnamon.

Tea   PAREVE

Microwave Oven Directions
For one serving:
   It is faster and more economical to heat water for a single cup of tea in the microwave oven than on your range. Fill a mug or cup with hot tap water. Place in microwave oven and cook on high setting 1½ to 2 minutes or until water is steaming hot. Add tea bag and allow to steep before serving.

To brew a pot of tea:
   When brewing a pot of tea it is faster and more convenient to boil the water on top of stove. The microwave oven, however, can be used to prepare the teapot (provided the pot contains no metal or metal trim). Put ½ cup (125 ml) hot tap water in the teapot. Place teapot in microwave oven and cook on high setting 1 to 1½ minutes or until water is boiling. Wait a minute, then pour out the water. The pot is now hot and ready to brew tea. Measure 1 teaspoon (5 ml) tea leaves or use 1 tea bag for each 8 ounces (250 ml) of boiling water, plus one extra spoonful or bag "for the pot." Pour measured amount of boiling water over tea. Cover pot and allow to steep 3 to 5 minutes for black or green tea, 5 to 7 minutes for herb tea before serving.
                                                        YIELD: 4 to 6 servings

Fruit and Tea Medley   PAREVE

6 cups/1500 ml boiling water
6 bags Darjeeling tea
1 bag mint tea
⅓ cup/75 ml sugar
2 Tbsp/25 ml honey

1½ cups/375 ml orange juice
1½ cups/375 ml pineapple juice
2 tsp/10 ml lemon juice
1 lemon, thinly sliced

Crock Pot Directions In crock pot, pour boiling water over tea bags. Cover and let stand 5 minutes. Remove tea bags. Stir in remaining ingredients. Cover and cook on low setting 2 to 3 hours.   YIELD: 10 servings

HOT MILK DRINKS

Hot Cocoa   DAIRY

1 Tbsp/15 ml cocoa
2 Tbsp/25 ml sugar
Dash salt
½ cup/125 ml boiling water

2 cups/500 ml milk
¼ tsp/1 ml vanilla
¼ cup/50 ml whipped cream,
    for garnish

Microwave Oven Directions In a glass mixing bowl, combine cocoa, sugar and salt. Add boiling water and stir until sugar and cocoa are dissolved. Slowly stir in milk and vanilla. Place bowl in microwave oven and cook on high setting 2 to 3 minutes, until mixture is very hot but not boiling. Pour into cups and garnish with whipped cream.

Conventional Directions Combine sugar, cocoa, salt and water in a saucepan. Bring to a boil, stirring constantly. Stir in milk and vanilla. Heat, but do not boil.   YIELD: 3 servings

Quick Hot Chocolate   DAIRY

2 cups/500 ml hot milk
½ cup/125 ml chocolate chips

Blender Directions Combine ingredients in blender goblet. Blend on high speed until smooth. Transfer to saucepan and cook over low heat until chocolate is dissolved. Pour into cups and serve.   YIELD: 3 servings

Hot Chocolate Malted Milk   DAIRY

1 (8-oz)/(250 grams) milk-chocolate
    bar
5 cups/1250 ml milk
½ cup/125 ml malted milk powder,
    chocolate-flavored

1 tsp/5 ml vanilla
½ cup/125 ml whipped cream,
    for garnish

Crock Pot Directions   In crock pot combine all ingredients except whipped cream. Cover and cook on low setting 2 hours. Beat with rotary beater or hand mixer until frothy. Pour into cups. Garnish with whipped cream.

YIELD: 6 servings

COLD MILK DRINKS

Chocolate Milk   DAIRY

1 cup/250 ml cold milk

2 Tbsp/25 ml chocolate
    syrup

Blender Directions   Combine milk and syrup in blender goblet. Blend on high speed until frothy.   YIELD: 1 serving

Eggnog   DAIRY

1 egg
Dash salt
1 Tbsp/15 ml sugar

½ tsp/2 ml vanilla
1 cup/250 ml cold milk
Dash nutmeg

Blender Directions   Combine egg, salt and sugar in blender goblet. Blend on low speed a few seconds to combine. Add vanilla and milk. Blend on high speed until frothy. Pour into glass and sprinkle with nutmeg.

YIELD: 1 serving

Variation

Honey Eggnog   DAIRY

Substitute 1 Tbsp (15 ml) honey for the sugar.   YIELD: 1 serving

Ice-Cream Milk Shakes   DAIRY

1½ cups/375 ml cold milk
1 tsp/5 ml vanilla

1 pint (2 cups)/(500 ml)
    vanilla ice cream

Blender Directions   Place milk, vanilla and half the ice cream in blender goblet. Blend on low speed until mixture is smooth and creamy. Add remaining ice cream. Blend on low speed just until ice cream is mixed in. Serve immediately.   YIELD: 2 to 4 servings

Variations   Make the following changes in basic Ice-Cream Milk Shake recipe:

Chocolate Milk Shake   D A I R Y

1 pint (2 cups)/(500 ml)   ⅓ cup/75 ml chocolate syrup
   chocolate ice cream

Substitute chocolate ice cream for vanilla. Add chocolate syrup and mix as in basic recipe.

Fruity Milk Shake   D A I R Y

2 cups/500 ml fruit

Add 2 cups (500 ml) fresh or canned fruit, cut into chunks. Bananas, strawberries, peaches and pineapple make good milk shakes.

Malted Milk Shake   D A I R Y

¼ cup/50 ml malted milk powder

Add to basic recipe.   YIELD: 2 to 4 servings

Malted Milk   D A I R Y

2 to 3 Tbsp/25 to 45 ml   1 cup/250 ml cold milk
   malted milk powder

Blender Directions   Combine ingredients in blender goblet. Blend on high speed until frothy.   YIELD: 1 serving

Milk Shake with Egg   D A I R Y

1 cup/250 ml crushed ice   1 Tbsp/15 ml honey
1 cup/250 ml milk, or as needed   1 tsp/5 ml vanilla
1 egg

Blender Directions   Fill a tall glass with crushed ice. Pour in milk until glass is two-thirds full. Transfer milk and ice to blender goblet. Add remaining ingredients and blend on high speed until smooth. Pour back into glass to serve.   YIELD: 1 serving

FRUIT DRINKS

Apple Cider   PAREVE

2 quarts/2 liters apple cider
¼ cup/50 ml brown sugar
4 pieces stick cinnamon
1 tsp/5 ml whole cloves

1 tsp/5 ml whole allspice
Dash ground ginger
¼ tsp/1 ml grated orange rind,
   optional

Crock Pot Directions   Combine ingredients in crock pot. Cover and cook on low setting 2 to 5 hours or longer. Ladle into mugs directly from crock pot.

YIELD: 10 to 12 servings

The secret to making good lemonade is to dissolve the sugar thoroughly. This can be done by combining the sugar with an equal amount of water and boiling a few minutes, or by combining the sugar with the lemon juice and stirring until sugar dissolves. Serve lemonade with lemon slices, maraschino cherries or sprigs of mint for an attractive garnish.

Lemonade   PAREVE

1¼ cups/300 ml lemon juice
1 cup/250 ml sugar

7 cups/1750 ml water
1 cup/250 ml crushed ice

Blender Directions   In blender goblet, combine lemon juice, sugar and ½ cup (125 ml) water. Allow to stand several minutes. Blend on low speed 30 seconds (if sugar is not completely dissolved, wait 1 minute, then repeat process). Add 2 more cups (500 ml) water and the ice. Blend on low speed 30 seconds. Pour mixture into a large pitcher and add remaining water.

YIELD: 10 to 12 servings

Variations   Make the following changes in basic Lemonade recipe:

Apple Lemonade   PAREVE

6 cups/1500 ml apple juice,
   unsweetened

¾ cup/175 ml sugar

Substitute 6 cups (1500 ml) apple juice for the water. Reduce sugar to ¾ cup (175 ml) or to taste.

Limeade   P A R E V E

2 cups/500 ml lime juice

Omit lemon juice and substitute lime juice.

Orangeade   P A R E V E

3½ cups/875 ml orange juice

Substitute orange juice for the lemon juice. Reduce water to 3½ cups (875 ml). Sweetening may not be necessary. Lemon juice may be added for tartness.

Pineapple Lemonade   P A R E V E

4 cups/1 liter pineapple juice

Substitute pineapple juice for 4 cups (1000 ml) water. Less sugar may be required.   YIELD: 10 to 12 servings

Hot Lemonade Punch   P A R E V E

1 quart/1 liter Lemonade
1 quart/1 liter cranberry or
　cranberry-apple juice
⅔ cup/150 ml sugar, or to taste

2 Tbsp/25 ml honey
. 12 whole cloves
1 stick cinnamon

Crock Pot Directions   In crock pot combine ingredients. Cover and cook on low setting 3 to 4 hours. Remove spices. Serve directly from crock pot.
YIELD: 10 to 12 servings

Spiced Peach Punch   P A R E V E

1 can (46-oz)/1.3-l peach nectar
3 cups/750 ml orange juice
½ cup/125 ml brown sugar
2 Tbsp/25 ml lemon juice

3 sticks cinnamon
6 whole cloves
6 whole allspice

Crock Pot Directions   In crock pot combine all ingredients. Cover and cook on low setting 3 to 4 hours. Remove spices. Serve directly from crock pot.
YIELD: 10 to 12 servings

Vegetable-Fruit Combo   PAREVE

2 cups/500 ml fruit   1 tsp/5 ml lemon juice, or to taste
   or tomato juice   1 cup/250 ml crushed ice
1 to 2 cups/250 to 500 ml vegetable
   chunks (see variations below)

Blender Directions Put juice, vegetable pieces and lemon juice in blender goblet. Cover and blend at high speed until vegetable is liquefied. Remove cover and, with motor running, add ice. Continue blending until ice is liquefied. For a smoother drink, strain before serving.   YIELD: About 3 servings

Variations Try the following combinations when preparing Vegetable-Fruit Combo:

Carrot-Pineapple Combo   PAREVE

3 carrots, cut in small chunks
2 cups/500 ml pineapple juice

Celery-Tomato Combo   PAREVE

2 stalks celery,   2 cups/500 ml tomato juice
   cut in small chunks

Cucumber-Grape Combo   PAREVE

1 cucumber
2 cups/500 ml grape juice

Peel and remove seeds from cucumber. Cut into small pieces and use, along with grape juice, in basic recipe.

Green Pepper–Cranberry Combo   PAREVE

1 green pepper
2 cups/500 ml cranberry juice

Remove stem, seeds and membranes from green pepper. Cut into 1-inch (2.5 cm) chunks and use, along with cranberry juice, in basic recipe.

                                                    YIELD: About 3 servings

PARTY DRINKS

Hot Wine Punch   PAREVE

1 bottle sweet red wine
8 whole cloves
4 sticks cinnamon

1 lemon, thinly sliced
½ cup/125 ml orange juice
½ cup/125 ml brown sugar

Crock Pot Directions Combine all ingredients in crock pot. Cover and cook on low setting 3 to 4 hours. Serve directly from crock pot.

YIELD: 6 to 8 servings

Spiked Punch   PAREVE

1 quart/1 liter Apple Cider
1 quart/1 liter orange juice
½ cup/125 ml lemon juice
2 cups/500 ml sugar
2 cups/500 ml water

2 cinnamon sticks
1 tsp/5 ml whole allspice
½ tsp/2 ml whole cloves
2 Tbsp/25 ml brandy
1 cup/250 ml rum

Crock Pot Directions Combine all ingredients except brandy and rum in crock pot. Cover and cook on low setting 5 hours. About 15 minutes before serving, add brandy and rum. Serve directly from crock pot.

YIELD: 20 servings

Tipsy Lemonade Swirl   PAREVE

1 (6-oz)/(177 ml) can frozen
   lemonade concentrate
¾ cup/175 ml vodka
¾ cup/175 ml water

3 cups/750 ml crushed ice,
   or as needed
¾ cup/175 ml frozen strawberries,
   slightly thawed

Blender Directions Combine lemonade, vodka and water in blender goblet. Add crushed ice. Blend on low speed until well mixed and snowy consistency. Add frozen strawberries. Blend in 1 or 2 pulse, or quick on-off motions, until swirl effect is achieved. Serve immediately. YIELD: 4 to 6 servings

PASSOVER

The 8 days of Passover involve another, special type of separation of food in a kosher home. This is the separation between chometz and pesachdig foods.

During Passover Jews are not permitted to eat or to have in their possession any form of chometz. Even the smallest amount of chometz makes an entire product not permissible for Passover use.

Chometz is defined as foods made from wheat, barley, rye, spelt and oats, or any form of these grains to which a leavening agent has been added, or which has come into contact with liquid for 18 minutes (the amount of time it takes for the mixture to start to ferment and rise). Ashkenazi Jews also refrain from eating rice, corn, mustard, peanuts and all varieties of peas, beans and legumes. Sephardim do not consider rice and legumes chometz and eat these as part of their Passover diet. Matzah and matzah products replace bread and grains during this holiday.

The foods used during Passover must be carefully chosen. Every item must be pesachdig (free from chometz). It is especially important that all processed foods (including spices, baking items, etc.) be carefully supervised and certified as "kosher le Pesach" or kosher for Passover.

Be aware that not all your small appliances may be "kashered" or converted for Passover use. Unless the motor base of an appliance is completely covered in such a way that no chometz crumbs, spatters, etc., can enter the motor area, there may be difficulty in kashering it for Passover use. A rabbi should be consulted in individual cases.

A microwave oven without a browning unit is easily kashered for Passover by washing and cleaning well. Do not use for 24 hours; then place a utensil with boiling water in the oven. Allow to boil for several minutes, remove the water and wipe the oven dry.

Many Passover recipes, particularly cakes and desserts, depend on beaten egg whites for leavening. The ideal appliance to use for this task is the mixer. One suggestion is that a small, inexpensive hand mixer be purchased and reserved exclusively for use during the Passover holiday.

Several recipes are offered featuring the use of the blender and food processor. If you keep kosher, these appliances are reserved exclusively for Passover use or else the particular models you own are ones which can be properly kashered for Passover.

Charosets is a traditional sweetened mixture made from chopped fruits and nuts that is placed on the ceremonial seder plate during the Passover seder. It is designed to resemble the mortar used to make bricks, to "remind us of the bricks we made when we were slaves in the land of Egypt," and there are as many traditional charosets recipes as there are countries that house Jews. This particular recipe is easy to make and serves about 20 people.

Charosets   PAREVE

2 cups/500 ml walnuts pieces
3 large apples
4 Tbsp/50 ml sweet red wine,
   or to taste

4 Tbsp/50 ml honey, or to taste
½ tsp/2 ml ginger, or to taste
4 tsp/20 ml cinnamon, or to taste

Food Processor Directions   Insert steel blade in food processor and place walnuts in container. Process until nuts are finely ground, then transfer to mixing bowl. Peel the apples, cut into quarters and remove cores. Place apple pieces in container and process until finely chopped. Add apples to ground nuts, along with remaining ingredients. Combine well and taste to correct seasonings.

Serve charosets on the seder plate or on individual plates, allowing at least 2 tablespoon (15 ml) per person.   YIELD: About 20 servings

---

This particular knaidlach recipe is my family's favorite, but any similar knaidlach recipe will cook beautifully in the microwave oven, using this technique.

Knaidlach (Matzah Balls)   FLEISHIG

2 Tbsp/25 ml melted chicken fat
2 eggs
½ cup/125 ml matzah meal
1 tsp/5 ml salt

2 Tbsp/25 ml liquid
   (soup stock or water)
1 tsp/5 ml chopped parsley,
   optional
2½ cups or more/625 ml water

In a mixing bowl, mix fat and eggs together. Add matzah meal and salt. Stir until combined, then add liquid and parsley. Cover bowl and refrigerate 30 minutes, or until mixture is well chilled and easy to handle.

Microwave Oven Directions   Pour 2½ cups (625 ml) water into a large glass bowl. Place in microwave oven and bring to a boil on high setting, about 6 minutes. Wet your hands and form the matzah mixture into 8 small balls. Place the balls in the boiling water, cover with plastic wrap and return bowl to microwave oven. Cook on high setting 10 to 12 minutes. Allow matzah balls to stand, covered, 5 minutes before transferring to hot soup.

Conventional Directions   Bring 2 quarts (2 liters) water to a rolling boil, then reduce heat so water is at a simmer. Form matzah balls, as described in basic recipe, and drop into simmering water. Cover pot and cook 30 to 40 minutes. Transfer matzah balls to hot soup to serve.   YIELD: 8 matzah balls

Matzah Balls, Low-Fat Version   PAREVE

3 eggs, separated   ½ tsp/2 ml salt
¾ cup/175 ml matzah meal   3 quarts/3 liters water

Mixer Directions   Place egg whites in mixer bowl, attach beaters and whip on
high speed until whites are very stiff. In another bowl, combine egg yolks,
matzah meal and salt, mixing well. Gently fold the egg whites into matzah
mixture.

Bring 3 quarts (3 liters) water to a rolling boil, then reduce heat. Wet your
hands and form mixture into 10 or 12 balls. Drop into simmering water.
Cover the pot and simmer for 20 minutes. Transfer matzah balls to hot soup
to serve.   YIELD: 10 to 12 matzah balls

Mashed-Potato Matzah Balls   PAREVE

4 medium-sized potatoes,   2 eggs
  cooked and peeled   ⅔ cup/150 ml matzah meal
1 tsp/5 ml salt   3 quarts/3 liters water
Dash pepper

Mixer Directions   Cut potatoes into chunks and place in mixer bowl. Attach
beaters and mix on medium speed until potatoes are smooth. Add salt,
pepper and eggs and continue mixing on low speed. Gradually add matzah
meal until mixture becomes firm enough to hold a shape.

Bring salted water to a boil; reduce heat. Wet your hands to form mixture
into 12 small balls. Drop into simmering salted water and cook, covered, for
20 minutes. Transfer to hot soup to serve.   YIELD: 12 matzah balls

Variation   Make the following changes in basic Mashed-Potato Matzah Ball
recipe:

Meat-Filled Matzah Balls   FLEISHIG

½ cup/125 ml chopped   2 Tbsp/25 ml chicken fat
  cooked liver or meat

Mold potato mixture around small balls of chopped liver or chopped cooked
meat. Bake balls in a 375° F (190° C) oven 30 minutes. For a crisp surface,
brush balls with melted chicken fat before baking.   YIELD: 12 matzah balls

Matzah-Spinach Stuffing   P A R E V E

7 matzahs
1 cup/250 ml orange juice
2 onions
2 stalks celery
4 sprigs parsley
½ cup/125 ml nuts

¼ orange, cut in chunks
   (seeds removed)
1 lb/500 grams spinach, cooked,
   drained, and chopped
2 eggs, beaten
1 tsp/5 ml salt
Dash pepper

Food Processor Directions   Insert steel blade in food processor. Break 2 matzahs into container and process until they become coarse crumbs. Transfer to mixing bowl and repeat procedure with remaining matzahs. Pour orange juice over matzah crumbs, stir well and set aside.

Peel onions and cut into chunks. Place in container along with celery (cut into chunks) and parsley sprigs. Process until finely chopped. Add to matzah mixture. Place nuts in container and process until finely chopped. Add to matzah mixture. Place orange pieces in container and process, using pulse button or quick on-off motion, until coarsely chopped. Add orange and remaining ingredients to matzah mixture. Stir until well combined. Makes enough stuffing for 2 chickens or 1 turkey.

YIELD: About 10 cups (2500 ml)

Mandlen (Soup Nuts)   F L E I S H I G

4 Tbsp/50 ml chicken fat
½ cup/125 ml hot water
1 tsp/5 ml salt

Dash pepper
1½ cups/375 ml matzah meal
4 eggs

Mixer Directions   Melt chicken fat and combine with water, salt and pepper in a small mixing bowl. Set aside.

Place matzah meal in mixer bowl and attach dough hook. With mixer running on medium speed, gradually add chicken-fat mixture. Add eggs, one at a time, and continue mixing until well blended. Continue until mixture forms a ball and clears sides of the bowl.

Roll dough between your hands into long, thin ropes, about ½ inch (1.25 cm) thick. Break off ½-inch (1.25-cm) pieces of dough and arrange on a greased baking sheet.

Bake at 400° F (200° C) 30 minutes or until brown. Serve in hot soup.

YIELD: 8 servings

Gefilte Fish Ring   PAREVE

3½ lbs/1.5 kilos fish fillets
1 large onion
1 large carrot
1 rib of celery
2 tsp/10 ml salt, or to taste

½ tsp/2 ml pepper
¼ to ⅓ cup/50 to 75 ml
   matzah meal
2 eggs, beaten

Microwave Oven Directions   Very finely grind the fish fillets, onion, carrot and celery (using finest blade of a food grinder or steel blade attachment of food processor). Add remaining ingredients and mix thoroughly.

Divide mixture in half. Take a 9-inch (23-cm) glass pie dish and place a glass cup (custard cup) in the center. Form half the fish mixture into a ring around the small cup. Repeat the procedure with a second pie dish and the remaining fish mixture. Cover with wax paper.

Cook each fish ring in microwave oven on high setting 12 to 15 minutes or until firmly set. May be served warm or cold.

Conventional Directions   Prepare fish mixture as described in basic recipe and press into 2 greased loaf pans. Bake at 450° F (230° C) 15 minutes, or until fish liquid is bubbling, then lower heat to 325° F (160° C) and bake 30 minutes longer.   YIELD: 6 to 8 servings

Macaroon Salad Dressing   DAIRY

12 Coconut Macaroons
2 cups/500 ml sour cream
¼ cup/50 ml sugar

¼ cup/50 ml brown sugar
½ tsp/2 ml lemon juice

Blender Directions   Place macaroons in blender goblet and blend at medium speed until coarsely chopped. Add remaining ingredients and blend on low speed just until mixed. Refrigerate overnight to allow flavors to blend. Serve on fruit salad.   YIELD: About 3 cups (750 ml)

Passover Blintzes   PAREVE

3 eggs
½ tsp/2 ml salt
1 cup/250 ml water
½ cup/125 ml matzah cake meal

1 to 2 cups/250 to 500 ml
   prepared Blintz filling
   (see Variations)

Blender Directions   Place all ingredients except filling in blender goblet and blend on high speed until smooth. Pour a small amount of batter into a hot, greased frying pan. Cook on one side, then turn out of pan onto a towel.

Place a spoonful of prepared filling (see Variations listed below) on cooked side of Blintz. Roll up Blintz, folding in sides. Fry again, in greased pan, turning to brown both sides.   YIELD: 8 to 10 Blintzes

Variations   Use the following mixtures as fillings for Passover Blintzes:

Cheese-Filled Blintzes   DAIRY

2 cups/500 ml cottage cheese
1 egg
½ tsp/2 ml salt

1 Tbsp/15 ml sugar
1 tsp/5 ml cinnamon
4 Tbsp/50 ml butter

Combine cheese, egg, salt, sugar and cinnamon, and use as a filling for Blintzes. Melt butter in a frying pan and fry Blintzes on both sides.

Jam-Filled Blintzes   PAREVE

1 cup/250 ml preserves or jam

Meat-Filled Blintzes   FLEISHIG

1½ cups/375 ml chopped cooked
   meat, liver or chicken
Salt and pepper to taste

1 egg, beaten
4 Tbsp/50 ml chicken fat

Combine chopped meat, seasonings and egg, and use as a filling for Blintzes. Melt chicken fat in a frying pan and fry Blintzes on both sides.

YIELD: 8 to 10 Blintzes

Passover Noodles   PAREVE

8 to 10 unfilled Blintzes

Fry blintzes as directed in basic recipe then allow to cool. Roll up each blintz and cut crosswise into ¼-inch (.6-cm) strips. Serve in hot soup.

YIELD: About 4 cups (1 liter)

Fruit Bread   PAREVE

3 pieces matzah
1 cup/250 ml apple juice
1 small apple
¾ cup/175 ml sugar

¼ small lemon, seeds removed
 (or ½ tsp/2 ml grated lemon rind
 and 2 tsp/10 ml lemon juice)
3 eggs, separated
⅓ cup/75 ml raisins

Food Processor Directions In a large mixing bowl, crumble matzah into very small pieces. Slowly pour apple juice over matzah, stirring to blend. Allow mixture to stand a few minutes until matzah is softened.

Insert shredding disc in food processor. Quarter the apple, remove core and place apple pieces in feed tube. Use pusher to guide the apple onto the cutting disc to shred fine. Add to matzah mixture.

Insert steel blade in food processor. Combine sugar and lemon in container and process until lemon is finely chopped. Add to matzah mixture. Add egg yolks to matzah mixture, stirring until well combined. Stir in raisins.

In a separate bowl beat the egg whites until stiff. Fold, by hand, into matzah mixture.

Microwave Oven Directions for Baking Pour into an ungreased glass baking dish and place in microwave oven. Cook on medium setting 25 to 30 minutes or until top is firm and springy to the touch.

Conventional Directions for Baking Pour into a greased baking dish. Bake at 350° F (180° C) 1 hour.   YIELD: 6 servings

Farfel-Fruit Kugel   PAREVE

2 cups/500 ml matzah farfel
3 eggs
⅔ cup/150 ml sugar
¼ cup/50 ml sweet red wine
2 Tbsp/25 ml orange peel
2 Tbsp/25 ml oil

½ tsp/2 ml salt
½ tsp/2 ml cinnamon
2 apples, cored and thinly sliced
¼ cup/50 ml raisins
¼ cup/50 ml chopped walnuts

Microwave Oven Directions In a large mixing bowl, soak farfel in cold water for a few minutes. Drain and squeeze into a paste. Beat eggs, sugar and farfel until thick. Stir in remaining ingredients. Pour mixture into a glass dish and place in microwave oven. Cook on high setting 10 minutes.

Conventional Directions Grease a baking dish. Prepare mixture as described in basic recipe and pour into greased dish. Bake at 350° F (180° C) 30 minutes.
                                            YIELD: 4 to 6 servings

Matzah Kugel   FLEISHIG

3 matzahs
Warm water
2 Tbsp/25 ml chicken fat
  or peanut oil
1 Tbsp/15 ml minced onion
2 Tbsp/25 ml chicken cracklings
  (grebenes) (see explanation under

recipe for Chicken Fat in Gravy
and Savory Sauces chapter).
3 eggs, well beaten
½ tsp/2 ml salt
Dash pepper
1 Tbsp/15 ml sugar, or to taste

Break matzahs into small pieces and soak in warm water 5 minutes or until softened. Drain thoroughly and set aside.

Melt chicken fat in frying pan and sauté onion until brown. Add to matzah mixture, along with remaining ingredients. Mix well.

Microwave Oven Directions for Baking Turn mixture into an ungreased glass dish and place in microwave oven. Cook on high setting 15 minutes or until set.

Conventional Directions for Baking Turn mixture into a greased baking dish. Bake at 375° F (190° C) 45 minutes or until browned. YIELD: 4 to 6 servings

Matzah Cheese Kugel   DAIRY

4 matzahs
Warm water
4 eggs
1 cup/250 ml cream
1 cup/250 ml milk
1 cup/250 ml cottage cheese

½ cup/125 ml sour cream
¼ cup/50 ml sugar
Dash salt
1 cup/250 ml shredded
  yellow cheese

Microwave Oven Directions Break matzahs into small pieces and soak in warm water 5 minutes or until softened. Drain thoroughly and set aside.

In a mixing bowl, beat eggs with cream, milk, cottage cheese, sour cream, sugar and salt, until well blended and mixture is smooth.

In a glass dish, place a layer of matzahs. Cover with a layer of the cheese-and-milk mixture and sprinkle with shredded cheese. Repeat, using remaining ingredients; however, reserve some of the shredded cheese to use later as a topping.

Place dish in microwave oven. Cook on medium setting 20 minutes or until firm. Sprinkle reserve cheese on top. Allow to stand 5 minutes.

Conventional Directions Grease baking dish. Prepare mixture as described in basic recipe and layer in the dish. Top with cheese. Bake at 350° F (180° C) 40 minutes or until kugel is puffed and brown.   YIELD: 6 servings

Chocolate-Orange Cake   DAIRY

⅔ cup/150 ml butter
¾ cup/175 ml sugar
3 eggs
½ cup/125 ml cocoa
1 cup/250 ml almonds,
   finely ground

1½ Tbsp/20 ml fresh grated
   orange peel
¼ cup/50 ml orange juice
1 cup/250 ml matzah cake meal
Chocolate Glaze Topping
   (see following recipe)

Mixer Directions Place butter and sugar in mixer bowl. Attach beaters and mix on medium speed until mixture is creamed and fluffy. Add eggs, one at a time, beating well after each addition. On low speed mix in remaining ingredients except glaze.

Grease an 8-inch (20-cm) round cake pan and line bottom with wax paper. Pour cake batter into prepared pan and bake at 375° F (180° C) 25 minutes. Cool in pan for 30 minutes then turn onto cake rack. Peel off wax paper and cool completely before serving. To serve, top with Chocolate Glaze Topping.   YIELD: 1 layer cake

Chocolate Glaze Topping   DAIRY

½ cup/125 ml cocoa
⅓ cup/75 ml butter

¼ cup/50 ml honey

Mixer Directions Combine cocoa, butter and honey in a saucepan. Cook over low heat, stirring constantly, until mixture is smooth. Pour into mixer bowl and beat at medium speed until thickened. Pour glaze evenly over cooled cake.   YIELD: About 1 cup (250 ml)

Date-Nut Torte   PAREVE

8 eggs, separated
1½ cups/375 ml sugar
1½ cups/375 ml nuts,
   finely chopped

3 cups/750 ml pitted dates,
   finely chopped
¼ cup/50 ml matzah cake meal
Chocolate Glaze Topping
   (preceding recipe), optional

Mixer Directions   Place egg yolks in mixer bowl. Attach beaters and mix on medium speed until yolks are thick and lemon-colored. Add sugar and beat until mixture is thick. Combine nuts, dates and cake meal, then add to egg mixture, mixing well.

In a separate bowl, beat egg whites on high mixer speed until stiff. By hand, gently fold egg whites into date-nut mixture.

Pour batter into a greased tube pan. Bake at 325° F (160° C) about 60 minutes. Cool before removing from pan. Serve plain or with Chocolate Glaze Topping (see previous recipe).   YIELD: 1 large tube cake

---

Meringue shells are very delicate and very fancy pastries, designed to hold fruit or prepared fillings. They are made from stiffly beaten egg whites, which are baked until they are dry and brittle. These can be made ahead of time and stored in airtight containers.

Meringue Shells   PAREVE

4 egg whites, at room temperature
1 cup/250 ml sugar

1 tsp/5 ml lemon juice

Mixer Directions   Place egg whites in mixer bowl. Attach beaters and beat on high speed until egg whites are in soft peaks. With mixer running, add sugar, 1 tablespoon (15 ml) at a time. Add lemon juice. Continue beating until egg whites are stiff and glossy.

Grease a baking sheet and cover with heavy paper. Form the egg-white mixture into shells, using a pastry tube or spoon.

The best way to bake shells is to place in a preheated 475° F (245° C) oven. Immediately turn off oven and allow shells to remain, undisturbed, 8 hours or overnight. A faster method is to bake the shells at 225° F (110° C) 1 hour, then allow shells to remain in the oven 1 hour longer after the heat has been turned off.

Carefully remove paper from bottom of shells. To serve, fill with fruit or flavored cream filling. YIELD: 6 large shells or 12 small (3-inch or 8-cm) shells

Fancy Cake Mixes   PAREVE

Mixer Directions   Many excellent "kosher le Pesach" cake mixes are available, both for Passover and year-round use. These mixes are pareve and
require only the addition of eggs and liquid. To add your own personal
touch to a Passover cake mix, try one or more of the following suggestions:

Increase the number of eggs called for, from 1 or 2 to about 6. Separate the
eggs, mixing the beaten yolks with the cake mix and liquid. On high mixer
speed, beat the egg whites until stiff, then carefully fold into the cake batter.

Add one or more of the following to the prepared cake mix:

> ½ to 1 cup/25 to 250 ml chopped nuts
> ½ cup/125 ml raisins, dates or chopped prunes
> ½ cup/125 ml freshly grated coconut (see food processor method
>   for Grated Coconut)
> 1 teaspoon/5 ml grated lemon or orange peel
> 1 teaspoon/5 ml cinnamon

Substitute for the required amount of liquid one of the following:

> Sweet red wine
> Apple juice
> Orange juice
> 1 banana, peeled and mashed (to substitute
>   for ¼ to ⅓ cup [50 to 75 ml] of the required liquid)
> Double-strength black coffee

YIELD: 1 "fancy" cake

Nut Cake   PAREVE

1⅓ cups/325 ml sugar	1 Tbsp/15 ml lemon juice
8 eggs, separated	1 cup/250 ml finely ground
1 tsp/5 ml grated lemon peel	almonds
	½ cup/125 ml matzah cake meal

Mixer Directions   Place sugar and egg yolks in mixer bowl. Attach beaters
and beat on medium speed until mixture is thick and smooth. Add lemon
peel and juice, mixing well.

In a separate bowl, beat egg whites on high mixer speed until stiff. Fold
egg whites, almonds and matzah cake meal by hand into batter.

Turn cake into a greased tube pan, or greased and wax-paper-lined 9-by-
13-inch (23-by-33-cm) baking pan. Bake at 350° F (180° C) 1 hour.

YIELD: Large 1-layer cake

Sponge Cake   PAREVE

6 eggs, separated   ½ cup/125 ml matzah cake meal
1⅓ cups/325 ml sugar   ½ cup/125 ml potato starch
⅓ cup/75 ml water   ½ tsp/2 ml salt
1 tsp/5 ml lemon peel   Chocolate Glaze Topping
2 Tbsp/25 ml lemon juice   (page 328), optional

Mixer Directions   Place egg yolks in mixer bowl. Attach beaters and beat on
low speed until thick and lemon-colored. Beat in sugar, then water, lemon
peel and lemon juice. Combine dry ingredients and gradually beat into yolk
mixture.

In a separate bowl, whip egg whites until stiff on high mixer speed. By
hand, fold the egg whites into the cake batter.

Turn batter into an ungreased tube pan. Bake at 325° F (160° C) 1½
hours. Invert pan on a wire rack and, without removing cake from pan,
allow to cool. When thoroughly cool, remove cake from pan. Serve plain or
drizzled with Chocolate Glaze Topping.   YIELD: 1 large tube cake

---

Every Passover the nursery school at our synagogue has a midmorning seder
to which all the parents are invited (but mostly only the mommies attend).
For the past half decade I have attended with one or more of my children.
One year, while the rabbi, cantor and children were enthusiastically singing
about Pharaoh and frogs, all the Moms were quietly circulating and copying
this particular recipe for Passover Brownies.

Passover Brownies   DAIRY

1 cup/250 ml sugar   ⅓ cup/75 ml cocoa
½ cup/125 ml butter   ½ cup/125 ml matzah cake meal
2 eggs   ½ cup/125 ml chopped nuts

Mixer Directions   Place sugar and butter in mixer bowl and attach beaters.
On medium speed cream mixture until light and fluffy. Add eggs and beat
well. Add remaining ingredients and beat until mixture is well blended.

Microwave Oven Directions for Baking   Pour batter into a glass baking dish.
Cover dish with wax paper and place in microwave oven. Cook on high
setting 8 minutes or until firm.

Conventional Directions for Baking   Turn batter into a greased 8-by-8-inch
(20-by-20-cm) baking dish. Bake at 375° F (190° C) 25 minutes.

YIELD: 16 squares

Coconut Macaroons   P A R E V E

3 egg whites   Dash salt
½ cup/125 ml sugar   2 tsp/10 ml water
1⅓ cups (about ¼ lb)/325 ml
   freshly grated coconut
   (see food processor method
   for Grated Coconut)

Mixer Directions   Place egg whites in mixer bowl and attach beaters. Beat on
high speed until soft peaks form. Continue beating and very gradually add
sugar. Beat until egg whites are stiff but not dry.

Combine coconut, salt and water. Carefully fold into beaten egg whites.

Drop by teaspoonfuls onto a greased baking sheet. Bake at 300° F
(150° C) 25 minutes, or until cookies are lightly browned. Wait until cookies
are nearly cooled before removing from baking sheet.

YIELD: About 20 cookies

Variations   Add the following to basic Coconut Macaroons recipe:

Chocolate Coconut Macaroons   P A R E V E

2 Tbsp/25 ml cocoa

When egg whites are stiff, beat in cocoa, before adding coconut mixture.

YIELD: About 20 cookies

Matzah-Meal Pie Crust   D A I R Y

1 cup/250 ml matzah meal   Dash salt
3 Tbsp/45 ml sugar   ½ cup/125 ml butter, melted
1 tsp/5 ml cinnamon
   (or less, if desired)

Microwave Oven Directions   Blend all ingredients together. Press mixture into
a 9-inch (23-cm) glass pie dish. Place in microwave oven and cook on high
setting 4 minutes, or until set.

Conventional Directions   Blend all ingredients together and press mixture into
a 9-inch (23-cm) pie dish. Bake at 375° F (190° C) 15 to 20 minutes or until
golden brown.   YIELD: One 9-inch (23-cm) pie crust

A crunchy nut crust is the perfect complement to an apple or other fruit pie filling. Any kind of nut, or combination of nuts, may be used to make this crust. Nuts contain a great deal of oil, and as the nuts are processed this oil is released. No butter is needed to hold the crust together.

Passover Nut Pie Crust   P A R E V E

2 cups/500 ml ground nuts   ¼ cup/50 ml sugar

Food Processor Directions   Insert steel blade in food processor and place nuts in container. With motor running, gradually add sugar through the feed tube. As processing continues, oil is released from the nuts and forms with the sugar into a workable paste. Use your fingers to press this mixture into a 9-inch (23-cm) glass pie dish.

Microwave Oven Directions   Place in microwave oven and cook on high setting 2 minutes.

Conventional Directions   Bake at 375° F (190° C) for 10 minutes.

YIELD: 9-inch (23-cm) pie crust

Freshly grated coconut is a delightful snack and adds a distinctive flavor and texture to many recipes. You can grate coconut yourself in a food processor or blender and toast it in the microwave oven. Store fresh coconut in the refrigerator.

Grated Coconut   P A R E V E

Break open the shell of a fresh coconut. (This is not always easy. Try driving nails into the three shiny black dots on the "face," then remove the nails to allow the liquid to drain out. Usually, at this point, if you tap the coconut with a hammer it will split in two pieces lengthwise. Heating the coconut in a 325° F (160° C) oven for 10 to 15 minutes may also facilitate opening it. If these methods fail, try a power saw or an ax.) After draining out the remaining liquid from the open coconut, use a sharp knife to cut out the white meat. Discard peel. Cut coconut meat into 1-inch (2.5-cm) squares.

Food Processor Directions   Insert steel blade in food processor. Place coconut squares in container and process until finely grated.

Blender Directions   Start the blender motor running at high speed. Drop squares of coconut into the goblet and process until shredded to desired consistency.

YIELD: 1 lb (500 grams) coconut meat yields
about 5 cups (1250 ml) shredded

Toasted Coconut   PAREVE

1 cup/250 ml freshly grated coconut

Microwave Oven Directions   To toast coconut, spread 1 cup (250 ml) coconut between layers of paper towels. Cook on high setting until coconut is lightly brown, about 1 minute, stirring well after 15 seconds.

Conventional Directions   Spread coconut on a baking sheet and place in a preheated 325° F (160° C) oven about 10 minutes.

YIELD: 1 cup (250 ml) toasted coconut

Coconut Macaroon Pie Crust   DAIRY

Coconut Macaroon cookies,   3 Tbsp/45 ml butter
   to equal 1⅓ cups/325 ml crumbs

Food Processor Directions   Insert steel blade in food processor. Place cookies in container and process until finely chopped. Cut the butter into chunks and process until mixture is blended into a workable paste, about 5 seconds. Press this mixture into a 9-inch (23-cm) pie dish.

Microwave Oven Directions   Bake at high setting 2 minutes or until set.

Conventional Directions   Bake at 300° F (150° C) 20 to 25 minutes, until golden brown.   YIELD: 9-inch (23-cm) pie crust

Variations   Add the following ingredients to basic Coconut Macaroon Crust recipe:

Chocolate Macaroon Crust   DAIRY

2 Tbsp/25 ml cocoa   2 Tbsp/25 ml liquid (milk,
⅔ cup/150 ml sugar   juice or water)
3 Tbsp/45 ml butter

Add cocoa and sugar to cookies before processing. Add butter and liquid. Process to achieve paste consistency.

Nutty-Coconut Crust   DAIRY

½ cup/125 ml finely chopped nuts   YIELD: 9-inch (23-cm) pie crust

PASSOVER PIE FILLINGS

Many of the pie filling recipes presented in the Desserts chapter can be adapted for Passover use in the following manner:

Dried Apricot Pie PAREVE

Substitute ¾ cup (175 ml) apple juice for the nectar. Apricots, raisins, juice, lemon peel, water and sugar may be simmered on low heat until soft. Substitute 3 tablespoons (45 ml) potato starch for the cornstarch in basic recipe.

Apple Streusel Pie PAREVE

The filling recipe may be used during Passover without any change in ingredients. Prepare streusel topping with 1 cup (250 ml) matzah meal and ⅓ cup (75 ml) butter.

Cottage Cheese–Pineapple Pie DAIRY

Omit pineapple tidbits and garnish pie instead with a sour-cream topping. To make topping, combine until smooth 1 cup (250 ml) sour cream, ¼ cup (50 ml) sugar and ½ teaspoon (2 ml) lemon juice.

Lemon Meringue Pie PAREVE

Substitute ½ cup (1 stick, 125 ml) butter for margarine in basic recipe for filling.

Orange Chiffon Pie PAREVE

Orange Chiffon Pie may be used for Passover without any change in filling ingredients.

Strawberry Pie DAIRY

When preparing strawberries, omit confectioners' sugar and substitute ½ cup (125 ml) granulated sugar. When preparing the glaze, substitute 1 tablespoon (15 ml) potato starch for the cornstarch.

CHILDREN'S CHAPTER

All recipes personally tested by Judy, Michael and Joshua London.

All of the recipes in this chapter can be made in either the microwave oven or the blender, because these two appliances produce the fastest results and children do not have to wait long to sample the fruits of their labors.

These recipes range from the very simplest Cinnamon Baked Apple and Fabulous Fast Fudge to recipes a little more interesting for the older child to cook, such as Snappy Crackle Bars.

For a child who loves grilled cheese sandwiches, here is an alternative that involves no frying pan or spatula to wash.

Toasted Cheese Sandwich DAIRY

2 slices bread, toasted   1 slice yellow cheese

Microwave Oven Directions   Place the cheese between 2 slices toasted bread. Place on a paper napkin and cook on high setting in microwave oven 15 to 30 seconds, or until cheese is melted. YIELD: 1 serving

---

These spicy, crisp sticks make an excellent snack.

Hot Diggety Doggy Sticks FLEISHIG

1 hot dog

Microwave Oven Directions   Cut the hot dog into long, thin strips. Try to cut at least 12 to 16 strips per hot dog. Spread strips on a paper towel in a single layer. Cover with a second paper towel and place in microwave oven. Cook on high setting 2 minutes for a chewy stick and 3 minutes for crisp sticks.

YIELD: 1 serving

Variation

Hot Dog Chips   F L E I S H I G

Food Processor Directions Insert slicing disc into food processor and guide a partially frozen hot dog through the feed tube. Spread the chips on a paper towel and cook as above.   YIELD: 1 serving

---

I have included in this section directions for using the food processor to prepare Peanut Spread. I feel compelled, however, to add a reminder that the food processor is *not* a toy for children to play with. The steel blade is as potentially dangerous as the sharpest of kitchen knives, and supervision and caution must be used.

Peanut Spread   P A R E V E

1½ cups/375 ml salted peanuts
1 Tbsp/15 ml vegetable oil

Food Processor Directions Insert steel blade in food processor. Place nuts in container and process until a paste begins to form. Scrape the sides of the container with a rubber spatula, add oil and continue processing until desired consistency is reached.

Blender Directions Place peanuts in blender goblet. Blend on high speed until mixture is smooth, using a rubber spatula to keep ingredients flowing into the blades. When desired consistency is reached, add oil and blend until smooth. Store, covered, in refrigerator.   YIELD: 1 cup (250 ml)

Variations Add the following ingredients to prepared peanut spread, processing again until smooth.

Banana Peanut Butter   P A R E V E

1 banana

Chocolate Peanut Spread   P A R E V E

½ cup/125 ml chocolate chips

Honey Peanut Spread   P A R E V E

1 tsp/5 ml honey, or to taste   YIELD: 1 cup (250 ml)

Caramel Apple Sticks   PAREVE

1½ lbs/750 grams caramel candy   8 to 10 medium red apples
  chews   8 to 10 wooden sticks
1 Tbsp/15 ml water

Microwave Oven Directions   Place caramels and water in a glass bowl. Cook on
high setting in microwave oven 5 to 7 minutes, stirring occasionally, until
caramels are melted and mixture is smooth.

Push a stick into stem end of each apple. Dip apples into hot caramel,
turning to coat entire apple. Place on greased wax paper to cool.

Conventional Directions   In the top half of a double boiler, over boiling water,
place caramels and water. Cook, stirring constantly, until candy is melted.
Proceed as in basic recipe.   YIELD: 8 to 10 servings

Variations   After dipping apples in hot caramel, roll in the following:

Coco-Caramel Apple Sticks   PAREVE

1 cup/250 ml shredded coconut

Crispy-Caramel Apple Sticks   PAREVE

1 cup/250 ml crisp rice cereal

Nutty-Caramel Apple Sticks   PAREVE

1 cup/250 ml finely chopped nuts
                                                   YIELD: 8 to 10 servings

Cinnamon Baked Apple   PAREVE

1 medium-size red apple   1 red lollipop, crushed
1 tsp/5 ml cinnamon-sugar

Microwave Oven Directions   Cut off the top ½ inch (1.25 cm) of the apple and
remove the core. Sprinkle cinnamon-sugar and the crushed lollipop into the
center of the apple. Place apple in a glass bowl and cover bowl with wax
paper. Place in microwave oven and cook on high setting 3 minutes. This
will be very hot, so allow to cool slightly before eating.   YIELD: 1 serving

For a special dairy treat, top Hot Fudge Banana Boats with whipped cream and a cherry.

Hot Fudge Banana Boats   PAREVE

2 bananas, slightly firm
1 tsp/5 ml lemon juice
4 Tbsp/50 ml Hot Fudge Sauce
  (see recipe in Sweet Sauces
  and Fillings chapter)

2 Tbsp/25 ml chopped nuts

Microwave Oven Directions   Split bananas lengthwise and place in a glass baking dish, cut side up. Sprinkle lightly with lemon juice. Drizzle Hot Fudge Sauce over top. Sprinkle with chopped nuts. Place in microwave oven and cook on high setting 30 seconds or until sauce is hot.   YIELD: 4 servings

---

Children are fascinated watching cupcakes cook in the microwave oven. One cupcake is ready in just 45 seconds!! Six cupcakes "rise and shine" in 2½ minutes—hardly enough time to lick the spoon.

Early-to-Rise Cupcakes   DAIRY or PAREVE

1 package cake mix, any flavor

Microwave Oven Directions   Prepare batter according to package directions. Cupcakes may be baked in a variety of containers, including:

    Microwave oven cupcake pans, lined with individual paper liners
    Custard cups, lined with individual paper liners
    Styrofoam cups
    Ice cream cones with flat bottoms
    4 paper liners stacked together, for each
    Coffee cup, lined with an individual paper liner

Fill the containers about half full of batter. Cook cupcakes on medium-high setting, 45 seconds for 1 cupcake, 2 to 2½ minutes for 4 cupcakes and about 2½ to 3 minutes for 6 cupcakes.

  Use frosting from any recipe to top the cupcakes and decorate frosting with colored candies, sprinkles, gumdrops, jelly beans, chopped nuts or chocolate bits.   YIELD: 1 package yields about 2 to 3 dozen cupcakes

This is a delicious gift idea for grandma or teacher that even a preschooler can make.

Fabulous Fast Fudge　　　　　　　　　　　　　　　P A R E V E

1-lb box/(500 grams)　　　　　　　　¼ cup/50 ml water
　confectioners' sugar　　　　　　　　　or nondairy creamer
½ cup/125 ml cocoa　　　　　　　　　1 tsp/5 ml vanilla
½ cup (1 stick)/125 ml
　pareve margarine

Microwave Oven Directions　In a glass mixing bowl, stir sugar and cocoa together until very well blended (if the sugar is not finely distributed, there can be lumps in the fudge; stirring is faster than sifting).

Make a well in the center. Put margarine and water in the well. Do not stir. Place in microwave oven and cook on high setting 2 minutes, or until margarine is melted.

Use a wooden spoon to stir and blend fudge mixture. Add vanilla and mix well.

Spray a large paper plate with a nonstick aerosol coating (or grease an 8-inch/20-cm dish). Pour fudge onto plate. Take a piece of plastic wrap and cover top of fudge. Place hands on top of the plastic wrap and smooth the fudge to the outer edges of the plate. Refrigerate about 30 minutes and cut into 1 inch (2.5-cm) squares.　　　　　　　　　　　YIELD: 1 lb Fudge

Variations　Make the following changes in basic fudge recipe:

Chocolate-Coconut Fudge　　　　　　　　　　　　P A R E V E

½ cup/125 ml shredded coconut

Add coconut with vanilla and mix well.

Chocolate-Mint Fudge　　　　　　　　　　　　　　P A R E V E

½ tsp/2 ml mint flavoring

Substitute mint flavoring for the vanilla.

Nutty Fudge　　　　　　　　　　　　　　　　　　　P A R E V E

½ cup/125 ml chopped nuts

Add chopped nuts with vanilla and mix well.

Peanut-Chocolate Fudge PAREVE

½ cup/125 ml crunchy peanut butter

Add crunchy peanut butter with vanilla and mix well. YIELD: 1 lb Fudge

---

When the children and I first concocted this recipe we sent a copy to my sister-in-law, Auntie Sherrie. She was a newlywed and always looking for "simple" recipes. According to her husband, Uncle Danny, he has enjoyed this treat for dessert, found chunks tucked into his lunch box and has even been served it for breakfast.

Snappy Crackle Bars PAREVE

1 (6-oz)/(168 grams) package
  chocolate chips
½ cup (1 stick)/125 ml
  pareve margarine

¼ cup/50 ml honey
3 cups/750 ml crisp rice cereal

Microwave Oven Directions In a glass bowl, combine chocolate chips, margarine and honey. Place in microwave oven and cook on high setting 3 minutes or until chips and margarine are melted, stirring once every minute. Stir until mixture is smooth. Stir in cereal, coating well. Pour mixture onto a greased dish and refrigerate until firm. Cut into squares to serve.

YIELD: About 16 pieces

Chilly Jelly Whip PAREVE

1 package kosher imitation-jel
  dessert, any flavor

¼ cup/50 ml hot liquid
  (water, fruit juice or nectar)
4 cups/1 liter crushed ice

Blender Directions Place imitation-jel in blender goblet. Add hot liquid and blend on low speed until jel is dissolved. Stop blender. Add ice. Cover and blend at high speed until mixture is smooth and snowy. Serve in tall glasses with straws. YIELD: 4 to 6 servings

---

Juicy Slush PAREVE

1 (6-oz)/(177 ml) can frozen juice
  concentrate, partially thawed

4 cups/1 liter crushed ice

Blender Directions Put juice and ice in blender goblet. Cover and blend on high speed until mixture is the consistency of snow. If necessary, use a rubber spatula to scrape sides of goblet and guide the ice to the blades. Serve immediately in a cup with straws and spoons. YIELD: 4 to 6 servings

Fruity Milk   D A I R Y

1 cup/250 ml milk
1 serving fruit or juice (see Variations)

Blender Directions   Chill milk and fruit thoroughly. Combine in blender goblet and blend on high speed until frothy.   YIELD: 1 serving

Variations   Use the following items to equal 1 serving fruit or juice in basic
Fruity Milk recipe:

Banana-Milk   D A I R Y

1 banana, cut up

Fruit Juice and Milk   D A I R Y

2 Tbsp/25 ml fruit nectar
   (apricot, pear, peach, etc.)

Grape Juice and Milk   D A I R Y

⅓ cup/75 ml grape juice
¼ tsp/125 ml lemon juice

Orange Juice and Milk   D A I R Y

½ cup/125 ml orange juice

Decrease milk to ½ cup and add ½ cup orange juice.

Strawberry Milk   D A I R Y

½ cup/125 ml sliced fresh strawberries
2 tsp/10 ml sugar   YIELD: 1 .serving

BABY FOOD

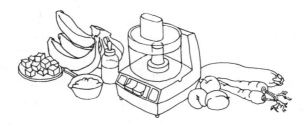

If you live outside a large city, finding kosher baby food can present a problem, especially strained meats and junior dinners.

A microwave oven, blender and food processor can all be used to great advantage in preparing, cooking or reheating food for baby.

Storage space was one problem I encountered in making homemade baby food for my first child. Usually my baby food recipe filled up several empty baby food jars, and the question arose of what to do with the leftovers. These little jars can take up more freezer space than anticipated and it takes a long time to thaw and reheat frozen baby food conventionally (it certainly seems like a long time if baby is impatient!).

One solution to the storage problem (I discovered with Baby Number Two) is to freeze the baby food in ice-cube trays. When the food is frozen, break it into cubes and store the food cubes in a plastic bag in the freezer. This makes storage a bit more compact, but the thawing-reheating problem still remains.

The microwave oven (which arrived in my life shortly after Baby Number Three) is a tremendous asset in preparing baby food. Not only does it defrost and warm the frozen food quickly but it can also be used to cook small quantities of fresh food, eliminating leftovers.

MICROWAVE OVEN BABY FOOD GUIDE

Warming a Bottle
To heat a bottle of formula from the refrigerator requires approximately 20 to 30 seconds on high setting. Shake the bottle slightly and test the temperature before feeding baby.

Heating a Jar of Baby Food
Before you heat a jar of baby food, always remove the metal lid. One jar of food, at room temperature, will warm to serving temperature in 15 seconds on high setting. If the jar has been refrigerated, it will take approximately 30 seconds. Be sure to test the temperature and stir the food well before serving baby.

Homemade Baby Food
It takes less time to cook baby's food fresh from scratch in the microwave oven than to remove a jar from the freezer, thaw and reheat. Very small, one-serving, portions of food may be cooked in the following manner:

· Wrap the food in plastic wrap (no additional liquid is needed)
· Place food in microwave oven and cook on high setting
· Cook according to the following time chart:

Beets, 1 small, peeled and quartered	1 minute
Carrot, 1 small, peeled and chunked	1 minute
Spinach, several leaves, washed	45 seconds
Squash, 1½-inch (4-cm) cube	1½ minutes
Potato or yam, 1 small, 3 oz (90 grams)	3 minutes

BLENDER BABY FOOD GUIDE

With the blender it is a simple task to prepare wholesome, appetizing food for baby, without the additives and fillers of commercially prepared food and at a much lower cost.

Basic Recipe—Fruit   P A R E V E

¾ cup/175 ml cooked fruit
2 tsp/10 ml water,
  or syrup from fruit

Blender Directions Put ingredients into blender goblet and blend on low speed until smooth. To test consistency, rub a small amount between your fingers. If mixture is not fine enough, blend some more. As baby grows older, less water will be needed to blend with the fruit and less blending time will be used to achieve a junior-type texture.   YIELD: 1 serving

Basic Recipe— Meat or Vegetable

FLEISHIG or PAREVE

½ cup/125 ml cubed cooked meat
  or vegetable

4 to 6 Tbsp/50 to 75 ml broth,
  formula or other liquid

Blender Directions   Put ingredients into blender goblet and blend on low speed until smooth. The amount of liquid given is needed for small babies. Decrease amount of liquid as baby grows older.   YIELD: 1 serving

Basic Recipe—Junior Dinner

FLEISHIG

½ cup/125 ml cubed cooked meat
  or chicken
2 Tbsp/25 ml cooked vegetables
  (carrots, peas, spinach,
  squash or celery)

½ cup/125 ml chicken soup,
  broth, water or other liquid
4 Tbsp/50 ml cooked rice

Blender Directions   Put all ingredients into blender goblet and blend at low speed until mixture is thoroughly pureed. Heat before serving.

YIELD: 1 serving

FOOD PROCESSOR BABY FOOD GUIDE

The food processor, like the blender, can be used to puree cooked fruits, vegetables and meats for baby food. When using the food processor to make baby food, the following procedure is best: Insert steel blade into food processor, place the food and liquid in the container and process until smooth. Heat the food before serving.

As baby grows older and able to tolerate coarser textures, foods may be processed raw, using the steel blade or shredding disc. Heat the food before serving.

Junior Chicken Dinner

FLEISHIG

½ cup/125 ml cooked chicken,
  cut into cubes

¼ cup/50 ml cooked carrots
2 Tbsp/25 ml chicken broth

Food Processor Directions   Insert steel blade in food processor. Combine ingredients in container and process until smooth. Heat before serving.

YIELD: 1 serving

Junior Hamburger Dinner   FLEISHIG

½ cup/125 ml crumbled   ¼ cup/50 ml mashed potatoes
   cooked hamburger

Food Processor Directions   Insert steel blade in food processor. Combine ingredients in container and process until smooth. Heat before serving.

YIELD: 1 serving

Junior Lamb Dinner   FLEISHIG

½ cup/125 ml cooked lamb,   ¼ to ½ cup/50 to 125 ml green peas
   cut into cubes   2 Tbsp/25 ml broth or water

Food Processor Directions   Insert steel blade in food processor. Combine ingredients in container and process until smooth. Heat before serving.

YIELD: 1 serving

PART THREE

MENUS
AND OTHER
INSTRUCTIONS

MENU PLANS FOR HOLIDAYS AND EVERYDAY

The following menus are suggestions for planning complete breakfasts, soup and salad lunches, dairy suppers and holiday dinners, using modern kitchen appliances. An asterisk (*) indicates a recipe found in this book. Add beverage of your choice.

BREAKFAST MENUS

Using the Microwave Oven

1. Orange and grapefruit sections
   * baked eggs
   * forever yours bran muffins
   * raspberry refrigerator jam

2. * Stewed apricots
   * crunchy granola with milk
   toast
   white and yellow cheese slices

3. Fruit juice
   * fried eggs
   smoked fish
   * cornbread
   * classic strawberry jam

4. Fresh strawberries
   * perfect custard
   shredded wheat cereal

Using the Food Processor

1. Cantaloupe slices
   * gourmet omelet
   * no-knead honey white bread
   butter and honey

2. Sliced bananas with raisins
   * cheese waffles
   butter and hot syrup

Using the Blender

1. * Banana blender drink
   whole-wheat toast
   * pineapple-peach marmalade

2. Orange juice
   * buttermilk pancakes
   butter and hot syrup

3. * Mocha blender drink
   * caraway-cheese muffins
   butter and jam

4. * Pineapple-carrot juice
   * fried egg
   whole-wheat toast

Using the Mixer
1.   Honeydew melon
   *   bagels
        lox (smoked salmon)
        cream cheese

2.   Fresh fruit
   *   scrambled eggs
   *   buttermilk biscuits
        butter and jam

Using the Crock Pot
1. *   Stewed prunes
   *   poached eggs
        rye toast and butter

2.   Grapefruit juice
   *   oatmeal (with cinnamon
          and milk)
   *   ginger-orange bread

SOUP AND SALAD LUNCH MENUS

Using the Microwave Oven
1. *   Old-fashioned cream of
          tomato soup
   *   fruity jel salad
        saltine crackers
   *   brownies

2. *   Cabbage borscht
        tossed green salad
   *   black bread
        fresh fruit, cookies

3. *   Pareve split pea soup
   *   egg salad
        matzahs
   *   sourdough chocolate cake

Using the Crock Pot
1. *   Lentil soup
        mixed vegetable salad
   *   pumpernickel bread
   *   dried apricot pie

2. *   After-Thanksgiving turkey
          soup
        lettuce and tomato salad
   *   pumpkin bread
        fruit and jel dessert

Using the Food Processor
1. *   Sweet and sour borscht
   *   Israeli vegetable salad
   *   no-knead whole-wheat
          bread
   *   sesame-seed candy

2. *   Cream of potato soup
   *   old-fashioned cole slaw
   *   rye bread
   *   peanut butter cookies

3. *   Mushroom-barley soup
   *   chicken salad
   *   brioche
   *   apple strudel

4. *   Onion soup
   *   egg salad
   *   zucchini bread
        fresh fruit platter

Using the Blender
1. * Quick mixed-vegetable
        soup
   * dairy cole slaw
   * graham bread
   * chocolate blender cake

2. * Blender borscht
        lettuce salad
   * Russian dressing
   * rye bread
   * orange chiffon pie

DAIRY SUPPER MENUS

Using the Microwave Oven
1. * Tuna-olive quiche
   * green beans
        hot rolls and butter
   * fruitcake miniatures

2. * Salmon circle
        baked potato
   * cheese sauce
   * fresh peas
   * pecan pie

Using the Food Processor
1. * Pizza
        spinach salad
   * Italian dressing
        carrot and celery sticks
   * juicy-fruity freeze

2. * Spinach-cheese latkes
        tossed salad
   * low-calorie dressing
   * cranberry fruit mold
   * oatmeal cookies

Using the Blender
1. * Crêpes with tuna salad filling
   * mushroom sauce
   * fresh asparagus
        carrot and celery sticks
   * sesame nut bars

2. * Manicotti
        tossed green salad
        garlic bread
   * strawberry sherbet

Using the Mixer
1. * Cheese soufflé
   * cinnamon baked apple slices
   * fresh broccoli
   * herb bread
   * pound cake

2. * Artichoke with mayonnaise
   * noodle kugel
        peas and carrots
   * crescent rolls
        fresh fruit platter

Using the Crock Pot
1. * Macaroni and cheese
        spinach salad
   * chocolate-chip cookies
   * dried fruit compote

2. * Cheesy noodle-vegetable
        bake
   * pickled beets
        tossed green salad
   * oatmeal cookies

MICROWAVE OVEN DINNERS

It is easier than you might think to coordinate and cook complete dinners in the microwave oven. Best results are usually obtained when food items are cooked one at a time and allowed a standing time for "aftercooking" while other items are being cooked. Because complete microwave oven meals are often cooked "out of sequence," here are some tips and timing suggestions to use as a guide:

1. Chilled Foods
Foods which will be served chilled or at room temperature should be cooked first. This includes most desserts, cakes, cooked salad dressings, etc.

2. Foods to Reheat
Foods which can be reheated should be cooked earlier, then warmed just before serving time. In fact, many foods improve in flavor when reheated. This includes casserole dishes, chili, spaghetti sauces, gravies and other sauces, soups, etc.

3. Dense Foods
The denser the food item, the longer it will stay hot after cooking. Large roasts, poultry and certain thick vegetables, including squash, corn on the cob, cauliflower, can be cooked early. If properly covered after cooking, these items can stay hot for 30 minutes or longer.

Proper coverings are important to help foods retain their heat after cooking, if they will not be served immediately. Cover meat and poultry with a tent of foil, shiny side toward the food, after you remove it from the microwave oven. To keep vegetables hot, do not remove the plastic wrap covering, as a great deal of steam and heat are held underneath. After microwave oven cooking, cover the vegetables with a second piece of plastic wrap or a piece of foil.

4. Delicate Foods
Delicate foods which cannot be reheated should be cooked last. This includes fish and eggs. Warming bread and rolls, etc., should also take place just before serving.

5. Cook and Hold
Many microwave ovens have a special warm setting or a probe which holds food at a serving temperature for long periods of time.

MICROWAVE OVEN DINNER MENUS

Meat Dinners

1. * Standing rib roast
   * potato kugel
   * French-style green beans
     with mushrooms
     sliced tomatoes and onions
   * pecan pie

2. * Beef stew
     tossed green salad
     hot rolls and pareve
     margarine
   * brownies with favorite hot
     fudge sauce

Ground-Meat Dinners

1. * One-dish spaghetti
     tossed green salad
   * sourdough French bread
   * strawberry sherbet

2. * Meat "loaf"
   * baked potatoes
   * glazed carrots
   * pareve peach whip

Poultry Dinners

1. * Oven-"fried" chicken
   * rice pilaf
   * Israeli-style zucchini in
     tomato sauce
   * pound cake with cherry sauce

2. * Barbecued chicken
   * hot potato salad
   * green beans
   * blueberry "can-do" pie

3. * Chicken with rice
   * fresh asparagus
   * corn on the cob
     sliced tomatoes
   * French dressing
     applesauce cake

4. * Orange-glazed duck
   * kasha with mushrooms
   * broccoli-carrot vegetable
     platter
   * orange angel food cake

Fish Dinners

1. * Poached salmon
   * curried rice
   * succotash
   * pumpkin pie

2. * Baked fish in mustard sauce
   * baked potatoes
   * brussels sprouts
     marinated cucumber slices
   * sourdough chocolate cake

HOLIDAY DINNERS

Holiday meals in a Jewish home are traditionally heavy—often lasting through 5 or more courses. The following menus, however, follow the modern trend toward lighter meals, limited to 3 or 4 courses. All of the traditional holiday favorites are included. Only that old, traditional, overstuffed feeling and some of the mountainous leftovers have been removed.

ROSH HASHANAH

1. *First-Day Dinner*
   wine for Kiddush
   * round challah
   * Sophie Sway's Roumanian
     gefilte fish, with horseradish
   * rolled rib roast
   * potato kugel
   * glazed carrots
   * French-style green beans
   * honey cake
   coffee   tea with lemon

2. *Second-Day Dinner*
   wine for Kiddush
   * round challah
   * sweet chicken soup with
     noodles
   * orange-glazed duck
   * sweet potatoes
   * asparagus
   * green garden salad
   * holiday apple cake
   coffee   tea with lemon

YOM KIPPUR

1. *Meal Before the Fast*
   * challah
   * chicken soup
   * kreplach with chicken
     filling
   * boiled beef (essic fleisch)
   * noodle kugel
   * peas
   * pareve peach whip
   coffee   tea with lemon

2. *Meal to Break the Fast*
   orange juice
   * bagels   challah   rolls
   lox   smoked whitefish
     herring
   cream cheese   white cheese
   * scrambled eggs
   * dried fruit compote
   * honey slices
   coffee   tea with lemon

SUCCOT

wine for Kiddush
* challah
* knishes
* stuffed cabbage
* stuffed acorn squash
* rice Pilaf
peas and onions
* apple strudel
coffee   tea with lemon

HANUKAH

* challah
* mushroom-barley soup
* lemon-glazed Rock Cornish
  hens
* potato latkes
* applesauce
* succotash
* cole slaw
* marble cake
coffee   tea with lemon

PURIM

1. Purim Seudah (feast)
* challah
* chicken soup
* kreplach
* pot roast
* rice kugel
* zucchini-onion bake
* hamentaschen
  wine   brandy   liqueur

2. Shalach Manot treats
* hamentaschen with prune
  filling
* hamentaschen with poppy
  seeds
* sugar cut-out cookies
* poppy-seed candy
* very good sesame-seed
  candy
  roasted peanuts
  fresh oranges
  dried apricots and prunes

PASSOVER

1. First Seder
  wine for Kiddush
  matzah
* gefilte fish with horseradish
* traditional roast turkey with
  matzah-spinach stuffing
* orange-glazed carrot coins
* broccoli
* sponge cake
  coffee   tea with lemon

2. Second Seder
  wine for Kiddush
  matzah
* chicken soup with knaidlach
* roast brisket with horseradish
* matzah kugel
* asparagus
* beets
* chocolate-orange cake
  coffee   tea with lemon

YOM HATZMAUT
(Independence Day)

* chatzelim
* hummus
* falafel balls
* pita bread
  tossed salad
* tahinah dressing
* kibbee (lamb)
  French-fried potatoes
* Israeli-style zucchini with
  tomato sauce
  fresh fruit platter
* very good sesame-seed candy

SHAVUOT

  wine for Kiddush
* challah
* sweet and sour borscht
* blintzes with cheese filling
  sour cream
  strawberry jam
  fresh fruit platter
* cheesecake
  coffee   tea with lemon

SHABBAT

1. *Friday Dinner*
    wine for Kiddush
    * challah
    * gefilte fish with horseradish
    * chicken noodle soup
    * Shabbat roast chicken
    * potato kugel
    * glazed carrots
    * peas
    * fruit compote, cookies
      coffee   tea with lemon
3. *Se'udah Shlishit* (third meal)
    * challah
    * egg salad
      tuna salad
      tomato slices
      fresh fruit
      cookies
      tea with lemon

2. *Saturday Kiddush*
    wine for Kiddush
    * challah
    * chopped liver on lettuce
      leaves
    * cholent
    * fruity jel salad
      pickles   olives
    * cole slaw
    * sponge cake
      tea with lemon

SPECIAL DIETS

Today many people are on special diets for various reasons. Some wish to lose weight or to feel healthier, while others are following a special diet as part of the treatment of disease. For whatever the reason a person has to adhere to a special diet, the use of modern appliances can be very valuable in preparing appetizing meals. The dieter and the rest of the family can eat according to their needs without too much wear-and-tear on the resident chef.

In this chapter 6 commonly used special diets are discussed in their relationship to traditional Jewish cuisine and how modern appliances can be used to best advantage. These special diets are High-Fiber Diet; Low-Saturated-Fat, Low-Cholesterol Diet; Low-Sodium Diet; High-Potassium Diet; Vegetarian Diet and Low-Calorie Diet.

HIGH-FIBER DIET

Cellulose or vegetable fiber has a regulatory function in the diet by aiding and regulating elimination. Although some foods are completely digested by the body, some plant foods pass through the digestive system virtually unchanged. Persons who follow a high-fiber diet should emphasize whole-grain cereals, raw fruits and vegetables.

Traditional Jewish diets have always contained a high amount of fiber. Ashkenazi Jews (descendants of Yiddish-speaking Jews from central and eastern Europe) enjoy a variety of grains, legumes and breads, including rye and whole wheat. In addition, there is a fondness for certain foods not generally included in many American diets, such as cholent and kasha. Seeds such as poppy and sesame are often included in holiday dishes.

The preferred diet of Sephardic Jews (descendants of Ladino—Spanish—Arabic-speaking Jews) and many Israelis is also high in fiber, with a great emphasis on salads, fresh raw fruits and vegetables and such items as bulghor wheat. Any tourist who has visited Israel will agree that sunflower seeds (garinim) are the favored food on buses and in movie theaters.

The use of a blender and food processor can be very valuable in following a high-fiber diet. High-fiber parts of foods not generally eaten, such as citrus pulp and rind, can be incorporated into recipes by use of these appliances (recipes for Harvest Bread and Orange Juicy Drink). Foods which have been finely chopped in a food processor or blender generally need less cooking.

Using a mixer with a dough hook to make homemade breads can be a good way to incorporate extra whole grains into the diet.

The following list may be used as a guide in selecting foods for a high-fiber diet:

FOODS HIGH IN FIBER	FOODS LOW IN FIBER
fruits (especially if eaten with skins)	sugar
	meat
vegetables (especially if eaten with skins)	fats
	white bread
legumes	breakfast cereals which are highly milled
whole-wheat and rye breads	
whole-grain cereals (bran, oatmeal, shredded wheat)	

LOW-SATURATED-FAT, LOW-CHOLESTEROL DIET

Cholesterol is a lipid, a fatlike substance which circulates in the bloodstream. It is one of the substances found in deposits on the walls of arteries. When these substances are deposited in large amounts it is called atherosclerosis.

Accumulation of these deposits in the heart can lead to serious heart damage. Although some research has shown that the consumption of high amounts of saturated fats (primarily animal fats) tends to raise blood cholesterol, it is difficult to lower the cholesterol level of the blood simply by diet. (However, a diet which emphasizes the intake of polyunsaturated fats—liquid oils of vegetable origin—is often recommended.) Other factors must also be considered, such as the amount of exercise, overeating or obesity, and the stress and strain of life.

Jewish diets are traditionally high in saturated fats—particularly because of the use of rendered chicken fat (schmaltz), whole eggs and cheeses. Here are some suggestions and substitutions for incorporating unsaturated fats into the diet:

Pareve margarine can be used as a substitute in almost any recipe calling for chicken fat. In this book every recipe that calls for chicken fat also offers a low-unsaturate alternative, such as pareve margarine or oil. Some of the recipes in the meat and poultry chapters call for browning meat or vegetables in chicken fat; however, in every instance vegetable oil may be used as a substitute. When you are shopping for margarine, carefully read the list of ingredients on the label. Always select a margarine which lists liquid oil as the first ingredient.

Egg substitutes or egg whites can be used in many cake or casserole recipes which call for whole eggs. Be aware that, although many of the commercial egg substitutes are kosher, they are dairy products and may not be eaten with meat or fleishig foods.

Chocolate contains cocoa butter and is very high in saturated fats. For a low-cholesterol alternative, substitute the following for 1 ounce (30 grams) unsweetened chocolate:

> 3 Tbsp (45 ml) cocoa plus 1 Tbsp (15 ml) oil, or
> 1 teaspoon (5 ml) chocolate extract

Meat, when eaten, should be very lean and trimmed of excess fats. The white meat of chicken, turkey or fish is a much better food choice for this type of diet.

The microwave oven can be a great help to persons trying to lower the cholesterol level of their diet. In conventional cooking, fat is added to food both for flavor and to keep foods from sticking or burning on hot pans. In the microwave oven, where foods do not burn, this fat can be eliminated, or vegetable oil or pareve margarine can be substituted.

The following list may be used as a guide in selecting foods low in saturated fats:

Foods High in Saturated Fats	Foods Low in Saturated Fats
fatty meat, fatty fish	skim milk
chicken fat	margarine (if made from liquid
egg yolk	vegetable oil)
cream	vegetable oils
full-milk cheese	corn
	cottonseed
	peanut
	soybean
	safflower

LOW-SODIUM DIET

Sodium plays an important role, along with potassium, in maintaining normal osmotic pressure and water balance between the body fluids and cells. Also, about 90 percent of the basic ions in blood plasma are sodium ions. This means that sodium is a factor in fluid retention and fluid balance in the body and also plays a role in maintaining normal blood pressure.

Tablet salt (sodium chloride) is the major source of sodium in American diets. In a low-sodium diet the use of table salt is eliminated or greatly reduced, and all obviously salty foods must be avoided. Many other foods have a high sodium content even though they do not have a particularly salty taste.

Following a strict low-sodium diet means giving up many favorite Jewish dishes, such as lox (smoked salmon), herring, deli meats such as salami, corned beef and pastrami, and also eliminating pickles.

In order for meat to be kosher, blood must be drained off in a process called kashering (see "Guide to Kashering Meat and Poultry" in "How to Keep Kosher"). The kashering process involves either soaking the meat and then coating it with a coarse kashering salt for a period of time, or else salting the meat lightly and then broiling. Persons on a salt-free diet usually kasher meat by the broiling method, without prior salting. Meat which is soaked in water for two hours after kashering by the salting method becomes dietetically salt-free.

The crock pot and the microwave oven are excellent appliances to use when cooking foods for a low-sodium diet. In both of these appliances extra liquids are not cooked away. This means that much of the natural flavor of the foods is retained and usually less seasoning, including table salt, is needed to give food taste. In this book, most of the microwave oven recipes give directions for withholding salt until after the cooking process is completed. This is because a sprinkling of salt on top of the food can draw out extra moisture and toughen foods.

The low-sodium dieter can take comfort in the fact that the food industry produces a wide variety of canned and packaged low-sodium products, including tuna fish, vegetables, fruits, peanut butter, etc.

The following may be used as a guide in selecting foods which are low in sodium:

Foods High in Sodium	Foods Low in Sodium
meats, fish and poultry that are pickled, cured or canned	meats, fish and poultry that are fresh and lean
salted butter and margarine	unsalted butter and margarine
processed cheeses and spreads	unsalted cottage cheese
canned vegetables	fresh vegetables
canned tomato juice	fruit and fruit juices
corn flakes, wheat flakes	unsalted breakfast cereals
MSG, soy sauce, Worcestershire sauce	most spices and herbs (not salt blends)
saccharine or artificial sweetener	sugar

HIGH-POTASSIUM DIET

Potassium is widely distributed in all foods except fats and oils. A deficiency in potassium is seldom seen in a healthy person; however, medications such as diuretics (often prescribed along with a low-sodium diet) and certain hormones may cause potassium deficiency if efforts are not made to replace potassium in the diet.

The blender can be used to make quick high-potassium beverage snacks. Add 1 teaspoon (5 ml) cream of tartar (potassium bitartrate) to an 8-ounce (250 ml) glass of tomato, orange or grapefruit juice, and blend until smooth and frothy. For a refreshing high-potassium beverage, try a Banana Blender Drink (recipe in Breakfast Foods chapter) or a Vegetable-Fruit Combo (see Beverages chapter), both delicious blender drinks.

The following list may be used as a guide to selecting foods high in potassium:

Foods High in Potassium	Foods Low in Potassium
fruits—especially bananas, apricots and dried fruits	breads
juices—tomato, citrus, prune	cereals (except bran)
meat and poultry (light meat only)	highly milled grains
fish	oils and shortening
vegetables—especially yams, squash, broccoli and cauliflower	

VEGETARIAN DIET

Jewish law (halacha) does not approve of a vegetarian diet. The enjoyment of life's pleasures, moderated by the restrictions of Jewish law, are not only condoned but encouraged. Eating meat, particularly on Shabbat and holidays, has always been a substantial part of the Jewish dietary practice. There have always been those, on the other hand, who for one reason or another have chosen vegetarianism. This practice has become particularly widespread among Jews in modern times.

In the book of Genesis, we learn that Adam and Eve were vegetarians in the Garden of Eden. We know from their experience that even a fruit and vegetable diet can cause problems, if you don't follow certain important rules.

There are many types of vegetarian dieters. All vegetarians eat vegetables, fruits, cereals, breads, yeast, legumes, nuts, seeds, and vegetable oils. If the diet also contains milk, dairy products and eggs, in addition to fruits and vegetables, receiving adequate amounts of calcium, protein and vitamins A and D usually presents no problem. A person who follows this type of diet is called a lacto-ovo vegetarian.

The major dietary concern of strict vegetarians (vegan) is preventing a deficiency in Vitamin B_{12} and zinc, because these two nutrients are found mainly in foods of animal origin and the body is unable to manufacture them independently.

Persons who follow vegetarian diets soon learn how to combine foods so that combinations of incomplete proteins found in plants act together to form complete proteins similar to those found in animal foods. The more restrictive the vegetarian diet, the greater care must be taken to study and learn the nutrient content of food and food combinations.

The blender has long been a favorite kitchen appliance of vegetarians because of its ability to liquefy many foods. Foods which are blended or processed in the food processor often need less cooking, resulting in a greater retention of certain vitamins.

The microwave oven is extremely useful, particularly in its ability to cook vegetables to the tender-crisp stage. The method of cooking vegetables given in the Vegetables chapter of this book eliminates the need to add extra liquid; the vegetables cook by steaming in their own moisture and most nutrients are not diluted or washed away.

LOW-CALORIE DIET

Obesity, or overweight, is the number-one nutrition problem in the United States today. It is caused by consuming more calories than the body is able to utilize. These excess calories are stored as body fat. "Calorie" is the term for a unit of the energy used by the body, as well as the energy values of food. In order to lose weight, the food intake must be less than the body's energy requirements, forcing the body to burn stored fat for energy.

When a person decides he needs to diet to lose weight, the first impulse is to try to lose it as quickly as possible. Most people did not gain their excess weight overnight, but rather gradually over a period of time. A similar gradual change is also the healthiest way to lose weight. Changed eating habits, developed during this dieting period, may mean that the weight loss will be permanent. Fads and quick-weight-loss diets are usually temporary measures that seldom result in a permanent weight loss and may actually be harmful to the body.

Some specific suggestions for a low-calorie, weight-reducing diet are to reduce the consumption of sweets, starchy and fatty foods and to eat food in their natural state, without added calories in the form of sugar or fat.

Here are some specific suggestions for preparing foods on a low-calorie diet:

Reduce fats in the diet by cooking with a microwave oven. Foods will not burn or stick when cooked by microwaves, so extra fat is seldom required in cooking. For top-of-the-stove or conventional cooking, use Teflon-coated pans. If a pan does need to be greased, use an aerosol nonstick vegetable coating rather than butter.

Enjoy skim-milk-and-fruit combinations in a blender milk shake. Combine ingredients in blender goblet and begin blending on high speed. Add 2 or 3 ice cubes, one at a time, blending until shake is thickened and frothy. For a rich, satisfying meal-in-a-glass, add 1 egg and blend until frothy.

Use the blender to make a thick, satisfying Quick Vegetable Soup, a combination of low-calorie vegetables with hot skim milk or reconstituted soup powder.

Place 1 cup (250 ml) buttermilk and ¼ teaspoon (1 ml) favorite seasonings, such as oregano, pepper, basil, and some lemon juice in blender goblet. Blend on low speed until smooth and use as a dressing for salads, cooked vegetables or eggs. This dressing may be thickened with 1 teaspoon (5 ml) unflavored imitation-jel dessert.

If you enjoy whipped-cream dessert treats, try substituting reconstituted powdered skim milk (directions for mixing with liquid are on the package) or well-chilled evaporated low-fat milk. Flavor milk with vanilla or lemon juice. Use the mixer to beat these liquid cream substitutes until very stiff and use in recipes calling for whipped cream.

Even though your diet may supply an adequate supply of nutrients, occasionally you may still feel ravenously hungry between meals. When that "must-eat" feeling comes, try to choose a low-calorie food to snack on. Use this list as a guide to selecting foods which, when eaten in moderation, are relatively low in calories:

Low-Calorie Foods

Fruits:	Vegetables:	Fish
Boysenberries	Bean sprouts	Matzah (1 whole matzah has the
Grapefruit	Cabbage	same number of calories as one
Raspberries	Cucumbers	slice of bread, but is much more
Strawberries	Green beans	filling)
Watermelon	Green onions	Cereals (unsweetened, ready-to-eat)
	Lettuce	Skim milk
	Mushrooms	Buttermilk
	Peppers	Cottage cheese
	Rhubarb	Popcorn (without butter!)
	Spinach	

HOW TO KEEP KOSHER

The following explanations are intended as a guide to the observance of kashruth *(the Jewish dietary laws)*. Only a rabbi is qualified to offer guidance and answer questions concerning any aspect of kashruth.

SETTING UP A KOSHER KITCHEN

Things You Will Need

First, choose your two favorite colors, one for milchig and one for fleishig, and carry out your color scheme. You will need two each of the following items. These items must be designated milchig or fleishig and may not be used interchangeably.

TWO SETS

Dishes
Silverware
Knives
Kitchen utensils (you may want three sets here—the third for pareve use):
　Measuring cups and spoons
　Wooden spoons
　All plastic and rubber items
　All metal items

Cookware
    Metal pots and pans
    Corning Ware and pyrex casserole dishes

Bakeware (in this case the two sets are for milchig and pareve)
    Cookie sheets
    Cake pans
    Pie dishes
    Loaf pans for bread

Serving trays and bowls
Condiment holders
    Sugar bowls
    Salt and pepper shakers

Can openers
Plastic or rubber kitchen items
    Sink basins or liners
    Drain racks and liners
    Silverware holders
    Tupperware and storage containers
Sponges and scouring pads
Dishtowels
Plastic tablecloths (cloth tablecloths and napkins may be used
    interchangeably if laundered between uses)
Placemats

ONE SET

Only one (or one set) is needed of the following items because they are
used only for pareve foods:
    Water glasses (although some families prefer two sets)
    Coffeepot
    Tea kettle and teapot
    Canister set
    Sifter
    Vegetable peeler
    Kitchen scale (cover the top with foil or plastic wrap before
        measuring meat or dairy foods)

Wine goblets
Items for observance
    Candlesticks
    Kiddush cup
    Challah plate, cover and knife

New Dishes—Toweling

If you are starting out with everything brand new, the procedure for setting up a kosher kitchen is simplified. Brand-new items made from earthenware, wood, rubber or plastic may be used immediately. New metal or glass items should be "toiveled" in a ceremony formally called "t'vilat kaylim." This is the process of immersing items in a mikveh (ritual bath), river, lake or ocean (under conditions specified by a rabbi). The following blessing is recited:

Baruch atta adonai elohaynu melech ha-olam asher kidshanu b'mitzvotav v'tzivanu al t'vilat kaylim.

Blessed art Thou, Lord our God, King of the Universe, Who has sanctified us by His commandments and commanded us concerning the immersion of a vessel.

Used Dishes: Kashering

If you have been maintaining a nonkosher kitchen and decide to start keeping kosher, some items may be "converted" or kashered. Many items which have been made nonkosher through accident or misuse can also be kashered. This guide to kashering may be applied to converting some items from chometz to pesachdig for the Passover holiday.

Only a rabbi can determine if an item can be kashered and which method to use. His decision is based on the materials used in making the item, how it is constructed, what it is used for and how it was made nonkosher.

Used or nonkosher items which normally *cannot* be kashered include:

Earthenware
Enamelware
China
Plastic
Porcelain
Items of other materials which contain grooves, narrow spaces, glued-on parts and hard-to-get-to crevices (i.e. sieves, graters, funnels, etc).

Items which possibly *can* be kashered are made from:

Glass
Metal
Wood

There are several methods by which nonkosher items may be kashered. Before any item can be converted, it must be thoroughly cleaned and set aside for 24 hours. (This also includes kosher items that will be used in the kashering process, such as large pots or tongs. Separate pots are needed to kasher meat and dairy items.) Pots to be kashered should have all handles and removable parts taken off. Covers and lids should be prepared in the same way.

The major methods used for kashering are:

Purging or Boiling This method is often used for pots, saucepans, and silverware. Each item must be completely immersed in a full pot of actively boiling water, with sufficient water to equal 60 times the volume of the item being immersed. The item is then rinsed in cold water. If the item to be kashered is a large pot which cannot be dipped or immersed, the pot itself is filled to the brim with boiling water so that the water overflows. Hot stones are frequently used as part of this process, and a rabbi should be consulted concerning their function and use.

Glowing Frying pans, baking sheets, ovens, ranges and spits are commonly kashered by this method. The entire surface of the item is slowly subjected to the heat of fire until it is red hot. Many families use a propane torch (blowtorch) for this purpose.

Immersion in Cold Water and Burying an Item These two additional methods of kashering are sometimes used. Glassware that would break if dipped in boiling water is immersed in a pot of cold water for 3 days, with the water being changed every afternoon. Certain metal items, particularly knives, are buried in the ground for 3 days. The item supposedly returns to the elements and is like a new item when found. A rabbi should be consulted concerning both of these methods of kashering.

Preparing and Using Appliances
Oven An oven is kashered by glowing. This may be accomplished either by use of a blowtorch as described above under "Glowing," or by heating the oven cavity, burners and broiler to the hottest possible setting, then maintaining this temperature for 30 minutes. A self-cleaning oven is automatically kashered by glowing during the cleaning process. A continuous-cleaning oven differs from a self-cleaning, and a rabbi should be consulted concerning the proper method of kashering.

Although some authorities recommend the use of separate ovens for milchig and fleishig, it is a general practice to use one oven for both milchig and fleishig—but at different times. The oven racks may be used interchangeably for milchig or fleishig, but should be kept clean and spills should be wiped up immediately. Milchig and fleishig foods should not be baked together in the oven.

Refrigerator and Freezer A refrigerator and a freezer are considered kashered after thorough washing and scrubbing. The only precaution in using a refrigerator is to try to avoid spills or leaking from food containers. It is best to wrap food or place it in a storage container before placing it in the refrigerator or freezer.

Dishwasher There is some controversy concerning the kashering of electric dishwashers. Some rabbis maintain that one dishwasher may be used with two sets of racks—one for milchig and one for fleishig and that the dishwasher should be "rinsed" between uses. Other rabbis maintain that only separate dishwashers should be used (in other words, use the dishwasher for fleishig and wash milchig dishes by hand, or vice versa). Consult your rabbi about kashering a dishwasher for year-round use and for Passover.

Preparing Work Surfaces and Storage Areas

Sinks If a sink is made of metal it can be kashered by purging. The method used is to pour boiling water over every square inch of the sink. Because the water should be boiling at the same time it is being poured, an electric tea kettle or coffeepot, still plugged in, is a good solution, but *use carefully!*

If you have a double sink, an accepted practice is to make one side milchig and one side fleishig. If you have one sink, the sink should be considered nonkosher and should be used with plastic or rubber liners or fitted basins. Two sets are needed, one for fleishig and one for milchig. If you have the opportunity to install a new sink, select one made of stainless steel, which is best for kashruth purposes.

Counters Counters made of nonporous materials can be kashered by the purging method. The same technique used to kasher a sink can be employed here.

Storage Areas Every drawer, cupboard and pantry shelf that will hold food, dishes or cookware items should be cleaned and lined. Many items can be used for lining, including shelf paper, contact paper, foil, rubber mats, linoleum or (temporarily) paper towels.

Fleishig and milchig items should be stored separately. If many people use the kitchen, it may be a good idea to label each shelf (at least until everyone is familiar with the arrangement).

SHOPPING GUIDE

Purchasing kosher food today is quite different from purchasing during grandmother's time. We are fortunate to have an enormous variety of frozen, canned and processed kosher foods available to us. Grandma, however, was luckier in one respect—she always had a clear knowledge of which foods were kosher and which were not. Today that decision is often difficult.

Unprocessed Foods

Foods which are sold unprocessed, in their natural state without additives, are easily identified as kosher. This includes such items as fresh fruit and vegetables, eggs, flour, fish (from kosher species) and milk.*

Processed Foods

Most processed foods contain additives. Additives are derived from many sources, and the origin of the additive determines whether the product it is used in is kosher or nonkosher; and, if kosher, whether it is fleishig, milchig or pareve. Although two items may appear similar on a grocery-store shelf, one may be kosher and the other with a different additive may be nonkosher.

Although this book does not go into the various types of additives, including emulsifiers, stabilizers, flavoring and neutralizing agents, etc., the reader should be aware that the decisions involved in determining if an item is kosher are very complex, requiring a detailed knowledge of biochemistry as well as halacha (Jewish law). In addition to supervision of basic ingredients, rabbinic supervision is required for the entire process if the item is to be sold as kosher because impurities may be introduced into a food at any point during the production, processing, packaging or storage of the product.

Commonly used canned fruits and vegetables, which are processed seasonally in canneries producing only fruits and vegetables, do not usually present a kashruth problem. These items include peas, carrots, asparagus, peaches, pears, etc. Other canned foods, however, may not be kosher because they are processed in plants which produce varieties of the same item that contain nonkosher meat and cheeses. These items, which require rabbinic supervision, include tomato juice, ketchup, prepared sauces, soups, baked beans, Chinese foods, including bean sprouts and chow mein noodles.

Frozen fruit juices and frozen vegetables without sauce are kosher.

Two additional categories of foods which present special kashruth problems are grape products and cheese.

The use of grape juices, jellies, vinegar, wines, brandies and other foods which are derived from grapes need special supervision and certification to assure that they are kosher. Only grape products which are prepared and handled exclusively by observant Jews may be considered kosher.

Cheese which contains rennet (a product derived from the lining of calves' stomachs) always requires a special kosher certification. Other dairy products, because they often contain nonkosher additives, such as gelatin, always need a special certification to insure that they are kosher.

---

* Most American Jews accept the opinion that the American dairy industry supplies pure cow's milk, unadulterated by the milk of a nonkosher animal. The European dairyman could not always be trusted to fill his milk quota without resorting to the milking of his mare or even his sows, so Jews did not use milk from gentiles without supervision. There are still those who prefer orthodox Jewish supervision of the milking process, and milk produced under such supervision, Chalav Yisrael, is available in some large cities.

Heksher

Most processed food and food products need to have a special rabbinic certification before they can be considered kosher. This certification by a recognized rabbinic authority is called a heksher. A heksher means that the ingredients used in the food are kosher and that the processing was officially supervised.

The heksher appears on the product label in the form of a symbol. Some of the symbols and the authorities or organizations they represent are:

Ⓤ   Union of Orthodox Jewish Congregations of America
    116 East 27th Street, New York, NY 10016

Ⓚ   Organized Kashruth Laboratories
    P.O. Box 218, Brooklyn, NY 11204

The UOJCA publishes several pamphlets and directories which are very useful and valuable sources of information. Included are: *Kosher Products and Services Directory, Industrial and Institutional Directory, Passover Products Directory* and *The Kashruth Handbook for Home and School,* which includes a complete list of kosher fish.

In addition to these two main groups, there are a profusion of other individuals and groups that offer kashruth certification, many of which use the symbol K to signify kashruth endorsement. Because K is not a copyrighted symbol it can be used by anyone. While most of these other organizations are highly reliable, there is the possibility of misuse. When there is a doubt, it is a good idea to check with the product manufacturer for more specific information.

The appearance on a label of the symbols Ⓒ and Ⓡ mean copyright and registered trademark, respectively. These are legal symbols and have nothing to do with kashruth.

Labeling

In addition to the above heksher symbols, certifying that a product is kosher, other symbols are standardly employed to denote if the product is milchig, pareve or fleishig. The following symbols are used:

Milchig   The capital letter D following the heksher symbol means that the product is milchig or dairy. Be aware that not all milchig products use this symbol. Often, in order to determine if a product is milchig or pareve it will be necessary to evaluate the list of ingredients.

Nonfat dry milk solids, whey, lactose or sodium caseinate listed on the label signal a dairy product. The addition of these substances in a product, as well as the presence of rennet as an additive in cheese, requires special kashruth supervision and certification.

Pareve   The word "pareve" (in lower-case letters) will often appear following the heksher symbol on a label. Many products, particularly chocolates, margarines, cake mixes, baking items and nondairy products should not be assumed to be pareve unless the label specifically states this.

Fleishig   The word "FLEISHIG" (in capital letters) will appear on a label denoting a fleishig or meat product.

The Kosher Butcher Shop

The maintenance of a kosher butcher shop, as well as the sources of the meat supply, must be under rabbinic supervision. All kosher meat must be ritually slaughtered and inspected.

Most butchers will, upon request, kasher meat and poultry for you. This takes about 1½ hours, so don't arrive close to closing time and expect this service. Hamburger must be kashered by the butcher before it is ground. If the meat you buy has not been kashered, you can cook it by broiling or you can kasher it yourself.

GUIDE TO KASHERING MEAT AND POULTRY

You must not consume any blood, either of fowl or of animal.
Leviticus 7:26–27, 17:10–14

Jewish law considers blood to be the repository of life itself. Although the Torah allows the eating of meat, it is forbidden for a Jew to consume the blood of an animal. Meat and poultry may be kashered (the removal of blood) by one of two methods.

Kashering by Soaking and Salting

The salting procedure should be done within 72 hours of slaughter. However, if the meat is thoroughly rinsed with water, it may be held an additional 72 hours. After that time it may only be kashered by broiling.

You will need a basin for soaking the meat and a rack for draining it. These items should be set aside for this purpose only.

A special coarse-grain kashering salt must be used for salting the meat. This can be purchased from a kosher butcher. In addition, many markets and delicatessens carry this product.

All inside parts of poultry should be removed before kashering and should be soaked and salted separately. The gizzard as well as the heart of an animal must be cut open and cleaned before kashering.

The procedure for salting and soaking meat is:

- Soak the meat in cool water for one-half hour.
- Salt the meat on all sides with coarse kosher salt.
- Drain the meat on an inclined surface for one hour.
- Rinse off all the salt in cold water.

Kashering by Broiling

Proper broiling of meat extracts all blood, rendering the meat kosher. The broiling may be done over or under a flame or in an electric oven or broiler.

Liver, because of its high blood content, can be kashered only by broiling.

The racks which are used to kasher meat may not be used to broil meat which has already been kashered by salting and soaking. Separate racks must be used for this purpose.

To kasher meat and poultry by broiling:

- Rinse the meat in cold water and sprinkle very lightly with salt.
- Place the meat on a grill, rack or spit that allows the blood to drain off.
- Broil the meat until the entire piece is at least half done and not just the surface, turning to broil both sides.
- Rinse the meat again after broiling.

After the meat or liver is broiled, it may be fried or cooked with other foods.

The purpose of kashering, by either method, is to remove the blood. What remains is regarded as "meat juice" and may be consumed. The meat may be served rare, medium or well done to personal taste.

People on a salt-free diet usually kasher meat by broiling without prior salting. However, meat which is soaked in water for two hours after kashering by salting becomes dietetically salt-free.

INDEX